MANAGERIAL PREROGATIVE AND
THE QUESTION OF CONTROL

D0841175

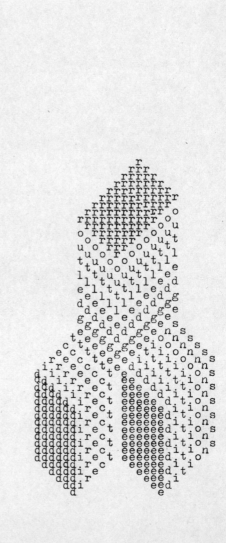

# MANAGERIAL PREROGATIVE AND THE QUESTION OF CONTROL

JOHN STOREY
Trent Polytechnic

ROUTLEDGE & KEGAN PAUL
London, Boston, Melbourne and Henley

First published in 1983
by Routledge & Kegan Paul Plc
39 Store Street, London WC1E 7DD,
9 Park Street, Boston, Mass. 02108, USA,
296 Beaconsfield Parade, Middle Park,
Melbourne,3206, Australia, and
Broadway House, Newtown Road,
Henley-on-Thames, Oxon RG9 1EN
Printed in Great Britain by
Redwood Burn Ltd,
Trowbridge,Wiltshire

ISBN 0-7100-9203-2

# CONTENTS

# PREFACE

This book is about the contemporary struggle over the control of
work. Accordingly, it is a study of the capitalist labour process.
The last couple of decades have been witness to a dramatic clash
over the control of production; the much-vaunted managerial resurgence came hard on the heels of the second shop stewards' movement
which had just reached its zenith. De-manning and new work practices have been forced through in a context of redundancy, plant
closures and high unemployment. But to interpret the real social,
political and economic significance of such events demands that they
be placed in historic and theoretical context. One version sees
managerial prerogative as having suffered secular erosion; in contrast, Braverman and his followers view the twentieth century as a
period of inexorable degradation of work, the ascendancy of Taylorism and the destruction of immemorial craft prerogative. Marx's
theory of real subordination of labour and Weber's rationalisation
thesis would seemingly lend support to the latter account.

Our analysis of the modern labour process reveals, however, a
more complex picture. It is shown to be necessary to go 'beyond
Braverman' - and Friedman - and in so doing also to reappraise the
marxian analysis. The theoretical strand running through the text
is dialectical. There is an unwavering focus upon managerial
strategy and worker resistance. Braverman, it is argued, reified
Taylorism as the device in capital's mission to secure control over
the labour process. Garnering the myriad critical reviews of the
Braverman thesis, we argue that their ostensible variety obscures
an underlying consistency - that the shortcomings of Braverman's
influential thesis results from the absence of a dialectic. One
central consequence is an over-rationalised conception of managerialism. The thrust of our argument is that managerial control is in
fact more precarious and more variegated. The concept of 'managerial prerogative' is subjected to close scrutiny. It is treated as
pivotal in the ideological armoury of modern capitalism. But again
its status as a legitimating device is shown to be not unassailable.
An ineradicable question-mark hangs over the control *by* management
over the labour process and also over the control *of* management
itself. So while the analysis is wide-ranging and one which certainly subscribes to the logic of a political economy of work con-

trol, another kind of amendment is made to past analyses of the
control of work and the capitalist division of labour, namely, a
more central focus is given to the activity of *management* albeit
linked to a thoroughly sceptical appraisal of practical managerial
'strategy'.

The book is addressed primarily to graduate and undergraduate
students of the social sciences, in particular to those studying
industrial sociology, industrial relations, and organisation theory.
It is intended to dissolve the traditional boundaries between these
'disciplines' with a view to defying the re-erection of the familiar
barriers.  While the underlying thrust is sociological the analysis
is intended to be radical and to cast doubts upon the territorial
integrity of even that broad church.

I would like to thank the Social Science Research Council for
grants which financed the research out of which this present book
grew.  I am indebted also to the librarians at Trent Polytechnic,
in particular to Linda Dean and Alison Smith.  Valuable comments
upon the manuscript were made by Howard Gospel of the University of
Kent, Stephen Wood of the London School of Economics and by Peter
Cressey and John McInnes of Glasgow University.  Students and colleagues at Trent Polytechnic shaped the final outcome immeasurably.

# Chapter 1

# CONTROL AND THE LABOUR PROCESS: TOWARDS A DIALECTICAL APPROACH

In both marxist and non-marxist scholarship there has been until recently, a remarkable neglect of the managerial control of labour. Even today this neglect stands only partially remedied. Yet in the current conjuncture with a deep recession emboldening top management in a resolve to reverse the post-war challenge from below, this issue demands even more urgent analysis. Interpretation of contemporary developments in work control has been significantly hampered by this relative theoretical hiatus. (1)

Indices of a more hawkish managerial approach are legion. Ironically, the man who was persuaded by Tony Benn to act as chairman of the KME workers' co-operative (though he remained for less than a month) has articulated the new mood more forcibly than most. At a seminar he convened for managing directors and personnel managers, Len Collinson, a director of numerous companies and a chairman of Collinson Grant Consultants, declared:

'Managers for 20 years have had a buffeting and bashing from governments and unions and have been put into a "can't win" situation. Many have been fire-fighting and many have given in. We have an opportunity now that will last for two or three years. Then, the unions will get themselves together again; and the government like all governments will run out of steam. So grab it now. We have had a pounding and we are all fed up with it. I think it would be fair to say that it's almost vengeance.' (2)

This 'new reality' has been developing for a decade or so, a decade which has been witness to a dramatic volte-face in industrial relations. The much-vaunted 'challenge from below' has been sublimated by talk of a 'managerial resurgence'. Attention has shifted from stoppages at Ford, BL and other favourite hot spots to a new litany of redundancies, closure plans, new working practices and disciplinary codes. In a more than literal sense Red Robbo (Mr Derek Robinson, the erstwhile Longbridge convener), has been supplanted by Michael Edwardes. In the 1960s and 1970s the figure at centre-stage was the shop steward; by 1980 Geoffrey Armstrong, Director of Industrial Relations at BL, could present a lecture on the new industrial relations in that company without once even mentioning shop stewards. (3) BL have secured shopfloor ballot approval for the Edwardes 'streamlining plan'; they have introduced

new working practices;  and they implemented a scheme that dilutes
the power of the shop stewards. (4)  Following a protest or 'riot'
in November 1980 at Longbridge, 8 shop stewards were sacked.  The
strike of 1,500 workers which followed was greeted with warnings
that strikers would be replaced by the unemployed from the Birming-
ham dole queues.  These are just a few instances of a tougher managerial stand at BL.

Meanwhile at Ford UK a similar pattern was being enacted.  In response to a series of unofficial stoppages, most notably at Halewood, Ford introduced a new disciplinary code.  The code provided
for the suspension without pay of workers who failed to operate
normally or failed to carry out an instruction from a supervisor.
Moreover, the code further stipulated that management would then
request other employees to re-man the job which had stopped.  If
the request was refused, lay-off without pay would then commence
for all employees who could not be 'gainfully employed'.  'This approach does not in any way alter the company's normal policy of applying progressive disciplinary action to individuals.  It is a new
sanction directed at employees who act unconstitutionally by stop-
ping work' (Ford Supervisors' Bulletin, Halewood, 14 November 1980).
Of interest here too is that the new measures were introduced, as
far as the unions were concerned, as 'disciplinary fait accompli' -
i.e. without negotiation or discussion at the FNJNC.  Indeed, the
company's tough attitude is revealed by the fact that they were
determined to announce their intentions directly to all employees,
prior to the union's proposed meeting to discuss the matter. (5)
Of course, following a strike, the new disciplinary code was in the
end withdrawn - but not before it had been used.  In its very first
utilisation of the code Ford suspended 22 men at Halewood who refused to obey a foreman's instruction to cease switching jobs.
Workers swop jobs to break the monotony, but they are only allowed
to do so officially if production targets are being met.

Similar developments were meanwhile occurring in other major
companies.  Peugeot was able to close the Linwood plant with a minimum of resistance.  At British Steel, Ian MacGregor secured agreement
for his 'rescue plan' which inter alia involves new working practices, elimination of over-manning, reduced absenteeism and overtime
and intensified working arrangements.  Again the tactic of a personal letter to the workforce was deployed, and again the threat of
liquidation was used.  MacGregor's approach is reminiscent of the
Edwardes style - perhaps it is no coincidence that MacGregor was
originally on the BL board before he went to BSC.  Stiffened by the
wider economic situation, management has an enhanced opportunity to
push through its control plans without resistance.  As Ian MacGregor
wrote in the final paragraph of his personal letter to all employees:  'To do the things we have to do without major interruption or
controversy, we must have the total co-operation of the workforce.
If the plan is put at risk, we may end up having to take much more
drastic action' (12 December 1980).

Managers in general may not be seizing the opportunity to the
extent that consultants like Len Collinson would like to see, but
the general reversal cannot be doubted.  Strikes have fallen and
unemployment has risen;  pay settlements were roughly half in 1981
what they were in 1980;  de-manning proceeded apace;  the full

impact on the trade unions has yet to be gauged.  1980-81 saw a fall
in union membership largely because of the sheer loss of jobs.   The
TGWU lost 8 per cent of its membership - i.e. nearly 200,000.   The
role of the shop steward has been questioned more intensely not only
by BL management but by other employers and more publicly by Richard
Dixon of the CBI.

These examples are but particular instances which signal further
developments in the continuing drama of management and the question
of control.  The persistent struggle for control and the rival
proclamations of asserted 'rights' can be claimed as a, or perhaps
the, central issue in the whole study area designated as 'industrial
relations'.  As Beynon observed - 'This conflict over rights is a
fundamental one and permeates union-management relations' (1973:
114).  The title of this present book intimates that control is precarious, that a secure situation of being 'in control' cannot be assumed.  On the contrary, its perpetual incompleteness and its subjection to question is to a varying extent the norm.  Employment
situations imply some control *by* management;  yet there is frequently also some struggle so that the control *of* management's arbitrary
exercise of its 'prerogative' is also in question.

But despite these considerations and despite the events briefly
depicted, there has been as noted at the outset a general neglect
of management control strategies by industrial relations analysts.
Speculation on the reasons for this neglect cannot be allowed to
detain us at this point but a few observations are necessary.
Within marxism, for example, it has been suggested that, with its
gaze firmly fixed on the replacement of capitalism, naturally little
energy has been devoted to exploring possible developments emerging
in control and resistance at the point of production.  Moreover,
Coombs (1978) has added that the long neglect of the labour process
within marxism stemmed not from 'mere isolated error' but reflects
a fundamental distortion in orthodox marxist analysis perpetrated by
the Second International and by Soviet Marxism.  This distortion he
identifies as derivative from an uncritical acceptance of economic
and technological determinism (Coombs 1978:81).  In so far as this
is true, and it is only at best a rough generalisation, the intricacies of strategy and counter-strategy would tend to be overlooked.
Sociology for its part seemed to allow the problem to fall between
two stools - macro-structures of class relations on the one hand and
the micro-relations of informal groups on the other.  That amorphous
body known sometimes as 'organisation theory' tended to obscure the
study of management control as a problem area because it took it so
much for granted.  The problematic lay elsewhere - usually in further 'rationalising' formal organisational structures.  The academic
study of industrial relations similarly had its eyes diverted towards the 'problems' of trade unions, industrial conflict and collective bargaining.

Of late, however, the general theme of the control of work has
been exciting ever-mounting attention.  This is particularly so
within the marxist-informed literature but also, though to a lesser
degree, outside it.  Michael Poole (1975) approached the subject of
workers' participation from a 'power perspective'.  Bowen (1976)
used the concept of control to interpret relationships in the steel
industry.  Boreham and Dow (eds) (1980b) have marshalled a collec-

tion of papers which straddle economics and sociology while addressing the general theme of the impact of capitalist crisis on work
experience.  Purcell and Smith (1979) edited a number of essays on
industrial relations which sought to address the theme of 'the control of work' - theoretical development did not, however, seem to be
a prime target.  Purcell and Earl (1977) in an earlier paper advanced clear conceptual guidelines on the theme of control and controlling.  Interesting and provocative studies which illuminated the
theme of work control also emerged in Beynon (1973) and Nichols and
Beynon (1977).  Additional recent works of note include Nichols
(ed.) (1980), Edwards (1979) and Hill (1981).  And forthcoming ap-
praisals of cognate interest include Wood (ed.) and Gospel (ed.).
This last collection examines managerial strategies in industrial
relations from a historical perspective. (6)

Parallel to the shift in focus in industrial relations towards
the question of control, and to the explanation of that control in
terms which situate it within the wider logic of capitalism, has
occurred a similar shift in the organisational studies literature.
This field, long-noted for its managerialist assumptions and problematics, has spawned a critical wing (Clegg and Dunkerley 1977;
Clegg and Dunkerley 1980; Salaman, 1979; Benson, 1977).  Some of
this radical organisational literature has been concerned explicitly
with questions of control and power (Kouzmin, 1980;  Goldman and Van
Houten, 1980;  Singleman, 1980).  Even a cursory review of the
papers gathered together under the first two editions of the 'International Yearbook of Organization Studies' (1980a and 1980b) will
reveal the shift intimated here.

This critical strand of organisational literature has reformulated the central problems.  The erstwhile strenuous efforts to
generate an all-embracing organisation theory which would be ap-
plicable to all 'types' of organisation (hence the superfluity of
typologies and taxonomies), are now declared redundant - and indeed
misguided.  Thus Salaman observes:

a genuine sociology of organisations is not assisted by the
efforts of some organisational analysts to develop hypotheses
about organisations *in general,* lumping together such diverse
examples as voluntary organisations, charities, political parties
and employing organisations.  Such an ambition results in gener-
alisations of an extremely high level of abstraction.  It also
*obstructs* the analysis of those structural elements which are
dramatically revealed in employing organisations but not necessarily in all forms of organisation (1979:33).

This interest in the organisational processes of capitalist employment relations inevitably brings these 'new' organisational
theorists in alignment with a similar development in industrial
sociology;  in the kind of economics generated by the Conference of
Socialist Economists in the UK, and the Union for Radical Political
Economists in the United States, and into general alignment with the
radical strand of industrial relations' theorising.

Harry Braverman's (1974) 'Labor and Monopoly Capital' has of
course been the catalyst for much of the contemporary debate within
the marxist and neo-marxist corpus.  He eloquently traces the degradation of work which was wrought by scientific management techniques in the service of monopoly capital.  Braverman is vitally

significant for his contribution in re-igniting debate on the managerial control of the labour process - a phenomenon essentially unexplored since Marx's elaboration in 'Capital'.  Of course he alone
was not responsible for the intense interest recently aroused on the
theme of hierarchy and the fragmentation of labour.  Marglin (1971),
Gorz (1972) and Katherine Stone (1973) had already produced significant theses in this area and Braverman utilised these.  R.C. Edwards
(1972) was also producing cognate work and has continued to do so
(1975, 1976, 1979).  In general terms the theme of control of the
capitalist labour process has flourished.  In the USA it has found
particular expression in the 'Review of Radical Political Economics', 'Telos', and 'Radical America'.  In Britain, the theme has
been given close attention in the journal 'Capital and Class' and
in the CSE's collection of readings under the title 'The Labour
Process and Class Strategies' (1976).

Subsequent investigations have identified important shortcomings
in Braverman's account despite acknowledgment of its seminal contribution (Friedman, 1977;  Palmer, 1975;  Brighton Labour Process
Group, 1977).  In essence there are three central complaints which
unfold in these and the many other related treatments and reviews of
Braverman. (7)  Foremost is his general neglect or at least minimisation of worker resistance. (8)  Trade unions, for example, are
dismissed in a couple of lines (1974:10).  But it is not only his
neglect of unions which his critics identify here.  They complain at
the portrayal of capital as essentially uncontested at any level.
Friedman (1977) finds this particularly misleading;  he argues that
Braverman requires a theoretical revision.  The interplay between
control and resistance in varying situations generates a force which
actually shapes the nature of the control system itself.  The second
criticism often made is that Braverman places too much emphasis on
Taylorism as the sole or main thrust of capital's control strategy.
As Nichols observes, 'there are other forms of control as well as
de-skilling and capital has more shots in its locker than Braverman
implies' (1977:194).  And Coombs suggests, the obsession with
Taylorism 'underestimates capital's room for manoeuver' (1978:84).
The third type of complaint from Braverman's critics fixes on his
failure to locate adequately the alleged incipient tendency towards
Taylorism in concrete historical contexts (Elger, 1979).  Elger contrasts this with an account which suggests Taylorism developed in
response to the crisis at the end of the last century.

It is important to recognise that these three problems are in
fact *interrelated*.  The neglect of worker resistance and the exclusive focus on Taylorism and de-skilling indicates not only empirical shortcomings (see for example the evidence produced by
Palmer, 1975) but points up a key theoretical weakness.  So far,
despite a plethora of apparently disparate criticisms no one seems
to have attempted to bring these together in order to allow a new
stage for theoretical advance.  Instead there have been partial attempts to 'correct' for shortcomings in Braverman.  Par excellence
in this regard was Friedman's (1977) delineation of the two major
strategies utilised by employers - direct control and responsible
autonomy.  These criticisms are themselves vulnerable to the kind
of counter-claim made, for example, by Zimbalist (ed.) (1979) who
mounts a vigorous defence of Braverman.  He maintains that Braverman

was well aware of worker resistance and of the modifications made to
the Taylor system.  It was not these 'details', however, which concerned him but rather the general ideological thrust and impact of
Taylorism.  While short-term tactical manoeuvres might exist the
underlying scientific management philosophy still rules.  'Responsible autonomy' had already been taken into account by Braverman and
treated accordingly as 'only a short-run and often cosmetic variation' (Zimbalist 1979:xxi).  Hence Zimbalist views the case studies
collected in his own book as reaffirming the Braverman thesis and as
contributing to the task of putting flesh on the skeletal form. (9)

I will argue, however, that it is not merely a question of fill-
ing out the details of Braverman's scheme that is required.  Rather,
fundamental theoretical amendments are needed.  There remain basic
problems in Braverman's account. (10)  Managerial strategies are
quite varied - and frequently for valid reasons.  The thesis of an
incipient tendency towards deskilling remains suspect.  Braverman
concentrates much of his analysis on the plans, propaganda, sales
talk and conceptualisations of the agents of rationalised working
and thereby avoids addressing the problems of implementing such
schemes.  He, like Marglin, tends to reify de-skilling as an abstract imperative.  In consequence analysis of managerial control
strategies is insufficiently located within a wider theoretical
scheme which would permit investigation of why control was required
and under what circumstances it would be pressed home.  The unevenness across sectors and within sectors is accordingly underemphasised and its significance underexplored.  Equally, managerial strategies are not situated in the contexts of particular periods or
against the backcloth of the theory of valorisation and accumulation.  The  real subordination of labour as explained by Marx faces
contradictions - again these are left untouched by Braverman's
scheme.

The argument advanced in this book is that the most productive
way to embrace the fruits of Braverman's work while at the same time
taking account of the key shortcomings indicated by his critics, is
to adopt a *dialectical* approach.  This it is argued offers the best
chance at this time of understanding the dynamic nature of the control of production.  It allows also consideration of the wider
social and economic context within which control strategies are
shaped.  It should permit a better consideration of the resistance
of labour and the reciprocal interrelationship between control and
resistance.

Despite Braverman's recognition of Marx's own 'genius at dialectic', his own book remains essentially deterministic and unilinear.
As Gavin MacKenzie observes, 'Braverman's own analysis is one-sided
... it is devoid of dialectical under/or over-tones' (1977:249).  In
proposing a dialectical method to cope with the interplay between
the material world and active human construction, and between
management control and worker resistance, I have in mind the sort
of framework which is developed in Benson (1977), Lukács (1971),
Heydebrand (1977) and Allen (1975).  In particular it is proposed
to construct a framework which calls attention to the 'totality',
the social construction of reality, and contradiction.  These three
are treated as elements of the overall dialectical approach.  They
accordingly find reflection in each subsequent chapter, though cer-

tain chapters will tend to draw more heavily upon different aspects.
Thus 'totality' tends to be explored most fully in the chapter on
the context of work control (Chapter 5).  Social construction is illuminated particularly in the chapters on management prerogative and
the strategies of management control (Chapters 6 and 7).  Contradictions are drawn out in Chapter 2 on the real subordination of
labour and Chapter 8 on struggles and resistance.  The dialectical
approach directs attention to *social interaction* with a prefigurative world constructed by forebears.  While action is thereby influenced and constricted it is not determined.  The maintenance of an
inter-subjective reality requires perpetual reconstruction.  This
occurs, however, within an interconnected whole - a 'totality'.
This contains inherent contradictions such that actions taken to
alleviate a perceived problem trigger complex related forces which
may create new problems.  Under a more fully developed model of
dialectical materialism the rifts and tensions would mount until a
cataclysmic crisis engendered a 'de-totalisation'.

To adopt a dialectical view here is not to denigrate the idea of
a general and persistent 'thrust for efficiency'.  Indeed this is
central to our account.  But it does imply that the application
tends to be strategic and adaptive.  It implies that the 'dull compulsion of economic relations' is mediated by technological opportunities, emulation, opposition and resistance, opportunism and
sheer irrationality and incompetence.

A dialectical approach offers a way forward.  Much 'radical
organisation theory' has remained content merely to catalogue the
shortcomings of orthodox theory (see, for example, Salaman, 1978).
Other work has elements of a dialectic method - highlighting for
example, contradictions or totality - but fails to develop the approach (Cressey and MacInnes 1980;  Friedman 1977).  Still other
work while sketching the basis for a dialectical view (Benson 1977)
has remained essentially at the middle level, viewing organisations
themselves as totalities (Burrell 1980:98).  In this introductory
chapter the elements of the dialectic can only be schematically
presented.  It is more fully developed in the following chapter and
elaborated in the rest of the book.

*Totality* was used particularly by Lukács (1971) but also by Hegel
and Marx.  In essence it denotes the idea that social behaviour must
be considered as part of a wider process of historic social formation which, through complex interconnection constitutes a whole.
The totality is reflected in each of the parts, and the parts in
turn have their reflection in the whole.  Currently this means that
the social relations at the point of production must be understood
with reference not just to the organisation, nor even the 'society'
but to the global capitalist mode of production which enjoys fundamental hegemony.  It is the logic and constraints of this totality
which inform the social control of work within each establishment.
Accordingly there is an interrelationship between economic, political, social and ideological forms.  The consequence of this for work
control and managerial prerogatives is that workers seeking to shift
the frontier of control and challenge managerial rights are likely
to find these buttressed by interlinking elements of the totality.
Thus the operation of the money market, the role of the state, the
wider cultural, political and ideological apparatuses, are likely

to be inimical to such a challenge.  Overall, the implication is
that the social phenomenon of work control must be studied relation-
ally.

This is not to suggest that managerial control under capitalism
is absolute.  Control structures and strategies typically contain
their own inherent *contradictions*.  Braverman implies de-skilling is
almost an objective or end in itself.  Yet this cannot be so.  Capital (accumulated, dead labour) requires living labour to continue
the cycle of production and valorisation.  In the final analysis the
inanimate factors of production must be placed in the hands of
living labour if surplus-value is to be realised.  There are circumstances where relative surplus-value is enhanced with a skilled
labour force:  the desiderata of control and surplus-value thus
contradict.  Marginalism may also imply that after a period of
rationalisation, structures are produced which resist further rationalisation;  any subsequent drive to increase relative surplus-value
may thus be stymied.  It is the combination of contradictions which
Althusser viewed as the basis for a 'ruptural unity' (Althusser and
Balibar, 1970).  This may explain why Braverman remained optimistic
(in 1976) despite what he saw as the current lack of resistance.

But the third facet of our dialectical scheme, *social construction,* may intervene here.  'Ruptural unity' may be impeded by a
series of measures consciously and deliberately designed to reduce
tensions and conflicts.  Accordingly, significant adjustments to the
system may occur as crises mount.  At the organisational level, for
example, a deterioration in labour relations or labour supply may
well induce a sober reappraisal and consequent corrective action.
The 'social construction' aspect of our dialectical scheme ranges
of course over an area much wider than this.  Most crucially it
reminds us that consciousness is not merely epiphenomenal.  Thus,
while 'society' (the product of human interaction) most certainly
acts back upon its producers, this does not cast them as merely
puppets or as helpless victims.  The dialectical facet we are here
calling 'social construction' points up the scope for liberating
actions.  Moreover, this aspect of the dialectic sharpens awareness
of the *social* nature of the conflict emerging from contradictions.
This is because the road of human destiny is seen more clearly as a
social product and therefore the interest groups which fare relatively poorly may perceive the source of their disadvantage.  Many
other ramifications are involved but for now one crucial point must
be noted:  the dialectical element of social construction emphasises
the fact that repressive structures of work organisation and the
whole technology of production arise not inexorably and therefore
unalterably but as a social product and so amenable to change.
Marxist theory recognises the contradiction between the worker as
a commodity and as a conscious human subject 'to be the driving
force of class struggle ... it is a dialectic we must capture'
(Gintis 1976:37).

To capture such a dialectic permits and demands progress beyond
Braverman.  A reformulation of this kind requires starting afresh
from the fundamental base constructed by Marx.  In the 1873 Postface
to the Second Edition of 'Capital' Marx declares, 'My dialectical
method, is in its foundations not only different from the Hegelian
but exactly opposite to it' (1976:102).  He proceeds to explain how

Hegel 'mystifies' the dialectic by elevating the notion of the
'Idea' to prime place, whereas for Marx the material world displaces
this:  'it must be inverted', he argues, 'in order to discover the
rational kernel within the mystical shell' (Marx 1976:103).   Marx
famously enhances and alters therefore, the Hegelian dialectic. (11)
More importantly here, he does so while paying close regard to the
characteristic features and developments in the capitalist *labour
process*.   Managerial control can best be understood from this basis.
In 'Capital' volume 1, having examined commodities and money in Part
One and the transformation of money into capital in Part Two, Marx
initiates an analysis of the production of surplus-value - i.e. he
moves from the sphere of circulation into the sphere of production.
This latter entails a study of the labour process - a sphere which
as noted has been generally neglected apart from Braverman's re-
opening of the issue.   Marx identified two spheres - that of exchange (or circulation) and that of production.   The latter continued to be a 'hidden abode' despite Marx's attempt to lead us from
the 'noisy sphere where everything takes place on the surface' into
this 'hidden abode of production on whose threshold there hangs the
notice "No admittance except on business"' (Marx 1976:279-80).

   The 'two spheres' are further contrasted in terms of authority
relationships.   The 'sphere of circulation or commodity exchange ...
is in fact a very Eden of the innate rights of man.   It is the exclusive realm of Freedom, Equality, Property and Bentham ...',
whereas when we steal into the hidden abode, the sphere of production, a significant transformation is made evident:

> He who was previously the money-owner now strides out in front as
> a capitalist;  the possessor of labour-power follows as his
> worker.   The one smirks self importantly and is intent on busi-
> ness;  the other is timid and holds back, like someone who has
> brought his own hide to market and now has nothing else to expect
> but - a tanning (Marx 1976:280).

This relatively neglected second sphere is to be the focus of the
present analysis.   However, this should not imply that it can be
treated in isolation from the other sphere.   Marx's intention was
not to suggest that the sphere of exchange was indeed in any absolute sense a realm of freedom and equality;  his purpose was to
dramatise the contrast between the spheres.   However, the full
interplay between control and resistance can only be appreciated
if both spheres are considered together.   Job control must be placed
in the context of the economic system, the role of the state, the
deployment of science and technology, the ideological network and
other facets of the cultural, political and economic totality - in
short a *political economy* of work control is required.   This point
has, of course, become more evident as the recession deepens.   The
question to be addressed is how contemporary analysis should come to
terms with this truth.   One lesson is clear:  the relatively 'unde-
veloped' scheme portrayed in Braverman (1974) will not suffice.

   This must at the very least, be augmented with the work of some
notable theorists ignored by Braverman, or more correctly, a new
departure must be made.   As Bill Schwarz (1977:164) observes,
'Braverman's general refusal to confront post-Marx marxists is particularly frustrating.'   This is a telling comment.   Something more
than psychological 'frustration' is involved;  there is a more

literal frustration of understanding as a result of a failure to
engage with the works of for example Gramsci, Lukács and Habermas.

Widening the analysis in this way implies attention also to the
work of Weber.  His famed analyses of the 'rationalisation process'
and of domination deserve consideration in the attempt to come to
terms with developments in management control techniques.  As
Lazonick argues, despite Marx's penetrating analysis 'he neglects
the role of cultural and political development in reinforcing and
reproducing ... domination' (1978:1;  see also Elger 1979).  The
value of a dialectical approach soon becomes evident when his work
is confronted.  Curiously, this figure so often used to emphasise
the 'role of ideas' in human society, to illustrate the genesis of
social action theory and to exemplify the subjective, creative element in human existence, is the same person who carried the rationalisation thesis to such lengths that even his own heavy pessimism
was fully exercised.  Conjuring an image of modern man in his 'iron
cage', entangled in a bureaucracy allegedly as inevitable under
socialism as under capitalism, Weber seems to arrive, however un-
willingly, at a position where the independent, creative capacity
of man is occluded.  The only possibility for cutting through the
'metaphysical pathos' is through a recognition of creative man as
a first step to his reawakening.  Inevitably, given capital's in-
dulgent use of formal rationality in its control strategy, this
theme must be given close attention.  The rationalised pursuit of
surplus-value has become a characteristic feature of modern life.
In their varying ways Marx, Weber and Taylor re-work the theme.
It is, however, the variation between them, and the ambiguities
within, that lead today to contrasting interpretations and confusions apropos the kernel of the dynamic element.  Does it lie in
the desire for control?  Is it the pursuit of profit?  Is it the
class struggle?  Or is its source in the forces of production?  A
dialectical model would allow an interplay between these kind of
forces.  Managers as key social actors would be seen as important
not only because of their strategies but also because of their
*reading* and *interpretation* of other forces which to a large extent
shape the control system.  Control is in the last analysis a means
towards the attainment of surplus-value.  Hence, along the way the
rigorous pursuit of scientific management may be relaxed if and when
this appears advantageous for valorisation.  Elbaum demonstrates how
in steel production bosses were content to allow retention of old
craft control methods - until that is Bessemer production techniques
became available.  Given the change in the organic composition of
capital, it was too risky to allow control to lie outside centralised hands, and further, there had to be an intensification of
production techniques to compete with other manufacturers in the
use of socially necessary labour time.  But even these sorts of
contrasts are not absolute, because there remains the opacity of the
choices facing fallible people and because there is some degree of
flexibility between alternative paths to meet similar criteria.

It will be argued then that a return to Marx is necessary in
order to start from fundamentals, but that certain emendations to
the orthodox marxian model are required.  The role of managers will
be raised here in a way which would seem impermissible if the conflict were viewed only as engaging capital and labour.  From a tra-

ditional perspective managers would seemingly present an inappropriate target for analysis:  Marx appears to lend weight to such a
view.  He writes, 'the *mere* manager who has no title whatever to the
capital whether through borrowing it or otherwise, performs all the
real functions pertaining to the functionary capitalist as such.'
(12)  This conceivably could lead us to an argument which deliberately neglected management because the priorities and forces
shaping their actions are seen as emanating from outside themselves.
Managers as functionaries or agents could be viewed as constrained
by, for example, market forces, such that fear of takeover or replacement ensures relatively predictable and conformist behaviour.
Therefore, it might be maintained that the appearance of control
over the levers of power should not be mistaken for actual control.

There is some merit in such arguments.  It is certainly no part
of our remit to maintain that senior managers comprise a new ruling
class (an interpretation of their social location is made in Chapter
5).  It is argued here, however, that to restrict the focus to capital and labour can direct much needed attention from managerial
strategies, and from the processes whereby capital's priorities are
mediated.  Without this, theorising may obscure and distort the
actual experience of control and resistance as lived at the point
of production.  It is precisely this dialectical interplay of control and resistance which has to be brought into focus.  There is
a need to clarify the *how* of management control.  It will indeed be
argued that the central rationale of the managerial function is precisely this activity of control.  The problem for the purchasers of
'labour' is threefold:

   (i)  to extract actual work or labour from the 'labour power'
   potential purchased in the market.  Hence labour has to be separated from its carrier;
   (ii)  to render malleable and tractable the labour which is in
   fact extracted.  It must also be made predictable and sustain-
   able;
   (iii)  to counter resistance both of an individual and collective
   kind which may emerge as a direct consequence of actions adopted
   under (i) and (ii).  This task may and probably will call for
   strategies rather different from those at the first level.

All these tasks fall to management.  Hence the capitalist labour
process involves management as a sine qua non.  Accordingly, Edwards
(1979) observes that to keep employees 'working diligently is itself
a major task employing a vast workforce of its own'.  Conflict
arises

   over how work shall be organized, what work-pace shall be established, what conditions producers must labour under, what rights
   workers shall enjoy, and how the various employees of the enterprise shall relate to each other.  The workplace becomes a
   battleground, as employers attempt to extract the maximum effort
   from workers and workers necessarily resist their bosses' imposi-
   tions (Edwards, 1979:13).

The battleground image may in many instances, and for a variety
of reasons to be explored later, be somewhat exaggerated and inappropriate.  Nevertheless, the nature of the task falling to management is made clear here by Edwards.  With increasing organisational
complexity, direct control through ownership and command becomes im-

possible.  The function of accumulation today is divided into specialist sub-functions of production, quality control, personnel
management, industrial relations management, operational research,
work study and accountancy.  Thus it can be argued that the managerial function interpreted in this wide sense deserves serious attention.

Managerial control is additionally bolstered by state control and
by complex interlinking with a cultural and political ensemble which
disguises domination as a rational response to technical problems.
As Habermas observes in 'Toward a Rational Society', 'The manifest
domination of the authoritarian state gives way to the manipulative
compulsions of technical-operational administration' (1971:107).  So
while a certain link is forged between Marx, Weber and Habermas, the
point also contains an amendment to the traditional Marxian scheme.
State involvement, for example, can no longer be considered as
merely epiphenomenal.  And Habermas departs from Marx's model by
effecting a shift from the economic base to the superstructural
level.

Lazonick (1979) mounts a related critique which again illuminates
the need for a revamped dialectical approach.  In what has to be acknowledged as at least a novel attack upon Marx, he argues that:

Marx in fact committed an error which is all too common in the
social sciences.  He derived his conclusion of the omnipotence of
technology in the subjection of labour to capital from an uncritical acceptance of capitalist ideology, instead of using his
own theoretical framework for an empirical investigation of the
interaction of the relations and forces of production (Lazonick
1979:258-9).

So mirroring Weber's 'metaphysical pathos', one comes away from Marx
and Braverman with an image wherein 'the capitalists essentially get
their way' (1979:231).  In this work I wish to remain more open-
minded about the degree and efficacy of resistance.

Antonio Gramsci provides some corrective here.  He asserts,
the mechanical forces never predominate in history, it is the
men, the consciousness and the spirit which mould the external
appearance and always triumph in the end ... the pseudo scientist's natural law and fatal course of events has been replaced
by man's tenacious will (quoted in Althusser and Balibar, 1970:
120).

In spite of Zimbalist's defence of Braverman, empirically there
does remain at least cause to doubt whether labour power at the
point of production has seen a secular progression towards intensified control (Davis, 1975;  Montgomery, 1979;  Palmer, 1975;
Lazonick, 1979;  Storey, 1980).  Of course much would depend on
one's comparative reference point. (13)  Measured against an idealised artisan control almost any contemporary centrally planned and
mechanised work situation would 'show' such a 'trend'.  But if we
compare decade for decade, as do a number of the studies quoted, the
unilinear 'tendency' does indeed seem debatable.

From a dialectical position this would not be a matter for surprise.  The real subordination of labour under the capitalist labour
process (examined more fully in the following chapter) contains its
own internal contradictions (see for example Cressey and McInnes,
1980).  Absolute removal of subordinates' initiative would render
them, except in the most stable and predictable of circumstances

frequently immobile and inactive, and even more frequently operating
'inefficiently'.  Further, even before this absolute point was
reached one might expect the onerous nature of an enhanced real control to provoke resentment and resistance - either individual, collective or both.  The forces of production, as Marx recognised, do
not advance alone, they are in dialectical relationship with the
relations of production.  As the 'fetters' begin to bite, adjustments might well be expected before an absolute rupture had chance
to occur.  Another implication of adopting a dialectical approach
derives from the observation that capitalists do not *primarily*
desire control as an end in itself but rather as a means of realising surplus-value.  At certain periods this may be seen as best
achieved by compromise and even the relaxing of past controls in
order to get the work out.  In this way variations in market conditions both cyclically and between sectors will find reflection in
the control pattern.  Uneven development between sectors will be a
related phenomenon, as will uneven development between countries
which may permit the 'export' of rigorous controls to developing
countries and the relaxation of controls in particular sectors of
metropolitan centres.

So the dialectical method must be sensitive to the *strategies* of
the actors on both sides.  These 'strategies' may at times be little
more than emulation, or experiment.  For employers this will normally involve a calculation of the relative pay-off from a contemplated
action for control and for surplus-value.  These may or may not be
coincidental on any particular occasion.  For example, Weber's
formal rationality may optimise control at the expense of productiveness.  The *twin* objectives of control and surplus-value are
recast into two types of rationality by Gordon (1976).  He notes the
pursuit of both 'quantitative rationality' (surplus-value) and
qualitative rationality (i.e. maintaining adequate levels of control).  Labour power has to be transformed by the capitalist into
actual work or labour.  Not only is there a certain *porosity* which
control is designed to counter, but additionally there is always the
danger under alienated capitalist labour that labour will be turned
to 'illegitimate' ends - for example, production for use rather than
production for profit or safe working conditions may be accorded
'too high' a priority (Brighton Labour Process Group, 1977).  It is
for these types of reasons that control over labour power is essential.  So the dynamic element in the path of control strategies is
not just the technology or forces of production but the class struggle itself and the strategies which this generates (Stone 1974:165).

Equally, the need for a dialectical method is realised when one
notes the imprecision created by a reliance on a conceptual tool
such as 'forces of production'.  This provides only a crude guide to
the major variations in the control of the labour process, variations which can only be accounted for by a further concept such as
uneven development.  Thus Elbaum and Wilkinson (1979) find major
differences between the control of steel production in Britain and
the United States.  Indeed, the logic of the work of Marglin (1974)
and Stone (1974) is that the forces of production, far from being an
independent prime causal variable, are themselves subject to manipulation.  As a general tendency, capital seeks to separate *conception*
from *execution*.  This is necessary to counteract the kind of 'devi-

ations' in the labour process noted above.  But there may be occasions and circumstances where valorisation, and the objective of
real subordination of labour, conflict.  One type of circumstance -
film production - is explored by Chanan (1976, 1980).  Elsewhere,
real subordination may proceed apace because employers *believe* it
will serve their interests and long-term goals.  Thus it has not
sufficiently been recognised in all of the discussion concerning
'work humanisation' and job enrichment that these experiments in the
*re*-structuring of jobs only occur because of a much longer legacy of
active '*de*-structuring'.  Locked into low-trust control systems, employers are naturally sceptical (as are employees) as to whether
partial reversals can succeed in the face of the wider tide.  But
in pursuit of valorisation some are prepared to *consider* it.

In sum, our stress on *strategy* is integral to the dialectical
method.  Just as it has been argued that the control process is not
fruitfully viewed as linear and unproblematic, so too with the related concept of formal rationality.  To succumb to visions of its
inevitability is equally to fall victim to bourgeois ideology which
fails to separate sectional interest from rational method.  To
effect a break from the 'strong streak of technological determinism
in both bourgeois and orthodox Marxist traditions' (Gordon 1976:35)
requires attention to a dialectical stance with emancipatory potential.  Anticipating somewhat our later argument, it might here be
signalled that close attention to Habermas's work and in particular
to his theme of 'communicative competence' will be fruitful.  The
*critical* stance here adopted implies a belief in *alternatives* but
the issue is complex, for, as Offe argues, capitalism in a way does
serve everyone's interests in so far as they receive real benefits
as members of a given capitalist society.  This whole question of
*interests* is developed at greater length in Chapter 2 where it is
tied into the analysis of rationality.  Here it may be noted, however, that while marxist interpretations have criticised subjective
conceptions of interest in liberal theorising, certain dilemmas
remain within the marxist conception itself (Balbus, 1971;  Stolzman, 1975;  Crouch, 1979b).  The argument that any gains in working-
class power which do not simultaneously undermine capitalism have to
be 'added to capital's side of the balance sheet' Crouch (1979b:34)
regards as flawed.  As he observes, the claim that working-class
interests will only be adequately met after a revolution is unfortunately a statement outside the realm of social science.  The
'rationality' of displacement has two provisos:  'reasonable expec-
tation' that domination will be eliminated or reduced and second
that the 'material advantages already gained by the class within
capitalism are not put in jeopardy' (Crouch 1979b:35).  Clearly
these are stringent criteria.  They present hurdles that were absent
when Marx could note the proletariat had nothing to lose but their
chains, or when Robert Tressell could argue his Mugsboro' painters
and decorators had nothing to risk but their rags.

In our argument, the path suggested will be an enhancement of
'practical rationality' based upon an advance in communicative competence.  The conception of 'rationality' used will have to cast
off the obfuscations engendered in Weber's writings.  An emancipatory rationality implies attention to and debate of ends and objectives as well as of means.  This kind of discourse would only be

possible through enhanced opportunities for communications - both in
channels available and the 'competence' of the communicators.   On
this latter, as Goodey argues, a *people's* revolution as distinct
from a revolution from above requires not only objective conditions
but also subjective *capabilities* (Goodey 1974:28).  This is not
merely a naive call for more 'education';  the dialectical method is
clear here in confronting the objective conditions with the subjective capabilities.  As Kurzwell expresses it in summarising Foucault, 'Salvation, if any, can be through knowledge, knowledge that
will grow on the ruins of our own epoch' (1977:417).  As with the
stance taken by Habermas, this is Foucault's response to the dilemma
posed by extant repressive 'socialist' states and 'free' societies
where citizens are subject to a more subtle and pervasive domination.  This type of learning and theoretical development as a reciprocal of action and vice versa is integral to the dialectical programme.  It is *praxis*.  A 'rational society' implies, then, an open
and considered interplay between technique (expertise), objectives
and values.  This argument is in line with that advanced by Hearn
(1978) who recasts 'rationality' in such a way as to distance it,
one might even say rescue it, from the Weberian category.  He
writes, 'practical rationality or the rationality of consciousness
rests not on technical rationalization but on the expansion of the
space and the time available for political discourse and critical
dialogue' (1978:44).  The distinction between technical rationality
and practical rationality is drawn from Habermas and Gouldner.  The
first term denotes calculated pursuit of given or taken-for-granted
goals, whereas, the second, 'practical rationality', denotes a process of enlightened reflection on the choice of goals through non-
distorted (political) communication.  This kind of rationality as
Habermas (1970) notes is possible only 'through *removing restrictions on communications*.  Public, unrestricted discussion, free from
domination of the suitability and desirability of action-orienting
principles and norms in the light of the socio-cultural repercussions ...' (1970:118).  Just as the capitalist may weigh the antici-
pated repercussions arising from the mix of 'quantitative' and
'qualitative' rationality, so too the outcome for the working class
in throwing-off capitalist control is by no means certain.  It is
not necessarily a choice between 'standard of living' and freedom
from coercive interference.  As has been noted, alternative relations of production may outstrip the productiveness of capitalist
relations of production (Braverman 1974;  Marglin 1974;  Gordon
1976;  Hearn 1978).
   The debate then on the capitalist control of work is far-reaching
in its implications.  It cannot be reduced to a discussion of de-
skilling.  It cannot be confined to the point of production nor
indeed the sphere of production.  It cannot be educed as a mystical,
incipient tendency wherein it has already been predecided that 'the
capitalist always wins'.  To escape from these restrictions it has
been argued, requires a dialectical approach.  This requires in the
first instance a return to the fundamental base furnished by Marx -
most notably in his analysis of the labour process.  It entails more
forthright attention to contradictions, to management strategy, to
uneven development, to resistance, and to the political economy of
work control.

# Chapter 2

# RATIONALITY AND THE REAL SUBORDINATION OF LABOUR: WEBER AND MARX

This chapter is not intended to review even in a modest fashion the works of Marx and Weber but rather to extract from each basic theoretical propositions on forces of production, rationalisation and strategy in order to advance the dialectical approach. The analysis presents a number of amendments to the schemes put forward by each writer although Weber's is subjected to the more radical alteration.

## MARX AND THE REAL SUBORDINATION OF LABOUR

Until recently attention to the work of Marx tended to focus on certain well-trodden macro-themes relating to class conflict, social change and the displacement of capitalism. But since Braverman (1974) there has been renewed interest in turning attention from the sphere of exchange to the sphere of production. In his foreword to 'Labor and Monopoly Capital' Paul Sweezy recommends a parallel study of 'Capital'. This is because herein Marx develops what has turned out to be a rather neglected analysis of the capitalist labour process. He moves directly from a discussion of commodities and the nature of value to the examination of the part played by labour. Hence in chapter 7 of 'Capital', volume 1, Marx begins his explanation of the labour process and the valorisation process. He observes that the purchaser of 'labour power' can only consume it by 'setting the seller of it to work'. In order for the capitalist to realise a profit he must indeed set work which will result in the production of commodities, i.e. use values. The basic process occurs 'independently of any specific social formation', because labour per se is 'first of all a process between man and nature' (Marx 1976:283). In the pages which follow Marx develops his case that it is living labour which generates use-values, i.e. goods and services. It is not things per se which are vital but labour. Thus,

> a machine which is not active in the labour process is useless. In addition it falls prey to the destructive power of natural processes. Iron rusts; wood rots. Yarn with which we neither weave nor knit is cotton wasted. *Living labour must seize* on these things, *awaken* them from the dead, change them from merely possible into real and effective use-values (1976:289).

Indeed, raw materials and the instruments of production (two of the
three 'elements' in the labour process - the third of which is 'purposive activity' or work) are themselves merely products of past
labour.  Thus, out of the labour process come products, which are
in turn to be seen as 'objectified labour'.  This is normally obscured - unless something goes wrong:

>   whenever products enter as means of production into new labour
>   processes they lose their character of being products and func-
>   tion only as objective factors contributing to living labour ...
>   it is by their imperfections that the means of production in any
>   process bring to our attention their character of being the pro-
>   ducts of past labour.  A knife which fails to cut, a piece of
>   thread which keeps on snapping, forcibly remind us of Mr. A, the
>   cutler, or Mr. B, the spinner (1976:289).

Having established the centrality of 'living labour' in the production of use-values, Marx goes on to establish its centrality to
the production of exchange-value and especially surplus-value under
capitalism, and also to establish the crucial features of the labour
process under the social formation called capitalism.  Herein two
features become characteristic:  first, the worker operates under
the *control* of the capitalist and, second, the product is now the
*property* of the capitalist.  Under this second, labour power itself
is a product or commodity belonging to the capitalist 'not the
worker its immediate producer.  Suppose that a capitalist pays for
a day's worth of labour-power;  then the right to use that power for
a day belongs to him, just as much as the right to use any other
commodity, such as a horse he had hired ...' (1976:292).  Thus the
capitalist appropriates both the labour power and the product which
is worked upon.  Marx likens this to the fermentation process:  the
capitalist mixes the 'living agent' of labour to the 'lifeless constituents' of the product and as with the wine in his cellar he owns
the agent and the product.

But the whole point of the exercise for the capitalist is not to
produce use-value but surplus-value and to do this he must generate
exchange-value.  Marx calls this process of transformation the
'valorisation process' - literally the value-building process (Wert-
bildungsprozess).

At this point in his argument Marx again reverts to elaborating
his labour theory of value.  This has been much misinterpreted by
bourgeois economists as a theory of relative prices.  Nevertheless,
there are other problems attached to Marx's theory of value, the
elaboration of which would be inappropriate here (Cutler et al.
1977;  but for a vigorous defence see Becker 1977).  It is, however,
necessary and valid to sketch certain aspects of the theory of value
at this point.  For Marx, value is determined by the socially *neces--*
*sary* labour time taken to produce the commodity.  The 'socially
necessary' time will be the average or normal time given the extant
level of knowledge and technology.  Therefore,

>   if a capitalist has a foible for using golden spindles instead of
>   steel ones, the only labour time that counts for anything in the
>   value of the yarn remains that which would be required to produce
>   a steel spindle, because no more is necessary under the given
>   social conditions (1976:295).

If for example the normal conditions prevailing are those where

'self-acting mules is the socially predominant instrument of labour
for spinning, it would be impermissible to supply the spinner with
a spinning wheel' (1976:303).  Moreover, it is only living labour
which can create surplus-value;  the other factors of production
such as the cotton itself or the proportion of spindle worn down by
friction only realise their equivalent direct exchange-value.  So,
exchange of equivalents is not valorisation:  this requires the
capitalist to retain a day's labour power for the price of say,
half a day (in Marx's own example).

It is the surplus labour which creates capital, and it is on account of this that the labourer is exploited.  Marx explores the
spiral (as distinct from circular) process whereby the 'trick' is
performed:  that is, money is transformed into capital.  First money
is turned into commodities (the instruments and materials of labour
but most importantly labour power itself), then a new process begins
wherein the old commodities (themselves as we saw earlier being dead
labour) are transformed into new commodities, these are sold for
more money and with part of this the whole cycle begins again.  Thus
the valorisation process is a step beyond the mere replacement of
labour power with an equivalent.  This, observes Marx, would be
'simply a process of creating value;  but if it is continued beyond
that point it becomes a process of valorization' (1976:302).

The overall phenomenon comprising the *unity* of the two processes
- labour and valorisation - Marx terms the 'production process' or,
more specifically, the 'capitalist process of production'.  This
embodies certain immanent characteristics highly pertinent to our
analysis.  It is necessary to sketch these out before turning to the
central part of Marx's framework to be used in our model - namely
the tendency towards the real subordination of labour under capitalism.

It may appear somewhat ironic, given the attention lent to the
exploitation of labour under capitalism, that one of its peculiarly
distinguishing features under this mode of production is that it is
formally 'free'.  Thus, unlike social conditions of slavery, feudalism and other instances of patently 'forced' labour where exploited
classes literally owed their labour power to their masters, under
capitalism there is a labour *market* in which the workers are, at
least in formal terms, free to offer their labour power for sale to
anyone who wishes to buy it, and for limited *contractual* periods.
So labour is free in the sense that, unlike the situation with slave
or serf, it is not irrevocably tied to any one particular master.
Moreover, there is a measure of freedom in that, unlike the slave
and serf again, the worker under capitalism is not compelled by
direct political and/or physical force to make him work.  In their
stead, of course, the limits to his 'freedom' are clear enough.  Cut
off from the means of independent subsistence the wage labourer is
subject to economic compulsion to sell his labour.  On the question
of 'free labour' Marx quotes T.R. Edmonds who in 'Practical, Moral
and Political Economy', makes the point succinctly:

A free labourer has generally the liberty of changing his master:
this liberty distinguishes a slave from a free labourer, as much
as an English man-of-war sailor is distinguished from a merchant
sailor ...  The condition of a labourer is superior to that of a
slave, because a labourer *thinks* himself free (cited in Marx
1976:1027).

And in a nice twist to the distinction without a difference Edmonds makes a profound point concerning the irrationality and anarchy of the market:

> the master of the slave understands too well his own interest, to weaken his slaves by stinting them on food;  but the master of a free man gives him as little food as possible, because the injury done to the labourer does not fall on himself alone but on the whole class of masters (Marx 1976:1027-8).

Though in real terms, therefore, labour is to a large extent 'unfree' (Marx used the term wage-slaves) the notion of its freedom to contract as an equal partner with a purchaser of labour has served crucial ideological purposes.  Not least of these has been in the realm of managerial prerogatives, as we shall see in Chapter 6.

Marx went on to distinguish certain other key elements of capitalist production, elements which can also be viewed as stages in its development.  These were:  co-operation, the division of labour, the use of machinery and large-scale industry.

> [Co-operation] only begins with the labour process, but by then [workers] have ceased to belong to themselves.  On entering the labour process they are incorporated into capital....  The *socially* productive power of labour develops as a free gift to capital, whenever the workers are placed under these conditions, and it is capital which places them under these conditions. [Because of this it appears as] a power which capital possesses by its nature (1976:451).

Referring back to pre-capitalist forms of co-operation, Marx distinguishes them on account of the unfree labour argument, and also on account of common ownership.  Co-operation under capitalism offers advantages to the capitalist in his attempt to realise surplus-value.  These advantages emerge from common use of buildings and other fixed capital, so even without changes in working methods capital gets its 'free gift'.  But subtle changes do tend to occur - a 'new power' arises 'from the fusion of many spirits into a single force, mere social contact begets in most instances a rivalry and stimulation of animal spirits' (1976:443), masons passing bricks along a line are more productive than if each carried his own separately and independently.  Furthermore, certain industries have 'critical moments' such as at harvest time when a mass of concentrated labour is very productive.

Significantly for our theme, the shift from the initial subjection of the individual labourer which occurred only as a formal result of not working for himself, becomes a more real subjection with the arrival of co-operation of many labourers.  Now the 'command of capital develops into a *requirement* ... that a capitalist should command in the field of production is now as indispensable as that a general should command on the field of battle' (1976:448).  The massification of labour is capital's doing, it confronts the labourers as a strange external plan, and direction becomes inevitable.  For this purpose managers are appointed who 'command in the name of capital.  The work of supervision becomes their exclusive function.' (1976:450).

Marx takes the argument further and posits not merely co-operation but the division of labour which occurs in the stage of manu-

facture.  He distinguishes here between general social division of
labour through the exchange of different commodities, and the technical division of labour in workshops under manufacturing, this
being 'an entirely specific creation of the capitalist mode of production' (1976:480).  The increases in productivity this change in
working practices allows have been documented by Adam Smith and other
classical economists.  Marx argues additionally, however, that the
implication of a rising output with the same number of hours is the
creation of 'relative surplus-value'.  Crucial also is the point
that the changes in production methods can actually change the
social relations of production under capitalism.  The original disparate social relations between the owner of the means of produc-
tion/exploiters, and the non-owners/exploited, is heightened and
exacerbated by the fragmentation of work, the loss of skill and the
general degradation of work under capitalism.  This was of course
the theme developed by Braverman.

The third stage in Marx's schema is that of machinery and large-
scale industry.  'Machinofacture' transforms the worker into an ap-
pendage, that is, it is responsible for a crucial *inversion*.  'In
handicrafts and manufacture, the worker makes use of a tool;  in the
factory the machine makes use of him' (1976:548).  There is a pre-
scient and ironic observation made by Marx on a comment by J.S.
Mill, one which finds echo in the current debate on micro-process
technology.  Marx quotes Mill's 'Principles of Political Economy'
wherein some doubt is raised as to whether 'all the mechanical in-
ventions yet made have lightened the day's toil of any human being'.
As Marx retorts, that was by no means its purpose!  Why the surprise?  Marx observes how the power of the master is increased while
that of the worker is diminished by the system of machinery, science
and the mass of social labour.  'The technical subordination of the
worker to the uniform motion of the instruments of labour' com-
pounded by barrack-like discipline brings the 'labour of superintendence to its fullest development' (1976:549).  The driving purpose behind all this intensification of labour, the machinery, the
discipline and the superintendence, is to raise relative surplus-
value.  The changes in the labour process which we have adumbrated
represent the replacement of merely formal 'subsumption' (or subordination to use a clearer term) with 'real subordination' (1976:
645).  This phrase expresses the crucial shift under the capitalist
production process from merely legal ownership to *actual* and *direct*
control over labour.  Marx develops this distinction between formal
and real subsumption in the Appendix to 'Capital', volume 1.  As
Mandel writes in his introduction to this manuscript (originally
intended as Part 7), understanding of 'Capital' has been significantly augmented by this recently-published work.

The merely *formal subordination* of labour occurs at an early
stage in the development of capitalism.  It exists when the social
relations of capitalism displace guild or feudal production and the
capitalist purchases the legal right to labour power but effects no
real change in the existing labour process.  Under these conditions
'surplus-value can be created only by lengthening the working day,
i.e. by increasing absolute surplus-value' (1976:1021).  *Real subordination* on the other hand can create relative surplus-value.
Here, the actual form of production is altered and 'a *specifically*

capitalist form of production comes into being' (1976:1024).  This, as we have noted, transforms and augments the corresponding *social relations* of production.  The contrasts between the two types of subordination may be summarised as below:

| Formal subordination | Real subordination |
|---|---|
| 1  Early capitalism. | 1  Advanced capitalism |
| 2  May merely incorporate pre-capitalist work methods. | 2  New production processes specific to capitalism. |
| 3  Realises absolute surplus value. | 3  Realises relative surplus value. |
| 4  Static. | 4  Dynamic. |
| 5  Capitalist has legal title to ownership of labour power. | 5  In addition to legal title capital actively directs labour. |

Each of these points has been raised but the fourth and fifth require further comment.

The dynamic nature of real, material subordination is promoted by the repeated revolutions in the mode of production, in productivity, in the application of science and technology and in the relations between capitalist and worker.  Marx notes the tendency towards large-scale social production and in the consequent rise in the required minimum amount of capital.  There is a tendency, he argues, for all branches of industry existing merely under formal subordination to be taken over.  As production is undertaken not for need but for valorisation, there is an inherent tendency for crises of over-production.  The intensification of the labour process and the introduction of labour-saving machinery promotes a further consequence - the augmentation of the industrial reserve army of the unemployed.

So the subjection of labour to capital in the labour process helps build the industrial reserve army;  in turn the subjection is made more possible by the sobering impact of the presence of that army.  The significance of the real subordination of labour under capitalism for the function of management can now be identified.  Under formal subordination the capitalist had the formal *'right' to manage*, but only with real subordination does he gain the wherewithal or capability to do so.  Indeed, given the dynamic character of the specifically developed capitalist mode of production (CMP) the capitalist can no longer be content merely to be the formal owner, he *must* direct and manage the accumulated labour, i.e. he takes on this new *function*.  Moreover, he is equally compelled to step up the level of real subordination.  As this proceeds and the control of production is seized from the artisan, management has to assume responsibility for the conception, design and ordering of the process.

The target of discussion - the capitalist labour process - may be conceptualised as at the centre of the dialectic between the forces of production and the relations of production.  The changed *social* relationship whereby the capitalist increasingly takes direct com-

mand and subordinates the worker in a real material sense has repercussions and indeed is augmented by strategies which involve changes
in the *forces* of production.   These changes in turn have further
ramifications for the nature of the social relations of production.

The consequences of all this for the worker is experienced in the
fragmentation of work, loss of initiative, self-direction and control, de-skilling and degradation.   In sum, whereas under formal
subordination he was alienated from the product of labour, with real
subordination he is also alienated from the process.   Management
looms large in the new capitalist production process.   But the
actual implementation of the claimed prerogative to control in a
real and direct sense turns out in practice to be essentially problematical.

In consequence of this last point it will be found necessary to
make certain emendations, and more modestly, to pose certain questions against the formal marxian model as here outlined.   The explication of such requires space and can therefore only be properly developed over the course of this work as a whole.   But a couple of
pointers may be briefly posted.   Firstly, the ideal typical account
of the real subordination of labour requires *situating* historically
and in accordance with concrete social contexts.   To a degree this
kind of task, that of re-working marxian theory to adapt it to developing conditions, has of course continued ever since Marx's
death.   Thus shortly after Engels, Kautsky and Plekhanov had
rounded-out the marxian schema, the next 'generation' had to re-
adapt it in order to respond to the markedly changed conditions of
imperialism, expansion and the transmogrification that came to be
called monopoly capitalism.   Lenin, Trotsky and Hilferding emerged
to perform this task.   But it was the rise of Western marxism that
led to far more significant shifts in marxist interpretation.   Paradoxically, the key figures such as Colletti, Althusser, Lukács and
Marcuse wheeled about and reversed the direction of Marx's own
journey from philosophy to political economy.   As academic philosophers, they engaged in the practice of 'reaching behind' Marx to
draw intellectual nourishment from his philosophical antecedents.
Althusser drew upon Spinoza, Colletti upon Kant, Lukács upon Hegel
(McClellan 1979;  Anderson 1976).   Equally, such writers freely drew
upon contemporary and novel theories - instanced by Marcuse's skil-
ful joining of Marx and Freud.   In the last few years critiques and
reformulations have grown more trenchant, abrasive and wide-ranging.
Thus, Cutler et al. (1977 and 1978) seek to identify a host of deficiencies in marxist theorising.   Their project was to 'explain the
failure of marxist theory to come to terms with the changes that
have taken place in capitalist social formations since the turn of
the century' (1977:2).   They submit that the problem goes deeper
than a mere failure to build onto Marx.   Rather, many of the central
concepts in 'Capital' are actually 'obstacles' to the theorising
required to interpret modern capitalism.   These concepts turn out
to be those of 'economic agents', of 'value' and of the 'laws of
motion'.

At this stage we might signal a different kind of amendment.   The
minimisation of trade-union and working-class resistance in 'Capital' may be forgiven, for it reflects the relative quiescence of the
time in which it was prepared.   But inattentiveness to resistance

today may have more serious analytical consequences.  It is likely,
for instance, to lead to a shallow view of the accomodative and
adaptive capacities of modern capitalism.  Unchallenged, the system
is presumed to travel the path of its own internal logic.  Marx was
of course not suggesting the inviolability of capitalism.  Quite the
contrary, he sketched its catastrophic demise.  The Historic Tendency of Capitalist Accumulation contains the 'immanent laws of capitalist production' which lead towards expropriation and centralisation.

> Along with the constant decrease in the number of capitalist mag-
> nates who usurp and monopolise all the advantages of this process
> of transformation, the mass of misery, oppression, slavery, de-
> gradation and exploitation grows;  but with this there also grows
> the revolt of the working class, a class constantly increasing in
> numbers and trained, united and organized by the very mechanism
> of the capitalist process of production.  The monopoly of capital
> becomes a fetter upon the mode of production which has flourished
> alongside and under it.  The centralization of the means of pro-
> duction and the specialization of labour reach a point at which
> they become incompatible with their capitalist integument.  This
> integument is burst asunder.  The knell of capitalist private
> property sounds.  The expropriators are expropriated (1976:929).

But this scenario, given the experience of the last hundred
years, at least requires juxtaposing with changes that have occurred
in trade-union organisation and state activity.  Development of the
capitalist *system* with its complex institutions of state and culture
may serve to mute some of the potential challenges to the capital-
labour relation that may be built up in the mode of production
(Lazonick 1978).  Indeed, trade unions and working class political
parties may function to integrate workers into capitalism.

The cultural and political institutions such as family and
schools may, on the other hand, develop contradictory tendencies.
They could themselves become arenas within which class struggles may
be engendered.  These institutions, forged in the early period of
class struggle, could consequently form the scene of its renewal.
Whichever scenario was to develop, it is certain that an adequate
interpretation is not now possible without a dialectical perspective, which encompasses the complex and interrelated institutions
of modern capitalism.  Moreover, the perspective must treat them as
a totality.  The essential point is that there is need for a clearer
articulation of the relationship between workplace control practices
and the wider socio-political context.

This raises the second point.  It will be suggested that, in so
far as a base-superstructure metaphor is still tenable, a subtle
shift towards the superstructural is in order.  The division of
labour, the deployment of machine technology, hierarchy and the
whole panoply of domination in current social relations of production may be regarded as 'objectifications'.  These are created and
re-created through human interaction.  Admittedly, to lean towards
insights from hermeneutics and critical theory in this way is in
part to disinter the materialism-idealism debate.  Althusser's case
for a structuralist reading of Marx has been noted.  He locates
Marx's 'epistemological break' as occurring in 1845.  This he describes as 'the mutation of a pre-scientific problematic into a

scientific problematic' (1969:32).  Althusser's own predilection, of
course, is for the science of materialism.  His theory of 'contradiction and overdetermination' and 'determination in the last instance by the economy' has become well known.  He uses the term
'Theory' to designate the *science* of dialectical materialism, and
reserves the term 'philosophy' for ideological philosophy (1969:
162).  In 'For Marx', he bears witness in a manner reminiscent of
Lenin to the

profundity of this principle:  that determination in the last instance by the economy is exercised according to the phases of the
process, not accidentally, not for external or contingent
reasons, but essentially for internal and necessary reasons, by
permutations, displacements and condensations (1969:213).

But in rejecting the humanism of Marx's early work, Althusser
discounted the forces of ideology and human action.  It was, however, precisely these forces which other theorists, most notably
Antonio Gramsci, chose to stress.  Gramsci believed the movement to
subvert class exploitation (i.e. revolutionary action) should and
must begin in the everyday lived world of the working people.  He
emphasised the subjective creative face of marxism.  This entailed
a focus on the ideological dimension and political struggle - i.e.
he directed attention to the superstructure.  Gramsci's praxis was
intimately tied to the workers' councils in Italy.  In his 'Prison
Notebooks' he denounced crude materialism as 'evolutionist positivism' (1971:426).  Indeed, he saw the belief in economic determinism
as an *obstacle* to progressive action.  He wrote,

it may be ruled out that immediate economic crises of themselves
produce fundamental historical events, they can simply create a
terrain more favourable to the dissemination of certain modes of
thought and certain ways of resolving questions ... (1971:184).

This kind of perspective is relevant here because of the need in the
context of the control of work and the degree of resistance to explain the nature of the constraints to further resistance.  Rejection of the reification implicit in structural determination is
allied to the emancipatory spirit inherent in critical theory -
especially that of Jurgen Habermas.  But it would be wholly false
to engage here in a game of picking optimists and pessimists.  Contrary to the theme of increasing clarity of class relations implied
in Marx's outline described above, Habermas and Marcuse explore the
opacity of domination under advanced capitalism.

Noting the ascendancy of science and technology, Habermas interprets their role as a 'substitute ideology for demolished bourgeois
ideologies' (1971:115).  He refers in the latter to the exploded
myth of 'equal exchange' (as explained earlier under Marx's framework).  Managers increasingly rely less on the 'rights' of formal
ownership as a legitimating device and more on the claimed neutrality of technical rationality and instrumental action.  This theme is
best explored with reference to Weberian categories.

Before turning to a consideration of his work let us just briefly
summarise our review of Marx.  We stated that his theoretical scheme
constructed around the labour process provides an indispensable key
to the unlocking of the intricacies of work control.  He starts with
the vital distinction between 'labour power' and 'labour'.  This is
followed by an unravelling of the differences between the labour

process under capitalism and earlier forms. Essentially the argument turns on the concept of the real subordination of labour in pursuit of relative surplus-value. This involves the agents of capital taking command and working out ways to take conception, planning and direction away from workers who thus take on the character of mere instruments. This development is heightened under machinofacture wherein the historic 'inversion' occurs so that tools and machines are no longer controlled and manipulated by workers but instead the worker is controlled and manipulated by the capitalist machines. A critical assessment of the Historic Tendency of Capitalist Accumulation, we argued, pointed-up the need for certain emendations to Marx's scheme. Accordingly the insights afforded by Gramsci and Habermas were noted. Further exploration of these must await a review of the work of Weber because it is he who has exercised most influence on the theorising which has occurred on the 'role of ideas' and the question of rationality - bourgeois and otherwise.


WEBER:   RATIONALITY AND DOMINATION

The structural subordination of workers to capital so clearly elaborated in the Marxian opus finds a peculiar refraction in the work of Weber. Weber's rationalisation thesis is famously posed as the towering counterfactual to historical materialism. The concept became 'the great guiding line not only of his sociology but fundamentally of his whole system' (Loewith 1970:109). Indeed, 'To Weber rationalization signifies the fundamental character of the occidental style of life' (ibid.). Its multi-faceted aspects encompassed the Protestant Ethic, the experimental scientific method, the codifying of government administration and the very growth of capitalism and bureaucracy. Each contributed to the literal disenchantment of modern society. In his exhaustive historical and comparative studies he found 'no analogue' to industrial capitalism's purposive instrumental rationalism with its explicit objectives and ordering of means (Bendix 1966). In this key respect he departs from the marxian account: it is rationalisation per se which is pivotal; it finds articulation in capitalism and bureaucratic control of commodified labour and is itself the sine qua non of these developments.

This much is well known; less well understood - indeed much misunderstood - are the *implications* of Weber's ubiquitous term 'rationality' in the realm of work control and its potential subversion. In this book we will be examining a range of 'rational' managerial control systems and equally, we will be assessing the type and effectiveness of worker responses to such controls. Inevitably the question must arise: to what extent does the (even partial) refutation of 'rational control' constitute an irrational action? Are employees who, for example, collectivise to counter or restrict such managerial strategies inevitably undermining some category of reason? Are managers the custodians of the 'logic of efficiency' and those who oppose them the benighted possessors of a 'logic of sentiments'? Or is it, alternatively, that the so-called 'formally rational administrative systems contain a substantive

bias' in management's favour? (Forbes 1975). Each of these stances
has been adopted in the industrial sociology literature and the
whole question of rationality in this area can only be described as
a quagmire. However, given the questions posed above it is necessary to attempt to steer a way through. Weber's work has been used
as 'proof' that appropriation of the worker and hierarchical domination are inevitable. Equally, as with Forbes above, and additionally by Marcuse (1965), it has been denounced as ideologically biased
in favour of capital.

The source of the diverse interpretations cited above largely
reside in the work of Weber himself, whose writings are replete with
the term 'rational' action. But this term carries shifting meanings. It was not, in fact, until the final year of his writing that
he settled on the dichotomy between 'formal rationality' and 'substantive rationality' - a dichotomy that has become axial in subsequent interpretations of Weber (Mueller 1979). Indeed, it is this
attempted distinction - only partially successfully executed - which
lies at the heart of the confusions regarding Weber's contribution
to interpreting the subordination of labour under capitalism.

In accord with his project on methodological individualism Weber
tried to delineate various ideal types of 'meaningful action'. (1)
Four types are of interest here. Two were unreflective and non-
rational (traditional and affectual action) and two were types of
rational action (Zweckrational and Wertrational). It is the latter
two upon which we must concentrate. This is what led him 'to the
discovery of the main axis of social action as well as of sociological theory: "utilitarian" external interests on the one hand
(as its "material" basis), and "idealistic" internal values on the
other hand (as its "ideological" superstructure)' (Mueller 1979:
152). In order to determine whether Weber was underscoring the
'necessity' for the real subordination of labour and was in fact
ideologically biased in favour of capital's continued domination,
it is necessary to clarify the construct's formal and substantive
rationality. *Formal rationality* denotes 'the extent of quantitative
calculation or accounting which is technically possible and which is
actually applied' (Weber 1964:184). *Substantive rationality* on the
other hand 'cannot be measured in terms of formal calculation alone,
but also involves a relation to the absolute values or to the content of particular ends to which it is oriented' (1964:185). This
'value rationality' (Wertrational) is that form oriented by ideal
interests, internal values and subjective feeling.

Now, Weber saw these two types of rationality as essentially in
conflict. Maximisation of formal rationality in social organisation
would militate against, and even in the end subvert, substantive
goals. Equally, priority accorded substantive or value-rational
social action would be inimical to the constraints of formal, rule-
based, calculative organisation. But there are problems in this apparently neat scheme. Is the formal rationality really neutral and
'absolutely indifferent to all the substantive considerations involved'? (1964:212). Is value-rationality the 'logic of sentiments'
which subordinates bring to the work organisation? Or is it that
'formal rationality is wholly suited to the needs and interests of
capitalists'? (Forbes 1975:224). Or again, does Weber's belief that
formal rationality is devoid of substantive bias imply that this ad-

ministrative machinery 'can function unchanged in a capitalist or socialist society'? (Cohen 1972:79). These kinds of questions find reflection in the contrary stances adapted by Forbes (1975) and Brown (1977). Brown critiques the Forbes's charge by maintaining that 'formal rationality does not correspond to a single substantive ethic' (1977:205).

Yet he apparently squares this in his own mind with an admission that 'formal rationality and laissez faire capitalism are *inseparable* in some respects' and that 'Weber made no attempt to disguise or justify the relationship between the spread of a *particular form* of formal rationality and the interests of the bourgeoisie' (Brown 1977:205, emphasis added). This seems to be having one's cake and eating it. Similarly Watson (1977) uses the distinction between these two types of rationality in order to elucidate the emergence and function of personnel managers in the present industrial order. They are viewed in functional terms, that is, as emerging to reconcile the tensions between a calculative formal rationality allegedly 'wholly suited to the needs and interests of capitalists' on the one hand and the substantive values and aspirations of the subject class on the other. If such an analytical scheme could be sustained it would imply that we could interpret the clash between managerial control systems and worker resistance as the conflict between two fundamental types of rationality.

But to frame the struggle at the point of production in such terms is to court a grave danger. It tends to mystify the nature of control by conflating the material interests of top managers with their allegedly independent control devices. Thus, unfortunately, this neat scheme must be questioned on a number of counts. It will not be found adequate to resolve the questions raised at the beginning of this section. There is an inconsistency in Watson's usage which, in part, derives from the confusions residing in Weber's own work. Weber writes: 'Bureaucracy offers above all the optimum possibility for carrying through the principles of specialising administrative functions according *to purely objective* considerations' (Weber 1948:215).

But there is an inherent ambiguity in the way the term 'formal rationality' is employed. At one time, it is, as in the quotation above, supposedly simply a means, a method of calculation, and is therefore inherently neutral. Yet at other times it is seen as coterminous with bourgeois rationality and bourgeois interests. Indeed, the whole point of Forbes's article is to demonstrate the laissez-faire bias in Weber's formal rationality concept. Forbes argues that 'structural subordination of the workers under conditions of a free market which operates upon the formal rationality of capital accounting is not devoid of a substantive ethic' (1975:220). On the contrary he claims, it is 'demonstrable that Weber's formal rationality did maximize a substantive ethic' (1975:225). If Forbes is correct, then the supposed 'tension' in industrial capitalism between formal rationality and 'substantive rationality' is a misleading obfuscation, because we are faced simply with a clash between *two* substantive rationalities - one which favours the values and interests of the bourgeoisie and one which favours the values and interests of the workers. To dress-up the former as being some qualitatively different form is merely to mystify this value conflict.

Hence, this same ambiguity finds reflection in Watson's model. He claims at one point that it is the 'paradox of consequences' that a neutral formal rationality subverts human values.  This is akin to the phenomenon noted by Merton, viz. the unforeseen dysfunctions of bureaucracy whereby because of strict observance of rules and red-tape, technical means can subvert original ends or even become ends in themselves (Merton 1949).  Yet at the same time we are told something different, namely, the problem is that 'the increasing rationalisation of Western societies in the hands of certain interest groups involves the increasing application of calculatively based techniques whereby those groups could further *their* interests' (Watson 1977:34, emphasis added).  Is it then, that formal rationality per se threatens substantive interests, or is it only because this special rationality is in the hands of 'certain interest groups'?  This latter interpretation leads him into accepting Forbes's judgment that 'formal rationality is wholly suited to the needs and interests of capitalists' (1977:27), without, one feels, accepting the full logic of Forbes's case.  For to do so would radically reduce the validity of sustaining the distinction, because we are dealing simply with a disguised form of substantive rationality. It also leads to further confusions.  Thus when Marglin argues that the division of labour and the rise of the factories was *not* the result of a search 'for a technologically superior organisation of work but for an organisation which guaranteed to the entrepreneur an essential role in the production process', this cannot be used to illustrate that technical rationality always serves the interests of the ruling group.  Clearly this is simply an instance of a straight-forward play for control, moreover, one which is by self-admission *unconnected* with the dictates of technical rationality.  Again it would seem that many of the actions viewed as 'formally rational' simply because they are deployed by managers, should rather be viewed not as depicting the clash of formal and technical rationalities but rather the clash between two opposing substantive rationalities.

Used so loosely, the terms 'formal and substantive rationality' can only lead to confusion.  Yet one must remember that Weber himself saw them as 'fundamental categories of sociology'.  At minimum, the constructs must be rescued from their ambiguities.  Steven Lukes doubts whether this mission can be accomplished.  He blames the obscurity upon Weber himself, whose 'uses of these terms is irredeemably opaque and shifting' (1970:207).  There is a good deal of truth in this remark, although I tend to concur with Arnold Eison (1978) that something may be rescued.  Eison sifts through Weber's work and redeems the general uses of the term 'rationality' with one exception.  The one 'confusion which remains' relates to the terms 'formal' and 'substantive' rationality.  This particular distinction he finds 'to be both theoretically confused and substantially biased' (1978:57-8).  Thus, even a would-be defender of Weber, one who reasserts the consistency and conceptual rigour of the rationality theme, finds that one aspect of it, namely the supposed 'focal' formal-versus-substantive idea, 'stands as perhaps the most confused and confusing concept in all of Weber's work on rationalization' (1978:61).  The potential value of this distinction as an ordering concept for our present analysis must, therefore, be doubted.

I now want to indicate the source (2) of these confusions and suggest a way forward.  The problem can be traced to two sources: (i) Weber's political writings and (ii) the way in which he bases the conditions for the development of formal (calculative) 'rationality' upon a series of *substantive* (value-biased) prerequisites.

Let us deal immediately with the latter.  Weber notes how the conditions for the maximum development of a rational capital accounting economy presuppose certain minimal substantive conditions. These include, he says, a market economy, the appropriation of the means of production by an owning class, and free labour.  Given that the supposedly neutral and objective form of calculative action is inextricably bound up with such a substantive base, it is hardly surprising that confusion has ensued.

His most well-known presentation of the technical superiority of bureaucracy in 'Economy and Society' is offset by his political writings where he forcefully argued two other tendencies, namely bureaucracy's inherent drive towards exceeding its instrumental function thus usurping the proper function of the politician;  and, secondly, the tendency of bureaucracy to reflect the class bias of a society, that is, to embody a social bias.  In these respects he was undoubtedly entering the contemporary political controversies by attempting to counterpose the German school of thought which was distrustful of political democracy and saw bureaucracy as the rightful focus of loyalty.  This was the German conservative position typified by Gustav Schmoller (Dronberger 1971).

In reacting to such ideas, Weber warned on many occasions of the dangers inherent in the spread of bureaucracy:  'All the economic weather signs', he wrote, 'point in the direction of increasing unfreedom' (Beetham 1974:46).  It was mainly in his *political* discourses that Weber's pessimism portrayed itself.  He enumerated its deleterious consequences:  dehumanisation and alienation, arising from the 'parcelling out of the soul' so that, 'it is the dictatorship of the official not of the worker that is - for the present at least - on the advance' (1974:71).

At the same time he was anxious to demonstrate the irrationality of socialism:

> where a planned economy is radically carried out, it must further accept the inevitable reduction in formal rationality of calculation which would result from the elimination of money and capital accounting.... This fundamental and in the last analysis unavoidable element of irrationality in economic systems is one of the important sources of all the problems of social policy, above all the problems of socialism (Weber 1964:215).

Moreover, he explicitly warned of other pathological consequences of socialism, which would, he claimed, reduce individual freedom, and curtail innovation and dynamism which are the by-products of entrepreneural and bourgeois activity.

Apart from the intrusion of his political concerns, a second course of confusion lies in his frequent assertions of the 'purely technical superiority of bureaucracy over any other form of organisation' (Weber 1948:214).  Indeed, this he claims 'has always been' the 'decisive reason' for its advance.  There is little doubt that Weber is not only describing the structural components of bureaucracy but also remarking on its functional consequences.  He writes,

Precision, speed, unambiguity, knowledge of the files, continuity, discretion, unity, strict subordination, reduction of
friction and of material and personal costs - these are raised
to the optimum point in the strictly bureaucratic administration
... (ibid.)

Not surprisingly, many commentators (for example Mouzelis) have
interpreted Weber as meaning that bureaucracy was 'the most efficient' form of administration.  If this was the case it would of
course carry clear implications for job control and other worker
attempts to limit or subvert its course.  These would, like Weber's
strictures on socialism, be then open to the charge of irrationality.  Albrow (1970), however, vehemently refutes this popular conception of Weber and assiduously develops the argument that formal
rationality does not mean efficiency - which implies recourse to
ends and not just means.  Undoubtedly the word 'efficiency' does
raise a wide range of connotations.  Nevertheless, Blau and Scott's
observation must remain valid:  the consequences of bureaucracy as
claimed by Weber, such as speed and precision, are not questions of
definition 'but questions of fact - hypotheses subject to empirical
testing' (Blau and Scott 1963:34).  This is so despite Albrow's
critique.  After all, research could show that where structural
components of bureaucracy, such as hierarchy and specialised spheres
of competence, are present to any marked degree, then the performance is not 'speedy' but slow!  As Beetham remarks, although
'Albrow denies that Weber was concerned with "efficiency" in his
bureaucratic model ... this seems as good a shorthand term as any
to summarize these characteristics' (i.e. continuity, reduction of
friction) (1974:91).  Actually the reason why it is not as 'good a
term as any' is precisely because this term, which Weber certainly
never explicitly uses but seduces others to adopt, invites attention
to substantive *ends* when the whole point of his dichotomy was to
separate 'formal rationality' from these.

A third source of confusion lies in the failure to distinguish
between technical rationality, formal rationality, and bourgeois
rationality.  It is by clarifying these that I hope to indicate a
forward path.

Action can be technically rational without being economically
rational.  Max Weber himself points this out, postulating as an
example a highly technical-rational machine (i.e. one which cannot
be faulted from an engineering point of view) which is designed to
produce nothing but atmospheric air, and therefore despite its technical elegance, is economically irrational.  If, however, one is
merely observing that capital has largely monopolised the use of
technical rationality, then this may be true but it is a different
point.  Even so it is a case which is only relatively and not absolutely true, for, as Banks has argued, 'The very techniques of
documentation and communication which have extended the coverage
of ruling class control have also made possible a greater trade
union defensive response to it' (1977).

In other words, technical rationality, techniques of calculation
and so on, are not inexorably tied to the interests of one class.
Geometry, algebra and the principles of mechanical engineering, the
railways, and the printing press, are not quintessentially bourgeois.  Formal rationality being purely a *means*, is, in principle,

of potential service to any human objectives.  Probity in financial
transactions, for example, is an important principle of accountancy
- a set of techniques viewed par excellence by Weber as an example
of formal rationality - yet probity can surely be an important means
of protecting community interests.  On the other hand, what does
tend to happen, is that, given a certain regime, be it an economic
system or a political mode of domination, the dominant culture (and
therefore the most influential values and norms) tends to reflect
the interests of that regime.  So, the techniques listed above tend
to be more predominantly exploited by one set of interests rather
than another.

Let us therefore draw the discussion to a close by delineating
four types of rationality.  Weber made occasional use of each, but
failed systematically to elucidate their differences.  His disciples
have if anything been more misleading than the prophet.  We should
distinguish between:  (i) *Technical rationality* - Weber used the
word 'technik', this obtains when there is a potential recourse to
science (1922:32).  The presence of a technical question (as in
Weber's example of whether to use iron or platinum for a machine
part) 'always means there is some doubt over the most efficient
means to an end', one problem being the achievement of optimum results with least effort.  For a technical question the only relevant
consideration is the scientific limitation 'bearing on the achievement of the particular end' (Weber 1964:161).  This differs then
from (ii) an *economic question*.  A question becomes 'no longer in
the present sense purely technical but *also* economic' when the question of relative scarcity of, for example, iron and platinum enter
the calculation, and when therefore the question of 'costs' becomes
a consideration.  Thus to elaborate the example we used above:

It would, for instance, be possible, as a kind of technical
amusement, to apply all the most modern methods to the production
of atmospheric air.  And no one could take the slightest exception to the purely technical rationality of the action.  Economically on the other hand, the procedure would, under normal
circumstances, be irrational because there would be no demand for
the product (1964:162-3).

(iii) *Formal rationality* - Weber (1922:58) uses the term:  'die
formal Rationalitak', and it constitutes yet a third type.  This
differs from 'technik' in that there can be no recourse to scientific knowledge in the sense of empirically verifiable statements
about the world.  Rather, we include here *contrived* formal logical
devices such as accounting, mathematics and chess.  For example, to
ask whether a pawn in chess 'can' move more than one space is not a
question amenable to scientific answer.  One can only refer the
questioner to the formal rules of the game.  (iv) *Substantive
rationality:* this has been discussed earlier and requires no amendment under this scheme.  It relates to the values and interests of
individuals and groups. (3)

Having developed this fourfold scheme, I found my attention drawn
to the fact that Mueller (1979) had also found it fruitful to split
Weber's Zweckrational category.  This he does by separating utilitarian purposive rationality from 'objective technical rationality';
he calls this latter type 'systemic' rationality.  So he ends up
with three 'mutually irreducible' types:  (1) Zweckrational which is

social, utilitarian-conative, based on material interest and a 'will
to power';  (2) Wertrational which is subjective, moral and idealistic;  and (3) *Systemic* rationality which is formal and based on
impersonal calculi or alogrithms and informed neither by material
interests nor by ideal values.  So the scheme I have proposed differs from his in that I have made a further distinction within the
category of action labelled 'systemic'.  It will be recalled that I
distinguished technical rationality where the prime consideration is
the scientific limitation 'bearing on a particular end' - (e.g.
whether to use iron or platinum in a machine part) - from formal
rationality where *contrived* systemic devices or rules are applied.
To conflate these two is to invite precisely the same kind of problems which Mueller attempts to avoid by separating utilitarian
conative Zweckrational action from systemically rational action.

The necessity for such fine reticulation of categories of rational action arises because Weber has provoked a debate which touches
a central nerve of modern industrial life.  Should economic rationality be accorded pre-eminence?  If so, which is more rational:
market or plan? (4)  If not, then what other rationality should be
accorded primacy?  Does the rationality of micro-interests aggregate
to a totality of irrationality?  Is modern technological rationality
inextricably bound with capitalist society?  (See, for example,
Levine and Wright 1980;  Balibar 1978;  Hearn 1978;  Cotgrove 1975;
Gordon 1976;  Schutz 1943;  Tenbruck 1980.)  In a sense then it is
the uncertain interlink between the various major themes in Weber
(rationality, bureaucracy, authority, domination) which inevitably
embroils any analyst of work control in his doings.  In 'Economy and
Society' he makes just such a link which provokes the kind of debates noted above.  He claims that 'capital accounting is ... associated with the phenomenon of "shop discipline" and appropriation
of the means of production and that means:  with the existence of a
system of domination' (1968:108).  In consequence of this kind of
statement the ideological manifestations find reflection in Taylorism and Fordism.  Managers as controllers claim special rights in
part as arbiters of 'rational action'.  The spectre of rationalised
domination haunts the would-be antagonist in a dual sense.  Rational
control implies immutability and such control assumes a visage of
logic and reason.  Equally, rationalised control implies that devices are honed to a fine, calculable precision.  Formal rationality
is harnessed to the real subordination of labour.  But in addition,
legal-rational order draws-in the representatives of labour and the
net is drawn even tighter with the codification of discipline.
Grievances, formerly questions of interest, are increasingly trans-
mogrified into questions of right.

Weber's obscurantism has provoked a neo-marxist critique
(Schroyer 1972, Marcuse 1965, Habermas 1971).  Thus, commenting on
Giddens's discussion in 'Capitalism and Modern Social Theory', Trent
Schroyer argues that Giddens fails to recognise the critique of
Weber's concept of rationalisation that resides in Marx's own work
(Schroyer 1972:114).  Similarly Hearn (1978) suggests that Weber's
conceptualisation is weaker than Lenin's which distinguished between
the 'rationality of consciousness' and the 'rationality of tech-
nique'.  Unfortunately this particular advantage was short-lived
under Lenin because the latter form of rationality was given inordi-

nate primacy.  The essential nature of such critique lies in the
categories of the rationality of production for 'profit' versus the
rationality of production for 'value'.  In concrete circumstances
the two may coincide but it is central to Marx's whole analysis that
they are essentially distinct.  At times Weber recognised this point
but it is his failure to sustain the clarity of the distinction
which makes his work problematic.  While I tend to think that Forbes
overstates his case in alleging Weber *equated* Zweckrational action
with laissez faire, Weber did invite such a misrepresentation.
Weber certainly begins by explicitly stating that there are 'substantive conditions' for the maximisation of the 'formal rationality
of capital accounting' (1968:107).  On the other hand it has not attracted sufficient comment that his discussion of this specific case
should not necessarily be read as formal rationality per se.  Rather
it seems Weber was exploring this one *application* of formal rationality.  After all, Weber's central problematic - and his own deep
personal concern - was the implication of rationalisation and domination for individuation (Seidman and Gruber 1977).  The trend he
saw filled him with a 'foreboding sometimes bordering on despair'
and this 'derived from his doubts about the rationality of rationalization' (Tenbruck 1980:314).

Nevertheless, the opacity introduced by Weber makes him a guilty
accomplice in the predicament that:  'At the moment, the impossi-
bility (in public discussion) of distinguishing between value and
material rationality is an index of the ideological function of
pluralist democracy' (Schroyer 1972:115).  Accordingly, his work has
served to *conceal* the contours of labour subordination.  There are
claims that it realises an '*unacknowledged* political domination'
(Habermas 1971:82).  The upshot is that 'the growth of expertise and
the nature of procedures within companies embody particular assumptions and priorities' which are inimical to the achievement of industrial democracy (Batstone 1979:268).

Thus Marcuse (1965) argues that Weber's construct is ideologically infused.  Habermas (1971) develops the analysis by claiming that
neither Weber nor Marcuse has satisfactorily explained the meaning
of the expansion of purposive-rational action nor satisfactorily accounted for it.  He uses new categories at the structural level to
find (a) that its meaning is a lack of emancipation in a wide sense
and (b) he accounts for it by elucidating the historic shifts -
first to a free market and then to state legitimation of 'welfare'
capitalism and the hegemony of technical discourse.  Habermas thus
explicates the 'scientism' of political life.  He observes that

A critical theory of society can no longer be constructed in the
exclusive form of a critique of political economy.  A point of
view that methodically isolates the economic laws of motion in
society, can claim to grasp the overall structure of social life
in its essential categories only as long as politics depend on
the economic base.  It becomes inapplicable when the 'base' has
to be comprehended as in itself a function of governmental activity and political conflicts (1971:101).

He envisages a potential for liberation through rationalisation
at another level - the interactionist institutional framework - by
removing restrictions on communications.  'Public unrestricted discussion, free from domination of the suitability and desirability of

action-orienting principles' would be promoted.  Such 'rationalisation' (the term is retained) would thereby 'furnish the members of
society with the opportunity for further emancipation and progressive individuation' (1971:118-19).

Such emancipation, however, would require the free public discussion of ends as well as means.  While commentators typically
interpret rationality (even in Weber - indeed, especially in Weber)
as implying means-ends calculation, in fact it is the *absence* of
debate about ends in formal and systemic rationalities which is so
problematic about Weber's writings.  Providing this kind of discourse did occur, however, then Marcuse's point may be accepted:
'technical reason could well become the instrument of the liberation
of man' (Marcuse 1965:15).  Man's unfreedom is a result of the assured synonymity of rationality and capitalist rationality.  The
prevailing industrial systems, East and West, become hegemonic because they high-jack reason and gird themselves with its aura of
inevitability.  The removal of restrictions on communications as
demanded by Habermas would, however, necessitate:  democratic
*channels* of communication;  a social order free from manipulative
domination;  and an enhancement of the communicative competence of
citizens which could only develop in a dialectical process with the
liberalizing of the institutional framework.  So this is not simply
a return to the slogan 'politics in command' but a reassertion of
our dialectical approach.  To believe in the possibility of emancipation implies a belief that technical rationality can be detached
from exploitative systems;  it implies that it can be saved from
corruption and it implies indeed that reason may itself be used as
an instrument to *expose* hidden interests and values.

# Chapter 3

# BRAVERMAN AND BEYOND

Direct heir to Marx's analysis of the real subordination of labour and progeny to Weber's rationalisation thesis stands Harry Braverman's 'Labor and Monopoly Capital' (1974). This book, by now widely hailed as a classic, has been described variously as: 'one of the two most important works of marxist political economy to have appeared in English in the last decade' (Rowthorn 1976); and 'a masterful contribution to the literature of social reality' (Heilbroner 1975). Yet the work has also attracted many critics (Nichols 1977; Elger 1979; Friedman 1977; Cutler 1978; Brighton Labour Process Group 1977; MacKenzie 1977). To be sure, each of these critics finds the book to be of an outstanding quality; none the less each also uncovers serious limitations. Thus, the Brighton Labour Process Group sees it as 'clearly a major step forward, but in our view further progress depends on the development of an adequate theory of the capitalist labour process, through which capital appropriates nature' (1977:3). Gavin MacKenzie submits that the 'lack of originality cannot be allowed to divert attention from the massive achievement that the book represents' (1977:248). And Nichols, whilst paying tribute to the 'great force' contributed by the author's own direct experience of work, finds that even this 'cuts two ways' (1977 : 192).

The kind of charges laid against the book are quite numerous. It is said to be 'deterministic' (MacKenzie 1977; Coombs 1978); it neglects worker resistance (Friedman 1977); its obsession with Taylorism ignores the rich array of alternative managerial control devices (Nichols 1977; Friedman 1977); its class analysis is defective and done better elsewhere (Coombs 1978); it not only is 'unoriginal' as noted above, and deterministic, but these shortcomings reflect a shaky theoretical foundation - particularly with respect to the valorisation process (Brighton Labour Process Group 1977; Elger 1979) and finally, for now, even Heilbroner, who described the book as 'masterful' could not help himself wondering about the neglect of a whole 'realm' - the political, ideological and sphere of consciousness (Heilbroner 1975).

This fairly extensive list of recommendations and criticisms is quoted here because I want to argue that: (i) the two sets of comments - high praise and rigorous criticism - are understandable and

warranted because the book *is* partial;  and (ii) intimately related
to this is that the myriad criticisms can be linked more coherently
if the key to the shortcomings is revealed.  The essential problem
it seems to me is the lack of a *dialectical* view of the control of
the labour process.  As Gavin MacKenzie suggests, the book 'is
devoid of dialectical under- or over-tones' (1977:249).  Thus the
work is significant and fascinating but it must be understood within
the framework of concepts we developed in the previous two chapters.
The process Braverman describes has to be located within the dialectical framework of:  totality;  contradictions;  and, yes, Heilbroner's 'realm' of ideology/politics, which I include within the
term *social construction*.  Thus I agree with Cressey and MacInnes
(1980a) who go partly down this road.  They note that while the discussion surrounding Braverman has mainly contented itself with qualifications and amendments what is required is a recognition of something more theoretically fundamental.  They conclude that the real
subordination of labour 'tendency' is in fact 'internally contradiction ridden' (1980a:12).  This inelegantly-expressed aspect of the
overall dialectic is identified as capital's *ultimate* reliance upon
workers such that 'contrary to the implications of the RSL argument,
capital has an active interest in suppressing its own dominance ...
in practice capital must surrender the means of production to the
"control" of the workers for their actual *use* in the production process' the workers' actual control of the 'detail of the performance
of their tasks ... never disappears altogether' (Cressey and
MacInnes 1980a:16-17).  Andrew Friedman (1977) is another who moves
part-way to a dialectical stance.  Unlike Braverman, Friedman seeks
'theoretical additions' to Marx's framework.
    This is because Marx did not deal systematically with changes
    within the capitalist mode of production which are the outcome
    of class struggle.  The importance of worker resistance lay for
    Marx in its potential for overthrowing capitalism.  But worker
    resistance has clearly forced accommodating changes *within* the
    capitalist mode of production, particularly since Marx's day
    (Friedman 1977:4).
So, while not developing a dialectical model as such - nor indeed
using the term - Friedman does explore the crucial interplay between
control strategies and resistance.  But the essentially economic
thrust of the analysis is directed towards questions of centre -
periphery and of uneven development generally.  Accordingly, sociological insights on the complex interrelationships at factory and
office level are ignored.  As Ken Roberts observes, Friedman's
interests 'do not lead far beneath statistics on trade union membership and industrial disputes' (1978:581).  Before we elaborate further upon the contradictions element as well as the other facets in
our dialectical framework it is necessary briefly to outline Braverman's own case.


'LABOR AND MONOPOLY CAPITAL'

Braverman's book focuses on the transformation in the labour process.  He himself notes the curious fact that while the central
theme in the first volume of Marx's 'Capital' is concerned with

the labour process (as we demonstrated in Chapter 2), this theme has
been largely neglected ever since.  Why should this be so?  Well,
not only have Marxists diverted their attention to other questions
such as periodic crises, the incipient revolution and the division
of the product of labour, but most important has been that the essential contours of the labour process have been taken for granted.
In the West the

> unionized working class intimidated by the scale and complexity
> of capitalist production and weakened in its original revolution-
> ary impetus by the gains afforded by the rapid increase of pro-
> ductivity, increasingly lost the will and ambition to wrest con-
> trol of production from capitalist hands and turned ever more to
> bargaining over labor's share in the product.

And even the revival of flagging radical interest following the
Russian Revolution was stymied by the Soviets' urgent uptake of
capitalist production techniques.  Given the gravity of the crisis
and the size of the task to be accomplished, 'the respect and even
admiration of Marxists for the scientific technology, the production
system and the organized and regularized labour processes of developed capitalism was if anything heightened' (Braverman, 1974:
10-11).

Under such circumstances, capital was given leave to proceed with
the degradation of work and to take for itself the control over the
labour process.  Thus would the historic mission from formal to real
subordination and the realisation of relative surplus-value be accomplished.  This process Braverman traces under four main headings.
These are:  the reorganisation of the labour process;  science
and mechanisation;  monopoly capital;  and occupational and class
impact. (1)

The reorganisation of the labour process entailed a persistent
onslaught on the workers' control embodied in craft skills.  Much of
the book's success may be attributed to Braverman's eloquent account
of how Taylor's scientific-management has been inexorably applied -
not as an inherently technically superior way of organising work,
but as a systematic device to subjugate labour to capital.  It describes how complex jobs have been incessantly broken-down into a
series of simpler ones.  This entails a shift from the historically
derived social division of labour to a detailed division of labour
within the workplace.  This is not a mere quantitative matter but a
qualitative shift.  Occupational distinctions are characteristic of
many types of society whereas 'the division of labour in the workshop is the special product of capitalist society.'  Within capitalism where the social division survives it is expressed in the form
of labour exchanged as commodities and is 'enforced chaotically and
anarchically by the market, while the workshop division of labour is
imposed by planning and control' (1974:73).  It is not merely the
breaking down of work into its constituent elements that is pertinent here.  A worker such as a tinsmith making a funnel might well
*choose* to fragment the task.  Rather, the point is that capital
carries this 'one step further ... not only are the operations separated from each other but *they are assigned to different workers*'
(1974:77).  This prepares the ground for the breaking of craft control, for the separation of conception from execution, for the sys-
tematisation of operations and the elimination of 'wasteful move-

ments', for paying the lowest possible rates to the detailed
workers.  If elements of skilled work perforce remain, at least
these can be isolated and cheaper labour hired to perform all of the
less skilled operations which are hived off.  J.R. Commons is quoted
to good effect in his description of this tactic in the meat-packing
industry:

> It would be difficult to find another industry where division of
> labour has been so ingeniously and microscopically worked out.
> The animal has been surveyed and laid out like a map;  and the
> men have been classified in over thirty specialities and twenty
> rates of pay, from 16 cents to 50 cents an hour.  The 50-cent man
> is restricted to using the knife on the most delicate parts of
> the hide (floorman) or to using the axe in splitting the backbone
> (splitter);  and wherever a less-skilled man can be shipped in at
> 18 cents, 18½ cents, 20 cents, 21 cents, 22½ cents, 24 cents, 25
> cents, and so on, a place is made for him and an occupation
> mapped out (Braverman 1974:81).

Thus the powerful message from Braverman is not just that jobs are
boring and alienating - this has been known by workers and even by
industrial sociologists, for some time.  Rather his message is that
work is like this designedly.  It is a phenomenon arising from the
class struggle over control.  It is within this thematic that the
discussion of Taylorism and technology occurs.

The detailed outline of Taylorism within Braverman's book is an
articulation of this theme which goes beyond the 'commonplaces' of
stopwatches and speed-ups.  For behind them exists 'nothing less
than the explicit verbalization of the capitalist mode of production' (1974:86).  Accordingly, it is 'impossible to over-estimate'
the importance of Taylorism in shaping the labour process.  It moves
like a hidden spirit so that the 'popular notion that Taylorism has
been "superseded" ... represent(s) a woeful misreading of the actual
dynamics of the development of management' (1974:87).  Indeed, if a
separate identifiable school of Taylorism cannot easily be recognised today,this is, 'apart from the bad odour of the name', because
its spirit is so pervasive it is no longer the property of one fac-
tion, but imbues the very bedrock of work design per se.

If there was a certain 'vanity' in the attempt to 'calibrate
individuals' and fragment their movements into standardised ther-
bligs in the attempt to treat the worker in machine terms as a
mechanism of hinges and ball-and-socket joints, this was appended
by a further twist in the degradation of work:  the inversion whereby machines and tools 'employ' the person.  Again Braverman draws
heavily and directly upon Marx's analysis of machinery.  This entails an emphatic reminder that it is the *social* relationship of
person-machine-person that requires discussion - this in two senses.
Much literature on machinery simply ignores the relationship with
the worker.  But secondly, machinery and especially automated
machinery, which in principle could have great *potential* in re-
storing the unity of control, conception, and execution, becomes
instead, under definite and concrete social relationships, an instrument for servitude.  In consequence this remarkable development
of machinery becomes 'the source not of freedom but of enslavement,
not of mastery but of helplessness, and not of the broadening of the
horizon of labour but the confinement of the worker ...' (1974:195).

The separation of intellectual work from that of execution is a
'technical condition' in so far as it is suited to profitability,
hierarchy and control.

The irrationality explored at this point by Braverman mirrors
closely the discussion concerning Weber in our previous chapter.
Braverman notes the absurdity of a situation where the proselytised
'solution' to 'crisis' is ever more productivity.  He points out
that 'no satisfactory level can ever be attained ... the very "efficiency" which produced the crises is seen here as the only answer
to it....  Here we have the reductio ad absurdum of capitalist efficiency' (1974:207-8).  Braverman seemingly agrees with our distinction between technical rationality, capitalist rationality, and
formal-calculable rationality.  This last, calibrating times, patterns and movements, could in principle be applied to any purpose.
And the distinction between technical and capitalist rationality
Braverman draws particularly well.  He observes how

> necessities are called 'technical needs', 'machine character-
> istics', the 'requirements of efficiency', but by and large they
> are the exigencies of capital and not of technique....  In reali-
> ty, machinery embraces a host of possibilities, many of which are
> systematically thwarted rather than developed by capital.  An
> automatic system of machinery opens up the possibility of true
> control over a highly productive factory by a relatively small
> corps of workers, providing these workers attain the level of
> mastery over the machinery offered by engineering knowledge, and
> providing they then share out among themselves the routines of
> the operation....  Yet this promise which has been repeatedly
> held out with every technical advance since the Industrial Revo-
> lution, is frustrated by the capitalist effort to reconstitute
> and even deepen the division of labour in all its worst aspects
> (1974:230).

In the less-penetrating third section, Braverman explains three
aspects of monopoly capital at the macro-level;  the changed structure of the modern corporation, the universalisation of market relationships, and the economic role of the state.  In large measure
this section reflects the framework of his mentors, Baran and
Sweezy.  The changed structure of the capitalist enterprise is
characterised by centralisation of capital and the concomitant
corporate divisionalisation.  The managerial functions of control,
marketing, administration and personnel become subdivided and separated to become entire divisions.  Each of these requires in turn
its own internal departments which 'imitate' the wider subdivisions
of the entire corporation.  Hence personnel, marketing and production may have their own accounting, clearing and maintenance sections.  The chapter on the universalisation of market relationships
argues the pervasive impact of the capitalist mode of production on
the individual, family, education, and other social spheres.  Capitalism transforms 'all of society into a gigantic marketplace'.

The final part of the book explores clerical work, service and
retail work, and other occupational shifts within the working class.
The chapter on clerical workers is the fullest;  it traces the same
pattern of routinisation, fragmentation and overall degradation of
labour as drawn earlier.  In Great Britain the growth in clerical
labour from approximately 70,000 (some 0.8 of a per cent of the em-

ployed) in 1851, to three million (almost 13 per cent) just over a
century later (1961), mirrors the developing function of these workers under monopoly capitalism.  They are agents employed to monitor
the flow of value creation in the labour process.  In turn, however,
these management functions of control and appropriation have themselves become labour processes and accordingly they too are subject
to standardisation.  William Henry Leffingwell's, 'Scientific Office
Management' (1917), is cited to illustrate this point.  No motion
was considered too trivial to time and rationalise;  the removal of
paper clips from correspondence was revealed to be inefficiently
performed.  The obsessive mental set promoted by such attentiveness
to detail is illustrated by one manager whose study of the evapora-
tion of ink from inkwells led to a calculation of potential savings
of one dollar a year if non-evaporating ink was used!  A more modern
'Guide to Office Clerical Time Standards' used by large American
companies such as GEC and General Tire reveals such fascinating information as the standard times for 'chair activity':  Get up from
chair .033 minutes;  sit down in chair .033;  turn in swivel chair
.009.  The mechanisation of office activity leads to even greater
similarity with factory work and Braverman convincingly argues that
the white-collar - blue-collar distinction is not only useless but
positively misleading.  Apart from the erosion of the gap in conditions of employment, his data reveals that clerical pay scales have
sunk to well below that of general operatives.  He has trenchant
points to make on service work and the notion of skill.  The census
data he shows to be crude on both counts.  The distinctions are
frequently meaningless because a worker performing exactly the same
function will be classified as 'service' or 'production' depending
simply on location - for example whether the operation is performed
in a restaurant, hotel, or in final preparation of a new product in
a factory.  In his 'final note on skill' he returns to his central
theme - the degradation of work.  He mounts a withering attack on
the notion of an increase in 'average skill' levels.  The official
statistics are misleading because whole masses of workers who are
merely associated with a machine become classified as 'semi-
skilled'.  The relationship between the dexterity and short-period
of training requisite for such positions bears no resemblance to the
old craft skills.  Braverman here reveals something of the craft
nostalgia which he is elsewhere at pains to deny.  But the essential
point remains, the long-term historic trend has been for the skill
previously lodged within craft workers to be appropriated by technology or destroyed by fragmentation and standardisation.

So no matter where he looks Braverman uncovers the essential
triumph of capital over labour.  Marx's ideal-typical 'real subordination of labour' Braverman finds largely accomplished in practice.  The 'General Law of Capitalist Accumulation' forming a 'dis-
posable industrial reserve army' is equally found manifest.  The
general law on both counts is seemingly complete, yet capitalism
survives.  Not surprisingly he was accused by some Marxist critics
as a pessimist.  Shortly before his death in 1976 he made a brief
reply to this charge in the 'Monthly Review' with a forthright
statement.  He declared:

I have every confidence in the revolutionary potential of the
working class of the so-called developed capitalist countries.

Capitalism will not, over the long run, leave any choice to these classes, but will force upon them the fulfilment of the task which they alone can perform (1976:124).

He recognises, however, that this prediction rests on an assumption that still further degradation of labour is in store.  Indeed, he frankly acknowledges it 'presupposes an enormous intensification' (ibid.).  But he has little doubt that it will happen, and, noting the quickened pace of change in the past few years he seems to suggest the time may not be so far off as he originally had thought.

As argued above, the book has attracted diverse points of critique.  It is here contended that the most fruitful miscegenation will emerge from a dialectical approach.  Braverman disallows himself such an opportunity from the outset by virtue of his self-denying ordinance - that his book is about the working class *in itself*, not as a class *for itself* (1974:27).  Inevitably given this self-imposed limitation he can only discuss what is done *to* the working class.  He cannot bring into view the working class or the trade unions as an active agency still less as a pro-active agent. It is with further elaboration of the social construction facet of the dialectical approach that we should begin.


SOCIAL CONSTRUCTION

Probably the most celebrated work to forge a dialectical link between the subjective and objective dimensions of reality is that by Berger and Luckmann (1967).  The work is apposite here for three reasons:  it illuminates the social construction dimension of the dialectical perspective;  it seeks even within this dimension to be dialectical;  and it heuristically sheds light even as it falters in its declared objectives.  This influential book has been seen as a popularisation of Schutz (Mennell 1974:46) but it also draws on Husserl's phenomenology and even on aspects of Durkheim.  Given the authors' aim to describe the process whereby reality is socially created and sustained, this book should carry significant humanistic and liberalising potential - and so it has generally been greeted and regarded.  Berger and Luckmann explore the process where subjective meanings become treated as objective facts and in this guise react back upon meanings.  This process they characterise in terms of the three 'moments' of:  externalisation, objectivation and internalisation.  Externalisation emerges from habituation in social activity.  Social actors create institutions and symbolic universes. Objectivation is the moment when these products of social interaction are reified and appear to assume an existence independent of the people who create them.  History itself 'as the tradition of existing institutions has the character of objectivity.  The individual's biography is apprehended as an episode located within the objective history of the society.  The institutions as historical and objective facticities confront the individual as undeniable facts' (Berger and Luckmann 1967:78).  Through the process of internalisation people experience, learn, and take-within themselves the meanings of the objectivated social products.  In emphasising this process Berger and Luckmann explicitly seek 'to bring to bear a dialectical perspective upon the theoretical orientation of the

social sciences' (1967:209).  This involves a complex interaction
between subjective human activity and objective social structure.
Consciousness is no mere epiphenomenon.

The 'Social Construction of Reality' has been received in the
main uncritically as a classic 'humanistic' work.  However, John
Welsh (1979) from a radical perspective, criticises the book on the
grounds that it is 'replete with repressive dimensions'.  Welsh
argues that it departs from a truly dialectical analysis in that it
elevates the objective over the subjective.  Moreover, it is deterministic in that the posited 'flow' of communication in the socialisation process neglects the possibility of reflexivity and removes
the possibility of individuals constructing alternative definitions
of self and society.  Equally problematical, maintains Welsh, is
that Berger and Luckmann treat 'successful socialisation' as the
compatible fit between external 'reality' and the consciousness of
the individual.  Only the subjective side of the equation is considered capable of illegitimacy.  In consequence, the emphasis tends
to rest on *adaptation* rather than *emancipation*.  Berger and Luckmann's treatment of 'reification' is thus drained of its critical
thrust.  Instead of presenting it as a historical account located
in, and legitimating, modes of production, they treat is as a normal
and invariate phenomenon.  Not only this but they seem to advance
the perspective that:

only in recent history has de-reification been made possible,
presumably through the scientific mode of consciousness as emergent in the capitalist phase of commodity production - an absurd
viewpoint given the discussions of reification in advanced industrial societies by Marx, Marcuse, Lukács, Picconne and others
(Welsh 1979:8).

Indeed, critical theory has undertaken the mission of pointing out
the ideological and repressive elements in advanced capitalism.

This critique has important implications for our analysis.
Berger and Luckmann have, in the main, failed adequately to confront
the problem of power.  This is something given close attention in
our next chapter.  Their treatment of reification conveniently ignores 'a number of historical examples of individual and group processes of *de*reification on the part of workers, peasants, intellec-
tuals and others' (Welsh 1979:8).  Such attempts at *resistance* and
reformulation must be given greater prominence.

Phenomenologically oriented sociology has a special place in
dialectical thinking.  Both Sartre and Lukács attacked the idea that
dialectics occurred within nature - a deviation found in the works
of Hegel and Engels.  In 'History and Class Consciousness', Lukács
criticised Engels's extension of the concept in this fashion and
argued that dialectical method was 'inseparable from the "practical"
and "critical" activity of the proletariat'.  The social construction element was thus central, dialection could only be developed by
social *praxis*.

Studies informed by phenomenology and critical theory reveal that
social control strategies based upon formalised rules are in practice a long way from enjoying completeness.  These studies provide
an important corrective to the metaphysical pathos induced by heavy
doses of Braverman.  Negotiative interaction limits the efficacy of
complete routinisation (Freidson 1977;  Kouzmin 1980).  Students of

'negotiated order' have stressed that theorists of formal organization 'tend to overestimate the more stable features of organizations
- including its rules and its hierarchical statuses' (Strauss et al.
1973:303). Such a focus is unrealistic, for one thing 'hardly
anyone knows all the rules'. Interactionist studies seem to reveal
that what passes for social order far from being an easy unproblematic accomplishment, requires on the contrary unremitting daily
effort. Social actors may or may not be 'streetwise' but they are
likely to be organisation-wise. They are capable of engaging in
tactics of withholding information, of withholding effort, of granting special favours and all of the other indulgencies and denials
which characterise everyday organisational life. There are other
studies which question the rather mechanistic assumption that rules
and formal structures actually succeed in determining behaviour.
Like Strauss above, Zimmerman (1973) criticises orthodox approaches
which ignore what rules actually mean to social actors and how they
use them. Zimmerman's ethnomethodological study illuminates how
actors use 'judgemental work' to accomplish actions 'essentially
satisfying provisions of the rule, even though the action may contrast with ... sociologists' ideas concerning the behavioural acts
prescribed or proscribed by the rule' (1973:262). Similar insights
from an ethnomethodological perspective are revealed by Bittner
(1973) and Sudnow (1973). The social construction of everyday life
within bureaucracies can also lead to 'indulgency patterns' which
vary the formal rules. Gouldner demonstrates how the rude disturb-
ance of just such a pattern led to strike action (Gouldner 1965).

The precarious status of organisation and social 'structures' is
explored by Golding (1980b). He treats the 'principle of control'
as a 'myth' which is 'merely a particular historical derivation of
doing organizing'. By 'myth' he refers to that social belief as
defined by Barthes: 'myth is constituted by the loss of the historical quality of things' (Barthes 1973:142). Thus managers although believers in 'the right to manage' had no access to historical reasons or source for this 'right'. The loss of social memory
could even help to 'depoliticise' the phenomenon. But there were
snags. Managers had to be careful not to violate other cherished
'myths', and equally they lost some of the initiatives of subordinates who used the managers' formal responsibility for decision
against them.

These few instances of social construction evince a healthy
scepticism of formalistic schemes. As Freund and Abrams (1976)
suggest, ethnomethodology and Marxism can be complementary, each
compensating for the other's shortcomings. Gramsci provided an
early lead in the rehabilitation of the subjective and creative side
of Marxism. He re-emphasised the political dimension and the importance of ideological struggle. But it was perhaps the Maoist
model of organisations which came closest to a radical wholescale
application of this message. The Cultural Revolution put 'politics
in command'. Mao encouraged mass activism to overcome bureaucratic
domination. Yeo-chi King (1977) explains how Maoist ideology dis-
placed economic determinism with 'human will'. It proffered a new
rationality - i.e. organisation is only rational when beneficial to
the masses. Its structural precepts were hostile to hierarchy, to
experts and to routinisation.

In the event of course, such actions have faced reversal in post-Mao China.  Paul Piccone argues that in a situation 'wherein both Russian and Chinese communism have exhausted themselves', Gramsci's is the best current hope for Marxism (1976:485).  Piccone emphasises the humanitarian and emancipatory merits in Gramsci's Marxism compared with the discredited Leninism.  He makes a telling contrast between the treatment given to Taylorism by Lenin and Gramsci respectively.  Lenin was mesmerised by the 'scientific achievement ... and the introduction of the best systems of accounting and control' (1965:259).  In consequence the new relations of domination in Soviet Russia 'far from being mere Stalinist deviations ... were to an extent already rooted in Lenin's partial and confused theoretical vision' (Piccone 1976:499).  Gramsci (1971), by contrast, in his essay 'Americanism and Fordism' approaches the subject of productive methods not as a purely technical problem but as a social relation.

A final point in this section on the social construction aspect of dialectics concerns the 'de-mythologising' which can only begin with a close attention to the actual history of the construction of managerial control.  Fortunately some very useful work of this kind is now forthcoming - (see for example:  Stone 1974;  Palmer 1975; Lazonick 1978 and 1979;  Goldman and Van Houten 1980;  Nelson 1975; Elbaum and Wilkinson 1979).  The constraint of space here permits only a brief illustration of this point.  The excellent study by Katherine Stone (1974) deserves special attention.  Her study of the origins of job structures in the steel industry reveals the control patterns to be the outcome of managerial strategies to surmount and counteract the homogeneity of the rank and file after the old skills had been destroyed.  De-skilling was only the start, for

labour discipline became a problem for the employers.  This was the two-fold problem of motivating workers to work for the employers' gain and preventing workers from uniting to *take back* control of production.  In solving this problem employers were creating a new labour system to replace the one they had destroyed (1974:164).

The devices concocted include job ladders, internal promotion, welfarism and the division between mental and physical skills.  Technology

plays only a minor role in this process.  Technological innovations by themselves do not generate particular labour market institutions - they only redefine the realm of possibilities.  The *dynamic* element is the class struggle itself, the shifting power relations between workers and employers. (Stone 1974: 165-6).

This central thrust of Stone's thesis is supported by Elbaum and Wilkinson (1979).  Their comparative study of the British and American steel industries reveals the divergences which developed between these two countries despite the common start point.  But of interest to the present concern with social construction is Elbaum and Wilkinson's amendment to Stone's claim that promotion ladders were entirely a management-imposed device to divide and rule.  They argue that workers themselves struggled hard to establish seniority rules as a device to control the labour supply (Elbaum and Wilkinson 1979: 292).

This point concerning control and resistance brings us to the second facet of the dialectical approach - that of contradiction.

CONTRADICTION

Here we may again pick up the Gramscian strand.  He wrote:
   American industrialists have understood all too well this dialectic inherent in the new industrial methods.  They have understood
   that 'trained gorilla' is just a phrase, that 'unfortunately' the
   worker remains a man and even that during this work he thinks
   more, or at least has greater opportunities for thinking, once he
   has overcome the crisis of adaptation without being eliminated;
   and not only does the worker think, but the fact that he gets no
   immediate satisfaction from his work and realizes that they are
   trying to reduce him to a trained gorilla, can lead him into a
   train of thought that is far from conformist (1971:309-10).
This witnesses Gramsci pursuing a theme rather neglected in Braverman.  There are in turn of course counter-tendencies such as habituation and wider socialising agencies, but these points we pick up in
the next section on totality.  For the moment our discussion hinges
upon the elements of contradiction inherent in the capitalist mode
of production.  The Taylor package itself was in a relationship of
some tension with certain managers' own perceived interests.  Thus
they resisted its introduction because they resented the implied
loss of *personal* control - despite the lure of profits and a control
of a more systematic nature.  In Britain in particular this stumbling block was encountered in the shape of the cult of the 'gifted
amateur' (Merkle 1968).

   The stress by phenomenologists on the reciprocal interaction -
that men produce society and are produced by it - is not sufficient
ground for labelling them dialecticians.  There is the extra dimension to be considered - namely intrinsic contradiction and negation.
Attention to this dimension does not have to involve the kind of
reification of history typified by Engels's 'Anti-Duhring'.  Marx
developed a far more subtle approach, as is reflected in his famous
lines:  'It is by no means "History" which uses man as a means to
carry out its ends as if it were a person apart;  rather History is
nothing but the activity of man in pursuit of his ends.'  Men and
women are not isolated individuals but comprise definite groups and
classes.  Their collective pursuit of their interests results in a
society marked by social inequalities which results in conflict and
crises.  Human definition of wants is conditioned by the existing
state of cultural and material conditions.  Marx's class conflict
model of society posits social change emerging from the conflicts
and contradictions within society.

   The rifts, tensions and inconsistencies which comprise contradiction are of a varied character.  There is a tensile relationship between the forces and the social relations of production;  between a
propertyless proletariat and a small but powerful ruling group;  between the buyers and sellers of labour power;  there is a contradiction in the bourgeois creation of its prime historic antagonist the
proletariat;  there is the contradiction between commodity as use-
value and commodity as exchange-value.  Thus in 'Grundrisse' we find
'as a value, the commodity is general, as a real commodity it is
particular' (Marx 1973:141).

   But the essential contradiction upon which we need to concentrate
here is that concerning the concrete application of the real sub-

ordination of labour.  Marx, Weber and Braverman have all in one
form or another addressed the rationalisation of the labour process
under capitalism, but they have not always explored its contradictions.  Yet these contradictions are to be found in the very application of the real subordination of labour.  For instance:

> The paradox of formal organisation is that it must not only
> reduce human variability to ensure role performance, but it must
> allow room for some variability and in fact encourage it.  There
> must be a supportive number of actions of an innovative, or rela-
> tively spontaneous sort (Kouzmin 1980:74).

Cressey and MacInnes (1980a:16) make a similar point.  It is, they
say, 'precisely because capital must surrender the use of its means
of production to labour that capital must to some degree seek a co-
operative relationship with it.'  They provide a basis for a critique of Braverman's single-minded emphasis on real subordination.
In order to enhance its chances of realising surplus-value, capital
must play down the commodity status of labour. (2)  Thus 'contrary
to the implications of the RSL argument, capital has an active
interest in suppressing its own dominance in the workplace ...'
(1980a:17).

This is surely correct.  Braverman may be said to have neglected
two factors here:  the need to avoid total demoralisation of the
workforce by pushing its advantage to the point of destruction and
second the fact that in many locations it met resistance well before
this point was reached.  In consequence of the resistance encountered, managers have had to devise a far more imaginative ensemble of
strategies and control devices than Braverman's scheme allows
(Nichols 1977;  Brighton Labour Process Group 1977;  Friedman 1977).
Palmer (1975) records how managerial techniques became more sophisticated, so that

> the efficiency drive of the 1920's became increasingly alien (in
> form if not in content) from the older unpolished sentiments of
> Frederick Winslow Taylor....  Capitalism, ever more perceptive
> than mere individuals, breathed a sigh of relief, for the new
> management was an effective vehicle in maintaining the structural
> continuity of the social order ... less rigid it (had) become
> more adaptable, more comprehensive, *more useful* (1975:40-1).

There is a developing literature documenting the resistance to
RSL encountered by rationalistic monopoly capitalism.  This literature spans the initial period of implementation of scientific
management and the period of contemporary struggles.  Historical
studies covering the phase of introduction include Davis's (1975)
study of the IWW's fight against Taylorism.  Significantly this
demonstrates that resistance was not restricted to skilled workers.
In a well-researched study, Montgomery (1979) traces the 'control
strikes' in the United States in the first two decades of this century - the early years of Tayloristic application.  He records the
'transformation of consciousness which generated these challenges by
enrolling five million into unions and infusing into their ranks a
widespread aspiration to direct the operation of railroads, mines,
shipyards and factories collectively.'  This was he maintains '
'itself the product of a decade of continuous struggle, the new
forms of which resulted from management's reorganization of industry' (Montgomery 1979:108).

Active resistance to real subordination was not so absent as an unwary reader might infer from Braverman.

Perhaps no other conflict epitomized the working class response to efficiency so cogently as the Illinois central and Hariman lines Railway Carmen's strike. Initiated in September of 1911, sustaining itself until June 28, 1915 and involving between 28,000 and 35,000 workers, the shopmen's strike is an important and neglected chapter in the history of American labour. The intensity of the struggle (as well as its epic duration) reveals, says Palmer (1975:42), the 'depth of hatred for capital's recent drive to rationalize production'.

The imaginative variety of employers' techniques for controlling labour in the face of such challenges, and the extent to which they clearly transcend the direct control techniques described by Braverman, have been documented in a number of sources. Donald Roy (1980) outlines the use of 'fear stuff', 'sweet stuff' and 'evil stuff' as three tactics used by management in the Southern United States to outwit unionisation drives. Fear stuff involves threats, rumours of closure, unemployment and lay-offs. Sweet stuff tactics promise promotion and other opportunities to be made available if unions are excluded. Evil stuff involves attacks on unionism per se through campaigns to link it with communism, corruption and violence. The elements of expedience and opportunity in the diverse forms of control are described by Hilary Partridge (1980) with reference to Fiat in Turin. Anti-strike bonus payments, 'quarantine' departments, racism, and favouritism are a few of the tactics she describes. There was an element of spontaneous reaction from the labour force. One worker describes how a colleague drew a line on the ground – a yardstick with which to measure speed-up on the line 'the worker would keep an eye on this line, and when he arrived at it he got off the assembly line ...' (1980:427). Of course in turn this was met by counter-reaction by Fiat management who moved the workforce around. 'Internal sackings' involved transferrals, enforced mobility and de-ranking. The unintended consequences aspect of dialectics is also nicely illustrated in this case-study. Fiat's recomposition of the labour force to work the new technology 'backfired' on the company, for the new Southern 'green' labourers were the ones most instrumental in generating the strikes and agitation of the late 1950s which culminated in the Turin general strike of 1962.

Fiat (of a later date) is also used by another writer who seeks to make a point concerning the dialectics of control and resistance. Thus, Friedman (1977b) draws a distinction between Volvo, where changes in work organisation were introduced by management, and Fiat, where 'the impetus came from the workers and the changes were only won after long struggles'. Indeed eventually worker initiatives previously confined to the plant level were extended to include 'initiatives concerning Fiat's overall investment policy and particularly its activity in Southern Italy'. This is all part of Friedman's wider thesis which critiques orthodox Marxist assumptions that direct control is continual and inevitable under capitalism. 'This view arises from a neglect of worker resistance as a force causing accommodating changes in the capitalist mode of production' (Friedman 1977b:43,45). So in addition to Direct Control (roughly

equivalent to the Tayloristic strategy explored by Braverman), there
is, says Friedman, a major alternative also utilised by management -
Responsible Autonomy.  This seeks to capture the potential of variable capital through such devices as group working and job enrichment.  It is, however, significant to note from our dialectical
viewpoint that RA just like DC is impossible as an ultimate ideal.
Contradiction remains in the form of 'the persistence of a fundamental tension generated from within' (1977b:53).

A final line of argument on the theme of contradictions is worth
considering.  Given the epistemological tenets of Bhaskar (1978), as
outlined by Burrell (1980), it would have to be admitted that it
would be extremely difficult if not impossible to demonstrate *empirically* that work-control processes have developed dialectically.
But equally, the same problem would confront the unilinear thesis.
A stalemate does not have to result from these observations.  What
can be done is to continue the kind of historical investigations on
the origin and development of control patterns as initiated by Stone
(1973, 1974), Marglin (1974), Montgomery (1979), Nelson (1975) and
many others.  Accounts of this kind tend to satisfy more adequately
the criteria of reason, internal consistency and symmetry demanded
by a realist philosophy of science (Burrell 1980:96).  Informed by
such accounts, Goldman and van Houten (1980) conclude that bureaucratic domination in American corporations was in fact a strategic
response to worker refractoriness and not merely a product of inexorable rational technique or even a straightforward unmediated adjustment to 'market forces'.  Nor does the unilinear account square
too well with the kind of qualitative assessment made by Miliband
(1978).  He discerns a 'state of de-subordination'.  This is defined
as a process in which people who find themselves in subordinate positions in factories, offices, hospitals, etc. do what they can to
mitigate, resist and transform the conditions of their subordination.  While this of course is an old phenomenon, Miliband sees it
as a 'much more accentuated and generalized feature of life in
Britain now than at any time since the first decades of the last
century' (1978:402).  Of course, there has been some reversal of
this with the deepening recession.  The 'refractory hand of labour'
has been chastised by technology and unemployment.  But this seems
not to be viewed as a stable solution - see for example the many
warnings to this effect from commentators in the 'Financial Times'
and 'The Times' - and in any case, as Miliband argued, the very
process of heightened de-subordination was always likely to provoke
a counter-response.

Nevertheless, at the time of writing, the employer strategy is
again shown to have its limits.  At BL the Metro line has been
halted by a strike over speed-up, and at Ford Halewood the plant
has been struck by a dispute over the attempted implementation of
the new 'disciplinary' code.  Both flagships of managerial resurgence are hit simultaneously.  In each case the confrontation concerns control issues.  And all this is occurring at the apparent
nadir in the fortunes of workplace shop steward organisation.

In sum, under the category 'contradiction' one finds a rather
more complex picture than that intimated under RSL.  It is a picture
replete with persistent tensions, with strategies and counter-stra-
tegies, with unintended consequences, and each of these feeding an

essential social dynamic.  The wider framework of this may be termed
the 'totality'.


TOTALITY

This concept used heavily by Lukács (1971) but also by Marx and particularly Hegel, points up the complex interrelations between
'parts' and 'wholes'.  Parts simply cannot be understood separately
from their relation to the whole;  in turn the totality is reflected
in each part.  It is the logic and constraints of the global capitalist mode of production which inform the social control of work
within 'separate establishments'.  There is an interrelationship between economic, political, cultural and ideological forms.  The precise working-out of the contradictions within the totality will vary
between societies and between work organisations within societies.
This will inevitably lead to uneven development and a variety of
forms in the control of work.
    The impoverishment of work, and its distortion under the capital-
ist labour process, cannot be understood solely at the interactionist level nor solely in terms of 'macro-structures'.  The process
has to be located within a wide analysis of the dynamics of capitalist production.  In this regard talk of 'levels' is purely an analytical and expository device - in fact mainly the latter, because
such a device can impede adequate analysis unless great care is
taken.  The dialectical interplay between interactionist 'controlling' activities and the wider social and economic framework which
I have in mind echoes the kind of theoretical work of R.C. Edwards.
In theorising 'discrimination' and 'segmented labor markets' he
generates a unity in the thesis that 'behaviour observed in the
labour market ("the sphere of circulation") reflects more fundamental processes in production itself ("the sphere of production").
To understand the labor market processes which "produce" group differences in incomes, unemployment, and mobility, then, we must investigate the institutional arrangements governing production - that
is, the social relations of production' (Edwards 1975:84).
    In his analysis, therefore, Edwards questions conventional market
theories which conceptualise markets as somehow 'external' and exercising 'constraint'.  In their stead he generates a theory which
unites the strategies and actions of the large corporations and the
labour markets they create.
    In somewhat similar vein Baumgartner, Burns and De Ville, in
their discussion of industrial democracy, argue for analyses which
locate work processes within the 'context - economic, political and
socio-cultural - of a *capitalist totality*' (Baumgartner et al. 1979:
173).  Thus they maintain that industrial democracy could only succeed if the 'liberation of work' and the 'liberation of political
power' are kept in mind as a 'dynamic totality'.  This entails
action which is multi-sphered (i.e. directed not only in the economic but the political and socio-cultural spheres), multi-level
(i.e. complementary action at enterprise level and the wider socio-
cultural level), and holistic (this means operating the above in a
simultaneous, systemic, fashion).  Consequently, action which for
tactical purposes proceeds in only a piecemeal fashion is likely to

be precarious and defective.  'Incompatibility' or 'mismatch' between spheres and levels may 'contribute to blocking or undermining
a genuine development toward the liberation of work' (Baumgartner et
al. 1979:213).  Thus the failures there have been so far in attain-
ing industrial democracy - not least, nor only, in Britain - could
be traced to a failure to develop 'holistic concepts and strategies
to bring about the transformation of social systems for the purpose
of human liberation' (ibid.).

This concept of 'totality' finds its fullest expression in the
work of Lukács (1971).  In 'History and Class Consciousness', he
argues that only with an approach 'which sees the isolated facts of
social life as aspects of the historical process and integrates them
in a *totality* can knowledge of the facts hope to become knowledge of
reality' (1971:8).  But this vantage point is not easily achieved in
a society which, characterised by division of labour and reification, actively promotes the partial and fragmented view.  Understanding is blocked by reification as for example in the fetishism
of commodities, and in consequence people themselves become things,
objects, not subjects.  In consequence, social relations become distorted.  The division of labour equally 'leads to the destruction of
every image of the whole'.  The problem therefore is not merely one
that resides in the perspective, a simple 'partiality' of view.
Lukács approvingly quotes Marx's own retort to criticisms that
'various factors are not treated as whole'.  Marx's riposte is that
such criticism is levelled 'as though it were the text-books that
impress this separation upon life and not life upon the text-books.'
(Lukács 1971:104).

Totality proper can only therefore be achieved by a class engaged
in a liberating struggle.  It entails
> the unity of theory and practice.  Action, praxis - which Marx
> demanded before all else in his *Theses on Feuerbach* - is in es-
> sence the penetration and transformation of reality.  But reality
> can only be understood and penetrated as a totality ... (Lukács
> 1971:39).

So vital was this concept and method of totality in Lukács's
scheme that he was able to claim:
> It is not the predominance of economic motives in the interpreta-
> tion of society which is the decisive difference between Marxism
> and bourgeois thought, but the point of view of totality.  The
> category of totality, the all-pervasive supremacy of the whole
> over the parts is the essence of the method ... (1971:27).

But as Allen (1975) notes, while Lukács here makes a valid point, he
was wrong to imply that the economic and the totality are separate
categories.  Instead, the 'view of reality as a totality follows
logically from accepting the causal predominance of economic factors' (Allen 1975:253).

In drawing upon this concept of totality it must again be emphasised that it is the *unity* of action and wider social 'structures'
which is being highlighted.  In much the same way as R.C. Edwards
posited the link between social relations in the factory and in the
wider society, so too must the discussion of action and social formations which follow be interpreted.  Totality implies a dynamic
theory, it implies placing 'down-to-earth, day-to-day tasks of
living' in context.

If every social situation possessed its own stimuli or none at
all then there could be no unifying causal determinant.  The
basic determinants, moreover, must have continuity over time
otherwise a rather odd form of empiricism would have to be prac-
tised, namely, that of discovering a succession of basic determinants ... a totality which is causally superior to its parts
then, is one which has historically determined structural determinants (Allen 1975:254).

The latter part of this quotation suggests that Allen is using a
rather more structuralist interpretation than is in my view warranted.  By 'totality' I intend to suggest a methodological precept
which directs attention to relationships between 'parts' and
'wholes'.  As Marx wrote, 'The relations of production of every
society form a whole' and can only in this way be understood.  Parts
only have meaning within their total context.  The part is in the
whole and the whole is in the part.  This approach can be more
clearly understood by contrasting it with earlier bourgeois social
theory which began with the fiction of the egoistic individual.  In
a 'Contribution to the Critique of Political Economy' Marx rejected
this form of social atomism and the 'preposterous' idea of 'production by a solitary individual outside society'.  Marx's method was
to begin with a pre-given whole, to *abstract* elements which comprise
this and derive thereby 'pure essences' – such as for example the
one basic relationship between capital and labour in 'Capital'
(Swingewood 1975).

There is a dialectical interplay between social action and the
concrete patterns of dominant social formations.  These latter are
seen as outcomes or objectifications of social interaction;  the
former are coloured and distorted by prevailing forms of domination.
Together they comprise the totality.  Thus, to illustrate, managerial actions and strategies in pursuit of instrumentality - exploitation, and the limited nature of the resistance to this - are *expressions* of the material context;  equally they actively *re-create*
these priorities, assumptions and 'constraints'.  Failure to recognise this promotes a reified conceptualisation of the social world
which tends towards the denial of the existential possibility of
reality as a fully *social* construction.  This latter invites comparison with Habermas's (1974:205), 'dialectical conception of
society as a historical process'.

There have in fact been some studies of work control which exemplify the importance of the methodology of totality.  Thus Rudin
(1972) demonstrates how the drive for hegemony of capitalist control
at the point of production was only part and parcel of a wider offensive which included weapons drawn from the moral, political and
cultural armoury.  He argues

Because the problem of worker loyalty and efficiency was not ex-
clusively economic or political in its roots, it would not yield
to economic or political reform.  Cultural reform was, therefore,
a necessary component of the business community's industrial pro-
gram, and this meant supplanting the traditional working class
ways of thinking and living for new business-oriented cultural
norms ... whether morality was conceived of as a means or as an
end, social control remained paramount as the ultimate goal of
the industrial reformers.  By 'uplifting' the workers' culture

out of existence, the business community hoped to create a cultural hegemony that would complement their dominance of other
areas of American Life (1972:73).

Lazonick (1978) even more forcibly demonstrates the necessity to embrace cultural and political developments in order to explain the
economic subjection of labour.  In fact it is a key characteristic
of capitalism that it tends to fragment society into separate
spheres.  This point echoes that made by Marx and Lukács.  The consequent thrust of Lazonick's paper is to argue that 'comprehension
of the nature of the system and its long-run tendencies requires an
analysis of the dialectical interrelation of economy, culture and
politics and their interpenetration into the various spheres of
social existence' (1978:2).  Accordingly, he ably explores the role
of the family, mass schooling and various political developments in
terms of the reproduction of labour subjection.  And the question of
the family is probed in order to locate the reason for its survival
once it became redundant as a production unit.  Mass schooling is
interpreted as a mechanism for social reproduction, the instilling
of values to induce passive acceptance of hierarchy and other facets
of the system.  The potential contradiction that schooling could,
however, also become an instrument for a very different purpose -
i.e. to challenge the status quo - is also noted.  In the political
'sphere' the subjection of labour was fought out at a public level
for half a century between 1790 and the 1840s.  In the main the
political challenge dissolved into collaboration, compromise and co-
option.

In the light of this analysis, the thesis advanced by McCoullough
and Shannon (1977) that the state is 'implicated' in organisation
activity, may be seen as a step towards the kind of perspective
which Lazonick has in mind.  McCoullough and Shannon critique the
voluntarist-instrumental conception of organisations with the associated view of organisations and the state as separate and independent entities.  Instead they proffer a conceptualisation of the
'protective' role of the state.  For his part, Lazonick views the
fully developed 'totality' perspective as, in the end, a challenge
to the deficiencies of Marx's focus on the economic.  He maintains:

Apart from the struggle over the length of the working day, one
would think in reading *Capital* that working-class organizations
including trade unions, simply disappeared in 19th century England.  If this were the case - if the very process of capital
accumulation simply destroyed the political and cultural forms
of resistance of the working class - then it would be justified
to analyse the real subjection of labour to capital strictly in
terms of the mode of production.  But the actual historical developments are much more complex and the failure to analyze them
leads to an underestimation of the importance of the capitalist
system as a whole in the reproduction of the capital-labour
relation (1978:5).

Thus Lazonick leads us from capitalist production to the totality of
the capitalist *system*.  While Lazonick's general thesis is sound and
useful, his critique of Marx's 'economic' focus is more debatable.
Swingewood (1975) presents a convincing case that if one goes beyond
'Capital' then Marx's methodology of 'totality' is in fact quite a
sophisticated dialectic.

The problem of the variations within the Marxist framework with
respect to labour and the historical developments within capitalism
is the topic raised for discussion be Elger and Schwarz (1980). The
contradictions in the accounts of Lenin, Gramsci, Braverman and
Sohn-Rethal are explained by situating their accounts historically.
Hence it is maintained that 'what Gramsci and Lenin failed adequately to confront was the historically specific and contradictory
features embodied in the monopoly capitalist socialisation and subsumption of labour and the forms of class struggle which develop on
that terrain' (Elger and Schwarz 1980:366). While Braverman is attacked for his 'celebratory notion' of the old craft form, Elger and
Schwarz for their part want to emphasise the differentiated forms of
current socialised labour.

One final point on 'totality'. It has radical political implications. Social change under this perspective implies something approaching 'de-totalisation'. An example of just such a total transformation is found in the displacement of feudalism by capitalism.
The conversion involved interdependent shifts in capitalisation,
demography, commodification, ideology, political institutions and
all aspects of social relationships. The ideological underpinnings
were provided by the intellectual work of Locke, Ricardo and Smith.
They helped identify the notion of private property and paved the
way for the subjection of labour. In sum, the category of 'totality' embraces the ideas that social analysis should focus on the
whole and the part; that social phenomena should be studied relation-
ally; and that the unit of analysis should be subjected to careful
reflection. Wallerstein (1976) in this regard argues that 'societies' are themselves inappropriate foci. Rather, recognition of the
operation of the world capitalist system is a prerequisite, he says,
to an adequate comprehension of social action. Meanwhile at the opposite extreme, work organisations may be regarded as 'mini-totalities' or 'structural ensembles' which themselves contain diverse
elements and contradictions. Thus while serving as integrative
mechanisms they equally face tensions and conflicts: paradoxically,
then, it is from organisations that capitalism derives its strength
- and its weakness (Burrell 1980:100).

In this chapter, we have attempted only the most programmatic
outline of the essential aspects of a dialectical approach. Ampli-
fication and further application are the subjects of subsequent
chapters. Thus aspects of 'totality' occur in chapter 4; of social
construction in chapters 5 and 6; and of contradiction in chapters
7 and 8.

Chapter 4

# WORK CONTROL IN CONTEXT

The course and outcome of the struggle to control the labour process is subject not only to the interaction of the parties but also
to the wider context.  Accordingly, it is now necessary to locate
these struggles within the totality.  In the first half of the chapter, connections are made with the wider configurations of power.
In the second half, an analysis is made of the ways in which the
central features of contemporary capitalism impact upon work control, and of the ways in which a reciprocal influence operates.


MANAGERIAL PREROGATIVES:  POWER OR AUTHORITY?

There are two key terms in the title of this book:  'managerial
prerogative' and the 'question of control'.  Both terms demand attention to the phenomenon of social power.  'Control' here denotes
the exercise of power.  When we talk of 'being in control' this
signals the successful end-result of applying power.  The present
participle 'controlling' suggests that someone is actively engaged
in applying power (Purcell and Earl 1977).  The purpose of this
section is to conceptualise power and its deployment so that the
nature of the relationship between managerial control and worker
resistance can be better appreciated.  Indeed, it can be categori-
cally stated that this relationship cannot be understood without
considering the nature and distribution of power.
    In the extensive literature on power it has been noted that there
is much contradiction. (1)  In the Parsonian view, power is a collective capacity to achieve common goals.  In contrast, under the
Weberian view, power is seen as the 'probability that one actor
within a social relationship will be in a position to carry out his
own will despite resistance' (Weber 1968:53).  These two views have
been categorized as 'power to' and 'power over' respectively
(Elliott 1976;  Dubin 1960). (2)  But the conflicts extend even
wider.  Roderick Martin (1977), among others, treats 'authority' as
a *type* of power, whereas Alan Fox regards this as 'Perhaps the most
persistent conceptual error' (1971:34) and although Fox cites
Giddens (1968) as a useful reference here, Giddens himself later
writes 'Authority may be one "base of power"' (1974:18).  The

54

premise that authority is a base for power is characteristic as it
happens, of the Parsonian perspective - it assumes that authority
precedes power.  Yet, as we will see in a moment, quite the converse
is postulated by conflict theorists who submit rather that power, in
fact, precedes authority.  Fortunately, among the conflicting interpretations, at least a certain pattern can be discerned.  Thus, the
Parsonian 'power to' conceptualisation has the twin additional attributes of regarding power as a non-zero sum phenomenon and also as
essentially based on consensus.  Conversely, the 'power over' school
tends to regard it as a relationship with zero-sum attributes and
based on conflict. (3)  But even within the 'schools' there are disputes.  For example, with the 'power over' perspective it has been
argued on the one hand that power can only be said to exist when its
effects are *consciously* promoted (Tannenbaum 1968;  Wrong 1968) and
on the other hand it is argued that power is exercised in fact to
more effect when it is unconsciously promoted (Lukes 1974).  Moreover, Weber's classic definition is typically interpreted to mean
that a relationship is only of a power kind when there actually is
resistance.  But Giddens (1974) maintains it is 'illegitimate' to
infer (from Weber) that power is only being used when resistance
from others has to be overcome (p.17).  Unfortunately, Giddens fails
to clarify whether he means by this (a) that Weber's conceptualisation is compatible with the Parsonian 'power to' idea, or (b)
whether, quite differently, he is referring to the possibility of
manipulation - the manoeuvering of people into non-self-regarding actions (to use Martin's term) without their being conscious of such.
   This latter area of discussion is, of course, crucial to the
analysis of managerial 'authority', 'legitimacy' and 'rights'.  I
would argue that power has both 'power to' and 'power over' possibilities.  Available definitions tend to fix on to only one or the
other.  In effect, they reflect different *problematics*.  This merely
means in part that the same term is being employed as a referent for
two entirely different aspects of social life.  But it has proved
notoriously difficult to extricate these usages.  This reflects the
fact that work organisations are characterised by both co-operation
and conflict.  Participants lower and higher typically have both
convergent and divergent interests.  In discussing organisational
'interdependencies', Bowen (1976) argues 'what seems to be required
is a model which demonstrates the simultaneous existence of conflicting and common interests' (p.68).  Bowen's thesis is in harmony
with the work of Lammers (1967) who sees power as a 'potentially ex-
panding resource'.  Accordingly Lammers (1967:201) claims 'power
raises' are comparable to 'wage raises'. (4)  Bowen wants to
'counter the suggestion implicit in conflict theory that the
presence of different interest groupings within an enterprise necessarily results in the use of power solely to further objectives at
variance with those of management'.  Recognition that there are
areas of conflicting interests 'need not, however, prevent these
parties from distinguishing areas of mutual interest suitable for
joint decision-making' (1976:71).
   One of Bowen's key mentors, Tannenbaum (1968), uses the term
'control' as broadly synonymous with power and influence.  His is,
essentially, a *behavioural* model which assumes intentionality as the
start point of the control cycle.  This cycle comprises:  the intent

of A, leading to an influence attempt, resulting in the behaviour of
B, that fulfils the intent of A.  In so far as this cycle occurs
then control may be said to have taken place.  Although Tannenbaum
refers to certain 'hidden elements' in the bases of power which
might help explain B's response, the focus of his model concerns the
more manifest elements.  The stress on intentionality is indicated
by Tannenbaum's point that the model has moral implications.  The
other key contribution from Tannenbaum is his 'control graph'.  This
measures the extent of control on the Y axis and locates different
personnel on the X axis.  With this tool he is able to graph the
discrepancies between actors' perceptions of the existing distribution of control and their ideal or desired pattern.  By shifting the
curves, the conceptual possibility of plus-sum as opposed to fixed-
pie allocations of power is dramatically made apparent.  On the
basis of trust, all parties can gain.  This is most easily conceived
if the negative is considered - i.e. where through mutual suspicion
everyone 'blocks' everyone else and therefore no one can fulfil
their potential or their interests.  Tannenbaum's model is thus
related to Blau's (1964) social exchange theory.  It offers a
rationale for productivity bargaining in that it acknowledges both
self-interest and interdependence.  But from a radical perspective
it could be said to gloss over the investigation of the asymmetrical situation prior to exchange.  In this sense it tends to be ahistoric and to neglect the possibility of a wider prefigurative structure of domination and non-voluntary exchange.

     In similar fashion, Bowen (1976) can be said to follow Tannenbaum
much too closely here.  For, Bowen states
     The premise of this book is that the regulation of work - its
     organisation, performance and reward *and the derivation of work
     goals* - is an essentially jointly regulated process between the
     employers (and managers) of labour on the one hand and the organ-
     isers of labour (trade unions) on the other (Bowen 1976:viii,
     emphasis added).
This is surely to exaggerate the extent of joint regulation which
obtains.  But Bowen continues 'Business objectives are negotiated
outcomes of the interplay of power and influence between the proper-
tied and propertyless of industrial life' (ibid.).  Even if one were
to interpret the term 'negotiation' here in its widest sense (see
for example, Strauss et al. 1973), the lack of recognition accorded
to the pervasiveness of market rationality and the wider structure
of domination, is evident in this assertion.  As with Tannenbaum, an
essentially behavioural level of power-relations is pushed to the
fore and obscures the view of what lies behind.

     Each of these studies reflect what, in the conflict theory liter-
ature, is called the 'collaborative ethic' (Thomas 1978).  This has
enjoyed a popularity among Organisational Development theorists who
have linked it with a range of positive outcomes - most notably
organisational effectiveness, and individual self-actualisation
(Lawrence and Lorsch 1967;  Blake and Mouton 1964;  Burke 1970).
Even the idea of graph techniques to represent shifts in control
curves as pioneered by Tannenbaum (1968) and utilised by Bowen
(1976) is mirrored in the conflict research of Kenneth Thomas
(1978).  However, in recent years, an increasing number of qualifications have been made to the collaborative ethic.  Inter alia these

have raised new doubts about the possibility of genuine collaboration without power-equalisation.  Some of this literature is 'managerialist' in the sense that the problematic addressed is that of
how to effectuate managerially-defined goals, but it is not entirely
so.  Thus, Chesler et al. proselytise the need for 'power-training'
in order to help surmount the mystification of the language of collaboration and the 'common good' which too often is used 'to mask
the prosecution of partisan self interest' (1978:88).  Power training would help articulate shared frustrations, foster new models of
organisation forms - such as worker-controlled factories and com-
munity-controlled schools and seek to 'de-mythologise those rationalisations for inequality that mythmakers have generated to legitimise the status quo'.  For these authors then, the critical goals of
conflict management 'extend beyond helping existing managers maintain an apparently orderly organisation and involve new answers to
the questions of management by whom, and management for what?'
(Chesler et al. 1978:88).

If we focus on the 'power over' aspect then, three interrelated
dimensions of power may be identified.  At the most basic, power is
exercised when two parties are in conflict and a decision is made or
an outcome is reached which favours the dominant party.  This asymmetrical relationship with an inherent potential for manifest conflict is expressed in Dahl's definition 'A has power over B to the
extent that he can get B to do something that B would not otherwise
do' (1957:202).  In organisational studies, this exercise of power
at the behavioural level is reflected in the work of Mechanic (1962)
and Crozier (1964) who identify power in the hands of 'lower participants' as a consequence of their immediate control over 'uncertainty'.  Crozier's maintenance engineers retained some discretion
over the duration of machine down-time.  In the terms used in our
previous chapter, the real subordination of labour for this particular group was not so far advanced as it was for other operatives.
Dahl, in his political studies of the exercise of power in the community, attempted to surmount the circularity of much power-elite
theorising, by re-focusing on observable behaviour.  But the simple
registration of wins and losses on contested issues is clearly a
partial view.  Thus, in the industrial sphere it would be a very
crude device to infer from a strike settlement that a particular
side had 'won' and was ipso facto the more 'powerful'.

It was to transcend this kind of problem that Bachrach and Baratz
illuminated a second face of power.  This one includes the more
subtle and less visible activity where 'A devotes his energies to
creating or reinforcing social and political values and institutional practices that limit the scope of the political process to ...
those issues which are comparatively innocuous to A' (1971:379).

Clearly, management are in a much stronger position to exercise
this kind of power.  They are more strategically placed to engage in
agenda-management.  Bachrach and Baratz's work allows some redress
of the shortcomings of the pluralist approach by re-focusing not
only on overt but also on covert grievances.  They permit investigation not only with respect to the fate of the items reaching the
agenda but also issues kept off the agenda.  Bachrach and Baratz
develop their case further in the article Decisions and Non-
Decisions:

> When the dominant values, the accepted rules of the game, the
> existing power relations among groups, and the instruments of
> force singly, or in combination, effectively present certain
> grievances from developing into full-fledged issues which call
> for decisions, it can be said that a non-decision making situ-
> ation exists (1963:641).

By this confusing term 'non-decision' the authors refer not to instances where A consciously decides against action but rather to
implement what Schattschneider terms the 'mobilisation of bias'. In
fact, they quote Schattschneider to this effect:

> All forms of political organisation have a bias in favour of the
> exploitation of some kinds of conflict and the suppression of
> others because organisation is the mobilisation of bias. Some
> issues are organised into politics while others are organised out
> (cited in Bachrach and Baratz 1971:380).

Bachrach and Baratz recognise, however, that in cases where a
previously latent submerged issue surfaces and gets pushed forward,
the decision-making process then activated may jeopardise the previously established mobilisation of bias (1963:642).

Lukes goes somewhat further and highlights a third dimension or
face of power. Whilst paying tribute to the 'major advance' made by
the two-dimensional view of power he says that it remains inadequate. The third dimension involves recognition that the most insidious power is exercised in such a way as to forestall the generation of grievances. It involves a forthright critique of the behavioural approach and allows consideration of the way 'potential
issues' are suppressed not only by agenda-setting or pre-emption by
a 'series of individually chosen acts' but also and most importantly, 'by the socially structured and culturally patterned behaviour
of groups and practices of institutions' (Lukes 1974:22). Lukes's
radical reformulation brings into view the shaping of preference and
cognitions such that subordinates 'accept their role in the existing
order of things, either because they can see or imagine no alternative to it, or because they see it as natural and unchangeable'
(1974:24). The agents of this form of power - that is including
managers - may themselves be unaware of the full part they play in
its perpetration.

It should be clear that when one turns from the exchange and
interdependence level of behavioural interaction, the dominant
agents and beneficiaries of the other two more hidden and institutional dimensions of power who come into view tend to be owners and
agents of owners - i.e. managers. It is not, therefore, simply as
Martin disingenuously observes that 'at the very least, few would
claim that workers have authority over management' (1977:115).
Rather, in addition to authority, the levers of power at the second
and third levels discussed above are essentially reserved for managerial use. Moreover, managerial prerogative is bolstered by the
fact that these hidden, institutionalised and insidious dimensions
of power are interwoven with and supportive of the fabric of authority which exists. In consequence, this interpenetration raises deep
problems when it comes to any attempt to stake out 'genuine' realms
of authority predicated upon legitimacy and consensus.

The 'mobilisation of bias' in the work world may be illustrated
by the compartmentalisation of issues and the institutionalisation
of conflict. Compartmentalisation of 'industrial' from 'political'

issues and of 'legitimate' from 'illegitimate' issues may be seen as
instances of the 'organising in' and 'organising out' referred to by
Bachrach and Baratz.  Hence Michael Mann observes:  'What we call
the institutionalisation of industrial conflict is nothing more nor
less than the narrowing down of conflict to aggressive economism and
defensive control' (1973:21).  Workers' demands that are not 'appro-
priately' framed in these terms will encounter particular problems
from both management and the organised trade union bodies.  'Un-
sophisticated' claims tend to be reformulated and pushed into well-
worn, familiar (and safe) channels.

But the cultural patterning noted by Lukes under the third dimension of power tends to ensure that 'non-negotiable' demands are not
generated in the first place.  Workers, in the main, accept the
configurations of industrial hierarchy, the extreme division of
labour, production for profit and not for need, market rationality
and material and symbolic inequality.  These are, by and large, perceived as 'givens' in the taken-for-granted world order.  Willis, in
'Learning to Labour' (1977), explores the uncertain path of socialisation for a group of teenage boys.  Ironically, even in their
rebellion against the middle-class cultural values of the school
with its emphasis on employment achievement and work as an expression of fulfilment and individuality, these 'under-achievers'
were fitting themselves realistically for the work experience available to them.  Their acceptance of the cash nexus and their celebration of manual labour over contemptible white-collar employment
uniquely eased their passage into the world of work.  The social-
conditioning power of societal institutions, such as the media,
schools, churches and families, helps generate a pervasive ideology.
So the cultural bias reproduced by managerial (and subordinate)
action and affirmation is not actually dependent upon any particular
manager's (or group of managers') strategies.  As Alan Fox indicates:  'power and social conditioning cause the employee interests
to accept management's shaping of the main structure long before
they reach the negotiating table' (1973:219).

Lukes's third dimension of power is related to Clegg's (1975) and
Clegg and Dunkerley's (1980) conceptualisation.  Clegg seeks to make
his case largely by mounting a wide-ranging critique of Hickson et
al. (1971) and their strategic contingency theory of power.  This
latter is within the behavioural approach to the explication of
power criticised above.  It maintains that power emerges because
organisations (here viewed as open systems) have certain 'needs' -
most notably, as rational systems, to cope with uncertainty.  The
division of labour and departmentalisation are facets of this
rational administration.  They allow specialists opportunity to cope
with diverse uncertainties.  But divisionalisation creates sub-unit
*inter-dependencies* and so, unlike the equilibrium-exchange models,
Hickson et al. (1971) posit situations of imbalance.  Hence a sub-
unit's 'power' depends on its centrality, substitutability and the
balance of dependence arising from the (diverse) 'coping' capabilities.  In this way, power becomes seen as the obverse of dependency.

Clearly this theory is a subtle admixture of different theoretical components:  systems, rationality, uncertainty, dependency, and exchange.  As Clegg rightly suggests, it is, however, a
seriously deficient theory of power.  Its primary shortcoming is
that it overlooks the fact that the organisational configurations

are pre-established and pre-based on wider 'rules'. It does seem
strange to suggest that the structural layout should determine the
source of power when one would certainly expect the reverse (Clegg
and Dunkerley 1980:444). In other words, Hickson et al. (1971)
adopt an essentially ahistoric and static model. It overlooks the
power of organisational structuring;  it adopts managerial definitions and deterministic assumptions about the supposedly unambiguous
'meanings' of environmental messages;  it takes organisational hierarchy for granted.

Clegg's alternative model is to conceive of an overarching structure of 'hegemonic domination' embodied in a system of 'rules'
within which structural power is exercised. This involves a conceptualisation of 'power' as a junior partner in a hierarchy of
domination. Hence the essence of the critique of the 'strategic'
contingency theory of power', of Blau's 'exchange theory', and the
'coping with uncertainty' theories of Thompson (1956) and Crozier
(1964) is that they only discern the surface level and neglect the
prefigurative and underlying 'deep structure'.

Clegg's case, which draws on Marx and Weber, is therefore essentially in line with our third dimension of power. Weber had argued
that social action was oriented by 'rules' and that these are 'without exception, profoundly influenced by structures of domination'
(Weber 1968:941;  Clegg and Dunkerley 1980:455).

There are, however, certain problems in Clegg's own exposition.
From our perspective his whole case is rather too deterministic. He
recognises that despite the shortcomings of exchange and contingency
theory there does remain the problem of explaining behavioural 'variance' from formal authority structures and dictates. Yet, at certain points, his enthusiasm to illuminate overarching domination im-
pedes his attempts to make sensible headway on this project. For example, he suggests that 'Just as with Crozier's maintenance men and
production workers, we can similarly say that the behavioural outcome is only possible because of some underlying rule(s) that people
use in constituting their actions. The manifestation of power is
enabled by an underlying rule' (Clegg and Dunkerley 1980:448). But
surely this cannot be true of all 'variance' in behaviour. Clegg
becomes misled by his example of the formal authority and 'scope for
power' of policemen in directing traffic. In the industrial sphere
dependence may arise from *incompleteness* in the real subordination
of labour - i.e. not because of any 'rule' but, if anything, because
of rule absence. It is therefore possible that the (partial) power
to exercise influence derives from the lack of rule. Moreover,
while Clegg talks of encouraging research strategies to explore
'variance' he seems to predetermine the outcome by declaring that
any power 'that employees have over and above, or outside of the
formal structure, is a capacity which is only possible within the
framework of hegemonic domination to which they would first have to
submit' (Clegg and Dunkerley 1980:482). In so far as this means
workers are constrained by the capitalist labour process, this is
true. But it tends otherwise to underestimate the potential for
worker resistance (this point is explored further in chapter 8).
Much would depend also upon what is meant by having to 'submit', but
as expressed it seems to rule out of consideration the possibility
of (say) the miners being able to prevent closure of 'uneconomic'

pits. It is a formula which underestimates the capacity of capitalism to make pragmatic adjustments and accommodations. Further, the
essential hierarchy of control in Clegg's scheme is domination -
rule - power. The notion of domination is expressive of the overarching structure of hegemony; rule is expressive of formal rationality and power is in consequence left as a rather circumscribed
phenomenon. But at other times, the term power is used in a wider,
more conventional sense, as in the statement 'power will be exercised to reassert control.... it is only when control slips, taken-
for-grantedness fails, routines lapse and problems appear, that
overt exercise of power is necessary' (Clegg and Dunkerley 1980:
481). Here, then, power is viewed as a resource not so much dependent upon 'rule' but, on the contrary, as a facility capable of
being deployed when 'rule' has miscarried.

And the fact of the matter, is of course, that hegemony is not
complete. There has been some decline in deference to those occupy-
ing formal positions of authority as Miliband (1978) has noted.
Workers cultivate a certain cynicism and remain suspicious of managerial motives. Workers' consciousness, as has been often observed
(Mann 1973; Parkin 1972), is typically ambivalent. Dominant values
are not so much embraced as 'modified'. As Parkin explains, 'The
tendency among the underprivileged is not to reject these values and
thus create an entirely different normative system, but to negotiate
or modify them in the light of their own existential conditions'
(1972:92). In consequence, workers who are seemingly happy to en-
dorse at an abstract level middle-class stereotypes of trade unions
and the malfeasance of strikes, infuriatingly maintain a mulishness
and impenitence when it comes to their own concrete situation
(Westergaard 1970; Nichols and Armstrong 1976; Cannon 1967). To
the extent that a subordinate value system does exist, it is associated with shared hardship in local working-class communities. Even
the dichotomous social imagery of 'us' and 'them' tends to be expressive in the last analysis of grim forbearance (Parkin 1972).
Subordinate values do not ordinarily represent an alternative vision
or a coherent replacement ideology. There is a measure to which
they may even serve to reconcile people to their status. But in
day-to-day situations, the point is that 'rule' cannot be assured of
unproblematic effectuation.

In similar vein, Mann explores the 'dualism' in working-class
meaning systems. He maintains that their willingness to subscribe
to certain aspects of dominant ideology such as the need for co-
operation in order to safeguard mutual economic interests is soberly
'realistic given the current economic system' (1973:68). 'Acceptance' is then essentially pragmatic. Acquiescence does not
necessarily imply a normative underwriting of managerial prerogatives.

The whole notion of a dominant ideology and the associated idea
of 'a primarily ideological incorporation of the labour force' is
attacked by Abercrombie, Hill and Turner (1980). They claim to find
the dominant ideology thesis 'empirically false and theoretically
unwarranted' (1980:1). They choose to situate explanation of
working-class action or inaction at the base rather than the 'superstructural' level. They maintain that today the dominant ideology,
such as it is, is less well defined than previously, and is to some

degree fragmentary and inconsistent;  thus its success in incorpo-
rating the working class is decidedly limited.  Moreover, the actual
context is 'elusive' and the private property component of Westergaard and Resler's 'core assumptions' (1975) is interpreted as a
legacy from an earlier stage of capitalism which may now be incompatible with the changed institutional structure of 'finance capitalism'.

They till over a considerable number of secondary empirical studies in search of dissension in working-class ideology.  And they
find it.  On balance they 'favour a view that gives working class
culture more autonomy than ideological hegemonists would grant it'
(p.143).  They instance bargaining claims which are dismissive of
managerial arguments regarding profitability and accordingly they
discern an elevation of 'social' over 'economic' criteria.  Under
'social' criteria are placed skill, need and customary differentials.  Aggressive wage-bargaining tactics, the persistence of the
view that the relationship between workers and management is based
on power rather than authority, and the low level of trust, are
taken as further evidence of the failure of incorporation at the ideological level.  It is noted, however, that this rejection of managerial values seemingly fails to elicit any practical consequences.
Indeed on the contrary, in quoting Willis's (1977) school study,
they observe the paradox that in rejecting the dominant culture
these boys penetrate the mystification whose function is to 'conceal
commodification'.  The boys appreciate and accept the cruel reality
that they are 'only labour power and that work can only offer them a
commodity status'.  In consequence, it is arguable whether this type
of 'rejection' of dominant ideology really amounts to anything.  As
Abercrombie et al. admit, the boys feel they are rejecting the dominant ideology 'at the very moment in which they accept the nature of
the economic system and their place in this' (1980:151).  Overall,
Abercrombie et al. set out to retrieve Marxism and sociology from a
thesis to which their own exegesis actually adds credence.  While
making the 'major conclusion that Britain is not in fact a cohesive
society' (1980:152), the authors find themselves having to explain
the 'ways in which social order and integration are maintained in
the absence of powerful consensual values' (p.153).  They run
through reformism, failure of the working class to generate a model
of an alternative society, and the fear of short- and medium-term
disruption from radical transformation.  These are the 'positive'
aspects.  'Negative' factors include divisions within the working
class, Labourism, and the Soviet-style socialism which 'discredits
the Marxist-Leninist alternative....  The demonstration effect of
Russian communism may promote aversion rather than endorsement' (p.
154).  Integration is also explained by realistic assessment of
economic survival under the present system, and in consequence there
must needs be some compliance with managerial decisions which is
'not of course, entirely voluntary and uncoerced' (ibid.).

It may be fairly claimed that Abercrombie et al. do more to amend
the 'dominant ideology' thesis than to negate it.  By careful selection of key elements it is possible to demonstrate considerable lack
of consensus among the working class.  But, at the end of the day, a
coherent alternative ideology is not sustained.  Tom Burns, in his
Foreword to the book, seems to recognise this.  He still wants to

preserve what he likes to call a 'weaker' version of the thesis, namely the ability of a dominant ideology to inhibit and confound the development of a counter-ideology.

In any case, the important point for our analysis is that with or without full ideological consensus, the material we have examined all casts doubt on the idea of genuine *legitimation* of managerial priorities and decisions.  Pragmatic acquiescence is a theme advanced not only by Mann and Parkin but Burns and Abercrombie et al. This being so, it has profound repercussions for the concept of managerial *authority*.  If Fox (1971) is right and authority is bound up with legitimacy, the absence of the latter threatens the existence of the former.  If acquiescence is not a sufficient guarantor of legitimacy, then this renders the foundation of authority as suspect.  Avoidance of glib talk of 'managerial authority' demands attention to the three interrelated questions - who legitimises what and how?  Generally, it is assumed that it must be the subordinates (workers) themselves who do the legitimising; they direct this at management by refraining from interfering in certain 'preserved areas' such as pricing and investment.  Thus Fox defines an authority relationship as one in which, 'the superordinate is perceived by the subordinate as having the *right* to make decisions which must be accepted as binding' (1971:34).  Conversely, power he regards as pressure or coercion to act 'against one's consent'.  The practical significance of this distinction, he maintains, is that, where authority obtains, there must exist some reciprocal 'obligation'. This means that persons legitimising authority feel obliged to obey and, indeed, accept the rightness or legitimacy of punishment if obligations are not fulfilled.  Conversely, power relationships generate a vicious circle of imposition, resentment, waywardness, further coercive sanction, further resentment and a renewal of the spiral. The essential point deriving from Fox is the stimulus to commence exploration of the cost-effectiveness of power versus authority.  He recognises that the latter requires 'cultivation' and in many circumstances, as for example in the case of short-term contracts, employers may simply not be willing (because they don't rate the pay-off as significant enough) to expend the required energy.  This weighing of 'costs' in terms of time, care and concessions against 'returns' in the shape of co-operation and legitimacy neatly exemplifies the penetration of economic rationality into human relationships.

In consequence, the much vaunted distinction between power and authority may, in certain contexts, be rendered highly suspect.  The employment relationship is subject to complex patterns of domination:  the difference between authority and power may turn merely on the degree of energy which managers 'invest' in order to mystify the relationship so power and authority should not be seen as mutually exclusive ways of structuring behaviour.  As Gouldner (1971:294) points out, 'legitimacy' and 'authority' never eliminate power; they merely 'defocalise it, make it latent'.  Power and authority therefore may both be viewed as that form of social relationship where one actor or group of actors is able to influence the behaviour of others in a way which gives net benefit of socially valued resources to the former.  It may be observed that this applies irrespective of the existence or otherwise of manifest conflict, irrespective of whether there is or is not conscious intent, nor does it mean that all of B's interests are necessarily sacrificed.  It does entail, however, an asymmetrical relationship characterised by inequality and the exploitation of wage-labour for valorisation would therefore always imply a power relationship.

It may be asked whether any industrial relationship can ever rest on authority.  Surely the possibility of some small workshop staffed by willing artisans happily working for a benign owner must be granted?  In essence the answer would turn upon the extent to which one could demonstrate genuine consent and legitimacy under these conditions of objective alienated labour.  Given a context of the commodification of labour, a dominant institutional framework, the capacity of a dominant group to shape meaning systems and impose its definitions of the situation, then the problem of furnishing proof of 'free choice' would seem insurmountable.  Reticulation of 'legitimate' spheres is elusive when power 'exists as a factor in the lives of subordinates shaping their behaviour and beliefs at every moment of their relations with those above them' (Gouldner 1971: 294).

Thus, to the question posed at the head of this section:  managerial power or authority?  the answer is power.


RE-CONCEPTUALISING WORK ORGANISATIONS:  POWER AND THE ORGANISATIONAL CONTEXT

Clearly much of the above argument has implications for the conceptualisation of work organisations.  In order briefly to identify the main strands of this 're-conceptualisation' (as distinct, that is, from that set of assumptions found in most organisational literature) four points should be noted.


(1)  Member attachment

We have departed in some wide measure from the standard inducement-contribution model (March and Simon 1958), which posits 'voluntary' exchange of time and effort for payment and other inducements.  The equilibrium tendencies and idea of voluntarism are rejected.


(2)  Organisational goals

In place of the normal assumption of organisational 'missions' reflecting their functional contribution to societal needs, the purpose of 'organisations' might more properly be regarded as to advance the sectional interests of the controllers and those on whose behalf they engage in controlling.  Alongside this mobilisation will co-exist the multifarious objectives of members including careerism, ego-expansion, the desire for an easy life, and other targets which may be pursued in contradistinction to the official goal.  These may involve actions in actual conflict with that goal, as for example, with output restriction, demarcation rules, sabotage, breaks for golf, attendance at Rotary and so on.  The consensual presumptions

contained in the term 'organisational goal'(s) are thus shown to be
suspect and in many cases false.


## (3)  Organisational structure

Administration theory treats structural attributes as manifestations
of rationality.  Accordingly, hierarchy, division of labour and
like-minded structural features are assumed to reflect the need for
social order and control rationally required if societal requirements are to be met.  This loops back to the Parsonian view of
organisational power as a societal resource for the attainment of
its goals.  Organisational structure then is regarded in rational,
legitimate and consensual terms.  But from a labour-process perspective formal organisational structure can be viewed as an institutionalisation of 'power over'.  Workers entering organisations are
exposed to control and direction.  Structure ossifies unequal influence, deprivation and reward.  Patterned inequalities in organisations are 'closely connected to variations in economic power (market
power, positions within the capitalist system of production);  and
they are related to political attitudes and culture.  In short they
are class-based' (Salaman 1981:200).  This aspect of organisation
structure as control is picked up again in chapter 7.


## (4)  Organisational rationality and market rationality

The notion of 'rationality' in administrative theory is treated
synonymously with 'efficiency'.  It intertwines means-end logic with
efficacy, economy of effort and resources, and 'reason'.  Weber's
(1968) ambiguity in his analysis of legal-rational bureaucracy has
much to answer for in this regard.  But he did indicate that this is
only one type of rationality and that in the main this particular
type rests on 'economic power for its foundation and maintenance'
(Weber 1968:942).  As argued in chapter 2, it would be a mistake
therefore, to assume that this type of 'formal rationality' necessarily optimises substantive interests.  On the contrary, it frequently subtracts from them.  In the same way, machinery and other
facets of technological structuring embody dominant interests.  The
forces of production thus shape the contours and experience of organisational life.  There is a symbiosis between work organisations
and the wider society:  organisations re-produce class society and
in turn, are constrained by it.  These organisations are designed to
produce surplus-value (this doesn't mean they seek to maximise
profit) and this is their sine qua non.  Accordingly, conglomerates
shunt resources around their organisations depending upon the relative yield.  Surplus-value is predicated, as we have seen, upon the
extraction of surplus labour - the process which produces class
struggle.  In contrast to conventional theory which viewed organisations as either rational attempts to find the most efficient mode of
operation or as a metaphysical expression of some mystical 'rationalisation process', neo-Marxist theory views them as 'the outcome of
a struggle between capital and labour over the rate of exploitation
of labour' (Gintis 1976:36).  This reconceptualisation of work

organisations reflects the category of 'totality';  it means that
they can only be fully understood in terms of the wider social
formation, a formation which they express and re-create.  It is to
an examination of the context of contemporary capitalism that we now
turn.


THE CAPITALIST MODE OF PRODUCTION

'Accumulate.  This is Moses and the Prophets!'  Marx's famous dictum
pinpoints the fundamental dynamic force which powers the capitalist
system.  This raison d'être of the system necessarily shapes the
whole context within which the labour process occurs.  It may be
argued that the changing contours of capitalism - covering such tendencies as increased concentration of capital, state interventional-
ism, cultural configurations, and the generation of crises and responses to crises, are implicated in this underlying dynamic.  It is
clearly impossible in a brief review to assess the general context.
Our objective rather, is to focus on the dialectical relationship
between the labour process and the 'driving fire' of competition.
    The 'contemporary form of the capitalist mode of production' may
be regarded as 'a working out of capital's attempts continuously to
reassert its control over the labour process in response to cyclical, social-historical forces that are interdependent with the process of capital accumulation' (Boreham and Dow 1980:20;  see also
Kay 1979).  Thus control over the labour process must be *situated*
within this wider context.  A useful perspective is made available
by E.O. Wright (1978) who examines 'impediments to the process of
continued accumulation'.  In a general sense these impediments are
always present, but at particular historic periods with a falling
rate of profit, these impediments amount to a 'crisis'.  There has
been much debate surrounding the identification of crisis - and in
particular, the distinction between it and a mere 'recession'.  The
Union for Radical Political Economics (1978), in their publication
'U.S. Capitalism in Crisis', essentially point to the structural
changes and institutional reformulations which occur in times of
crisis.  They observe:
    institutions are changing their shape very rapidly during the
    present period.  Corporations are shifting the location of their
    activities to such an extent that entire cities and regions are
    affected.  Labor unions are being forced to adjust their collec-
    tive bargaining policies' (URPE 1978:3).
Their list includes deterioration in services offered by municipal
governments and harsher policies from national government.  The
echo of these structural re-adjustments in Britain hardly requires
comment.  In Britain, the United States and other countries in
crisis, the economic and political systems will, as URPE observe,
be very different ten years from now as a result.  Whose crises is
it then?  Is it just a crisis from capital's viewpoint?  Hardly.
The point is that in order to resuscitate the accumulation process,
the kind of institutional re-adjustments referred to above are designed to shift the burden onto workers, claimants, and consumers.
Redundancies, speed-ups and  rises in prices all become manifestations of the underlying crisis - the falling relative rate of
profit.

The 'dynamic' nature of capitalism thus cannot be interpreted as a positive innovative phenomenon for all citizens. It embraces the 'long-waves' or cycles which have been debated most notably by the Soviet Deputy Minister Kondratieff in the 1920s, by Trotsky in the same period, and more recently by Gamble and Walton (1976) and Mandel (1978). The crisis period is used to mount a counter-attack upon the advances made by organised labour and to thin out the over-capacity in capital's own ranks (Gamble and Walton 1976;  Block and Hirschhorn 1979).

In consequence, the erosion of managerial prerogative which can occur - especially during boom periods - is largely contingent upon continued employment. And yet, these same forces tend, on the contrary, to ensure endemic instability. The ranks of the reserve army may rather suddenly be swelled by erstwhile protagonists. The disciplinary impact of such transition is likely to be accompanied by raised work standards for those who do remain within the labour process. Thus, the challenge from below always bangs its head against the ceiling of the employers' ultimate control over jobs: 'all the wiles in the world are powerless in the face of lay-off or redundancy' (Lane 1974:214).

And given the fall in pre-tax profit recorded by Glyn and Sutcliffe (1972:66) redundancy is precisely what might have been expected. They logged the continual decline in profits for each five-year period from 1950. The annual averages were as follows, 1950-4: 16.5%;  1955-9: 14.7%;  1960-4: 13%;  1965-9: 11.7%;  1970-4: 9.7%. It is precisely the disruption of accumulation and the falling rate of profit which has been defined as central to 'marxian crisis theory' (Wolf 1975;  Zimbalist 1975). The significance of slow-down and the importance of dynamism is well known by capitalists too. As the General Motors Corporation have expressed it:

Economic progress is like a wheel,
When it loses speed it wobbles and
When it stops it falls, kerplunk.
(Cited in Wycko 1975:14.)

For accumulation to proceed, 'capital must win its battle for control over production' (Conference of Socialist Economists 1976:2). As the CSE points out, the present crisis is not just about some inherent cyclical tendency for the rate of profit to fall.

In Britain, for example, substantial sectors of the organised working class have consistently and successfully challenged the power of capital to introduce 'rationalisation' or 'Fordisation' as the price for higher wages. In sectors where rationalisation has been introduced the conditions of work have been resisted on a scale which, echoed throughout the advanced industrial countries, has seriously undermined capital accumulation (1976:2).

There is, in consequence, a vital dialectical link between the labour process and the wider context. As the CSE (1976) suggest, the degree of resistance at the point of production can promote 'impediments' to the accumulation process, thereby helping to slow the economic 'wheel'. But equally, in the reverse direction, the way out of the Great Depression at the end of the last century was, as Sohn-Rethel (1976) reminds us, not just imperialism but an increase in labour exploitation at home. Thus while increased resistance at the point of production may obstruct accumulation, the

space eventually created tends to be used by capital to attack the
very same points of resistance.

To cope with such problems, capital has looked to the state for
assistance.  Classic depictions in industrial relations emphasised
a 'tradition of voluntarism' (Flanders 1974) and of 'laissez-faire
collectivism' (Kahn-Freund 1969).  But as the state becomes increasingly interventionist under conditions of late capitalism, these
characterisations are rendered less relevant.  Equally, even the
historical validity of such depictions implying a tripartite model
which includes a 'neutral' and 'independent' state has, in any case,
come under challenge.  For example, Hyman argues that it was always
a 'non-intervention in favour of capital' (1975:132).  In other
words, under conditions prevailing in mid-nineteenth century at the
zenith of laissez-faire, non-intervention did not mean neutrality,
rather, it spelled endorsement of prevailing bourgeois dominance.

Under conditions of crises, the role of the state in the twentieth century has been markedly different.  We have witnessed an increasingly *interventionist* state anxious to stabilise an unwieldy
political and economic order.  Keynesian policies chiselled one
major landmark;  the Beveridge commitments in social policy and
full-employment carved another.  With respect to the role of law in
industrial relations Kahn-Freund (1969) classified three types of
state intervention.  The auxiliary function comprised those measures
designed to support the 'autonomous' system of collective bargaining;  the regulatory function enacted a code of substantive rules
and terms of employment;  and the restrictive function circumscribed
certain kinds of actions or to put it more favourably, provided
'rules of the game'.  Because there are various types of intervention, it is misleading to assume that more (or less) intervention
is necessarily favourable, or unfavourable to labour.  But, as the
Müller-Neusüs;  Habermas and Offe debate reveals, the problem of
conceptualising the state within capitalism goes much deeper.

Müller and Neusüs (1975) attack what they term the 'reformist'
interpretation of the modern state.  This, they maintain, is the
'illusion of state socialism' (state socialism being used here to
denote an advanced type of 'welfare' state existing under capitalism
as distinct from a 'socialist state' which refers to a situation
where at least in a formal sense the objectives are explicitly anti-
capitalist).  Müller and Neusüs claim that in the history of the
labour movement the conception of the state as relatively independent has been the foundation of 'revisionist strategy'.  Revisionists believe in the talk of 'democratic processes'.  They allegedly
conceive of the state as a 'sacred vessel' that can just as easily
be filled with socialist as with capitalist contents.  Revisionists
also reject the idea that the CMP can only be negated by revolutionary working-class action; they envision the transforming potential
of the state apparatus.  But Müller and Neusüs, for their own part,
see the state as inherently incapable of resolving the fundamental
*contradictions* between wage labour and capital.  The deepening
crisis, moreover, means this fact will not be concealed for much
longer;  the state will be exposed as irrevocably tied to the interests of capital.  It has to maintain 'business confidence' - meaning
it has to guarantee the potential for continued exploitation.
Crisis conditions rule out the possibility that workers might seek

redress from the state on questions of work speed and the intensification of the labour process.  Thus, the illusion will wane.  Meanwhile, they accuse Habermas and Offe of mystifying the situation
through their 'politicism'.  That is, these two are seen as over-
emphasising the political dimension at the expense of the economic.
This can only serve to divert attention from the fundamental contradictions within capitalism.  This challenge, of course, has long
been levelled at the Frankfurt School.  The break of Critical
Theory with traditional Marxism was predicated on a model of late
monopoly capitalism which 'meant the collapse of base and superstructure and consequently, the de-emphasis of the production process as the exclusive locus of class struggle' (Heydebrand and
Tummons 1975:4).  In consequence, for Critical Theorists, class
struggle is manifested in the totality so that contradictions between labour and capital are seen as having been transformed.
These contradictions now become manifest as 'legitimation crises'
(Habermas) and/or as conflicts on the periphery of the point of production (Offe).  It is for these reasons that it is necessary to
consider the whole context of the labour process.

In 'Legitimation Crisis', Habermas (1976) broadens the debate
well beyond that advanced by Müller and Neusüs.  He outlines the
susceptibility of capitalism to a number of diverse 'crisis tendencies'.  These comprise (in addition to economic crises) rationality
crisis, legitimation crisis and motivation crisis.  In truth it
would be a distortion to label Habermas a 'revisionist'. (5)  Claus
Offe (1975) equally rejects the polemic waged against him.  He re-
iterates his position that 'concern for the "general welfare" of
capitalist society as institutionalized in the state apparatus reduces economic antagonism' but refutes the alleged connection with
classical revisionism (1975:105).  It is 'no accident' he maintains,
'that the political conflicts and revolutionary perspectives relevant in the U.S. today result from the institutional conditions of
non-realised labor power' (1975:108).  He refers here to the non-
productive surplus labour power that cannot be realised but is situated in repressive locales such as ghettos, worthless training programmes, the military and authoritarian welfare institutions.  The
state acts to prevent crises outside the strictly economic.  The
state apparatus, that is, has wide-ranging stabilising functions.
Like Habermas, Offe reaffirms that the political economy of late
capitalism has suppressed contradictions in the production sphere
but in consequence it has to face a more diffused front across the
whole of social life.

Noting that most recent theorising on the state has been within
the Marxist tradition, Colin Crouch (1979b) finds several aspects
unsatisfactory.  The theory of 'overloaded government' whereby democratic governments face instability because of excessive demands
from their citizenry, represents one of the few conceptual advances
for the pluralists.  Meanwhile, within the neo-Marxist perspective
the theory of the 'corporate state' has enjoyed predominant attention.  The recent decline in economic fortunes, and the consequent
difficulties in absorbing rising expectations within the economic
sphere, have prompted greater state intervention - not least to
regulate industrial conflict.  Corporatism is thus widely regarded
as a capitalist strategy to regulate threatened instability.  Crouch

notes the wide measure of overlap between corporatist theory and
Marxism but also 'more surprisingly' he observes the
   considerable rapport between marxists and proponents of the overloaded government thesis.  Reactionaries and radicals alike cele-
   brate the same evidence of discomfiture in the political compromise which has kept them both at bay for so long, even if at the
   end of the celebration they retire to opposite corners (Crouch
   1979b:24).
A major difference though, is that for Marxists the new state role
is seen as prompted by capital's urgent interests and not as a response to popular demand.
   But within Marxism itself there are diverse interpretations -
even among that branch which acknowledges some 'relative autonomy'
of the state.  For Poulantzas (1975) this is necessary in order to
cope with the 'fractions' within capital.  This role may demand at
times the state sacrificing particular fractions in the general
interests of capital.  The French structuralist position typified by
Poulantzas is found, none the less, too inflexible for Crouch.  He
refers to Miliband's (1977) account as more realistic in that it
allows for some measure of working-class influence.  Although, as
Crouch rightly observes, 'unfortunately, however, this mainly
emerges in Miliband's empirical accounts.  At the level of theory
he is 'silent' (1979b:29).  He is critical of Miliband for failing
at the theoretical level to distinguish between authoritarian and
liberal-democratic forms.  This, it will be noted, reflects the
Müller/Neusüs-Habermas-Offe debate.  In large measure, therefore,
Crouch aligns himself with the more subtle Habermas-Offe camp in
positing a more complex model of symbiosis between state and capital.  The shortcomings of the orthodox Marxist stance he relates to
an 'underlying paradox:  the unwillingness of most marxists seriously to discuss social change.  Too much has been invested in the
dramatic idea of revolution....' (1979b:31).  This paradox lies at
the heart of Müller and Neusüs's attack on Offe and Habermas.  These
latter theorists do not deny the possibility or desirability of
revolutionary change but rather they should be seen as 'trying to
articulate new foundations for revolutionary change commensurate
with the conditions of contemporary capitalism' (Heydebrand and
Tummons 1975:5).
   The state role, then, with respect to the private accumulation
system, is complex.  As O'Connor (1973) observes in 'The Fiscal
Crisis of the State', the state apparatus is faced with the complication of the dominance of multi-national corporations whose interests may depart drastically from those of the competitive sector.
O'Connor sees the state as in a necessary yet contradictory relationship with the private accumulation system.
   The wider context within which the labour process is located has
been for over a decade now a milieu characterised by 'impediments'
to the accumulation process.  It has witnessed a decline in profits
and, consequently, a decline in investment.  The upsurge in shopfloor militancy was met with a state response which has oscillated
between incomes policy, the 'reform' of collective bargaining and
industrial relations, and outright repression.  Corporatism has not,
then, been the sole option.  Hence the strategy Crouch (1977) termed
'bargained corporatism' was soon to give way to a monetarist strate-

gy. But even before this shift, there had been attempts - many from
within the labour movement - to formulate an alternative economic
strategy - the AES. Exponents included the Cambridge Political
Economy Group (1974), Hodgson (1979), the Trades Union Congress (see
various annual 'Economic Reviews'), and the London Conference of
Socialist Economists Group (1979). The kind of 'alternative' which
emerged in practice from the Conservatives has heightened interest
in a socialist alternative - see for example Rowthorn (1980b),
Trades Union Congress (1980) and the Conference of Socialist Economists (1980a). Of course, there is no coherent alternative strategy
which would secure full agreement within the labour movement - or
even among those whom Swartz (1981:102) denotes as 'serious socialists' - but the mounting crisis has provoked a re-awakening which
has been manifested in formulations which have some measure of
accord. (6) These seek to respond to government policies designed
to restructure relations between capital and labour along lines more
favourable to the former.

The economic crisis and the kind of state role so far described
are not the gratuitous results of some 'misguided' policy but can
rather be seen as logical components of an essentially capitalist
economy which has become increasingly peripheral. The dialectical
relationship between the struggle at the point of production and the
wider socio-economic institutions has meant that worker gains have
provoked responses (or inactivity) at higher levels. Investment has
fallen, output has followed suit and unemployment has, therefore,
risen. Unemployment can be viewed as both cause and consequence of
British industrial relations' practices. The relative militancy and
relative success in instituting restrictive work practices in comparison with more quiescent labour forces, in turn, serves to dis-
courage capital. In consequence, it has been argued that 'the
government has been forced to precipitate an economic crisis in a
slightly desperate, but none the less rational attempt to lay the
basis for future growth under capitalist conditions' (CSE 1980a:3).
This analysis reflects that made by Gamble and Walton (1976). The
implication is a labour movement locked within a context which
transmogrifies its very successes.


THE CAPITALIST CONTEXT AND SOCIALIST STATES

Radical analysis by definition must quarry deep to locate the fundamental sources of alienation, inequality and other characteristic
features of contemporary labour. But to locate the structural
source in 'capitalism' is far from sufficient. Inevitably, many
students will interpret the term 'capitalist society' as denoting
Western societies in contradistinction to the extant self-styled
Eastern European 'socialist societies'. Does capitalism have
politico-geographical boundaries such that the Soviet Union and
its satellites are excluded? To fail to confront this issue today
is to be guilty of unconscionable neglect. Yet much discussion has
bandied the term around quite glibly. The imprecision is discom-
forting because some kind of counter-factual must be evoked. In
academic circles it is more or less taken as read that an as-yet-
to-be-attained state of socialism is the counter-factual, in quest.

But, in popular discussion, the dichotomy turns upon the politico-geographical dimension: Western Capitalism-Eastern Communism.  To ignore these divergent usages is not only to sow confusion, it is to miss some vital theoretical issues.  If these societies are not included in the genotype 'capitalism', how can it be claimed that work degradation and alienation is an offshoot of capitalism per se when it is known that these are also characteristic features of the Eastern European countries?  If these societies are included, then this decision demands much sharper attention to the definition of 'capitalism' and its essential elements.

In the so-called socialist societies, Braverman observes, there is 'an organisation of labour differing only in details from that of the capitalist countries so that the Soviet working population bears all the stigmata of the western working class' (1974:12).  And additional evidence comes from other sources to the effect that the Soviet Union and the Eastern European countries have not transformed the labour process.  Extreme division of labour and oppressive supervision are reported by Haraszti (1977) and Holubenko (1975). Despite the revolutionising in the sphere of the means of production, the 'Soviet bureaucracy, uses formidable methods to subdue and atomize the working class, scientifically track it down and destroy every embryonic form of its opposition' (Holubenko 1975:5).  A somewhat more optimistic view is taken by Lane and O'Dell (1978), who point to the attempts to design organisational structures which depart from the Weberian ideal-type.  But even these writers qualify heavily.  So, for example, they observe, 'In practice, however, we doubt whether the Party does have this superior role and it seems more likely that it often becomes much more a tool of management closely identified with the fulfilment of the factory's economic plans.  There is a tension between theory and practice' (1978:39). Later, they point out the fairly self-evident fact that property-conditioned alienation is absent (as it must be by definition). 'But other forms of alienation are evident' (Lane and O'Dell 1978: 136).  And yet, as Chris Goodey (1974) points out, there has been a history of significant spontaneous protest in the Soviet Union - most notably in the Factory Committees around 1920.  This history, he maintains, has been 'hidden and ignored' because of 'dogma and the most rigid form of orthodoxy' (1974:27-8).

Apart from the device of ignoring the issue, one other classic way out of the dilemma is to treat these societies as simply 'variants of capitalism' (Hyman 1976:85).  Thus, one hears of 'state capitalist societies'.  The problem is that to treat them as variants demands much greater attention than is commonly devoted to the importance or otherwise of the supposed vital elements of the materialist 'base' - most notably the private ownership of the instruments of production and the role of the anarchic market mechanism.

Salaman (1979) at least has the merit of addressing the question. He maintains that the argument of his book, which firmly links 'dominating forms of organisational structure' with 'capitalism', is not weakened by the simultaneous existence of similar forms in the Soviet Union.  Why not?  He furnishes two different answers. First, that the Soviets chose to emulate the West and then 'over time of course, these work practices became established within the USSR' (1979:36).  The second argument, however, denies that the

Soviet Union is, in any case, a socialist society:  it 'represents
something less than a fully-realised socialist society - a tran-
sitional or possibly mis-directed form' (1979:37).  So the problem
is largely removed by re-definition:

> Clearly, the relevance of the Soviet case to the argument under
> consideration (of the close links between capitalism and hierar-
> chic inegalitarian, organisational structures) is greatly reduced
> if the USSR is seen as not being genuinely socialist.  This is
> the position adopted in this book (ibid.).

But there is an element of tautology here.  How do we know it is not
'genuinely socialist'?  By the use of what criteria?  The answer
given is that although it has abolished private ownership, it re-
tains hierarchical, inegalitarian and repressive structures.  In
fact, the 'pervasiveness and persistence' of these forms 'is in
fact, one index (but by no means the only one) that the societies
concerned have not achieved socialism' (Salaman 1979:37).  The problem, however, is not what label these societies carry.  The issue to
be tackled is that despite the removal of private ownership, the
suppression of the market and the other concomitant elements of capitalism in a forthright cataclysmic revolution, the profound shift
in social relations one would have expected under conventional Marxism did not occur.  At the minimum, one has to draw the lesson that
the revolutionising of these structural features is not sufficient
although they may be necessary in effectuating such an emancipation.
Or one could reverse this and say that capitalism is sufficient but
not necessary as a base for the alienation of labour.

Tom Burns and Veljko Rus (1979) draw a similar lesson.  Socialism, they note, is

> presumed to overcome these (Capitalist) contradictions through
> the abolishment of private ownership and the substitution of a
> planned economy for a market economy.  The liberation of work is
> assumed to be an automatic outcome of such macro-societal chan-
> ges.  In the 'Socialist countries' with public ownership and
> planned economies, the prevalence of totalitarian theories and
> practices which ignore or even deny the possibility of alienation
> in work is not perhaps surprising.  The character of all parts of
> the social system is considered to be pre-determined by the
> nature of the total system.... (1979:4-5).

Burns and Rus draw theoretical lessons from this;  in our view it
also has implications for praxis.  It suggests support for the case
advanced by Habermas and Offe and less support for that made by
Müller and Neusüs.  The import of ideology, the media, schooling and
other facets of culture and politics are underscored.  Hegemony and
domination as experienced at work can no longer be expected to be
negated automatically with the abolition of private property and
substitution of planning for the market.

Certainly, the declared policy of economic competition with the
West has implications for the structuring of work in so-called
socialist societies.  Fleron and Fleron (1972:84) say it leads to
an even greater reliance on capitalist administrative and management
methods.  Another point is that in addition to Lenin's famous statement that 'We must organise in Russia the study and teaching of the
Taylor system and systematically try it out and adapt it to our
ends' (Lenin 1965:259), it should be noted that some of the key

figures put in charge of emulating American industrialism in Lenin's Russia, were, in fact, Americans (Fleron and Fleron 1972:83). Thus, emulation was certainly a factor. However, it is not necessary to claim that the Soviet Union is a 'variant' of capitalism (to do so, as we have said, is to urgently require further reconsideration of the key features of capitalism) rather, it is possible to claim that the exploitation of labour can result from a number of different causes and social systems. Our focus upon western capitalism therefore, is not initiated because it is the only source of domination but because it largely sets the scene for most of the world's contemporary socio-economic system.

CONCLUSION

In order to understand the struggle for control over the labour process, it is necessary to locate that struggle within the wider totality. It had been noted earlier that the 'negotiation of order' has to be related to the wider configuration of power. Accordi ;ly, the complex structure of power and authority was explored in the first part of this chapter. Attention was focused on the hidd dimensions of power and it was argued that managers are more sua tegically placed to manipulate these more covert levers. Even overt manipulation may not be required in the main, for the power of capital rests largely on the fact that the major societal mechanisms and assumptions operate routinely in its favour. The wider framework of hegemony was therefore emphasised, although it was argued that for a number of reasons this is far from complete.

The conclusion was drawn that a realistic assessment of contemporary work relationships must focus on power rather than authority. The implications of this for understanding organisations were then explored. The 'reconceptualisation' which followed picked out the implications for member attachment, organisational goals, structure, and rationality.

Then, broadening the argument still further, organisations themselves were located within the capitalist mode of production. The focus adopted was the dynamic nature of capital accumulation and the conflicts generated by 'impediments' to the same. The dialectic between resistance, crisis and capital's consequent strategies to react to these 'impediments' was emphasised. This entailed a discussion of the interventionary state, crisis management, and alternative economic strategies. Underlying characteristics of capitalist societies were surfaced and the question concerning the Soviet Union was confronted. It was concluded that the experience of work is intimately tied to the dynamic nature of capitalism which is currently hegemonic, while it was recognised that work degradation can additionally occur for other reasons.

# Chapter 5

# MANAGEMENT

It is perplexing to find that, although by definition industrial
relations must involve a relationship between at least two parties,
one of the key dramatis personae has been studiously ignored - or
more correctly taken for granted - by analysts.  Textbooks which
lavish detailed attention on the intricacies of trade-union structure, government and finance, and which probe and prod the shop
steward to reveal his most intimate secrets, intentions, age, education, tenure and so on, blithely ignore the other half of the
equation - i.e. managers and employers. (1)  It is more significant
than mere 'oversight' that, despite the superficial titular balance
of 'The Royal Commission on Trade Unions *and* Employers' Associations', the main thrust of intensive inquiry was directed at the
trade unions and their loci of power.  The fact that no one thought
to pose to management the kind of questions directed at stewards
indicates where the 'problem' was thought to be located.  Until very
recently the neglect continued;  thus in the 1979 revision of his
text, Hugh Clegg concluded:  'The truth of the matter is that the
study of management in industrial relations is in a primitive state'
(p.164).

In a paper entitled An Overview of the Study of Management in
British Industrial Relations, Wood (1981) constructs an interesting
analysis built around the treatment of management in the industrial
relations literature.  He notes that four types of explanation have
been put forward for the neglect.  These refer to:  the historical
legacy of a subject which originated with the study of trade unions;
a research access problem given managerial secrecy;  ideological
predilection which manifests itself in a disquietude which reasons
that to study management is somehow to support its existence;
finally and conversely, that academics have viewed employers and
managers as non-problematic.  Wood essentially is satisfied with
none of these although he finds most sympathy for the first and the
last.  His main argument is that there are more *theoretical* reasons
for the neglect of management;  it arises, that is, from the prevailing interpretation of the nature of industrial relations, one
which regards the subject as merely confined to the study of the
system of rule-making in the Oxford-school tradition.  Hence there
has not been so much a 'neglect' of management in the sense of

'oversight' or in the sense of a gap to be filled; rather it could
be argued that management has been 'studied to the extent that is
warranted by this theory' (p.6).

The post-Donovan literature such as that by Turner et al. (1977),
and McCarthy and Ellis (1973) does in fact accord management a vital
and central role in developing strategic reform of company industrial relations.  But as Wood (1981) points out, the model of management used is essentially unexplicated, unanalysed and poorly researched.  So while it is true that management has been neglected in
terms of academic research, they have actually been allocated a central role in policy formulations.  Thus management have been charged
with the responsibility of formalising a coherent long-term indus-
trial-relations strategy.  The Donovan Report itself set this ball
rolling in that it charged management with the task of centralising
negotiations, of gaining control over labour costs and with generally seizing the initiative in industrial relations as a whole.  Wood
convincingly makes the case that much of the critical assessment and
emendation of Donovan has in fact in the main merely extended its
central logic and has continued to treat management in the same way.
Thus Bullock and the management-by-agreement thesis represent an attempt to extend the *scope* of involvement of workers.  But the increasing responsibility placed upon managerial shoulders from the
'pluralist' position - most especially the exhortation to generate
a more thorough-going IR strategy which is an integral part of a
more wide-ranging corporate strategy - is ironically now likely to
focus more critical attention on management per se.

There are in fact already certain signs of developing inte
in the management role.  An SSRC study group was formed to examine
'the management function in industrial relations'.  This group held
a conference at Cumberland Lodge in December 1977.  Consequent to
this meeting certain areas were identified for analysis and the
results are to be published in a collection of papers edited by
Thurley and Wood (forthcoming).  Hill (1981) has a chapter on
Managerial Goals and Organizational Structures, and in 1980,
Poole and Mansfield edited a collection under the title 'Managerial
Roles in Industrial Relations:  Towards a Definitive Survey of
Research and Formulation of Models'.  The subtitle was certainly a
mistake.  There is only one brief reference to Braverman, none to
Friedman and no mention of Barnard or Fayol - despite papers which
seek to cover The Management Task, and Management Control.  None
the less there are some useful insights in the book and they are
discussed later in this chapter.  Poole, Mansfield, Blyton and
Frost (1981) have also now reported more fully on their sample
survey of members of the British Institute of Managers.  The
report provides general information on managerial recruitment and
attitudes.  Other signals of the heightened interest in the managerial role in industrial relations can also be traced.  The British Universities Industrial Relations Association found the subject
sufficiently central in contemporary importance to commission one
of its periodic Review articles on the topic (Purcell 1982;  and
Purcell forthcoming).  Significant also are the publications by
Turner et al. (1977), Freedman (1979), Timperley (1980) and
Purcell and Smith (eds) (1979), each of which indicates a shift
of attention towards the managerial side of the equation.  Equally, Storey (1980) contains chapters on management, managerial prerogatives and the means of managerial control.  The quickening

pace of interest in managerial labour policies is reflected also
in some re-orientation in the work of labour historians (see Gospel
(ed.) forthcoming;   Chandler 1977;   Hannah 1980;   Mailing 1980).

In the media too, managers have been projected centre stage.   The
recession has dimmed the light of the stewards and new expectations
are directed towards managers who are expected to emulate the pug-
nacity of Michael Edwardes.   The 'Financial Times' commentator, John
Elliott, notes how 'for too long in the past managers did not feel
strong enough to run their factories efficiently' ('Financial Times'
14.4.81).   Now, he counsels, is the time to advance the managerial
resurgence, but he warns that managers must act subtly to avoid a
backlash.   He quotes senior managers who talk as if union docility
is to be a permanent feature;   as if ministerial propaganda of a
'new sense of shopfloor realism' reflected a real situation.

Of course, as we suggested in chapter 1, there might be an argument that 'management' have been deservedly neglected in industrial
relations because their role is severely constricted under the impersonal chivvying of market forces.   Wayward or 'soft-hearted' behaviour by managers which blatantly disregards 'what needs to be
done' will result in displacement, takeover, or ignoble demise.
Managers must remain alert to situational demands.   Evidence is
lacking that managers have been able or willing to adopt markedly
different objectives from entrepreneurial predecessors.   The pursuit
of profit remains an undiminished guiding force.   It is the underlying principle defining 'rational' action.   Even the supposed alternative goals of growth and higher market share can be viewed as
interlinking ones which allow a sounder base for profitability.
Moreover, it could be argued that the more sophisticated specialists, 'professional managers' and analysts merely provide more refined analytical techniques for an attuned responsiveness to market
forces.   In consequence, the 'divorce of ownership from control',
and the 'managerialist thesis' having been found wanting (Child
1969a;   Zeitlin 1974) - why bother to focus on managers when the
concept of Capital might well suffice?

This is a question which was found pertinent to the discussion on
Braverman where it was argued that he misleadingly equated Taylorism
with capitalism and with management strategy in toto.   It was suggested that a more dialectical approach was required, and that managerial action in specific historic and concrete situations reveals a
more richly varied pattern of work control.   There are in consequence a number of reasons why the managerial role in industrial relations deserves analysis.   First, if an explanation of behaviour
was allowed to rest only on market 'forces' there would be little
cause to examine any of the parties and institutions in industrial
relations because they too operate within a market context.   In any
case the 'environment' does not provide unambiguous messages - its
'meanings' must be interpreted.   Second, even if managers are highly
responsive to market exigencies, the actual process whereby the
function of labour control is effectuated still requires analysis.
Third, it remains important to see how managers legitimise their
superordinate position and how they legitimise their endeavours to
exercise control.   The debate about the supposed divorce of ownership from control does not detract from the crucial importance of
the controlling function itself.   If owners still retain direct influence, the study of managerial action is important because they
are cast as agents of control.   On the other hand, if ownership has

been dissipated or the owners have withdrawn from direct influence, then managers would be even more directly in command.  Fourth, there is of course fierce debate concerning the extent to which managers are subject to constraints and the extent to which they can exercise choice. (2)  The constraints aspect is emphasised by contingency theory (Burns and Stalker 1961;  Woodward 1965).  The scope for choice is reflected in an article by Child (1973), but even more so in Wood (1979).  As Wood points out, contingency theory (even in its revamped form à la Bowen (1976) and Legge (1978)) essentially 'renders choice redundant.  Its notion of organizational choice is deceptive, for the effective form of organization is dictated by situational imperatives' (Wood 1979:354).

It is not only the orthodox Marxist model, then, which diverts attention from managerial action-choices.  Ironically, by adopting overly rationalistic assumptions, even managerialist models also serve to disguise and suppress the truly *political* choices.  Fifth, in its departure from the classic model, modern economic thought constructs a theory of monopoly capitalism and its variants of imperfect competition, which restores a greater measure of importance to the discretion and control of managers (Cyert and March 1963; Baran and Sweezy 1966).  For increasing industrial concentration has meant that the character of economic activity 'has come to depend more on the planning of activities *within* firms and less on competition in the market' (George 1974:39).  This, in turn, implies that 'managerial decision-making within the firm has become a much more important matter for investigation' (ibid.).


THE NATURE OF 'MANAGEMENT'

Part of the reason for the confusions which abound in this area is the use of the same term for an activity, an occupational group and a hierarchical level demarcating special status and authority (Harbison and Myers 1959).  Much controversy surrounding the value, necessity, or otherwise of 'management' in fact simply derives from protagonists attaching themselves to one or other of these meanings and proceeding to argue at cross purposes with one another - hence the confusion surrounding Alistair Mant's (1977) Delphic pronouncement that there should be 'no management'.  Unless the term is disaggregated it is difficult to see what this might mean.  Alistair Mant, who has himself been heavily engaged promoting what is known as 'management development', wages a highly critical attack upon the way the British have sanctified 'the magic brotherhood'.  'The real puzzle', he argues, 'is to understand why we downgrade so many of the jobs that really matter whilst building around the idea of management a plethora of myths, shibboleths and incantations which our most successful competitors seem able to do without' (Mant 1977:3). (3)  The meaning that the term 'management' has accrued in Anglo-American and British colonial culture has been highly damaging, he argues, to this country's económic performance and social harmony. British managerial ideology, according to Mant, is embedded in English class snobbery.  He maintains it is all of a piece with the pernicious dichotomies between white collar versus blue collar, clean versus dirty, U versus non-U, pure science versus applied, and so on.  Hence management in England has absorbed the idea of being clean and generalist, a state of being rather than an activity.  It was not always so.  Both Mant and Raymond Williams trace the etymological derivation of the term.  In the sixteenth century it carried the Italian meaning of the word 'meneggiare', referring to the handling of horses.  In the seventeenth and eighteenth centuries the French meaning evolved which referred to careful housekeeping ('majordome').  Only late in the nineteenth century was the word 'management' used in the business context.  As Williams notes, it came to cloud and mystify the frank dichotomy between 'masters' and 'men' (Williams 1976).  The even more pointed terminology of 'master' and 'servant' was enshrined in an Act of 1824 which made workers liable to imprisonment for breach of contract.  Via the relatively muted term 'employer' to the now popular term 'manager', the journey led to an apparently more neutral function.  Thus, these linguistic shifts carried powerful ideological overtones.  The British Institute of Management has been doing all it can to assist in this regard.  So, its official definition of management (1966) emerged as:  'Responsibility for judgement of the decision in effectively planning, motivating, and controlling operations towards known objectives attained through efficient co-operation of the personnel concerned.'  As Mant observes, 'it certainly isn't English and to be fair, it must have been larded together by a committee' (1977:12).  Nevertheless, it illustrates the linguistic muddle with regard to the word 'manager'.

To locate recent studies on the nature of the managerial task one has to be rather eclectic.  Sources include the anecdotal works of industrial magnates, journalistic pieces detailing managerial intrigue, and a voluminous literature in the classic managerial mode. This last essentially began with the work of Henri Fayol, a French mining engineer, in 1916.  He delineated five key elements:  planning, organising, commanding, controlling and co-ordinating.  Management consultants like Brech, Gulick and Urwick gave this schema wider currency, and even more recent writers such as Rosemary Stewart and Peter Drucker have shown themselves to be heavily influenced by Fayol's work.

These formalistic writings have been heavily criticised recently by industrial sociologists who point out that many of the aphorisms of the classical school are neither descriptively accurate with regard to real managerial work nor do they serve as a useful guide to action.  Realism has been pursued by those researchers who have used the case study method to elucidate the 'political' nature of the managerial function.  Dalton (1959), Sayles (1964) and Pettigrew (1973) each conducted observational studies which shed light on lateral as well as vertical lines of conflict in managerial work. That is, they revealed how managers are exposed to relationships of conflict, both with their colleagues and with their subordinates and superordinates.

There have been other key points of focus in pertinent studies. Amongst others, these include studies of entrepreneurs, of the decision-making process and of leadership.  But the studies which have the most immediate relevance are those concerning behavioural analysis.  These set out to depict precisely what it is that managers actually do.  This type of research began with Sune Carlson's study of nine Swedish managing directors in 1951.  He pioneered the use of diary-based methodology to analyse managerial work, and his study

was followed by Rosemary Stewart who conducted a more extensive
survey of 160 British managers in the mid-1960s.  Published as
'Managers and Their Jobs' in 1967, Stewart's research covered managers from over 100 companies and from all the main functional areas.
Variations were depicted in a fivefold classification of job types
which she depicted as:  emissaries, writers, discussers, trouble-
shooters and committee-men.  These titles are fairly self-evident
and require no description here.

This exercise in constructing a typology triggered off further
attempts.  Maccoby (1977) identified four types of managers:  the
craftsman, the jungle fighter, the company man and the gamesman.
The craftsman is enmeshed in the work ethic, he aims for quality and
thrift;  the jungle fighter's prime goal is power;  the company man
is reminiscent of Whyte's organisation man;  the gamesman is the new
man, the leading figure in Maccoby's study.  He is a dynamic stra-
tegist,'hyped-up' by the contest itself.  In the preface to the
British edition, Maccoby argues that in Britain, unlike America, the
centre stage is not occupied by the gamesman but by the jungle
fighter armed with tradition and besotted with rank and titles.  He
suggests that the British class structure militates against the ir-
reverent gamesman who loves innovation and risk-taking.  Maccoby is
pessimistic about British economic fortunes especially with regard
to innovation and competition.  He quotes in despair a British chief
executive whom he considers typifies the problem - a man bemoaning
the 'loss of authority' instead of actively seeking respect.

Henry Mintzberg (1973) produced one of the more systematic academic studies of managers in recent years.  On the basis of empirical study he concluded that 'managers' jobs are remarkably alike'
all being traceable to ten fundamental roles (1973:4).  These, such
as figurehead, liaison and so on, are reminiscent of Rosemary
Stewart's classification, albeit more elaborate.  By identifying
which of the ten roles are given salience by incumbents, Mintzberg
is able to derive a typology of managers - for example, 'real-time
manager' or 'team manager'.  The details do not concern us here but
it is worth noting that Mintzberg provides some basis for developing
systematic knowledge about types of managers and their likely interface with industrial relations' activity - a basis mirrored in the
work of Batstone et al. (1977) and their typology of shop stewards.
Mintzberg finds that being more involved with operating problems,
production managers experience greater fragmentation in their role
activities than other managers.  They spend more time in the
*decision* roles of disturbance-handler and negotiator.  In contrast,
the managers of staff specialists spend more time alone, more on
paperwork, more on their own speciality and generally therefore,
more on the *information* roles of monitor, spokesman, and dissemi-
nator. (4)

Overall, these recent behavioural approaches to the study of
management, utilising direct observation, activity sampling and
diary-based analyses, all tend to agree on certain basic points.
They each see the manager's job as characterised 'by brevity, variety and fragmentation' (Mintzberg 1973:5).  Consequently, there
seemed little evidence here of sophisticated construction of strategy.  This is a significant point - especially when it is remembered
that the studies we have quoted investigated top-level managers and

were not confined to middle levels where such characteristics might
have been more readily expected.  These studies tend to furnish
evidence that analyses of the Braverman types may have adopted a
rather over-rationalised conception of management-man.  In addition, the behavioural studies also note the predilection managers
have for active and interactive patterns of behaviour, and for a
reliance on the spoken word rather than writing, thinking or planning.

The contention that in reality managers conduct a rather less
sophisticated strategy than they are often credited with finds significant support in a recent survey by the Bradford University Management Centre.  From a sample of 10,000 members of the Institute of
Industrial Managers, the Bradford group found British managers engaged in a very lacklustre take-up of available control techniques.
In fact, despite all the discussion among sociologists of Taylorism,
over a third of the respondents used no work study at all.  'Work
study is a topic taken for granted;  it's assumed that everybody
uses it ... this (assumption) is found to be untrue' (Lockyer et al.
1981:32).  Other techniques have an even lower take-up by British
managers - only 6 per cent used Predetermined Motion Time Studies
(PMTS);  less than 20 per cent of companies with under 250 employees
used any form of method study.  Overall, the Bradford team found
that British managers ignore even basic techniques and spend most
of their time on routine.

This rather amateurish approach is reflected too in the findings
of a study of directors by Anne Spencer (1981).  She found directors
willing to say that boardroom decisions were reached in a fashion
'like any sort of dinner party' (1981:51).  The bigger decisions -
involving for example expenditure in the region of £10 millions -
frequently attracted less comment and discussion because members of
the board felt they lacked expertise.  (See also Winkler (1974) and
Anthony (1977).) (5)  Even at the megalith of rational capitalism,
General Motors, there was, according to the insider De Lorean, no
forward planning to speak of ... policy-making was often shallow and
insignificant (1979:7).

An attempt has been made by Judi Marshall and Rosemary Stewart
(1981) to transcend the 'over-rationalised' view of management.
They note Schutz's (1967,1972) distinction between 'scientific
reasoning' based on second-degree constructs and 'everyday practical reasoning'.  Marshall and Stewart seek to elucidate this
latter aspect of management by eliciting managers' own accounts.
Using semi-structured, tape-recorded interviews of eighty-six middle
managers from three manufacturing companies, they discerned three
categories of perspective.  The first, which they term 'job analysis', encompasses those perspectives which rested on detailed de-
scriptions of tasks within the job.  The second, termed 'focused',
comprised perspectives which picked out major priority areas such as
customer satisfaction.  The third, termed 'holistic', embodied those
perspectives of a highly abstract nature such as defining the management job as coping with or promoting change.  In addition, the
researchers picked out different ideas on how jobs should be tackled
or what they term 'working strategies'.  These ranged across a
continuum from 'reactive' to 'proactive' - i.e. from relatively
passive and short-term approach to a 'shaping' long-term approach.

Overall, they found some very diverse approaches to managerial work.
The 'brevity, variety and fragmentation' finding by Mintzberg was
reflected in the prominence of 'hustle and bustle' in the Marshall
and Stewart study.  The correlation between job perceptions and
working strategies was not apparently very marked and also of interest was that the role of education and professional training did not
figure very prominently in the attempted explanations of the adopted
perceptions and working strategies.

Of course under the label 'management' are subsumed a variety of
tasks, roles and interest groups.  In addition, there are different
levels and types of managers.  In part these derive from a fragmentation of administrative tasks and functional skills which are
associated with the concentration of capital.  The 'technological
revolution' as C.W. Mills (1953:13) puts it, results in a 'demand
for specialists to handle the complicated institutional machinery
developed to cope with the complication of the technical environment.'  As I shall argue in the next chapter, there is an extent to
which 'managerial professionalism' may represent a strategic device
by particular segments of staff to advance their material and status
prospects.  'Professionalism' here is used as a resource under which
attributes of training, qualifications, a certifying body, a code of
ethics and a body of 'knowledge', are projected for tactical advantage.  Pettigrew demonstrates that specialisation is 'an emergent
process', a process subject to the 'negotiation of occupational
identities' (1975:274).

But whether arising from 'technical demands' or from occupational
politicking it is necessary to remember that there are differences
*within* management.  Rosemary Stewart (1976) has explored the 'contrasts in management', and it is additionally clear that the specialised management functions of production, sales, accountancy, and
management information, should warn us of the dangers of simplisti-
cally treating 'management' as a monolithic whole.  Much managerial
energy is consumed with the friction and stress which are generated
on an interdepartmental basis, on a line-staff basis and on other
intra-management dimensions (see Gowler and Legge 1975).

Clearly not all conflict within work organisations is management-
worker conflict.  Nor do all who carry the title 'manager' actually
'manage' others.  Nevertheless, given that our focus is on manage-
ment-worker conflict, much of the intra-management relationship will
necessarily be obscured.  Workers frequently do, for all intents and
purposes, confront management as a 'hostile totality' (Hyman 1976:
92).  The multifarious distinctions can serve to disguise a certain
unity of function which extends throughout the major part of managerial work.  The employment of the labour power of others and the
subsequent separation of conception from execution required an administrative hierarchy to effectuate the production of surplus-
value.  Large-scale operations which developed after the turn of the
century demanded a large managerial stratum.  The quintessential
role of managers therefore became, and to a large extent remains,
that of controlling.

Labour power comes in a form ineluctably attached to the worker.
Hence, unlike other 'commodities', labour is an uncertain factor
intrinsically possessing all the vagaries of the subjective individual.  Management must render the potential of labour power actual

and in a form which is malleable.  In addition, the concentration of
production under the phase of monopoly capitalism increases the
necessity for co-ordination and control.  The managerial and administrative strata increases accordingly.  While some are made responsible for direct and personal management of labour, others are
assigned to indirect, impersonal management of control systems (for
example, stock control, production planning, and budgeting).  In
either case, the essential function is the same:  controlling. (6)
As Cardechi (1977:130) observes, in both public and private enterprises in capitalist society 'it is the manager who is the non-
labourer/exploiter/non-producer/real owner ... opposed to the
labourer/exploited/non-owner/producer.'  The division between intellectual and manual labour upon which management is predicated is
itself, argues Sohn-Rethel (1978), an aspect of class struggle and
historical materialism.  He seeks to demonstrate the roots of intellectual activity in the 'social formation of its epoch' (1978:7).
The intellectual-manual division of labour and hence management,
will not, however, simply disappear with the abolition of private
property, but will have to be consciously liquidated (Sohn-Rethel
1978:169).


IN SEARCH OF MANAGEMENT STRATEGY

The inescapable interface between managers and their employees is
the control process.  Yet in theoretical terms this observation represents a relatively recent departure.  Under the classical economists' theory of the firm, no formal controls or instructions are
posited.  They were foreclosed by a focus on the self-regulating
operation of the free market.  It was a deterministic model which
presented the individual 'who intends only his own gain' as one 'led
by an invisible hand to promote ... the public interest'.  Thus in
'The Wealth of Nations' Adam Smith (1937) saw the price mechanism as
the perfect information device and allocative mechanism. (7)  Conscious regulation and direction were therefore unnecessary.  Modern
theories of the firm, however, interject a range of amendments.  The
monistic conception is replaced with a recognition of specialised
contributory individuals who are purposive, their behaviour not determined by an invisible hand.  Instead, conscious co-ordination is
required;  objectives have to be defined, people appraised of what
they have to do, and controlled in order to ensure their actual behaviour approximates that desired by the co-ordinator.  Thus from
black boxes to internal control systems.  One way to conceptualise
their purpose is to regard them as conscious attempts to translate
the messages of external market forces into the guides for action
otherwise known as internal operating procedures.  The name of the
game is conscious control.
   This concept requires further comment.  Although frequently used
interchangeably with power, power is more fruitfully regarded as a
capacity to influence, whereas control is a process (see for example
Millham et al. 1972;  Tannenbaum 1968).  When used in accord with
the classical writers on management, control refers narrowly only to
the monitoring and corrective action process.  This usage is manifested in the classical delineation of the managerial function which

segregate planning, organising, co-ordinating, commanding from controlling (see for example Elkins 1980;  Haimann, Scott and Connor
1978;  Certo 1980).  But more modern usage is that indicated by
Eilon (1979) and Kynaston-Reeves and Joan Woodward (1970) - that is
to utilise the term 'managerial control system' to denote each of
the major processes including planning, executing and appraisal.
There is in fact unusual interdisciplinary accord here, for modern
writers in accountancy and industrial engineering equally accept
this wider definition (Horngren 1975;  Shillinglaw 1972;  Maynard
1971;  Anthony 1965).  Shillinglaw, Woodward, Anthony and Hofstede
all concur in a three- or four-item classification of the management
control system.  Space does not allow their representation here.
Suffice it to say that their inconsistencies can be removed by re-
ducing the elements of 'controlling' to the following moments:
  1  Policy formulation and strategic planning.
  2  Execution;  supervising and directing current operations.
  3  Monitoring feedback, appraising and taking corrective action.
This kind of analytical breakdown is useful for it permits us to investigate the managerial control process by engaging with those
practical rationalities/management 'sciences' (in particular accountancy and industrial engineering) which are consciously designed
to advance managerial control.

  The first 'phase', policy formulation and strategic planning,
comprises that area often known as corporate strategy or business
policy.  Planning is here distinct from forecasting in that the
former is the more active and committed process of determining a
broad course of action.  Forecasting provides information for planning.  Haimann, Scott and Connor (1978) distinguish further between
grand strategy which involves long-term general overriding goals,
and strategy per se which is more specific and is concerned with the
planning and policy-making to effectuate the grand strategy.

  Formulating grand strategy would include responding to what
Drucker (1974) and Ansoff (1979a, 1979b) pose as the first question,
that of determining quite deliberately what business the firm is in.
More commonly, strategy is seen as of a piece.  Thus A.D. Chandler
defines it as 'the determination of the basic long-term goals and
objectives of an enterprise and adaption of courses of action and
the allocation of resources necessary for carrying out these goals'
(Chandler 1962:13).  This implies a rational process of choice.  It
therefore represents a challenge to cruder forms of contingency
theory. (8)  It implies, moreover, a goodly measure of consistency
and harmony between what Elkins (1980) terms the 'hierarchy of objectives'.  Clearly this provokes two key questions apropos industrial relations and the management of labour generally.  First, is
it realistic to assume the existence of a coherent 'strategy' in the
industrial relations area or is the operation normally characterised
by 'ad hocery'?  Second, even if there is a modicum of a planned and
long-term sequence of actions, to what extent does this 'strategy'
harmonise with other business objectives relating for example to
markets, production and technology?  Or is it the case that by and
large social integration is neglected or given a back seat to systems integration as Bowen (1976) implies?

  In fact the papers in Thurley and Wood (forthcoming) confirm that
doubt on both these points is justified.  Thus in one of the papers

Purcell, for example, implies that managers need *convincing* (by
quasi-government agencies such as ACAS and the erstwhile CIR) of the
need for an industrial relations strategy.  The rationale and
thrust of the Donovan Report would seem to accord with this point.
In an empirical piece Marsh and Gillies report that managers are in
actuality usually uncertain about their firms' policies with respect
to industrial relations - if indeed there are any ideas sufficiently
thought-through to justify such a term.  Marsh's findings echo those
of Mintzberg (1973) which characterised managerial work as marked by
brevity and fragmentation.  Wood (1980) warns that 'strategic control' should allow for the likelihood of a number of strategic plans
and he warns too of adopting an overly-conspiratorial view of management and an attribution to them of 'greater omniscience than perhaps they really have' (1980:60).  This is apposite given another
contribution to the same volume which maintains that there is a
'holding back' of technological innovation on a world scale because
'monopoly capital realizes' that automation may defeat the objective
of profit maximisation (Boreham 1980:30).  The level of attributed
global rationality here seems exaggerated and it tends to reify into
a monolith the *various capitals*.  The aggregate irrationality of
capital's endeavours is more convincingly portrayed in Hardin's
(1968) The Tragedy of the Commons.  Woods's (1980) account accords
more closely to our dialectical approach especially when he goes on
to adumbrate the potential for workers to (perhaps indirectly) influence managerial formulation of plans.  He develops a 'case for
considering strategy as something more than a plan outlined unilaterally and autonomously by management' (1980:63).

This permits, therefore, a model of competing corporate strategies and bids for influence, that is, an amended form of negotiated
order theory which allows for political and power dimensions.
Equally, one must allow space for other types of rational action
which are not necessarily coincident with the corporate, such as for
instance the pursuit of career interests.  In the light of such remarks does it make sense to talk of 'The Taylor Strategy'? (Merkle
1968).  If by this one conceives of a monolithic management team
hell-bent on implementing Taylor's doctrines then I think it would
not be permissible.  In fact Merkle himself discusses the degree of
managerial resistance to Taylorism (1968:65).  Palmer (1975) suggests that even by the 1920s control had become more sophisticated
than the cruder forms of Taylorism.  He offers the phrase 'the
thrust for efficiency' as more reflective of actual events.  And
Sohn-Rethel (1978) points out that it is mistaken to assume that
flow production is based on Taylorism.  Moreover, one must be careful in attributing a rather abstract, free choice of strategies as
if they were available à la carte.  More realistically, the interrelationships between hierarchy, technology, and control are, as
Offe (1976a:39) demonstrates, quite profound.  While in practice
management may not be as rationalistic as textbooks and manuals seem
to assume, it would be absurd to overlook the general capture by
capital of the conception function.  Planning and corporate strategy
are thus vital components in the overall control of labour.  It
would be a mistake to search for novel master-plans in the quest for
industrial relations' strategy of the character of, say, Boulwarism.
A fruitless trawl of specifically industrial relations' fishing

grounds should not be taken to signal that labour management proceeds without direction.  The control of labour, as we have emphasised, is effectuated on a much broader front than that!

The second moment of control, the directing and executing of
current operations, takes place in diversified form in modern corporations.  Organisations are typically departmentalised in order to
fulfil this part of the task.  Thus there will be separate works
organisation, supplies organisation, marketing and so on.  Some
functions are in fact purely concerned with controlling the activities of other functions.  So, for example, production control is established precisely for the purpose of controlling production at
every stage without itself actually executing any part of this.  The
costing and budgeting function is another specialised control function, organised to allocate, trace, monitor and regulate the distribution of resources.

The third 'stage' of control is to monitor feedback, to appraise
and evaluate this and to take, where it is deemed necessary, corrective action.  The language of management specialists is here instructive.  They talk of measuring 'variance' or 'deviance' from
planned performance targets.  This permits 'management by exception'
- i.e. ignoring minor deviations in order to concentrate more vigorously on those designated as a more serious threat.  Two types of
response can be made:  'corrective' for cases where direct control
has been inadequate, or 'adaptive' for cases where an unforeseen
contingency in a hostile environment calls for replanning.  The ap-
praisal/evaluative element utilises what is known, following Simon
(1957), as the 'scorecard function'.  This latter is used as an
instrument with which to reward or penalise particular performances.

What is significant about this whole control cycle is the scope
it allows for treating control problems as individual disciplinary
issues rather than as collective issues.  The process is designed to
cope with the contradictions of the labour process by treating them
as routine administrative and technical problems rather than as
social or political issues.

These points will be developed in chapter 7 where the *range* of
control devices is assessed.

THE GENESIS OF MANAGEMENT

The emergence of management as a self-conceived, separate entity,
distinct that is, from entrepreneurs and owners of capital, has been
one of the most remarkable developments of recent decades.  Their
importance has been adjudged as significant enough for them to be
conceived by some as a 'new class'.  Their own self-consciousness
has been raised;  indeed the British Institute of Management felt
emboldened enough, for example, to declare 1978 as The Year of the
Manager.  Yet what is remarkable is the rapidity of this emergence.
At the beginning of this century there was little justification for
thinking in terms of a distinct management group.  Industrial management arose in two stages:  first there was the genesis of the industrial entrepreneur at the beginning of the nineteenth century,
and only much later did the second stage take shape, that is, the
development of a separate group of non-entrepreneurial managers.

Industrial management of the first phase only developed when workers were brought from their homes to work together under one roof.  Pre-industrial merchant-capitalists had often employed thousands of men, women and children in their own homes by means of the 'putting-out' system (Thompson 1968:299).  In the first half of the eighteenth century in cotton textile manufacture, for example, merchant-capitalists distributed cotton to be spun into yarn, and then woven into cloth by domestic producers who used hand-operated equipment.  Sometimes the merchant owned this equipment as well as the materials which he circulated.  The transformation from merchant-capitalism to industrial capitalism came about with the onset of the factory system.  It was only under the latter form that the problem and function of management emerged:  i.e. management emerged with the problem of labour control.

There are now two contending theories concerning the actual instigation of the factory system.  Economic historians have normally suggested that the technological innovations of the Industrial Revolution required the demise of the scattered domestic hand-working system and its replacement by a centralised power-driven mode of production.  Thus, for example, one typical classic text explains the origin of the first factories by observing how, *'for technical reasons* small groups of men were brought together into workshops and little water-driven mills' (Ashton 1948:33, emphasis added).

More recently, however, it has been alternatively suggested that the origin of the factories should be traced not to technological determinants but simply to the desire of the capitalist to impose his control more directly.  Marglin (1974) has put this case forcibly and it has since enjoyed considerable popularity among sociologists.  However, I shall be supporting neither position but instead suggesting a third.  Meanwhile, Marglin's case requires elucidation. Marglin contends that the capitalist was moved to bring workers together in factories in order to substitute his own control for their autonomy and in order to impose further division of labour.  This then guaranteed to the entrepreneur an essential role as integrator of the work process and also led to enhanced work discipline, sustained effort, and sustained output.  The capitalist sought to avoid embezzlement and to organise the production functions in such a way as to ensure his own indispensability.  Fox also gives a clear statement of this alternative explanation:  'The emergence of the factory system owed as much to the desire for closer co-ordination, discipline and control of the labour force as to the pressures of technology' (1974:180).

The factory system, once ushered-in, required 'speed, regularity and attention' (Bendix 1956:39).  In a word, the factories required discipline, and this was supported by sanctions.  This was the managerial task.  Marglin's case is given weight by the fact that the early workshops 'were simply agglomerations of smaller units of production, reflecting little change in traditional methods' (Braverman 1974:59).  Indeed, large numbers of people employed in factories continued to use the old hand-working methods (Pollard 1965:8).

Sidney Pollard's scholarly and still unrivalled historical survey of the genesis of management confirms that the origin of the factories did not always have a technical base.  Rather, the attraction to the entrepreneur was to increase output (a) by imposing direct

supervision, discipline and control, and (b) by creating a new type
and level of division of labour (Pollard 1965:11-12).

Even this particular facet - the division of labour - has been
sceptically viewed by Marglin who adopts a more conspiratorial
theory. He writes:

> The Capitalist division of labour typified by Adam Smith's famous
> pin manufacture, was the result of a search not for a techno-
> logically superior organisation of work, but for an organisation
> which guaranteed to the entrepreneur an essential role in the
> production process, as integrator of the separate efforts of his
> workers into a marketable product (1974:34).

It seems unlikely, however, that these entrepreneurs sought control for its own sake. Certainly, they would not have viewed favourably their reliance on authonomous craftsmen. The early development of workshops outside the pale of guild restrictions testi-
fies to the desire to escape constraints. But, the growth of the
factories cannot simply be viewed in Marglin's terms alone. As we
have indicated, merchant-capitalists had previously 'employed' hun-
dreds, sometimes thousands, in domestic production. How can the
rush to the factories be explained at the particular time that it
occurred? After the potential of a series of mechanical innovations
became realised, mills grew rapidly. By 1822 the typical Manchester
cotton mill employed 100-200 and had an average per capita investment of about £80. Yet within the space of a mere ten years the new
mills contained on average 40,000 spindles which represented a capital investment of £80,000 - that is, about ten times the capitalisation per worker as a decade earlier (Chapman 1972). The mills did
not increase greatly in size as measured by numbers employed. The
'internal' economies of scale seem to have been fully exploited with
a workforce of about 200. Thus, the long history of merchant capitalism resting on the putting-out domestic system, and the rapid
capitalisation of the factories once the new-wave of factory building commenced, militates against too crude an interpretation of
Marglin's thesis that the capitalist was merely seeking to assert
direct control.

Furthermore, within the factories once they were built, the single
capitalist often used a system which enabled him to *evade* the exercise of direct control, viz. the sub-contracting system. For example, in the cotton mills the skilled spinners were put in charge
of machinery and engaged their own help. This contract-system per-
sisted well past the middle of the nineteenth century. Indeed, 'as
late as 1870 the immediate employer of many workers was not the
large capitalist but the intermediate sub-contractor' (Dobb 1947:
262). And contemporary surveys revealed that the substantial majority of operatives under 18 years of age were actually employed
by other operatives (Pollard 1965:43). If the capitalists' motive
in bringing workers together under a single roof was mainly to exercise *direct* control over them, it is rather strange that in the
early cases of aggregation of guild-journeymen and artisans 'the
work remained under the immediate control of the producers in whom
was embodied the traditional knowledge and skills of the craft'
(Braverman 1974:59).

Because of the remarkable persistence of the sub-contracting
system, it is only during the last one hundred years that the cur-

rently fashionable phenomenon of direct employment and direct management control has been the characteristic pattern.  Historically,
this too, may prove to be a transient phase.  The considerable
utilisation of 'contracting-out' in many of the firms I have studied
could indicate a potential future path.

Thus I argue that early industrial managers were not primarily
interested in the metaphysics of direct control per se.  They were
happy to avoid it when to do so would not jeopardise accumulation.
But when it was viewed as advantageous to assert control in order to
seize economic opportunities then control it would be.  This would
explain their contentment with the years of the domestic putting-out
system and the early factory period of sub-contracting.  When higher
levels of capitalisation were reached, however, they were no longer
prepared to allow sub-contractors to determine its utilisation and
earnings potential.  This interpretation accords with the thesis advanced by David Gordon (1976).  He confronts the 'efficiency' (of a
contingent kind given a particular context) versus 'control' argument.  He recasts the usual debate.  It is not a question, he says,
of competition or class struggle;  these are interdependent.  Capitalists seek both quantitative efficiency (the greatest physical
output from a given set of inputs) and qualitative efficiency (a
production process which best reproduces class relations).  Capitalists are forced 'to accept sacrifices in potential physical output,
given prevalent scarcities and relative factor prices, in order to
maintain worker discipline and reproduce their control over the
means of production' (Gordon 1976:24).

Before leaving the historical arena it remains necessary to
sketch the emergence of a distinct management function and a distinct management group.  The two did not necessarily occur concur-
rently.  Prior to the Industrial Revolution the practice of 'management' (as opposed to the social group) can be identified in many
quarters.  It had been exercised in the building of the Pyramids,
the construction of the Great Wall of China, and in the leadership
of armies.  But although industrial capitalism had been preceded by
earlier forms of joint-stock company (for example the East India
Company) and by the above forms of large man-management problems,
the combination of these features with one new element (the pursuit
of profit through a free market) made industrial capitalism unique.
As Pollard notes, one of its seminal ideas was the combination of
these factors whilst drawing upon the united efforts of formally
free labour (Pollard 1965:7).  In this sense management can be seen
as a novel product of the rise of industrial capitalism.

With the rapid spread of the factory system more and more workers
were drawn into its vortex.  By 1871 over half of the working population was employed in factories.  This mass of humanity presented
the entrepreneurs with a 'management problem'.  It was heightened by
the great merger waves of 1880-1918.  These metamorphosed the British economic structure (Hannah 1974).  By the First World War, the
foundations of the modern corporate economy had taken shape.  Accom-
panying the wave of mergers and take-overs has been a more than commensurate increase in the numbers engaged in managerial and administrative activities.  This has been a persistent trend common to ex-
panding and contracting industries alike (Thomas 1976;  Bendix
1956).  These groups have developed special management institutes,

they have engaged in training, education and qualification-seeking, and they have participated in the complication and elongation of managerial hierarchies (Child 1969a). Management, then, as a function increasingly became identifiable as something different from entrepreneurship itself. The line of this distinction has been variously drawn. Sometimes it is seen as demarcating tactical from strategic decision-making. Alternatively it is viewed as resting on a distinction between routine and innovation; or between manipulating the inner workings of the organisation and a more grand manipulation of the environment. If, however, one confines the problem to distinguishing between entrepreneurs and managers as *groups*, the distinction is much simpler, namely that the former risked and managed primarily their own capital, whereas the latter group of functionaries are employed as *agents* of capital to administer it to best effect. This now involves managers in both internal and external intervention.

The traumatic struggle whereby this newly emergent group sought to wrest knowledge and control from erstwhile self-directed workers and thereby carve out a role for itself is traced by Dan Clawson (1980). He demonstrates how capital's control 'was done primarily through the creation of management, a separate category of technical and supervisory personnel which essentially did not exist in the nineteenth century' (1980:1). Strife was inevitably to ensue from this heist. Management's hubristic defence of its 'right' to specify method, pace and quality is frequently blind to the fact that its roots reach only to the topsoil of history. Surveying the period between 1860 and 1920 in the United States, Clawson finds workers enforcing what they considered was a reasonable speed of work. So too with quality of work. This had traditionally lain with the craft-worker and management's attempts to change standards - usually in a downward direction - were also resisted. (9) As one moulder at a US government arsenal complained when ordered to take a short-cut by ceasing to nail the castings: 'That is going to hurt my character' (Clawson 1980:6). The ambiguity concerning who had the right to determine such questions as quality, method and speed was made very evident during the special Congressional hearings on the Taylor system. Management claimed it was now their function to determine such matters; the moulders disagreed. As one of the latter argued: 'Now, the point I wanted to bring out is that a military officer who is not a moulder would not be competent to instruct a man whom you testify is probably the best moulder in the arsenal....' As Clawson comments: 'That is, the workers rejected the very concept of management as an occupation and a skill separate from expertise in the work itself' (1980:7).

The turn of the century was in fact a watershed in the history of the labour process. In the nineteenth century - even at the end - there was very little 'management presence'. The current plethora of managerial personnel simply did not exist. The foreman or inside-contractor was 'almost the only level of supervision between the worker and the capitalist ... it is even inappropriate to use the term "management" - there was no significant category of non-workers who existed to manage and direct the details of the work' (Clawson 1980:7-8). The rise of management was to come with the development of control devices such as record-keeping, costing and planning.  Once again therefore we see that the twin phenomena of management and control are inextricably linked.


THE SOCIAL LOCATION OF MANAGERS

It is relevant to consider the available evidence concerning managers' social origins, education, rewards, social attitudes, social-class location, and the implication of these factors for their control function.  Earlier we reviewed the empirical studies of management activities (see especially Stewart 1976 and Mintzberg 1973).  In addition, there have been a few studies of British industrial managers as an occupational group sufficient to construct a tentative social profile.  As Mansfield (1980) observes, there have been five main studies:  the Acton Society Trust (1956);  Clements (1958);  Clark (1966);  Leggatt (1978);  and Melrose-Woodman (1978).  The picture which emerges is unfortunately somewhat blurred.  On the one hand there is Anthony Giddens's (1973) claim that executives come from 'a narrow background of economic privilege', whilst on the other, Clements, Clark and Leggatt present data suggesting a rather mixed composition.  Equally, evidence concerning the education of managers points to a group not particularly privileged when compared say to the professions or the civil service.  Thus only about one quarter of post-war managers have gained a university degree and of these the larger proportion are graduates in science or engineering.  Melrose-Woodman's survey of members of the British Institute of Management (4,525 in the sample used) shows 14 per cent to be graduates of Oxford or Cambridge universities.

   Given this general pattern of education, it is less surprising to find that the occupational career paths of managers, as sampled by the studies quoted, have often begun with a relatively early job take-up.  Sixty per cent of the BIM sample had started work by the age of seventeen.  Only 15 per cent started, however, in manual work, whereas around two-thirds started in clerical work.  A significant feature of the social profile revealed by all the studies was the sexual composition of management;  less than 2 per cent were female.  In a striking way this anachronism reflects the pattern of domination found in the early factories.  There, the overseers and spinners were male, not because of superior skill, but because of superior strength.  This was the asset wielded in fulfilling their function of maintaining order, application and control.  The enduring impression gained from an overall review of these studies, however, is one of 'heterogeneity':  the managers surveyed
   came from a wide variety of social backgrounds, they undergo different forms of education, their early careers vary considerably and they differ considerably in age, salary and affiliations to professional associations and trade unions (Mansfield 1980:19).
   The social profile again became complex, however, when in the following paper by Stewart, Prandy and Blackburn (1980) it is argued that the younger managers are more likely to have started as management trainees and equally they are more likely to have been to public school.  This rather mixed picture is reflected in the patchy and ambiguous flirtation of management with managerial trade unions and associations (Gospel 1978;  Farnham 1978;  Weir 1976;  Bamber

1976;  Hartman 1974;  Frost 1980;  Blyton 1980). One must infer
from the social profiles available that the control function of management does not rely on the existence of a homogeneous elite social
group.   Rather, the bonds which tie the social control networks of
work organisations are rather more functional in nature.  The managers themselves are subject to a managerial division of labour (de
Kadt 1976).  Equally, as Claus Offe argues, the development of
'task-discontinuous status organisations' means that hierarchical
control can rest on a series of 'peripheral' yardsticks.  There can
be symbolic substitutes for performance which reward not technical
accomplishment but demonstrated acceptance of the organisation's
power relations (Offe 1976a).  Insider evidence for this is forthcoming from John Z. De Lorean (1979), erstwhile Group Executive for
GM's car and truck group.  He graphically retells the pressures to
be a 'team player' on the fourteenth floor at GM world headquarters
in Detroit.  The actual executive job itself he claims to have been
empty and meaningless.

    Analysing the social location of managers by function, rather
than say by father's occupation, reflects the kind of analysis made
by Carchedi (1977).  Here, managers can be located by reference to
their service to the 'global functions of capital', that is, to the
surplus-value producing process.  Johnson (1977) utilises Carchedi's
approach to explain the potential diverse paths of the 'professions'.  Those professional occupations or congeries of tasks which
can be divided, simplified and routinised, display the characteristics of the 'collective labourer'.  However, those professionals or
managers who cope with 'indeterminacy' of a form and in a way which
coincide with the requirements of capital, may be located in a
rather different class.  Thus Carchedi and Johnson depart from the
rather crude ownership/non-ownership of the means of production
criterion to determine social class location.  Johnson explicitly
distinguishes, for example, routine accountancy work which corre-
sponds to the work of the 'collective labourer' from that work performed by those

    who frame such systems of financial control and supervise their
    implementation.  Such accountants fulfil a special function in
    relation to large-scale organizations which, while not necessari-
    ly involving them in 'line' authority, does include the creation
    of those systems of surveillance and control which are fundamen-
    tal to the process of surplus value production.... Even where
    the investment stake of such accountants is low or non-existent,
    they stand high in the organizational hierarchy with a large per-
    centage of their work activity relating to the global functions
    of capital (Johnson 1977:107).

Clearly this argument rests heavily upon the prior distinctions made
by Carchedi between the labour process which creates use-values, and
the capitalist labour process which produces surplus-value - i.e.
the crucial distinction made by Marx as outlined in chapter 2.

    In similar fashion Gorz (1972) in Technical Intelligence and the
Capitalist Division of Labour, says that it will not be possible to
locate technical, scientific and managerial labour within the class
structure of advanced capitalist society unless the focus is turned
on what *functions* these groups perform vis-à-vis accumulation and
the reproduction of capitalist relations.  In fact he explicitly

states that the determination of whether they
>  belong to the middle class or to the working class *must be made*
>  *to depend* upon the following questions ... is their function re-
>  quired by the process of material production *as such* or by capi-
>  tal's concern for ruling and for controlling the productive pro-
>  cess and the work process from above? (1972:28, emphasis added).
He posits further questions all of which turn on the distinction between socially 'necessary' labour versus the control and disciplinary function.  In similar vein Clawson (1980) traces the 'rise of
bureaucracy' to class struggle.

With each of these approaches one returns to a *class* analysis of
the managerial control of work organisations.  As Marx observed on
the subject of management, not all co-ordinating activity is a consequence of capitalism:
>  All directly social or communal labour on a large scale requires
>  to a greater or lesser degree, a directing authority, in order to
>  secure the harmonious co-operation of the activities of individu-
>  als, and to perform the general functions that have their origin
>  in the motion of the total productive organism as distinguished
>  from the motion of its separate organs.  A single violin player
>  is his own conductor:  an orchestra requires a separate one.  The
>  work of directing, superintending and adjusting becomes one of
>  the functions of capital, from the moment that the labour under
>  capital's control becomes co-operative.  As a special function of
>  capital, the directing function acquires its own special charac-
>  teristics (Marx 1976:448-9).
Marx thus distinguishes between two types of control activity - the
one associated with any large-scale co-operative labour process producing for use, and the other characteristic of a labour process
organised for profit.  He mockingly quotes that 'philistine' peri-
odical the 'Spectator' on its reportage of the Rochdale co-operative
which showed that workmen could manage themselves '... "but they did
not leave a clear place for masters".  Quelle horreur!'  Consequently, it is 'not because he is a leader of industry that a man is a
capitalist;  on the contrary, he is a leader of industry because he
is a capitalist.'  The managers, he notes, 'command in the name of
capital' (1976:450).  And later, in Volume III of 'Capital', Marx
argued that under joint-stock company capitalism 'money capital assumes a social character'.  Accordingly, the 'mere manager who has
no title whatsoever to the capital whether through borrowing it or
otherwise performs all the real functions pertaining to the functioning capitalist as such' (1959:388).

The celebrated debate on the 'divorce of ownership from control'
has been thoroughly raked-over by Child (1969b) and Zeitlin (1974).
The evidence points away from the idea of sociologically significant
'managerialism' whether of a sectional or non-sectional variety (to
use Nichols's (1969) terminology).  Certainly the metaphor of
'divorce' is inappropriate.  Some functional separation, on the
other hand, has undoubtedly occurred.  But even the extent of this
can be exaggerated.  Zeitlin (1974) for example, claims that a majority of American corporations are still controlled by ownership
interests.  Where some functional separation has occurred a number
of arguments are ranged against the notion that any significant
change in class relationships thereby results.  Thus partly because

of devices such as non-voting shares even an apparently small concentration of overall ordinary shares may be quite sufficient to
retain overall control;  top managers who are not large shareholders
in relation to the total share-distribution may nevertheless have a
large part of their own personal fortunes tied up in the company;
the managers of business enterprises must in any case respond to
similar market constraints as would face an owner-manager (Child
1969b:39-40).  In addition, top managers, according to Crompton and
Gubbay (1977) are likely to share the same social outlook and background as the shareholders.  The deduction that can be made from
these kind of points is that top management in a functional sense as
well as in other ways is constrained to behave in a manner which
sets it apart from ordinary workers.  'From the point of view of
management there are threats to profitability from a number of different directions' (Crompton and Gubbay 1977:67).  These are:

> price and quality competition in the product market, price rises
> in the factor market - particularly for labour, availability and
> cost of credit or share yield demand in the capital market, and
> danger of take-over or forced merger.  The best way to cope with
> these threats to profitability as such is to plan, calculate and
> organize methodically to maximize long-term profit;  the control-
> lers of the modern corporation are characteristically devoted to
> that cause.

In the light of its primary function to service the valorisation
process and to secure this in part by exercising control and surveillance over the labour process, management must be deemed to
occupy a position not only separate from that of the workers, but a
position decidedly within the capitalist camp.

While the *function* of managers and other 'professional' employees
must be the key determinant of class location the gross discrepancies in material advantage should not be overlooked.  As Frank Field
(1981) demonstrates, unequal advantage enjoyed by top management extends well beyond inequality of direct income.  'Under the cover of
supposed narrowing of differentials between managerial workers and
the rest the company welfare state has expanded considerably in the
past few years and most particularly for those on high earnings'
(1981:137).  Drawing on data compiled by the Royal Commission on the
Distribution of Income and Wealth, and on surveys by the consultants
AIC/Inbucon, Field demonstrates how top salary-earners are the ones
in receipt of expensive cars, free medical insurance, bridging
loans and free meals in the management dining-room.  The Royal Commission calculated that the average cost of 'fringe benefits' in
1975 contrasted markedly between the figures of under £1,000 for
salary-earners at the £5,500 mark, to nearly £7,000 for those earning over £24,000.

The multi-dimensional character of inequality is illuminated
further by Wedderburn and Craig (1974).  'The employing enterprise
is a hierarchy where income differentials are paralleled by other
dimensions' (1974:141).  These other dimensions relate not only to
dependability of income, but to the content of work, the exercise of
power and the kind of social relationships which people are involved
in at work.  So in addition to suffering gross disparities of
income, operatives must typically endure clocking-on to record attendance (92 per cent of operatives, 4 per cent of senior manage-

ment);  and pay deduction as a penalty for lateness (90 per cent of operatives, 0 per cent of senior managers) (1974:144).  The disparity between managers and workers extends also of course to the question of less favourable working conditions, the risk of industrial injury, wage-age curves, the chance of promotion, the degree of interest, responsibility and autonomy in the work itself and a host of other tangible and less tangible experiential factors.  The essential overall point is that empirical surveys of this kind tend to suggest that there are grounds for considering managers as in a distinct class location not only (albeit as we have argued, primarily) because of the *functions* they perform, but additionally in terms of the unequal life-style and 'life-chances' they enjoy.

Management nevertheless is itself subject to the dialectics of advanced capitalism.  The 'totality' of the dynamic built around surplus-value production is encapsulated in the managerial role. 'Rampant managerialism' (Anthony 1977) has been perpetrated in all spheres - health, education, home and leisure - all seem now to require 'management'.  It has become the leitmotif of advanced industrial capitalism.  The contradictions of management are ascertainable in the social location of managers and in the management function.  Managers are at once both hired labour-power and exploiters of labour.  The increased success enjoyed by them in exploiting labour also increases workers' 'resistance to the domination of capital and, necessarily the pressure put on capital to overcome this resistance' (Marx 1976:449).  Managers are caught in the trap of this contradiction.  Additionally, as formal and technical rationality increase, so does the opportunity for the routinisation of managerial jobs, and hence do managers become the victims of their own devices.  In a still more abstract sense, Horkheimer and Adorno in the 'Dialectic of Enlightenment' (1979), argue that commensurate with the conquest over external nature, the internal nature of those who gain ever higher triumphs becomes more deeply enslaved.  Fletcher (1973:135) points to managers 'worn-out literally, by work and worry'. (10)  Simultaneously perpetrators and dupes, the subject and object of constant reorganisation, rationalisation and redundancy, managers may reach a point where the clash between home life and work life begins to undermine the long-standing assumption of managerial loyalty to the system.  And thus may be triggered 'a middle class reaction against competition' (Pahl and Pahl 1971:262).  But such a point has not been reached.  The mounting crisis and the commensurate rise in managerial redundancy have been borne in traditional individualistic fashion.  Wood (1980) found how managerial redundants and early retirers behaved with great secrecy about their fate.  This was interpreted as a reflection of their own feelings of failure and stigmatisation.

Managerial stress and anxiety may paradoxically be increased by the 'success' of its own ideology.  The inviolability of the managerial rights paradigm and the glossy official corporate histories tend to be blind to the occurrence of past resistance (de Kadt 1976).  In consequence, each generation of managers is made to feel peculiarly responsible for the 'deteriorating' situation.

CONCLUSIONS

Managers, we found, had been subject to little academic study in
industrial relations.  This, following Wood (1981), was regarded
less as an outcome of simple 'oversight' and more to theoretical
shortcomings within the subject.  A number of arguments were then
put forward to justify a study of the managerial role and to dis-
count the idea of by-passing this through the subsumption of it
within the category Capital.  The central contention was that managers have considerable scope in determining the style and pattern
of control.  A host of recent studies of managers by people like
Mintzberg, Maccoby and Rosemary Stewart were reviewed and the variety and frequently re-active nature of much managerial work was
noted.  Doubts about the kind of rationalised strategic models advanced by Braverman and Friedman were accordingly increased.

Nevertheless, it was argued that despite contrasts between managers, a central character of managerial work - and especially that
part of the work concerned with labour - was that of control.  While
doubts were cast that a unified 'Taylor Strategy' was being implemented universally by management, the incessant,though tactical
rather than 'strategic',day-to-day campaign to render labour tractable was underlined.

The section on the genesis of management emphasised the relatively short time-scale during which this group had existed.  Particular
stress was laid on the traumatic transition period between about
1880 and 1920 in the United States and Great Britain during which
time the asserted 'rights' of an emerging management cadre to determine speed, quality and method of working were most acutely in
contention with the ancien régime of craft and insider-contractor
working.  Marglin's now-famous thesis was noted but the 'debate'
between the rival claimed priorities of 'efficiency or control' was
seen as somewhat sterile.  Building on Gordon's work, it was suggested that realising surplus-value was the underlying rationale
and control was inextricably tied to this and could not be sepa-
rated-out as an objective in its own right.

On the question of the social location of managers, the empirical
evidence from Melrose-Woodman and other surveyors of managerial
social backgrounds was considered.  The overall impression gleaned
from these was of greater measure of heterogeneity than might generally have been expected judging from general sociological literature
(e.g. Giddens 1973).  But on the basis of *function* and relating this
to the theoretical frameworks of Marx, Cardechi and Gorz, it was
noted that as agents of the global functions of capital, many managers, whether owners or not, must be allocated an antagonistic class
location to that of workers.  Equally, using the rather different
measure of material and symbolic reward, the wide discrepancies and
gross inequalities within the production system were noted.

Overall, 'management' was revealed as a complex phenomenon, a
function and a special occupational group.  In both its guises it
had elements in common with labour  and yet had elements distinct
from and antagonistic to it.  Management claims to be a partner, it
works *with* labour but also stands *over* it.  In an age which officially proclaims deep moral attachment to democracy, citizenship
rights and equality, the preservation of special managerial rights

and prerogatives would seemingly be vulnerable to challenge.  The
consideration of this issue comprises the subject of the next chapter.

# Chapter 6

# MANAGERIAL PREROGATIVE

The concept of 'managerial prerogative' has long been overdue for
analysis. There is no full-length British academic study of the
phenomenon. Three classic American tomes have obliquely mulled over
the problem but they have avoided defining it or probing its meaning
in any depth (Slichter, Healy and Livernash 1960; Chamberlain 1948;
Chandler 1964). The issue is an emotive one: within it are interwoven the two key strands of bourgeois ideology: private property
rights and the rights of contract.

Managerial prerogatives here will be used more or less interchangeably with the related terms 'management rights' and 'management functions'. The rights aspect is often asserted to derive from
property rights of ownership of plant and equipment with managers
acting as trustees for the legal owners. (1) The call for the preservation of managerial functions, on the other hand, is somewhat
akin to a demarcation claim. It relates to those functional tasks,
the possession of which helps give this occupational group its dis-
tinctiveness. It is no accident, of course, that these tasks essentially relate to the control function and that, therefore, this occupational group is delineated not only horizontally but vertically,
thus maintaining a hierarchical division of labour.

It is true that in the realpolitik of today, sober and sophisticated managers use the term 'managerial prerogatives' in public
statements with some diffidence. Nevertheless, its spirit infuses
a wide realm of managerial thinking and assertiveness. Spokesmen
extol the virtues of leaving industrialists free 'to get on with the
job'. Nor is the concept some offbeat fancy of a few isolated back-
woodsmen. The Conservative party gave official forthright support
to the doctrine in the policy statement 'Fair Deal at Work'. On the
subject of management it declared: 'Their fundamental prerogatives
- so often the subject of dispute and disruptive negotiation - would
be clearly set out in the Code of Practice. These would become
recognised and established principles - whether or not management
rights were incorporated in a collective agreement' (Conservative
Political Centre 1968:65). This was, of course, a vain hope. In
the event, the Code of Practice published by the Conservatives when
they came to office in 1970 did not 'clearly set out' nor indeed
itemise these prerogatives. (2) Although these rights are described

as 'fundamental' it is in fact very difficult to delineate them.
The examples given by A.I. Marsh in his 'Dictionary of Industrial
Relations' - i.e. hiring, firing, promotions, discipline, manning,
production control and decisions on overtime - can in many work-
places be shown to be subject to bargaining or indeed entirely subject to workers' unilateral control.  It is interesting also that
Marsh's list is clearly not meant to be exhaustive.  Indeed, it
omits all the strategic, financial and investment decisions which
management makes, presumably because these are taken for granted as
clearly belonging to management.  The implication is that only the
issues directly related to labour management, or having proximity to
the current frontier of control are here reasserted. (3)  A more
comprehensive definition from an American source which conducts a
vigorous defence of managerial prerogatives may be contrasted.  It
states:

> when we refer to management rights, we are talking about manage-
> ment's right to decide what is to be done, when, where and by
> whom.  Such as the right to move operations from one location to
> another, the right to determine the hours of work and the right
> to take all other decisions which are normally and traditionally
> the sole responsibility of management (Torrence 1959:1).

Despite occasional diffidence by managerial spokesmen, the rights
issue is, and has proven itself historically to be, a very real and
sensitive one.  As Beynon observed, 'This conflict over rights is a
fundamental one and permeates union-management relationships' (1973:
144).  Similarly, Aldridge argues that simply because the doctrine
itself is unclear, inconsistent and often compromised in practice,
does not detract from the fact that it has influential impact upon
behaviour.  After all, most belief systems are muddled and ambiguous.  'In this respect the doctrine of management rights is hardly
unique.  Its impact on industrial relations is extensive' (Aldridge
1976:37).  And Richard Herding (1972:223) ponders the possibility
that the conflict between managerial authority and job autonomy may
prove to be more far-reaching and permanent an issue than structural
wage conflicts in the capitalist system.  At GM, according to De
Lorean (1979:173), executives 'are almost paranoid about even the
suspicion that anyone but themselves is in control of the business'.
This included government and workers, and in respect of the latter
he found little but contempt from 'all layers of management'.  The
essence of De Lorean's case here finds support from no less a figure
than Alfred P. Sloan Jr.  In his classic autobiographical work, 'My
Years With General Motors', he writes, 'What made the prospects grim
in those early years was the persistent union attempt to invade
basic management prerogatives.  Our right to determine production
schedules, to set work standards and to discipline our workers were
all suddenly called into question' (1963:406).  The strident defence
and obsession with management rights is most legendary, of course,
at Ford Motor Company.  Tuchfeld (1969:16) observes:  'Ford have an
international reputation for labour disputes - derived some say from
a pathological belief in management rights'.  This has been explored
by Huw Beynon (1973).  But equally its pervasiveness emerges in a
more recent work concerned with industrial conflict at Ford (Friedman and Meredeen 1980).  For example, they cite pronouncements from
the Cameron Court of Inquiry, which was established in 1957 to in-

vestigate a dispute at Briggs Body Plant.  In its final report this
Inquiry referred to the company's 'general emphasis on discipline
and obedience (which) suggests an attitude of mind tending towards
regimentation' (Friedman and Meredeen 1980:28).  Similarly, the very
first recognition and procedure agreement at Dagenham in 1944 contained a management's rights clause as its opener.  The words have
been retained virtually unchanged in every subsequent agreement.
'Ford's continued assertion of managerial prerogative in the
achievement of efficiency through the unilateral right to determine
manning levels and workloads has long been a prime source of employee discontent and of unconstitutional action' (Friedman and
Meredeen 1980:27).  Indeed, at the time of writing (Spring 1981) the
Ford Halewood strike over the new Disciplinary Code, introduced to
curb unconstitutional action, was spreading nationwide to all Ford
plants.  From the Ford evidence to the Bullock Committee on Industrial Democracy, Friedman and Meredeen's inference that the company
has now adopted a new pluralist style seems somewhat premature.

The concept of managerial prerogatives may be seen, therefore, as
intimately tied to the whole question of management control over the
labour process.  Before we turn to examine in the next chapter the
range of managerial control techniques it is necessary to discuss
the attempts to legitimise the contours of that control.  This implies a study of managerial ideology; and the keystone of this particular arch is the doctrine of managerial prerogative.


PREROGATIVE AS IDEOLOGY

Control was indeed the essential managerial function from the earliest days of nascent industrialism - in all countries, and under all
social systems.  Industrialisation, like any great social movement,
had its beneficiaries and its victims; the former more often than
not were the ruling groups (Sutcliffe 1971).  Most participants in
Britain, as in Stalin's Russia, were victims.  Indeed, it has been
observed that 'there is no evidence that the mass of the population
anywhere has wanted an industrial society, and plenty of evidence
that they did not.  At bottom all forms of industrialization have
been revolutions from above, the work of a ruthless minority'
(Barrington Moore Jr 1973:506).  Numerous other studies have shown
the problem of labour-recruitment to have been a difficult one even
early last century despite the massive increase in population (in
Britain, between 1801 and 1851, the population increased from 8.8m
to 17.9m).  Of course the 'managerial problem' of recruitment was
only the start of it - there was the further problem of developing
and sustaining a disciplined industrial workforce.  The new factory
discipline had to be imposed, comprising speed, regularity, time-
keeping, and attention.  There is much contemporary evidence summarised in the Hammonds' book 'The Town Labourer' (1925), to indicate the harshness of factory conditions and the detail of employer
attempts to control.  Lengthy lists of coercive penalties for each
carefully scribed misdemeanour can occasionally be found off-printed
and framed, providing quaint memorabilia for some chic pub wall.
But no social system can survive in the long term by relying solely
on direct repression; those subject to rule must be persuaded to

legitimise, in some degree, the 'rightness' of the prevailing order:
'The strongest is never strong enough to be always master, unless he
transforms his Might into Right and Obedience into Duty' ('The
Social Contract', Rousseau 1947).  This process is made the easier
by a tendency among subordinates to find that the attribution of
'rightness' to a command system is functional also for themselves in
at least justifying continued submission.

The immediate context of most modern employment relationships is
that of large, hierarchical, complex organisations.  Some form of
subordination and discipline appears indispensable.  The way in
which sociologists typically explain the preservation of this order
is by recourse to the concept of 'ideology'.  Used sociologically
the term has a specific meaning.  Put simply, it denotes those ideas
and statements *which serve to justify* the actions or privileges of
an interest group.  Thus, Bendix defined 'managerial ideology' as:
'All ideas which are espoused by, or for, those who exercise authority in economic enterprises, and which seek to explain and justify
that authority' (Bendix 1956:2).  Similar formulations are offered
by other writers.  For example, Joan Woodward (1965:254) sees management ideology as serving 'a positive function in sustaining management as a social institution' (though the meaning of 'positive'
here is somewhat ambiguous).  McGivering sees it as 'a set of beliefs which management seeks to propagate in order to inspire acceptance and approval of managerial autonomy by the general public
and by specific groups of workers' (McGivering et al. 1969:91).

The theoretical formulation, constructed by Weber, and developed
by his disciple Bendix, may offer some insight.  It also leaves us
with some problems.  A point of essence is that power-holders who
have recourse to coercive instruments use ideology as a resource in
order to seek legitimacy for their position and their influence.
This raises an interesting problem at the organisational level.
Some kind of interactionist model is implied.  There are legitimising messages 'sent' via 'spokesmen', but there must, therefore,
also be some 'audience' or recipients.  Direct subordinates (organisational members) may reject these statements about the world
(definition of goals, priorities, etc.) whilst the wider population
(non-organisational members) may accept managerial definitions as
valid.  Can we then talk of the power being 'legitimised'?  There
is the added complicating factor, that whilst rejecting legitimacy,
the organisation subordinates may nevertheless act in accordance
with rules - i.e. act *as if* legitimacy were granted.  This may be
because 'significant others' in society - politicians, the law,
trade union leaders, churchmen, family members and other employers -
in accepting the order as legitimate, place *constraint* upon members
themselves.  There is the additional obfuscation that in acting as
if one accepts commands and rules as legitimate, one is, in that
very act, legitimising.  This is to ignore the subjective dimension
of authority.  Such actions (or non-actions) in-accord-with-rule,
are best viewed not as an aspect of authority.  As Rousseau pointed
out:  'if a man is constrained by Might to obey, what need has he to
obey by Duty?  And if he is not constrained to obey, there is under
this circumstance no further obligation on him to do so.  It follows, therefore, that the word right adds nothing to the idea of
Might.  It becomes in this connexion, completely meaningless'
(Rousseau 1947:245).

To bow to force then, is not to legitimise the powers that be.
For Rousseau the only foundation for legitimate authority is 'agreement'.  An interesting set of problems in turn emerges at this junc-
ture:  Who is party to the Agreement? How? When?  Over what range
of issues is their agreement to submit to authority?  Is it possible
to submit to authority 'in general', yet draw the line at certain
points?  To these problems we shall be returning.  For the moment
let it be noted that power is only here regarded as having been
granted a modicum of legitimacy, to the extent that recipients respond subjectively in some way to these ideas;  statements which
*seek* to legitimise only achieve a degree of 'legitimacy' when they
effect a change in people's meaning-systems.

The doctrine of 'managerial prerogatives' can be seen as one such
attempt to lay claim to wide-ranging rights.  Historically, its
emergence was prompted by the new circumstances prevailing in nascent industrial capitalism.  The welding together of features previously separated - such as large bodies of men brought together for
purposive activity;  the pursuit of least cost;  the use of formally
free labour;  and unified direction in pursuit of private profit -
all necessitated some such device.  The idea of prerogatives was a
device already partly forged.  The idea of a royal prerogative, for
example, had been canvassed for centuries.

Nowadays, 'managerial prerogative' is an emotive term and can
thus lead to wide misunderstandings.  When used in trade union circles, it can raise suspicions and protests that the user is implying
support of unilateral and arbitrary managerial action;  when used in
management circles, it can raise contrary fears that an attack is
being prepared on management's 'right' to manage.  For these reasons
alone, it may well be wise simply to avoid the term altogether.
However, in that it reflects an area of decision-making over which
management believes it should have (and acts as if it does have)
sole and exclusive rights of determination and upon which it strenuously resists any interference, then the term may serve as a useful
shorthand phrase for an important element in many collective bargaining situations.  Additionally, despite the apprehensions connected with its use noted above, it is a concept used by some participants on both sides, participants whose behaviour we wish to
understand.

Some managers have reported to me that they personally prefer not
to think in terms of rights.  This perhaps, represents a sagacious,
pragmatic stance.  Nevertheless, many important managerial spokesmen
have defined their interests in terms of rights and prerogative.  In
this section we briefly review these and the complementary statements made by trade unionists.  Their underlying rationale is subjected to critical analysis in the final section.

Managerial prerogatives have been defined as:
the name for the remaining portion of management's original
authority and is therefore the name for the residue of discretionary powers left at any moment in the hands of managers.
Every act which a manager or his subordinates can lawfully do,
and without the consent of the worker organisation is done by
virtue of this prerogative (Wood 1956:25).
In the American context the reference to the restraint of law is
more important than in this country - the Employment Protection Act

notwithstanding.  The reference to an 'original authority' is somewhat curious and not a little misleading.  In academic works the
term, whilst much employed, is rarely defined.  Chamberlain and Kuhn
(1965), to cite one of the more comprehensive and authoritative
works in this area, employ the term many times, and its implications
are discussed, but never its meaning.  Elsewhere, when a definition
is supplied it is almost invariably accompanied by polemic.  For example, one functional view sees management prerogatives as 'those
rights, or that authority, which management *must have* in order to
successfully carry-out its function of managing the enterprise'
(Hill and Hood 1952).  This may be contrasted with the definition
of prerogative as 'an *indefensible* and unquestioned right belonging
to a person or body of persons by virtue of position or relation,
and exercised without control or accountability'. (4)


MANAGEMENT VIEWS ON PREROGATIVE

Although the claim to managerial prerogatives has arisen as an issue
in its own right from time to time, it can more often be detected as
an unstated and undefined issue in many diverse struggles upon particular matters.  Only occasionally is it explicitly presented for
debate. (5)  At management conferences delegates normally content
themselves with a  solemn re-declaration that 'management must
manage'.  Justifications for this maxim, when they can be teased-
out, can be seen to rest on four pillars.  The first decrees that,
deriving from the rights attached to ownership of property, management as owners or agents of owners must have control over their
capital assets.  ('The right to do what one likes with one's own.')
As labour owns no part of these assets, the way in which they shall
be utilised is solely a matter for the owners and their representatives.  Early formulations of this doctrine were so sweeping as in
effect to deny any legitimacy to trade unions at all.  Borrowing
heavily upon the divine right dimension of the royal prerogative,
one American company director in 1902 stated his case as follows:
    The rights and interests of the labouring man will be protected
    and cared for - not by the labour agitators, but by the Christian
    men to whom God in his infinite wisdom has given the control of
    the property interests of the country, and upon the management of
    which so much depends (cited in Bakke et al. 1960:187).
    A second argument rests not so much on the Common Law of proper-
ty rights, as the statutory law of ownership responsibility.  In
Britain, Company Law, particularly the Companies Acts of 1948 and
1967, puts responsibility firmly in the hands of shareholders.  Additionally, the implications of responsibility resting with the
company for questions of safety contained in the Factories Acts, and
Health and Safety at Work Act, have also been claimed as reason why
authority must be concentrated in management hands.  L.C.B. Gower
(1969), in his 'Principles of Modern Company Law', indicates the
primary duty of directors to place the interests of shareholders as
paramount over those of employees, customers and others.  As Thomas
(1976:84) has noted, this position is confirmed by the 'News
Chronicle' case: 'When that newspaper was closed down, the Cadbury
family, the controlling group, sought to compensate the employees,

but this was successfully contested by one shareholder.' Statute also influences of course the composition of the board of directors; thus implementation of proposals for industrial democracy which have designs on this level of the firm would require changes in Company Law. This would apply even in respect of those proposals emanating from the EEC in the shape of its Fifth Directive.

The third set of justifications made for managerial prerogatives has been the one most favoured for recent deployment. This I will call the 'economic efficiency' argument and it contains several separate strands. They each tend to argue that it is in everyone's *interests*: consumers, shareholders, the nation, and workers alike, that managers be left alone to manage as they see fit. Management's way is the more efficient. This is said to derive first of all from their expertise and superior ability, resting in turn on their training and education - aspects considered particularly pertinent given the increased technical and economic complexity of present operating conditions. Thus, during a debate on company level collective bargaining, a representative of Plessey Telecommunications, 'emphasised that management and no one else had a fundamental responsibility for exercising a leadership function appropriate to present day conditions' (Hawkins 1971:207). The increased specialisation in management noted earlier, and the development of business studies degrees and graduate business schools, are further tendencies which might be expected to engender an exclusive management cadre. A separate management level is also argued to be more efficient for a second reason, namely, that it is a logical outcome of the division of labour. Bureaucracy implies specific spheres of competence, and a single line of authority which can co-ordinate varied efforts into a unified and optimal organisation process. A scalar chain of command is required to prevent separate departments sub-optimising at the expense of the whole. A fourth line of argument centres on the notion that there are persons naturally identifiable as 'leaders', and others who perform best when led. This is an aspect of the social Darwinism ideology which preaches the survival of the fittest. In this view, the modern businessman is seen as: 'A better fighter than most of us ... industry is the battlefield where the struggle for existence is defining the industrially fittest to survive' (Henderson, cited in Bendix 1956:256). This glamorisation of the manager has naturally made this a popular perspective, not least with managers themselves! Miller and Form (1964:186) elaborate on this ideology of top management -

a highly self-conscious group whose ethnocentrism leads them to believe that they have special gifts and attributes not generally shared by the population. The greatest of these is the ability to manage and organise people.... Top management is an authority-conscious group. Men at the top of the supervisory structure are consumed with decision-making and commanding. Yet they do not like to believe that men obey them because they have power ... they want to feel that they command because they are gifted to lead.

Bendix too, echoes this theme: 'Like all others who enjoy advantages over their fellows, men in power want to see their position as "legitimate" and their advantages as deserved.... All rulers therefore develop some myth of their natural superiority' (Bendix 1966: 294).

We see, then, that the managerial justification for prerogative rests upon property-rights of ownership which must be protected (and upon legal enactment which does in fact make them responsible for the company's activities) and, secondly, upon a series of 'economic efficiency' arguments.  Both of these streams of argument are traceable to the same spring:  the primacy of market rationality.


## TRADE UNION VIEWS ON PREROGATIVE

Trade union views on this matter are, to say the least, ambivalent. Many workers and their representatives clearly do accept *some* role for management to manage.  When trade unionists use the phrase as they occasionally do (see for example the Electricians' evidence to the Donovan Commission), they refer not to the right, but to the *duty,* of management to do the job for which they are paid.  The TUC itself has expressed such a view, stating that it 'is management's job to lead ... what is required is not a diminution in managerial authority but a new conception of how this authority should be exercised' (Trades Union Congress 1967:101).  Indeed, the aphorism that it is 'management's job to manage' is not only used by managers as a defensive statement of their role, but also by trade unions anxious to place responsibility firmly upon managerial shoulders.  This demarcates a 'permanent opposition' role for unions, allowing them the freedom to challenge whatever decisions are made, wringing modifications out of management but never actually engaging in industrial governance.
    Bob Wright, who used to be identified by the media as a leading left-winger among prominent unionists, has gone on record proclaiming the 'necessity of control'.  Although this must, he said, 'be balanced by the freedom which enables individuals to apply their own ideas, make their own critical analysis and draw their own conclusion while keeping in mind and making allowances for the wider needs of the community'. (6)
    Sometimes, this position is stated in a way which more forthrightly circumscribes the union role.  Thus the late George Meany, the popular American AFL-CIO leader, declared:  'A union exists to protect the livelihood and interests of its members.  Those matters that do not touch the worker directly, a union cannot and will not challenge.' (7)  He obliges further by specifying some of these issues:  'these may include investment policy, a decision to make a new product, a desire to erect a new plant, to reinvest or seek new equity.  But where a managerial decision affects a worker directly a union will intervene.' (8)  Many unionists in this country (and indeed in America) do not, however, view the problem so simply. There are numerous areas where managerial decisions will affect workers indirectly, and trade unions often aspire to influence such decisions.  Indeed, it has been said that 'Whatever reservations unions may have in connection with participation, they can be expected to favour the strengthening and widening of the scope of collective bargaining' (Clarke, Fatchett and Roberts 1972:114).
    The TUC expounded its view in 'A Programme for Action' (1969):
    Too often the background of industrial relations on the workshop
    floor is an outdated insistence by managements on their preroga-

tives to make decisions unilaterally, which in practice leaves
workpeople with no apparent alternative to applying sanctions in
the form of strike action.  Work-place representatives do not
regard procedures that automatically exclude many matters on
grounds of managerial prerogatives as reflecting the realities
of the industrial situation.  The only satisfactory method,
therefore, is to adopt procedures which are agreed by both sides
as providing a realistic basis for good industrial relations, and
which state clearly the matters which have to be taken through
the procedure ...' (Trades Union Congress 1969:para. 19).

*Which* matters are to be included, and which excluded from such exercises, is of course the nub of the debate.

Harry Urwin, Assistant General Secretary of the TGWU, gave an appraisal of union attitudes to the idea of prerogative when he wrote:

The history of collective bargaining has been marked by a
struggle between those seeking to maintain authoritarian management on the one hand, and the aim of working people to control
their own working environment.  Some of the most bitter disputes
in industry have been fought on the issue of 'Management Functions' in which employers have sought to impose their absolute
'right to manage' ... to insist that unions could only raise
issues following the act of management (1970:3).

Urwin clearly has in mind here the long struggles in the engineering
industry.  This provides a classic illustrative case of the conflict
over management rights.  It has been a long-standing clash dating
from 1850 until the present day and it has carried wide significance.  Accordingly, we review the history and progress of this
crucial battle in the next section.  We have seen from the statements made by employers and union leaders that the doctrine of managerial prerogative has figured centrally in their consciousness.
It is used as a device to further their perceived interests - for
some union leaders it is seen as preserving the institutional role
of permanent opposition for the unions.  Nevertheless, the two sets
of conceptions are not complementary, and major conflicts have revolved around the issue.  We now turn to review these and then
return in the final section of this chapter to an analysis of both
the doctrinal statements reported here and the history of the actual
struggles which have taken place.  The objective at that stage will
be to interpret the interplay of actual events and to draw out the
contours of principle which lie beneath the doctrinal assertions.
This will be achieved by providing a thoroughgoing analysis of the
meaning of 'rights' and the social process of their production.  The
engineering industry case study is illuminating for here the management rights issue became a veritable cause célèbre.


THE BATTLE OVER MANAGEMENT RIGHTS IN THE ENGINEERING INDUSTRY

It was in the engineering industry that the battle over management
rights was made most manifest.  Employers made explicit claims to
certain unilateral rights of action and after a series of long
struggles had these acknowledged in writing.  Engineering craftsmen
on the other hand, laid claim to property rights in their jobs and
in their skill.  Both sides sought to control the 'status quo' in

their own favour - the employers claiming the right to make changes
first and argue through procedure afterwards (with the changes meanwhile intact) and the unions claiming a different status quo - that
proposed changes would not be operative whilst a dispute concerning
them moved through procedure.  Not only was this a bone of contention in 1922, it was 'the stumbling block' (9) to a new procedure
in 1971.

Therefore, because of the manifest nature of the struggles on the
above issues in engineering, it is in this industry that meanings
which participants placed upon management rights questions can most
clearly be demonstrated. (10)  It is a story of strategic move and
counter-move by all the parties;  here organising, there breaking
ranks, in order to gain some advantage over opponent or competitor.

The craft-workers in this industry organised themselves early,
forming the Amalgamated Society of Engineers in 1851, one of the
'New Model' unions with an initial strong emphasis on mutual welfare
benefits.  They soon became the largest and most important union in
the country.  The first bitter struggle was joined in 1852 only a
year after their formation.  They lodged a demand for the abolition
of overtime and piecework;  this prompted the employers into a
temporary central organisation of their own whose object was patently to eradicate the union altogether.  Members of the employers' association pledged not to hire any union member, and further, to enforce the use of the notorious 'declaration' whereby employees and
prospective employees would sign their intent not to join a union.
Under these conditions workers trickled back to work.

The EEF itself was formed in 1896 and was used to impose the
famous nation-wide Great Lock-Out of 1897, described by one contemporary observer as 'The greatest struggle between Labour and
Capital that this country has ever seen' (cited in Clarke 1957:128).
Ostensibly, the conflict began over the length of the working day,
but it was viewed by employers themselves, and by union leaders, as
essentially a struggle over much deeper issues, most of these re-
volving around 'the real issue (which) was the limit of trade union
interference with managerial decisions' (Clarke 1957:128).  Certainly the months of build-up did contain strife on a wide range of
questions which involved, at heart, the issue of managerial prerogatives, and the conflict period itself (6½ months) not only saw the
continuance of this theme, but indeed saw its growth.  This is illustrated by the Board of Trade's own assessment:

> Though the immediate cause of the general dispute was the demand
> for the eight-hour day in London, the real questions at issue be-
> tween the parties had become of a much more far-reaching kind and
> now involved questions of *workshop control* and the limits of
> trade union interference (cited in Wigham 1973:55, emphasis
> added).

So the Board of Trade's conciliation attempts were refused by the
employers who issued instead their own demands relating to the
'freedom to run their own factories'.  This list of demands sum-
marises the unfolding of certain continuing themes.  The central one
was the employers' insistence on the 'principle of freedom to employers in the management of their works'.  The union response countered that managerial acts which affected their members should be
subject to prior agreement.

This aspect of the management functions' debate eventually became distilled into the 'status quo' issue.  Ironically it was the establishment of the formalised Procedure for the Settlement of Disputes which lasted from 1897 to 1971 that generated the status quo problem.  Whilst a question was being processed through the machinery, should conditions prior to the change be preserved or should management's decision stand?  The latter position was secured by the employers and it was enshrined in national agreements until 1971.  Other issues, yet surely ones which were an offshoot of the first, were mainly concerned with freedom of employment, manning, compulsory overtime, the imposition of piecework and the recruitment of apprentices.  The freedom of employment issue presaged the closed shop disputes of the 1970s.  The union in 1897 wanted to avoid discrimination against their members in favour of non-unionists, and to be able to limit non-unionists by refusing to work with them.  Employers in turn asserted their right to hire whom they so pleased.  The manning problem was again a precursor of a current live issue.  This arose out of craftsmen's fears in the face of increased machine work towards the end of the century.  To preserve their employment prospects, they demanded that any machine tool which was used to do work customarily done by a skilled man must be operated by a skilled man.  There was a concern here over 'dilution' through the use of unskilled labour to perform jobs, albeit with new equipment, which had previously been performed by skilled workers.  There was some attempt on this issue, by the Amalgamated Society of Engineers to claim 'ownership rights in the job' on the basis of custom.  Conversely, the employers claimed freedom to act in relation to these machines on the basis of ownership rights vested in property.

In the face of an increasing closing of ranks by employers, the ASE withdrew their claims and accepted the employers' terms of settlement.  After the agreement, the men could not in principle oppose piece-rates, limit the number of apprentices, or influence the manning of machines.  On the status quo which 'was seldom out of the minds of the two sides from 1898 to 1971', the terms of settlement decreed that while a question was going through procedure, work should continue on current conditions.  'This was held to mean conditions *after* the change that was being challenged not before it.'  (Wigham 1973:68).  This version of the status quo was not always opposed by trade unionists.  Indeed, the General Secretary of the ASE told his members in 1907 that, 'Pending settlement, somebody must say what must be done, and it seems to me that somebody must necessarily be the employers' (Wigham 1973:71).

Developments in the following decades were as much marked by government action as that of trade unions.  The Fair Wages Resolution of the House of Commons in 1891, which stipulated the insertion of a clause in government contracts to ensure current conditions in each trade were upheld, was greeted by the EEF in much the same way as the CBI in 1978 reacted to the 10 per cent 'guideline' clause.  The EEF sought to encourage members to refuse local authority and central government contracts which contained such a clause, which they saw as an infringement of management rights.  Another development, that of moves towards arbitration in industrial relations matters, met a response from the EEF by which they identified 'two sets of questions' - questions of 'principle' and questions of

'fact'.  The former 'arose out of rights and privileges' and are by
nature not open to arbitration;  whereas questions of fact which are
'determinable by circumstances' - such as the general alteration of
wages - may be open to the arbitration process.  The years prior to
the 1922 lock-out also saw the temporary suspension of management
rights during the war, and the growth of the shop stewards' movement.  The engineering industry gave early recognition to shop
stewards:  there was a formal agreement in 1919 which gave effect to
this and additionally provided for steward facilities and the establishment of works committees.

The 1922 lock-out was triggered by the issue of compulsory overtime.  The AEU were faced with a memorandum containing a clause
which gave the right to managers to stipulate overtime working.
Whilst allowing representation through procedure, 'meantime the
overtime required shall be proceeded with'.  The unions opposed
this, yet it was to become a clause in the agreement to survive the
next fifty years.  The Federation wrote to fifty unions - including
those not in dispute - with an ultimatum to be signed and accepted
within a matter of days.  The contentious clause read as follows:

The trade union shall not interfere with the right of the employers to exercise management functions in their establishments....
Instructions of management shall be observed pending any question
in connection therewith being discussed in accordance with the
provision referred to.

The AEU refused to sign and were locked out.  Other unions were per-
plexed.  'We cannot understand your reference to management functions', wrote the Amalgamated Moulders plaintively.

Significantly, in terms of the discussion above, the Federation
argued it was in the country's interest and that of the work-people
for the freedom of management to be maintained;  'dual control as is
now sought is incompatible with the proper working and efficiency of
an industrial establishment' (Wigham 1973:121).  A Court of Inquiry
on this dispute (aptly known as the Mackenzie Inquiry, as Sir
William was the only member) supported managerial rights to make
decisions on overtime.  This was seen as arising purely out 'of the
requirements of the work to be done' and as

to this necessity the managers alone are in a position to judge.
The National Agreement, allowing thirty hours in four weeks, implies that, up to that limit, overtime, granted its necessity, is
regarded as reasonable.  Up to that limit there *must be freedom
to the management to act in the exercise of their discretion*.

It was also noted that the employers regarded the AEU attempt to
secure prior consent to overtime as an attack on the 'whole principle of control' (Report of a Court of Inquiry Concerning the Engineering Trades Dispute, Cmnd 1653, 1922).

The AEU were locked-out for three months, but again individual
workmen who signed a slip accepting the employer's right to issue
instructions and the employee's duty to conform were accepted back.
The struggle again ended in the employer's favour:  the management
functions clause was signed.  The 1922 management function agreement
was to last unchanged for the next fifty years.  In domestic practice, of course, daily encroachments were made upon the supposed inviolate rights of management.  These grass-roots practical events
are the subject of a later chapter.  In terms of the current dis-

cussion on the battle over principle we can now bring the record up
to date.


DEVELOPMENTS SINCE 1971

The battle over management rights did not decline in importance
during the 1970s.  On the contrary, the issue flared up to a pitch
unattained at national level since the 1922 lock-out.  In December
1971 the unions abrogated the Procedure Agreement.  This dated back
to 1922 and indeed its main principles derived from the 1898 Agreement.  Both the unions and the employers agreed in 1971 that the
main 'stumbling-block' to reaching a new agreement was the problem
of management functions and the status quo.  At the final negotiating conference in September 1971, at which the unions gave notice
to terminate the old agreement, Hugh Scanlon spelled out:  'the main
issue on which we have broken down;  that is, status quo'. (11)
     Status quo is the counter which unions use to check the operation
of managerial rights.  Status quo provisions 'define the extent to
which the unions have a right - or the employers are bound - to
defer the implementation of certain managerial decisions until
either agreement is reached or the negotiating procedure has been
exhausted'. (12)
     The old procedure had been subject to much criticism;  this
centred around two main points.  First, that it was authoritarian,
and that it institutionalised managerial prerogatives.  This charge
rested on the constitution of the Local and Central Conferences.
Whereas most procedures in other industries provide for negotiation
in joint committees with equal numbers of employers and unionists,
the engineering 'conferences' involved unions and managers putting
their case to an adjudicating court consisting only of employers.
In practice the 'failure to agree' provision ensured that outcomes
were not always in the employer's favour.  The first criticism,
then, was that the procedure was a form of undisguised 'employer
conciliation'. (13)  The second was the inordinately protracted
nature of the procedure.  It took on average three months for a
grievance to reach the Central Conference Stage at York.  This
'ritualistic waste of time', (14) engendered pre-emptive unofficial
and unconstitutional action.  In consequence, the Engineering Procedure became the bête noire of the institutional reformers of the
1960s.  'We have in recent months', complained the EEF, 'been taken
to task by the Donovan Commission, by the National Board for Prices
and Incomes, and by the Government in its White Paper 'In Place of
Strife'. (15)
     The Federation were not disposed to accept that the procedure was
'totally anachronistic' but were prepared to review it, and accordingly the first formal negotiations for this purpose took place in
April 1969.  The criticism of 'employer conciliation' - the charge
that the procedure made the employers judge and jury in their own
case - they parried somewhat lamely by retorting that it 'at least
has the advantage of introducing external influences'. (16)  On the
question of management functions and the status quo, they maintained
that criticisms alleging that violation of the status quo by employers were causing the proliferation of disputes, and ignored the fact

that most matters moving through procedure were about money and that
the status quo was therefore inapplicable.

Hugh Scanlon replied by admitting that most of the issues in procedure did concern money but he denied that this made the status quo
inapplicable - indeed in these cases management insisted it applied
by ensuring the disputed sum was not paid during the course of procedure! He added:

I only make this point to illustrate.... If we are prepared to
say to you:  where we seek to make a change we are prepared to
agree that we will exhaust [the procedure] ... we think there is
a responsibility on you to respond in the same vein ... when you
wish to make the change ... for instance if you wish to dismiss
a shop steward. (17)

Such a stance, which implied to the employers that they were to
have no more rights of discretion than the unions, led them to issue
a press statement which alleged that the CSEU terms meant that 'management would have to seek agreement or exhaust the Procedure even
on day-to-day administrative matters to which a single worker ob-
jected'. (18)

The two sets of proposals were open to different interpretations
and this particular interpretation was rather an extreme one.  The
EEF, it should be made clear, were not unwilling to accept a status
quo clause, but they wished it to be rather narrower than the CSEU
version.  The old 1922 Agreement itself contained status quo provisions.  In order to clarify the conflict we need to juxtapose the
competing clauses:


1922 Agreement

   I   (a) The Employers have the right to manage their establish-
       ments ...
   II  (b) When the Management contemplates *alterations in recog-
       nised working conditions*....  The Management shall give the
       workpeople directly concerned, or their representatives in
       the shop, intimation of their intention and afford an oppor-
       tunity for discussion....  The alterations shall not be im-
       plemented until settlement has been reached or until the
       Procedure has been exhausted.

There was also a seven-day rule, which meant that proposed changes in material or method which would result in 'one class of work-
people being replaced by another' would not be implemented for seven
days if the move was disputed.

   (d) Questions arising which do not result in one class of work-
       people being replaced by another ... and on which discussion
       is desired, shall be dealt with in accordance with the Pro-
       visions for Avoiding Disputes and work shall proceed meantime
       under conditions *following* the act of the management.

In 1970 the EEF presented a draft agreement which contained new
proposals, ones which, they said, 'go further along the status quo
road'.

1970 EEF Proposal

>  Where an employer seeks to change ... an existing *system* of pay-
>  ment or a condition of employment which is either agreed or cus-
>  tomarily applicable ... or an individual worker's *condition of*
>  *employment* (unless the change required is in accordance with
>  agreed or established practice ...) the existing term or con-
>  dition shall be maintained until agreement has been reached ...
>  or procedure ... exhausted.  Nothing in the foregoing shall re-
>  quire management to invoke the procedure when carrying out its
>  responsibilities within the framework of agreed or established
>  conditions.  In such circumstances the decision of management
>  shall be implemented immediately.... (19)

These clauses, claimed the EEF, would give the protection sought
by the union 'without taking away from the employer those responsibilities he must bear ...'. (20)


CSEU Draft Status Quo Clause

>  It is accepted by the Trade Unions that Managements have the
>  right to manage and to expect all normal management decisions
>  concerning the efficient operation of the establishment to be
>  implemented by the workers immediately, except that any decisions
>  which alter the established wages, working conditions, practices,
>  manning, dismissals (except for gross industrial misconduct) or
>  redundancy, to which the workpeople concerned object shall not be
>  implemented, until the Local Conference procedure has been ex-
>  hausted.

The EEF negotiators claimed to see little difference in intention
between the two alternative proposals.  Hugh Scanlon, however, maintained that the employers' draft would leave the issue unchanged
from the existing agreement and that it 'envisages that the act of
Management will prevail ... and that we will carry out that act ...
whilst we discuss it with you....  It is that fundamental conception
we wish to change.' (Proceedings in Conference, Thursday 16 April
1970:11)

Much dispute then followed for months on end concerning the exact
nature of the difference between the alternative proposals.  The
EEF's version excluded dismissal, redundancy and transfer of employees from the status quo.  But the 'real crunch' came over who
would interpret when an 'existing system' (see EEF draft) was being
disturbed, and who would decide when an 'established practice' (see
CSEU draft) was established or not, and whether an agreement covered
it or not.  Mr Jukes, QC, Director General of the EEF, put to Mr
Scanlon a hypothetical case:  if a man was to be moved from Job A,
which had an agreed piece-work price, to Job B which similarly had
an agreed price but one which yielded not 'quite so much as Job A,
though it is agreed.  Would you say that management has the right
to do that or could the man object?' (ibid.:18)

Mr Scanlon replied:

Can the man object? - Yes.  But the practicalities of it are ...
although the man objects at this stage when he brings in the
steward he will expect the steward to say:  'This is the subject

of agreement between ourselves and the Management and therefore
you should accept the transfer.' (21)
Scanlon later pointed out that this would constitute the procedure
being exhausted.

Despite the abstruse nature of the difference between the draft
proposals, the real point of difference was that whereas the employers wished to preserve freedom to act first and talk later, the
unions wished to establish that the shop stewards should be party
to a series of shop agreements and understandings which would establish a framework within which management could act.  That Hugh
Scanlon wished to include custom and practice is made clear when he
said that 'established' conditions refer not only to agreements but
conditions 'hallowed, for the want of a better word, in practices
which are recognised even if they are not the subject of specific
agreements ...'. (22)  It must be said, however, that the determination of what is a 'recognised' practice merely puts the problem
back a stage further.

In the event, although the written drafts may appear somewhat
alike, the rift between the parties on this issue was such that although agreement was reached on all the other issues including a
shortened procedure, shop stewards, works committees, and so on, the
status quo problem prevented any agreement at all.  It was clearly
viewed as the central bone of contention and a major point of principle.  99 per cent of Association members voted to support the
EEF's decision 'to make no further concessions on the status quo
issue'. (23)  Thus the termination of the 1922 Agreement left the
industry without the framework of a procedure and, as Mr Jukes
solemnly pointed out, left it therefore without any nationally
agreed arrangements for the recognition of unions, shop stewards,
works committees or access to external stages of procedure.  Moreover, it made it more likely that if problems arose the parties
would fall 'back on the provisions of the Industrial Relations Act'.
(24)

The step was none the less taken.  Two years later in 1973, the
EEF convened a Special Conference to attempt fresh negotiations.
They floated the idea of a Procedure Agreement without a status quo
provision but of course this was rejected.  Scanlon said he could
not see how such an agreement would be 'worth the paper it was
written on'. (25)  Then the EEF proposed setting up a working party
with the status quo placed at the end of the agenda.  The CSEU
wanted this issue settled first, and indeed looked for some movement
from the employers towards the unions' 1971 draft clause as a pre-
condition even to establishing a working party.  The conference
therefore came to nothing.

Not until 1 March 1976 was a new agreement signed.  Informal
talks led to the abandonment of both proposed clauses, and surprisingly, the problem was resolved by adopting practically word-for-
word the TUC's formulation as found in their publication 'Good
Industrial Relations:  A Guide for Negotiators' (1973).  This simply
stated:

It is agreed that in the event of any difference arising which
cannot immediately be disposed of, then whatever practice or
agreement existed *prior* to the difference shall continue to operate pending a settlement or until the agreed procedure has been
exhausted (Trades Union Congress 1973, emphasis added).

The conflict generated by the Management Functions issue was such
that it took seven years from the initiation of negotiations for a
new procedure in 1969, to arrive at these few simple words!

The next section sets out to interpret the events outlined, and
the doctrinal statements made in the immediately preceding section.
This is done in terms of regarding 'rights' as emergent tendencies
arising from social rule-making which in turn is based on congeries
of group interests.


RIGHTS, RULES AND INTERESTS

Whilst the whole question of 'rights' in general terms has given rise
to a series of difficulties, the specific question of managerial
rights may be claimed as perhaps the most abstruse of them all. The
'rights' question has enjoyed a remarkable revival in recent years.
Yet its philosphical base extends only into relatively recent history.
Eighteenth-century manifestos, the work of men like Thomas Paine,
culminated in major Declarations of inalienable Human Rights in both
America and France.  The underlying philosophy was an ingredient of
a great liberal movement, part of the political, economic and theo-
logical convulsion which shook the ancien régime.  The American
Declaration enshrined the rights of citizens to alter or abolish
governments which failed to uphold the enumerated individual rights.

Nowadays the concept of human rights has become an international
issue of such import that its merits are weighed against the value
of detente itself.  The civil rights issue has become central in
Northern Ireland and in the United States.  The Civil Rights Act of
1964 in the latter country encompassed questions of employment,
religion, sex, race and national origin.  Yet the national debate
there continues;  the Bakke case (that of the white American initially denied a medical school place because of a racial quota
system) is but one example.  In England there has been legislation
on equal opportunities and Lord Hailsham has proposed a written
constitution, whilst others talk of a Bill of Rights.  The twentieth
century has also witnessed the assertion of numerous other rights,
for example, the right to education, the right to housing, the right
to work, and the continuance of the right to manage.

In attempting to come to terms with this last aspect and by
placing it in the context of the gamut of 'rights' in general, we
may note immediately that there are three main ways of approaching
the whole farrago of claims.  Lawyers seek only to determine if
there is a claim that can be substantiated in law.  But, for our
purposes here, this is rather limited because such determination
would not assist us in those cases in which rights are claimed and
sometimes honoured *outside* the law, or conversely, those instances
where a legal claim is judged to exist but where in practice the
corresponding action is not forthcoming.  Philosophers seek out
basic principles and try to ascertain the types of moral claims
which are made.  Sociologists are more concerned, however, to make
descriptive statements, and to trace the reasons why some groups
appear to accept a series of asserted claims, whilst others do not.
The studies of beliefs and meaning systems are relevant here.  It is
not the task of social analysis to settle the metaphysical question

concerning the existence or otherwise of absolute inalienable rights
or the existence of a natural law.  These concepts are relevant here
only to the extent that they provide points of reference or touch-
stones to which the parties appeal in order to defend their perceived interests. (26)   But Abrahamsson and Bromstrom are much more
affirmative in their submission that 'rights are social and legal
facts and can be subjected to scientific analysis' (1980:43).  They
consider and reject the 'positivist' position which in Sweden was
advanced by the Uppsala School and by Hagerstrom in particular.
Under the sway of German philosophers - particularly Hegel and
Nietzsche - criticism was directed at concepts like 'rights' and
'duties' which had no concrete real-world analogue.  They were thus
dismissed as 'metaphysical'.  The whole thrust of Abrahamsson and
Bromstrom's book, however, is to explore how the 'rights of labour'
can be made meaningful:  'economic democracy implies a transfer of
means of production from private to *collective* ownership, but to
which collective?' (1980:42-3).  Genuine industrial democracy, they
argue, implies transfer of ownership rights, but to whom - the
labour-force collective or the civic collective?  The essential
problematic of their book is on what *basis* should we make this
choice and what implication would flow from the choice.  Their
thesis begins with the authors taking a stand on the rights of
labour.  They argue that 'instrumental' value-judgments in social
science are not only acceptable but necessary;  the criteria rest
on the *consequences* of choice (1980:48).

Overall, the authors argue for the substituting of the 'rights of
labour' in place of the present liberal private ownership system.
It is a pragmatic case built on the consequences of allocating the
right to the ownership and disposal of the means of production.
'The principle of the rights of labour is the principle of reunifi-
cation of decision-making and executive power over production'
(1980:252).  This can be effected, they argue, on the basis of the
labour theory of value, leading to a radical interpretation of employee investment funds.  In the British context such a proposal
would sound fanciful, but Abrahamsson and Bromstrom give it some
credence in the light of the Swedish context.  They are critical of
the social democratic or 'functional socialism' approach which
strips the artichoke leaf by leaf.  This results in the problem of
what to do with the heart:  the right to private ownership of the
means of production.  The 'handling of this heart began' they state,
'with the discussion of employee investment funds and industrial
democracy in the 1970's' (1980:251-2).  The community, they suggest,
could beneficially complete this operation by re-allocating this
right.

Even more fundamentally, the concept of 'rights' has been alternatively analysed as 'entitlements';  second, as 'expectations';
third, as existing only when there is the power to secure the claim
(this is the position of the 'Realists'; (27)  and fourth, in functional terms.  This latter, the one reflected strongly in Abrahamsson and Bromstrom, has also been argued by Laski.  It has found support among apologists of management rights, who argue that these are
in the *national* interest and not just a sectional interest.  Laski
argues that rights are:
     correlative with functions.  I have them that I may make my con-

tribution to the social end.... The claims I make ... are
claims that are necessary to the proper performance of my functioning ... which ought to receive recognition because a recognisable public interest is involved in their recognition (Laski
1967:94-5).

This, of course, is the line argued by Abrahamsson and Bromstrom
who think they can demonstrate that the rights of labour can be
justified in precisely these terms. As we will see in a moment,
apologists of private ownership of the means of production feel they
too can make an equally sound case in the opposite direction. (28)

I want to argue here that, to understand rights in general and
managerial rights in particular, we will find it useful to locate
our analysis in the context of our earlier general framework.
Rights in this context relate to rules. Rights, duties, and rules
are all social products. Social scientists cannot make moral judg-
ments which pronounce that someone should be bound by a duty or
should have his rights recognised. These are moral or normative
statements. The social scientist can, however, make descriptive
statements. Thus rights and duties are important in our framework
in so far as they are part of the *meaning systems* of the actors we
are studying. They are significant if we can, therefore, produce
descriptive statements based on the *probability* of patterned behaviour. That is, the normative discourse of our subjects is of great
interest to us if it helps shape their actions. We can then describe when classes or groups will in all probability have their behaviour shaped in this way, and why it is that these groups and not
others will feel so compelled.

Sociologically, it will prove most appropriate and illuminating
to view rights as social rules. Rules prescribe behaviour, and although, like all prescriptions, and all rules, there will be occasions on which they are ignored or violated, this does not vitiate
the rule itself in more general terms. Different types of rules,
too, can be identified - moral, legal, and customary. Quite often
participants will, of course, regard these as interrelated. Though
the lawyer may show no interest in extra-legal 'rules', the social
scientist is quite properly inquisitive. Sociologists have long
been involved with norms, values, mores, tradition and folkways;
and these can comprise important constraints on behaviour irrespective of their legal position. Nor are moral and customary 'rules'
fully coterminous. Not all moral questions can be settled by determining majority view in Gallup-poll fashion. Claims to the
rights of minorities would often be discounted if this were the
criterion.

If there are extra-legal 'rules', then there can be extra-legal
'rights'. These must find their sanctioning, therefore, from some
source other than the law. Much of the classic formulaic work of
Elliot Jacques on the sanctioning of 'Authority' is founded upon
this kind of analysis. The rights of those holding authority derive
from the sanctioning of the authority structure according to
Jacques. This sanctioning process involves the making of agreed
*rules*. Sanctioning comes from without and from within. From without it derives from the sanctioning of the product (by customers)
and the task (by investors); from the government; from professional standards; from the community, which will not tolerate major

violations of its cultural standards.  It derives too from the
'contract' under which, according to Jacques, the individual employee signs his acceptance of a whole gamut of rules and documents.
From within, there is the 'sanctioning power of the task' (Jacques
1951:262) by which he means the imperatives deriving from the nature
of the task itself and the materials used.  This of course takes one
back to M.P. Follett's 'Law of the Situation'.  Elliot Jacques dis-
plays a glimmer of recognition that the task 'imperative' may not be
altogether unambiguous, but he resolves the issue with an ingenuous
assertion:  'Ultimately, top management is in the best position to
distinguish what is technically possible ...' (ibid.).  Finally,
sanctioning occurs from within, through the 'democratic sanctioning'
of joint consultation.  'The more far-reaching the control exercised
by the consultative system', he argues, 'the more complete the
authority vested in the executive system,' and this in turn 'can
assist the ability of management to manage' (1951:263).  This type
of control strategy can be seen to relate back to an admixture of
the direct control method and the employee-involvement method discussed earlier.

Whatever the merits or demerits of Jacques's scheme, it does involve a recognition that rules can be and are used to shape action,
and that in turn rules must be defensible in terms of society's
norms or in terms of some significant section of the community.  The
'right to manage' is, as we stated at the start of this section,
perhaps the most abstruse of all of the claimed rights we have
noted.  The reasons for this, and the grounds for this contention
can now be stated.

The first reason is that the claimed rights are peculiarly open-
ended.  If someone acts as creditor for a stipulated sum, then the
right vis-à-vis the debtor, and the reciprocal duty he has to repay,
can be easily stipulated.  The specificity, both of the duty owed,
and the person to whom it is owed, is high.  Lawyers designate this
as an *in personam* right.  But in the case of 'managerial rights'
(especially if we assume a large industrial concern), the precise
*person* to whom duty is owed is hard to specify, and the exact dimensions of the 'due' equally so.

Secondly, as we have noted, many employers based their 'management rights' on the fact of their property entitlements.  Now this
question of 'property rights' is at once fascinating and complex.
The claimed right of enjoyment of ownership is in the main a claim
to freedom from interference.  As we saw, the owners affiliated to
the Engineering Employers Federation claimed the 'right of non-
interference' in their property.  Lawyers call these proprietary
rights *in rem* rights:  they are not directed against any particular
individual such as a debtor who has a corresponding duty:  rather,
they are general rights of a negative kind directed at any would-be
transgressors.  This property-rights element in the claim to managerial prerogatives is clearly very different from the claim to a
right to demand a positive obligation from a specified person to do
something.

Property rights have been linked by their defenders to the question of individual liberty.  Aims, the Free Enterprise Organisation,
issued its own 'Declaration of Freedom - 1978' .  Each of the
signatories were managing directors.  They wrote:  'We, the under-

signed declare ... that without free enterprise there can be no
liberty.' The 'affirmation' continues by linking liberty, free
enterprise and democracy, claiming that each is 'being eroded by
State interference'.

A declaration-cum-affirmation does not, of course, have to do
more than declare and affirm. There is no compulsion to prove or
demonstrate the case. Nor is one provided. But more developed defences of private property rights can be found. Milton Friedman in
'Capitalism and Freedom' (1962) and Friedrich Hayek in 'The Constitution of Liberty' (1960) have argued the case in utilitarian terms.
They justify it with reference to valued ends - efficiency, liberty,
and freedom of speech. Locke tried to defend it in terms of basic
principles, i.e. rights of acquisition emerge because every man has
a property right in his own person and part of a person is his
labour, which, when 'joined' to an object, that latter becomes part
of his objectified self. So, if a thief steals an object someone
has made or grown he has stolen his efforts and in effect treated
him like a slave. That form of ownership of property which derives
from one's own accumulated past labour would in these terms therefore be justified. Apart from Locke's acquisition theory, (29)
other apologists have traced proprietary rights to the Hobbesian
social contract, and some have even argued that a property-owning
democracy within a competitive economy is the best way to fair distribution because it will ensure a rough correspondence between contribution and reward (Baldwin 1966). The anomalies of inherited
wealth, and the clear mismatch between effort, service and profit
have not made this latter line of defence the most popular. The
most significant recent book in this whole area has been Nozick's
(1974) 'Anarchy, State and Utopia'. Nozick argues that proprietorial rights are a defence against any imposed pattern of distribu-
tive justice. Imagine, he says, your own favoured distribution pattern - say everyone with an equal share - (position D1). Now, if
members acting freely agree to pay for extra service - perhaps to
someone working all of his leisure hours - then this will involve a
transfer of holdings, thus leading to distribution D2. Any attempt
at intervention to maintain the original distribution would therefore infringe the liberty of all parties to do as they pleased.

Two crucial problems with Nozick's thesis then arise. First, he
assumes too readily that 'holdings' or 'possession' necessarily involve the ownership rights of disposal. One can have access to
buildings, land, the use of goods such as transport and leisure
facilities, and the occupancy of jobs, without having the *additional*
right of disposal of these goods. In other words, whilst granting
use of, or even occupancy or possession of, some goods, we do not
necessarily also grant free right to do as one will. Thus, the community demands that owners of private land seek planning permission
before a major change is effected in its utilisation. Certain uses
of private property can create a nuisance to the surrounding community; in such cases the right to freedom of interference which the
owner claims may then be denied. That is, the community acting
through its political institutions creates a new 'rule' to protect
its interests. The interests of the property-holder in his rights
of ownership are overridden by an alternative set of interests.
This introduces the second point. The acquisition of some goods,

even if based on skill, diligence and expertise, does not justify
granting full ownership rights.  To use one of Nozick's own examples, if an individual through his display of all of these qualities
came to monopolise the water supply, the community would surely not
recognise his right to do with his 'own' as he pleased.  There would
have to be 'interference' to protect other liberties.  Hence, we
arrive at the crux of the issue:  what about the private ownership
of the means of production? (30)

Proprietorial rights in this special class of goods clearly involve a clash in liberties.  We cannot raise all of the arguments
concerning private property here and it is only appropriate to note
that there is a presumption arising from Nozick's thesis that ownership of this class of goods should be equally respected.  Yet, in
an industrial society, where the majority of people are dependent
upon the deployment of capital goods, their ownership clearly involves *power over others*.  Under pre-capitalist forms of property-
relations there were rights of access to common land and rights of
utilisation, for example, for grazing.  The enclosure movement restricted these rights.  Thus, the link between private property
rights and liberty is clearly problematic. (31)

When employers defend managerial rights in terms of ownership
rights, therefore, they are clearly exposing themselves to these
sorts of objections.  They amount to questions concerning how acquisition rights were secured in the first place;  to denials that
possession necessarily involves the granting of full ownership
rights;  and to the counterposing of one set of liberties with
another set.  The claim even to *in rem* rights - to freedom from
interference - may well, therefore, be denied and, of course, the
state already does 'interfere' in this way.  Furthermore, even if
full proprietorial rights were granted (a negative right), this
would not resolve the managerial problem of securing *obedience to
command* (which involves recognition of a positive right).  In 1922
when the Engineering Employers insisted upon their right to decide
when compulsory overtime would be worked, they were not seeking the
power to be left alone, but the power to *direct*.

In order to meet this desideratum of positive-active right, as
opposed to the more negative right to deter trespassers, the ideology of managerial rights contains three further elements.

(i)  First, there is the claim to duty arising from the employment
*contract*.  As Benn and Peters (1959) argue in their well-known text,
'rights', to be meaningful, must always be matched by a corresponding obligation or duty.  Thus they argue - 'the right of X is the
duty of Y.  To say that X has a right to £5 is to imply that there
is a rule which, when applied in the case of X and to some other
person Y, imposes on Y a duty to pay X £5 if X so chooses' (1959:
88).

Though this formulation purports to offer an underlying principle
concerning the existence of rights in general, this it cannot do.
There are some rights which can be said to exist even though there
is no person with a corresponding duty to reciprocate.  Thus, for
example, although one might claim the right to marry there is no
person labouring under the obligation or duty to realise this right.
But no matter;  although the formulation may not have universal ap-
plicability it does seem to apply in cases of contract.  The right

to drive away a car bought from a seller is only meaningful if there is a seller with the obligation, once having received money, to surrender the car.  The Engineering Employers sought to benefit from this source of rights when they prevailed upon workers to sign the 'Document' before they could return to work in 1922.  This document purported to take on the semblance of a 'contract' such that the employer would be granted the right to issue instructions, and reciprocally the worker had the 'duty' to conform.

As we have noted, however, the employment contract is a very peculiar sort of contract.  Whereas a car is a recognisable quantity, the purchase of labour does not entail the exchange of a specifiable item.  To a degree this can be overcome by a more detailed job definition:  thus 'X is hired to drive the Number 10 bus around the town', or 'X is hired to build walls for Y'.  But this does not tell us how much effort must be expended.  More problematically, such specificity is double-edged:  it undercuts that essential discretionary quality of the managerial task.  (Though it will be remembered from our narrative that the Mackenzie Report sought even to overcome this by asserting 'the freedom of management to act in the exercise of their discretion'.)  One of the other difficulties raised by philosophers in this regard is, however, something of a red herring.  Thus it has been claimed that:

> One could in theory come to think of the duties of his job as
> deriving from the 'employment contract' and therefore *owed* as
> obligations to the boss as promised.  This was seldom a con-
> vincing myth ... the 'employer' was so vast and nebulous he could
> hardly be conceived as the claimant of a personal obligation
> (Feinberg 1966:140).

This overlooks the concept of the corporate personality and, if acknowledged, it would equally deny the possibility of one company making a contract with another company.  Some philosophers appear not to have come to terms with bureaucracy with its delegation of duties and its hierarchy of command and this kind of limitation seems to arise from an excessive focus on individualism.  Feinberg does, however, raise a more fundamental problem which concerns the asymmetrical nature of the employment contract.  The duty to be bound by a contract normally presupposes that the contract was freely entered into, and, in a market analogy, that the parties could choose to go elsewhere.  Neither proposition of this model accurately reflects the realities of employment relations in modern industrial societies.  In the end, however, the main problem with the 'contract' idea is that the employment contract is normally so open-ended and unspecific.  The unions sought to counter this with the device of the status quo.  But in turn the employers limited this 'temporary veto' to a range of specific issues, and it will be remembered, excluded in 1971, items such as dismissal, redundancy and transfer, from its scope.

(ii)  A second weapon in the armoury of positive (i.e. active) managerial rights derives historically from the concept of 'status'.  Under the medieval social structure, the feudal lord had a right to his serfs' labour by virtue of their respective statuses.  Indeed, the obverse of the lord's rights were the 'dues' of the serfs.  Despite the demise of feudalism certain aspects of the wide-ranging obligations attaching to statuses were preserved in the master-and-

servant relationship which survived under capitalism.  The transition from one mode of production to the other was in the main paralleled by a movement *from status to contract* as the cement of social
relationships.  But, in the sphere of employment in particular, the
actual movement between these pure types has been less clear.  Hence
a peculiar admixture of diverse ideological bases survives.  Where
the contract is unspecific with regard to precise duties (as it
typically will be), management appeal to their status as managers to
determine the order of things.  Golding (1980) reveals how managers
at 'Wenslow Manufacturing' perceived a steady erosion of prerogatives which they believed to have existed from an ill-defined historic state when the sheer status of 'manager' was sufficient to
ensure that an order was obeyed.  Similarly, across the Atlantic,
managers of the Illinois Central Railroad 'regarded working class
rejection of efficiency measures as an encroachment upon managerial
prerogatives' (Palmer 1975:42).  That is, it was perceived not
simply as a breach of contract, or as one measure of efficiency as
against another, but as an outright flouting of legitimate status.
  (iii)  The third and final type of claim to positive managerial
rights of direction derives from a belief that expertise carries
entitlement.  The appeal made here is not to a licence attributable
to ownership, status, the solemnity of tradition, or the respect accorded to elders, but simply to pure pragmatism.  A number of
strands interweave to form this argument.  The case opens with the
perceived need to have a hierarchy of command, given conditions of
large-scale production.  It was a premise Engels found attractive,
as witnessed by his now famous assertion:  'Wanting to abolish
authority in large-scale industry is tantamount to wanting to
abolish industry itself, to destroy the power loom in order to
return to the spinning wheel' (Engels 1969:377).  Managerial prerogative is thus called-up to cope with inescapable organisational
imperatives.  Moreover, not only does this hierarchical division of
labour make sense in its own right (i.e. even if one assumed equal
distribution of talent the separation of tasks in this way would
still be productive) but specialisation enhances expertise.  It is,
however, further argued that, as talent is not in fact equally distributed, a meritocratic system is required so that those endowed
with superior talent will gravitate to commanding positions.  If the
whole community is to enjoy the fruits of their applied talents then
these experts must have their decisions more seriously regarded than
alternative formulations generated by the less gifted.  Failure to
enable this to happen will not only sabotage the particular decision
but will demoralise present incumbents and aspirants, thus negating
incentive.  A prejudicial effect may therefore be wrought on the
quality of future decisions.  To disallow or compromise managerial
prerogatives is thus to threaten the logic of the whole system.
  The defence of managerial rights couched in these terms is therefore an appeal to practicality rather than to moralistic feelings of
duty.  It is assumed that economic growth is a shared objective.
Managers are cast in the role of expert interpreters of a pre-
ordained technology and economic system.  They do not 'rule' for any
particular interest group;  they merely 'serve' by de-coding the
obscure requisites of industrialism.  Obsequiousness to managerial
rights is the price that even a democratic society must pay for the
material benefits which it enjoys.

Modern critics have picked energetically at this skein of arguments.  For example, Kouzmin (1980) seeks to explode the 'enduring
myth of organization and administrative theory ... that a formal
hierarchy of authority is indispensable for co-ordination within
complex organizations' (1980:130).  He questions how much real co-
ordination is achieved by contemporary hierarchies.  In similar vein
Engels has been particularly criticised for failing to differentiate
the conditions under which the exercise of authority can be considered oppressive.  An important distinction in this regard has
been drawn by Marcuse who makes a contrast between rational authority and domination.  The former is inherent in any division of labour
and he conceives of it as serving the advancement of the whole
social unit.  In contrast, domination is wielded 'in order to sustain and advance itself in a privileged position' (Marcuse 1968:45).
Managers' claims to be mere impartial translators of technological
and economic efficiency are rendered suspect by the attack from
Critical Theory on scientism.  The ambivalent defence of managerial
prerogative on the shifting grounds of property rights, and Tayloristic ideology of 'science', has rendered it especially vulnerable
to such attacks.  It was the disentanglement of these strands which
Habermas attempted in 'Toward a Rational Society' (1971).  He points
out that 'technology and science themselves in the form of a common
positivistic way of thinking, articulated as technocratic consciousness, began to take the role of a substitute ideology for the demolished bourgeois ideologies' (1971:115).  Managerial prerogative
as a substitute ideology has veered towards a claim on neutral
rationality of instrumental action.  But it still disguises a system
of domination.  Scientific-technical rationality is not necessarily
incompatible with the liberating potential of Habermas' second type
of rationality - that founded on interaction.  It could indeed serve
it.

# Chapter 7

# THE CONTROL OF WORK

This chapter seeks to explore and explain developments in managerial
control strategies by having recourse to a dialectical approach. (1)
It argues that orthodox organisational analyses and neo-classical
theories of the firm which try to explain current control structures
and devices in terms of technical and administrative imperatives are
misleading and ideological.  It will not, however, be part of the
purpose of this chapter to rehearse the deficiencies of orthodox
accounts of organisational structure.  This task has already been
performed elsewhere (Salaman 1978, 1981;  Kouzmin 1980;  Clegg and
Dunkerley 1980). (2)  Rather, an attempt will be made to move towards the development of a more radically informed and critical account of the patterns and structures of control.  This will draw
upon our earlier reconceptualisation of organisations which depicted
them not as neutral technical systems but as ensembles of formalised
action *designed to secure domination*.  In a neglected publication,
'The Art of Cutting Metals', F.W. Taylor articulates this in his
reference to the 'original objective ... i.e. that of taking the
control of the machine shop out of the hands of the many workmen
and placing it completely in the hands of the management' (cited in
Sohn-Rethel 1976:34).  Taylor re-states the message in his more
famous 'Principles':  'It is only through *enforced* standardization
of methods, *enforced* adoption of the best implements and working
conditions and *enforced* cooperation that this fast work can be assured', he wrote.  'And the duty of enforcing the adoption of standards and enforcing this cooperation rests with *management* alone'
(1911:83).

Work organisations therefore will be viewed as social outcomes
and more specifically as emergent properties of class struggle. (3)
In place of technological determinism our model posits social relationships shaping the technology which is created and which in turn
reacts upon social relations.  The model may be simply denoted thus:
social relations - technological developments - social relations.
This case is argued and developed on the basis of earlier theorising
which distinguished between the categories of labour power and
labour.  It is the essential function of management, it was argued
in chapter 5, to control, that is to translate labour power into
labour and thereby to realise surplus-value.  Steering the labour

process along the straight and narrow of valorisation demands real control to ensure that other substantive objectives do not confound its realisation.  This is accomplished through a variety of strategies and tactics - illustrated by key features of contemporary work organisations such as hierarchy, fragmentation of jobs, disciplinary codes and many other devices.

But while orthodox organisational theory is defective, Marxist theory, too, with regard to this problematic is itself 'not adequately developed' (Gintis 1976:37).  The submergence of the dialectic even in celebrated works such as Braverman's (1974), which treats de-skilling and the real subordination of labour as an incipient tendency, leads to an implicit attribution of a unilinear path for the juggernaut of capital.  All-powerful in the face of Braverman's 'passive and inert working class' (Schwarz 1977:161), capital would find little reason for pursuing variety in control methods.  And yet variety is what research does uncover (Edwards 1975, 1979;  Friedman 1977a and 1977b;  Nichols (ed.) 1980;  Goldman and Van Houten 1977;  Elger and Schwarz 1980;  Zimbalist (ed.) 1979).  Such variety demands attention to strategic choice (Child 1972, 1973).  This measure of choice is interpreted here as impelled by the drive for surplus-value within the dynamic context of labour struggle, fierceness of competition in product markets, capitalisation levels and so on.  These 'contextual' features, in turn, are neither static nor given but are the temporary products of earlier social action.  For example, the capitalisation ratio expresses the strategic substitution of dead labour for living labour.  But there is never absolute free choice at any given point in time.  Organisational 'context' just like organisational 'structure', is an expression of the working-through of contradictions historically and dynamically.  Organising is the processual character of 'organisation' which is a construct to signify a temporary outcome of practical activity.  As such, contexts and structures are always incomplete.  And although *social* products, at any one moment they nevertheless dialectically influence and constrain the strategic choices available at that moment.

Organisational 'structure' and other managerial devices such as rules and disciplining activity, are interpreted then, as strategies of control. (4)  But we are pointing to the variety in such devices and this variety requires explanation.  Essentially this is accounted for here as a product of two interrelated forces.  Organisation at the point of production is the locus of the contradiction between the forces of production and the relations of production.  As Marx observed in 'The Poverty of Philosophy':

The very moment civilization begins, production begins to be founded on the antagonism of orders, estates, classes, and finally on the antagonism of accumulated labour and actual labour.  No antagonism, no progress.  This is the law that civilization has followed up to our days. *Till now the productive forces have been developed by virtue of this system of class antagonisms* (Marx 1955:53).

Thus, the productive forces themselves, which include technology, tools, machines and the organisation of production in forms such as assembly lines, are products of the class struggle and react back dialectically upon the course of that struggle.  This implies change

and variety and it results in uneven development in control systems
(Elbaum and Wilkinson 1979;  Elger 1979).  It may be argued that
this unevenness is something more than 'a comment on the nature of
the competitive system' (Kilpatrick and Lawson 1980:93).  Contradiction does not denote a simple dualism or a metaphysical antinomy,
but a dynamic tension which is worked through and developed in historical time (Heydebrand 1977).  It develops in a processual way
from practical activity.  This activity of social construction does
not therefore produce 'structures' of an entirely rationalistic
character.  Their incompleteness in part expresses a series of 'unintended consequences'. (5)  Real subordination and complete formal
domination are never fully established;  they have always to be
strived for and struggled over.  Moreover, even where they are
nearly established, the very dynamism of capitalism means even this
partial dominance has continually to be re-established (Brighton
Labour Process Group 1977).  This restless search accounts for the
disparity between Henry Ford's $5 day tactic and Frederick Taylor's
dream of destroying common interest through individualised pay.  The
control strategies of industrial relations as argued in chapter 5
blur with general corporate strategy (see also Wood 1980;  Ansoff
1969;  Thurley and Wood forthcoming).  The relative success of
worker militancy in Britain has helped encourage capital development
in other countries such as Korea and Spain where labour costs are
lower and a more docile workforce is available, at least for the
moment (Kilpatrick and Lawson 1980;  Elbaum and Wilkinson 1979). (6)
Hence, of at least equal importance with Ford's disciplinary code
strategy at Halewood must be the extra room for manoeuvre the company gains by secretly deciding to replicate the building of the new
Ford Escort in Spain. (7)
    Moreover, not only is there a variety of control strategies be-
tween organisations, but there is within organisations a 'frequently
changing corporate structure ... to solve the problem of labour control' argues Maarten de Kadt (1976:19).  Based on his own experience
as an 'executive' in a large insurance company in North America, de
Kadt traces the shifting structural formations including divisionalisation, centralisation and departmentalisation which have been
and are used to deal with the labour problem.  Like De Lorean, de
Kadt joins the ranks of those 'blowing the whistle' on top management strategic thinking.  Works like these illuminating the functioning of organisational hierarchy (Stone 1974;  Marglin 1974;
Clawson 1980) and wider features of corporate structuring (Chandler
1962;  Channon 1973) should serve to emphasise the arbitrariness of
restricting a work control survey merely to the shopfloor labour
process.  De Kadt (1976) extends Chandler's (1962) analysis of
divisionalisation and other strategies whereby 'managers manage
other managers' (as pioneered by du Pont and General Motors, Standard Oil and Sears Roebuck) so that he can develop the explicit link
between corporate re-organisation and the control of labour.
    In addition to this point on the *organisational* level of control,
it is necessary to extend analysis even further in order to note
that control at the point of production must not be treated in isolation from the wider *totality*.  Partiality of this kind was and is
one of the key problems in orthodox managerialist analyses of organisations.  A view of organisational activity as merely expressing

technical problems and therefore missing the political element is
bound to be partial.  While Marxists have tended to neglect the
administrative control aspects of the labour process, scholars operating within what they take to be the Weberian tradition have in
contrast focused in blinkered fashion on bureaucratic devices to the
exclusion of societal contradictions of which these are but a part.
Braverman helped to remedy the neglect of the labour process, but
the intimate interrelationship between this and wider political and
cultural institutions was not sufficiently developed.  There are
examples, however, illustrating how characteristic features of the
capitalist labour process 'spill over' into wider cultural formations and how these in turn react upon the labour process.  Thus
Michael Chanan (1980, 1976) describes how capitalist priorities in
the labour process of film production, where capital tries to reduce
aesthetic labour to the status of ordinary wage labour, are mirrored
in the organisation of film production and in the final product.
Hence the owners use studio conditions to reduce films to genres and
standardised types which can be bought off-the-peg.  The constraints
on aesthetic objectives are at once a consequence of the capitalist
system of production and also designed to promote these conditions
(Chanan 1976:11).

The class struggle proceeds both at and beyond the point of production.  Continued appropriation of surplus-value requires reproduction of labour power in the cultural and political spheres.
These latter aspects have been fruitfully explored by Lazonick
(1977, 1978), Gintis (1976) and by Bowles and Gintis (1976).  Meanwhile, the dual focus on the point of production and the wider
social setting has perhaps been confronted best by Richard Edwards
(1972, 1975, 1979) and Edwards et al. (eds) (1975).  Edwards tackles
directly the farrago of control strategies used by employers and
relates these to the labour markets which are created and to the
wider capitalist system.

Overall, we are suggesting a dialectical approach to the interpretation of control.  Using the three sub-categories outlined
earlier - contradiction, social construction and totality - the
implications of such an approach may now be summarised.  The essential contradiction is that between the forces and relations of production.  In order to realise surplus-value, the agents of capital
must extract real labour from its potential form, labour power.  The
exploitative social relations established for this purpose militate
against the realisation of the full productive potential within the
forces of production.  Equally, the development of productive forces
is inhibited by the distorted social relations.  The dynamics of
these relations are but one part of a wider totality of antagonistic
relationships and institutions.  The agents of capital seek to construct ever more sophisticated strategies and technologies to surmount the resistance of labour.  But for a variety of reasons the
strategies are far from complete and the complex social processes
lead to the uneven development in control systems which research has
uncovered.  Accordingly, the purpose of the remainder of this chapter is to explore and explain more fully the social dynamics of the
*variegated* control strategies.

Managerial and employer control devices and systems have developed somewhat fitfully and unevenly over the last couple of centuries.

The complexity of the path and the variety of forms have been revealed more fully in Williamson (1975, 1980) and Chandler (1977)
than in Braverman's more simplistic account.  A schematic history
of developments in institutional arrangements and structures of control which management have used to maintain suzerainty over labour
is provided by Gospel (1981).  He explains how the putting-out
system had its advantages for the merchant in minimising capital
outlay, spreading risk, providing flexibility and avoiding the costs
and trouble of maintaining a workforce.  The over-concentration by
Marglin on the control advantages of the factory are also noted.
And on the point of variety of control systems, Gospel emphasises
that the putting-out system continued to exist side by side with
factory organisation.  Of note is that the extent of this varied
by sector.  For example in footwear, frame-knitting and some metal
trades, it continued into the mid-nineteenth century and in some
parts of the clothing industry it survives of course to the present
day.

   Significantly too, the factory did not coincide with direct control.  The insider-contracting system flourished into the twentieth
century.  Similar to it was the 'helper system' wherein a craftsman
hired assistants and paid them from his own earnings.  Again, both
systems frequently existed alongside direct methods of management.
Unevenness was once more a feature.  Various forms of sub-contractor
and helper systems existed in the coalfields well into the inter-war
years, in the car industry in the 1920s (Gospel 1981:9), and it
still survives in the building industry.  Even for direct forms of
control, the rationalised Taylor system was far from being the only
one in the 1920s and 1930s.  The 'bowler-hatted foreman' was a
formidable independent figure who could hire, fire and exercise
considerable dictatorial powers over labour in his own right.  And
at the other end of the scale employers evaded the responsibility of
controlling labour by shedding as much as possible on to employers' organisations:

   In a sense employers were subcontracting labour management to external organizations.  Top management came to rely on their associations, just as they relied on foremen, as a way of avoiding
   direct handling of labour matters.  This undoubtedly slowed down
   the development of internal management structures and enterprise-
   based industrial relations strategies (Gospel 1981:15).

   Increasingly, however, as enterprises grew in size and hierarchies lengthened, production managers, assisted in their different
ways by accountants and other staff, took more responsibility for
labour control.  And gradually welfare workers-cum-labour managers-
cum-personnel managers developed their position (Niven 1967;
Crichton 1968;  Watson 1977).  An associated factor of merger, takeover and growth was the multi-unit enterprise.  Corporate strategy
frequently dictated highly centralised financial control with a decentralised labour-management function (de Kadt 1976;  Chandler
1962;  Chanan 1973).  As Gospel (1981:20) points out, 'For senior
managers in the parent companies, especially where they might have
come from finance-capital backgrounds, it was easier to delegate
local labour responsibilities to former owners and their local managers' (Gospel 1981:20).  But some companies did centralise across
a much wider range of functions.  In Britain the most notable ex-

amples were ICI, Unilever and Dunlop.  Each of these developed centralised strategies and structures in the 1930s and 1940s.  Again,
the point to observe, however, is that these were mainly special
cases.  As Hannah (1980:53) observes, there were only a dozen such
firms by 1948.  Meanwhile in the United States a few key firms such
as GM, du Pont and Standard Oil were pioneering *de*centralised multi-
departmental structures and the corporate strategy of divisionalisation (de Kadt 1976;  Chandler 1962).  The strategic choice of a
centralised labour management function was made by ICI as early as
1927, and by the 1930s it was working on a uniform centrally administered wage structure (Gospel 1981).  As is widely known, the
rash of productivity bargaining in the 1960s precipitated a more
general move back to decentralised systems.  But once more in the
1970s and 1980s a centralising mood, typified by BL's activities,
has reversed the pendulum.

Overall, this survey emphasises the variety of structures and
strategies.  Moreover, it contests any notion of an incipient tendency towards an evolving pattern.  Variations between firms and
sectors are revealed;  variation within sectors is also uncovered;
and oscillation over time is seen to occur at all levels.  Finally,
to attempt to interpret à la Marglin these 'strategic moves' as
driven by the sole or even predominant purpose of securing greater
control over labour seems misguided.  Undoubtedly this would be one
objective of managerial strategy and structuring, but it would not
seem to be the primary, still less the only, one.  If the ensuing
discussion of the *variety* of contemporary control devices is to be
attempted within a dialectical framework, then attention must be
directed to their inherent contradictions, their relationship to
worker resistance, their 'choice' by employers, and their relation
to the wider totality.  It will be recalled from chapter 5 that
'control' is to be regarded in the wide sense:  encompassing the
whole cycle from planning, designing, directing and monitoring to
appraising, rewarding and taking corrective action.  I argue therefore that it is necessary to direct attention beyond the specifically titled personnel or labour relations managers if one is adequately to come to terms with labour control.  The circumscription of the
standard texts on this matter requires correction.  It will for example be fruitful to consider the implications of the work of management accountants and industrial engineers.  Each of these should
be subjected to rather searching scrutiny because they help to formulate strategy and structure in ways which impact forcibly on the
labour process.  The complete cycle of control from planning to monitoring and correcting is influenced by both of these functionaries.
Hence, whilst it is argued that it is wrong to adopt an 'over-
rationalised' conception of managers and management strategy, it
should be remembered that management nevertheless does have privileged institutionalised access to the levers of power.  The managerial ensemble of control strategies may be conceptualised as comprising simultaneous action on the two fronts of social relations
of production and the forces of production.  This involves manipulating (a) social relations - through, for example, the labelling
and social construction of deviance in order to discipline;  and
through the formalisation, standardisation and monopolisation of
information. (8)  Action on (b), the forces of production, is ef-

fectuated through the material means of production, for example, by
manipulating technology and the organisation of production.  The
relationship between worker and the means of production is 'inverted' under capitalism so that as far as possible the means of
production control the worker rather than vice versa.  Each area
is considered in the ensuing sections. (9)


DISCIPLINE

Discipline as a control device carries each of the three dialectical
aspects we have been noting.  Par excellence it illustrates through
labelling theory the phenomenon of social construction;  second, it
will be seen to be intimately bound to the wider totality and in
consequence its changing nature may be linked to the maturation of
capitalist society;  third, the unitary tenets on which a disciplining agent rests will be seen to be in contradiction with the plural-
istic assumptions of modern industrial relations.

From a work control perspective the essential point to note concerning discipline relates to the strategic attempts socially to
construct a dominant definition of reality whereby acts of challenge, recalcitrance, and resistance routinely attract a label of
culpable transgression.  Managers as agents, loosely and problematically 'mandated' to define and treat individual acts of deviance,
are thereby put in possession of a potentially potent control
device.  It is hardly surprising therefore that discipline perhaps
more than any other managerial 'right' or 'function' has revealed
the fundamental contradictions in liberal pluralism and in the
general strategy to institutionalise industrial conflict.

Pluralists argue that discipline 'ought not to be seen strictly
as a matter of managerial prerogative in which employees and their
representatives are allowed no say' (Ashdown and Baker 1973:49).
It is maintained that it is in the employer's own best interest to
secure joint agreement with trade unions on discipline.  Conversely,
discipline can be seen as the sine qua non of the managerial function.  As Harbison and Myers put it, the logic of industrialisation
'impels the employer to covet the role of rule-maker ... it requires
that workers take orders from management';  indeed the very raison
d'être or 'prerogative of management is to prescribe duties, assign
tasks, and get satisfactory performance.  For this it needs discipline' (Harbison and Myers 1959:48).  Today, of course, there are
some well-publicised restrictions on that 'coveted' role.  Both the
Trade Union and Labour Relations Act and the Employers' Protection
Act contain provisions to this effect.  Employers must furnish a
written statement giving the reasons for dismissal and the employee
has a right not to be 'unfairly dismissed'.  The onus falls on the
employer to demonstrate that there is a substantial reason for any
dismissal.  But, despite the imbroglio of regulations, it is important to note that in practice the impact of such legislation has
been much exaggerated.  The largest percentage of cases reaching the
Industrial Tribunals are from small, non-unionised firms.  In 1977
two-thirds of successful applicants received less than the equivalent of six weeks' wages and only one half of a percent were in fact
reinstated.

While management may 'covet' the disciplinary function as in the
last analysis essential to its role, the possession of this capacity
unilaterally to sanction is in some tension with the legitimacy it
seeks from pluralist doctrine.  Authority to discipline is a delicate plant requiring tender care.  In pursuit of its nurture, capital and state have devised formal procedures, a Code of Practice,
and Industrial Tribunals.  An illustration may be had by reference
to the ACAS Code on Disciplinary Practice and Procedures (1977a).
This appears unequivocal in its declaration that 'management is responsible for maintaining discipline'.  'However', it adds, rules
'need to be accepted as reasonable ... management should therefore
aim to secure the involvement of employees ...' (1977:2).  Again,
notice the pluralist position:  responsibility lies in management
hands, but it will find it pragmatically advantageous to 'involve'
unions and employees and to 'win' their co-operation in order to be
able to 'manage by agreement'.  To assist in this the Code provides
practical advice such as alerting employees to the rules, drawing up
a known systematic procedure, allowing for appeals, and stressing
that the essential objective should be not to impose sanctions but
to 'encourage improvements in individual conduct' (1977:3).  The
corrective philosophy is thus codified.

The conventional wisdom in the fields of labour law and personnel management suggests that since the early 1970s there has been
a shift from an older 'punitive' approach to discipline, to a
more modern, enlightened, 'corrective' orientation (Anderman 1972;
Ashdown and Baker 1973;  Freedland 1975;  Mellish and Collis-Squires
1976).  The punitive approach is said to have been characterised by
harsh and often arbitrarily imposed penalties.  These were invoked
for what would now often be regarded as trivial 'offences'.  In
Marshall's flax mills in 1821 'so strict are the instructions that
if an overseer of a room be found talking to any person in the mill
during working hours he is dismissed immediately' (cited in Ashdown
and Baber 1973:5).  A list of Mill Rules posted by a Haslingdon firm
in 1851 stipulated the following regulations and penalties:
> For any bobbins found on the floor, 1d for each bobbin;  for
> waste on the floor 2d;  any person leaving his work and found
> talking with any of the other workpeople shall be fined 2d for
> each offence;  all persons in our employ shall serve four weeks
> notice before leaving their employ, but the proprietors shall and
> will turn any person off without notice being given;  any person
> wilfully damaging this notice will be dismissed (Hopkin 1969:31).
The harsh abuses of the factory system have been well chronicled
(Hammond and Hammond 1925;  Hobsbawm 1968;  Thompson 1967, 1968;
Wing 1837).  'Discipline' included the beating of children (it was
noted earlier that spinners were male not because of special skill
but because of their physical capacity to control women and children).  Evidence of corporal punishment was attested before Sadler's
Parliamentary committee of enquiry (Wing 1837:9).  The Hammonds
noted that the beatings were often administered by workpeople themselves - often on their own children - a cruelty they attributed to
the heinous compulsion of the system (Hammond and Hammond 1925:33).

In contrast, the 'corrective' approach is said to be enlightened
and to effect a shift from retribution to education and reform.  The
basic tenet of the corrective approach rests on a formalisation of a

procedure which codifies the list of offences and penalties.  In
addition, the procedure should be jointly agreed, well-publicised
and fully understood.  A characteristic feature is the recommended
series of unambiguous written warnings.  Accordingly, a recent
article in 'Administrative Management' entitled The Delicate Art of
Firing, while reaffirming that firing like hiring and promotion and
other employment decisions 'is a management prerogative', nevertheless stresses the *cost-effectiveness* of constructing a 'paper trail'
of events leading to the actual firing (Hubbartt 1981:23).  Further
tenets of the 'corrective' approach include a careful investigation
of facts and an opportunity for appeal (Industrial Society 1978;
Incomes Data Services Handbook 1979;  ACAS Code of Practice 1977).

Radical analysts, however, have mounted a critique of accounts
such as these which postulate a newly emergent corrective approach.
Mellish and Collis-Squires (1976) for example, identify four problems in the 'reformist' literature:  an over-emphasis on procedure;
the assumed advantages of formalised procedures;  a managerialist
bias;  and the separation of discipline from wider aspects of control which 'as a result individualises what can be a collective
issue' (1976:167).  These elements might usefully have been more
coherently related. (10)  Scope for this resides in the last theme:
the others may be regarded as essentially tactics in its service.
However, in their 'alternative view' the authors fairly state their
case, namely 'that what is a disciplinary issue depends in part on
what management care to treat as such', it is also contingent upon
'whether employees collectively allow an issue to be treated as an
individual one' (1976:172).  The dialectical nature of discipline
as a control device is here made plain.

An additional gloss is furnished by Henry (1981).  He suggests
that, rather than interpreting recent manoeuvring as in continuity
with age-old conflict, the changes of the last decade or so should
be seen as signalling a more subtle alteration 'in the technology of
industrial social control' (1981:2).  He seeks to emphasise the
ideological aspect of discipline.  The keynote is taken from
Foucault (1977:215) who maintains:

> Discipline ... is a type of power, a modality for its exercise
> comprising a whole set of instruments, techniques, procedures,
> levels of application, targets;  it is a 'physics' or an anatomy
> of power, a technology (Foucault, cited in Henry 1981:1).

Accordingly, rather than shrugging off the 'new discipline' as mere
business as usual, this line of analysis suggests that, far from
being a minor component of work control, discipline should be regarded as a pervasive social technology underlying the continued
existence of capital's hegemony (Foucault 1977;  Melossi 1979;
Henry 1981).

This argument that discipline is no mere minor component of the
total battery of control devices but rather should be seen as inextricably woven into the whole fabric of social control, is given
extra credence by F.W. Taylor himself.  He astutely observed that
if a worker is baldly ordered to produce

> fifty per cent more pieces than he has in the past ... (it would)
> therefore be assumed by most people that he must work fifty per
> cent harder.  In this issue the union is more likely to have the
> sympathy of the general public, and they can logically take it up

and fight upon it.  If, however, the workman is given a series of
plain, simple and reasonable orders, and is offered a premium for
carrying them out, the union will have a much more difficult task
in defending the man who *disobeys* them (quoted in Clawson 1980:
12).

The ultimate 'technology of discipline' Foucault fround in Jeremy
Bentham's panopticon - the model architectural plan for a circular
prison with cells surrounding a central control point.  This allows
total surveillance.  Never knowing when they are actually being
watched, the inmates trim their behaviour to the assumption that
they are always watched.  They are 'caught up in a power situation
of which they themselves are the bearers' (Foucault 1977:201).  As
John Lea (1979) notes, the panopticon can be considered as a paradigm case of a type of control.  But factory control does not rely
on this particular manifestation.  The competitive market can be
seen as a 'sort of decentralized panopticon' (1979:79), i.e. finding
an equivalent in the knowledge carried by the bearer that his commodity (labour power) can be replaced by another. (11)  Thus the
capitalist is not prepared to meet the costs of total surveillance,
so the direct analogy of prison and factory breaks down.  And, nor
does he need to meet these costs because of the constraining force
of the labour market stiffened as it is by the weight of the industrial reserve army.  But the dialectical presence emerges with the
maturation of capitalism.  It may be hypothesised that the modern
system of capital accumulation based on relative surplus-value
increases 'the autonomous space available to the workers to further
distance the factory and factory life from anything approaching
panopticon' (Lea 1979:84).  In support evidence can be marshalled such as the use of automatic technology which frees the worker's mind to speculate upon his predicament and the increasing
reliance of capital on economic compulsion rather than direct
physical discipline.  This economic emphasis provides the basis for
reformism as the ideology for the labour movement.  The posited
'evolution of discipline' departs from an Orwellian State.  At best
- or rather at worst - the state under this scenario maintains only
a rudimentary and highly partial surveillance system standing 'in
readiness should the unstable parameters of monetization break down'
(Lea 1979:88).

In the main the same analysis is made by Melossi (1979), who
points out developments under the new structure of monopoly capitalism.  He argues that Marx's 'two spheres' - the sphere of circulation and the sphere of production - are increasingly occluded as
social control extends from the factory to permeate urban society.
Advertising, the mass media, the welfare state apparatus and more
subtle alternatives to incarceration such as probation and police
surveillance are instanced as expressions of this development of
the 'new discipline'.

Thus do contemporary deviance theorists expand the concept of
discipline.  Following Foucault, they identify it as 'neither an
institution nor an apparatus; it is a type of power'.  This type of
power is seen to develop with the changing nature of capitalism;  it
is a totality.

Even the more conventional analyses of the concept of 'discipline' are predicated upon the prior existence of social *rules*.

'Self-discipline', for example, implies behaviour in accord with rule.  To engage in active *disciplining* suggests that some infraction of a pre-existing rule has occurred.  Linking discipline to rules in this way helps to point up the control aspect, because the origin, nature and purpose of rules then become subject to public gaze.  It is clear from historical studies that work rules were designed to deal with a recalcitrant and fractious workforce.  Thus Josiah Wedgwood complained of 'slothful workmen' and Taylor complained of 'systematic soldiering' (McKendrick 1961;  Goldman and van Houten 1977;  Merkle 1968).  Given that discipline was targeted at such 'problems', it is evident that the line between it and the more general political issue of extracting surplus-value is, to say the least, blurred.  This is not, however, to be mistaken for the assumption that ruled governance was directed at maximising efficient operations.  As a number of studies have demonstrated, workers may need to violate rules in order to work more efficiently (see, for example, Bill Watson 1972).  And the obverse of this same coin is that workers may, as a sanction of their own, decide to 'work to rule'.  Or, rules may be used simply as a defence (Crozier 1964; Merton 1949).

Accordingly, discipline can be seen as a pervasive control device inextricably bound-up with the wider politics of work control, (12) but at the same time it too is subject to inherent contradictions. There is some difficulty in reconciling an irrevocable attachment to what is in the last analysis an employer-imposed discipline with the now widely held pluralist conceptualisation of industrial relations. The coalition model of the work organisation based on the idea of multiple interest groups legitimately pursuing their separate interests does not square easily with the idea of one of those groups having the right and responsibility to assume a superior position. The belief that ultimately 'management is responsible for maintaining discipline' invokes the unitary ideology that one party has the special moral and legal authority to designate and punish certain classes of action as 'misdemeanours', and that this is to be regarded not as imposing industrial sanctions but as merely applying 'penalties'.  Ideally, it *would* be 'cost effective' to secure joint agreement and to follow formal procedures (one may recall the discussion on 'cultivating authority' in chapter 4) but with or without that agreement, it is management which in the last analysis is going to be the agent *doing* the 'disciplining', management is not to be the party receiving it.


THE VARIETY OF CONTROL STRATEGIES

In addition to simple direct control and discipline there is a whole battery of control devices at managerial disposal.  This variety has led to analytical schemes which posit 'trends' in control patterns (Palloix 1976;  Braverman 1974;  Kynaston-Reeves and Woodward 1970; Offe 1976a) and it has alternatively led to attempts to account for contemporaneous uneven development in extant control strategies (Friedman 1977a, 1977b;  Edwards 1975, 1979).  Both types of endeavour, whether discerning general trends or unevenness, typically take as their prime referent the rationalised control structure

known as bureaucracy.  The key dimensions of bureaucracy - hierarchy, specialisation and division of labour, impersonality and
formalised rules - are expressive of its essential control function.
Accordingly, Salaman is able to observe, 'organizations are structures of control' (1981:143).  I am not proposing here to review
bureaucratic control per se as this has already been accomplished
elsewhere (Salaman 1981;  Clegg and Dunkerley 1980;  Mouzelis 1975;
Edwards 1979 and Albrow 1970).  Rather, in order to draw out the
point concerning managerial strategic choice, it is more appropriate
to consider the *alternative* control systems that exist within and
perhaps even beyond bureaucracy.  An explanation of the need to
resort to such alternatives might well be the contradiction between
formal rationality and worker resistance, as well as that between
the limits to innovation and flexibility implied by formalisation
and the adaptability required during the labour process.

ALTERNATIVES WITHIN BUREAUCRACY

Weber's writing gives the impression that bureaucracy is a unitary
whole.  However, as subsequent research has shown, bureaucracy as an
umbrella or generic term disguises the fact that within its embrace
may lie *alternative* control structures.  Primarily we should note
that centralisation (i.e. where all important decisions have to be
posted vertically up the hierarchy) may exist independently of a
control structure resting on formalisation (i.e. the resort to known
set procedures and regulations particularly of a written kind).  The
consequence is that an organisation which appears to be highly decentralised and perhaps less bureaucratic may in fact be highly
regulated because it relies heavily upon formalised procedures and
tightly drawn rules.
     Recent empirical and theoretical work has substantiated the view
that Weber's bureaucratic characteristics are not necessarily mutually dependent.  On the contrary, Stinchcombe (1970), Gouldner
(1954), Udy (1959), and Constas (1958), suggest that they represent
potentially alternative modes of control.  Stanley Udy recast the
specific characteristics and found that whilst some were positively
associated, others were actually negatively related.  He found three
bureaucratic specifics which did co-vary, these were hierarchy, the
presence of an administrative staff, and differential rewards according to office.  But this cluster was not associated with another
group of characteristics which he termed 'rational elements'.  I am
not concerned here with the labels he attached, nor with the hypothesis which he and another writer, Constas (1958) posited, i.e.
that there is in fact an opposition between 'bureaucratic' and
'rational' elements (although this again points to the contradiction
inherent in formalised control systems).  Rather, our present purpose is to note that even within the apparently unitary mode of
control commonly known as bureaucracy, some variation of control
patterns is possible.  This can mean the option to choose different
types of bureaucracy at *different* times (as exemplified in Gouldner's (1954) study) or, the choice of alternative control systems
within an organisation at the *same* time (hence a large construction
company may have a formal bureaucratic core and yet may also utilise

the labour-only sub-contracting system known as the 'lump' (Austin 1980).  This point may also be illustrated by reference to Gould-ner's (1954) 'Patterns of Industrial Bureaucracy'.  He delineates three types:  punishment-centred, representative and mock bureau-cracy.  The dynamic pattern of change traced by Gouldner at the gypsum plant suggests that a unilinear 'trend' is less convincing than a dialectical model which allows for oscillations in control strategies:  between tight routine and indulgency depending upon the level of activation of conflictual relations, which in turn, may rest upon management's interpretation of wider economic variables.

Pugh, Hickson and Hinings (1969) also provide evidence of 'varie-ties of bureaucracy'.  They distinguished between 'workflow bureau-cracy' and 'personnel bureaucracy'.  Under workflow bureaucracy management rely on impersonal control mechanisms such as formalised routines and procedures and the specialisation and delineation of roles.  Under personnel bureaucracy there is little formal struc-turing but instead managers resort to direction and surveillance, a strategy which is based upon a functioning and active hierarchy of command.

Again the point being stressed here is not that there is some-thing inherently conflictual between the various Weberian dimensions of bureaucracy (pace Udy) but rather that strategic controllers of work organisations have at their disposal even within the bureau-cratic mode, a range of control devices.  But the armoury does not of course stop there.  There are a range of control strategies which breach and therefore go beyond what is normally taken to be the bureaucratic.  They are not necessarily 'softer' because of that.  Indeed, if one follows Blau and Schoenherr (1971), it would be said that these non-(or less) bureaucratic 'insidious' forms of control are in fact more deadly in their embrace.  Significantly it is also frequently claimed that these 'new forms' of control are displacing the more longstanding bureaucratic forms.  Occasionally this is alternatively expressed prescriptively, that is, they should replace bureaucracy because the latter is outdated, inhumane or inefficient.

A whole collection of writers on organisations have adopted a bimodal framework in order to contrast bureaucracy with some al-legedly new form.  Thus Friedman's (1977a) direct control versus autonomous responsibility echoes an earlier litany which, inter alia, includes McGregor's theory X and theory Y, Likert's authorita-tive versus participative modes, Burns and Stalker's mechanistic versus organic, and Sofer's rigid versus flexible organisations.  Indeed, such dichotomies are so replete within the organisations literature, as to lend credence to Hickson's (1966) observation of a 'convergence in organization theory'.  The essential contrast is between low-discretion, rule-bound, hierarchical organisations versus high-discretion, low-specificity, decentralised modes.

Unlike many of the authors cited, we are not here concerned with which form is more 'efficient' under current conditions of alien-ation.  Rather, the dynamic of those control strategies which are apparently non-bureaucratic in character is the focus of attention.  This point may be illustrated by reference to Stinchcombe (1970), who contrasts bureaucratic and 'craft' administration of production, the former being treated as but one 'sub-type of rational adminis-tration' (1970:262).  He compares the centralised planning and

direct control characteristic of bureaucracy with the autonomy he
found on American construction sites.  In such locations, he argues,
control of pace, skill, and operative decisions (all three of which
he describes as the essential components of industrial discipline
anywhere) are more economically and rationally left to professional-
ly maintained occupational standards.  Using as a key index of
bureaucratic control the proportion of persons in the authority
structure who have 'special communication-processing positions'
(i.e. mainly typists, filing clerks, book-keepers and others who
process communications but do not initiate them), he finds that
whereas such persons comprise 63 per cent of administrative personnel in motor manufacture, the corresponding figure is only 20 per
cent in the case of construction.  The importance of this difference
is that these people are the ones who facilitate the control and
planning of work in large organisations and allow the close control
of the work process.  The important difference between the two control systems, and one that links back to the deskilling debate, concerns the type of administrative staff employed.  Stinchcombe finds
that in bureaucratised manufacturing the action-originators are
professionalised personnel who plan tasks and set standards thereby
removing these functions from the work crews.  Conversely, in construction he finds these facets of the job are more typically decentralised to the craft or foreman level.  Stinchcombe's illumination of the option of operating this alternative form of control
system in the construction industry might be open to the objection
that this industry presents a very special case and that large-scale
manufacturing industry would find bureaucracy to be technically indispensable.  But Clawson (1980) refutes such a suggestion.  He
meticulously traces the operation and demise of the 'insider contracting' craft system between 1860-1920.  Evidence is marshalled
to demonstrate that large-scale production did occur, and is therefore feasible, using this non-bureaucratic system.  Singer Sewing
Machine Company and Winchester Rifles, for example, each had plants
with over 2,000 workers apiece before 1900.  Output was also high
with Singer turning out 350,000 machines a year in the 1870s.  The
crucial point emerging from Clawson's work is that it suggests considerable *choice* of organisational form is possible and was indeed
exercised.  Now, he is not merely saying that social groups could
choose between a viable but not quite so technically efficient old
system, and an alienating but more technically efficient modern
system.  Rather, he maintains that bureaucracy is not technically
inevitable or superior.  It was introduced to advance the scope for
control;  it is thus an expression of class struggle.

Yet, whilst many of these writers appear to adopt an evangelical
mission to shift organisational structures from the mechanistic and
bureaucratic towards more flexible autonomous forms, Blau and
Schoenherr sound an insistent warning about the nature of the 'new
forms of power'.  The overt rules and sanctions of 'old fashioned
bureaucratic power' are replaced by perfidious devices such as
highly selective recruitment of conformist personnel.  This is
exemplified par excellence by W.H. Whyte's (1956) 'Organisation Man'
whose personality, dispositions, beliefs and family circumstances
are thoroughly screened during recruitment.  Where personnel are
hired who possess technical knowledge and an internalised obligation

to perform as management would wish, then crude direct controls can
be (at least partly) relinquished.  Recruitment of such 'pre-
programmed' personnel casts control into an indirect form.  Stinchcombe's work, above, indicated how 'craft lore' could reduce the
need for an administrative superstructure, but Blau and Schoenherr
seem to have in mind the recruitment of 'professional' workers in
high technology industries - personnel whose commitment to their
narrow specialism ensures that their efforts, although inner-direct-
ed, can be utilised by organisational controllers.  To date, shopfloor recruitment has not lent itself easily to this device although
employer blacklists represent a tentative step, and legislative
regulations on dismissal may engender a generally more cautious and
searching recruitment process in order to screen out potential re-
calcitrants.

An equally important indirect mode of control is the strategic
allocation of resources and personnel.  The importance of a venture
can be predetermined by the way the central planner distributes the
amount of funds, and the status of the persons he allocates to the
project.  Similarly, the setting of target dates which foreclose
further 'search' processes prior to a decision can additionally influence the outcome. (13)  The allocation device has been described
as 'the ultimate mechanism of organizational control' (Blau and
Schoenherr 1973:17).  We will have occasion to probe it somewhat
more deeply when accountancy control systems are examined.

A further subtle control device is the use of incentive systems
and performance reviews.  Payment-by-result schemes have long been
part of the arsenal of scientific management, but these can be
exercised in more disguised form.  Promotions and re-grading may be
tied to statistical records of performance;  operatives may be required to complete their own performance record sheets and these can
even form the basis of a certain degree of competition.  One of the
light assembly areas I examined in an engineering factory had the
practice whereby operatives (mainly female) were obliged to record
the number of 'jobs' completed.  It was considered a stigma to
finish the day with less than half the record sheet filled-in.  At
the opposite end of the scale there appeared to be little group
pressure to restrict output.  Performance review techniques at managerial level may assume a more 'participative' guise.  Thus under
management-by-objectives the individual is party to the forward commitment and partakes in a post mortem to discern the adequacy of the
actual performance.  The subject may even be party to refining the
surveillance and monitoring devices.  Control is thereby likely to
be enhanced next time around.

The net result which arises from the deployment of each or any
of the above indirect control methods is that although less rule-
bound, control may in effect not be diminished but heightened.  Thus
we are confronted with Blau and Schoenherr's famous paradox, 'we
today are freer from coercion through the power of command of superiors than most people have been, yet men in positions of power
today probably exercise more control than any tyrant ever has'.
(1971:13).  An expression of this 'new form of power' exists under
the label 'social technology'.

SOCIAL TECHNOLOGY

There is in fact no unproblematic label to cover the bundle of strategies normally embraced by terms like 'human relations', 'neo-human
relations', 'neo-Fordism' (Palloix 1976), or 'social technology'.
The latter is indicative of the control function we wish to emphasise but a drawback is that it implies other forms of technology are
somehow not 'social'.  However, by this term I mean to indicate the
standard human relations techniques which seek to channel the dynamics of inter-personal relations towards the serving of managerial
ends, and also the neo-human devices which offer a mite more latitude to find ways of meeting centrally determined goals.  Furthermore the label can be deployed to include attempts to use job en-
largement, job enrichment, and devices such as 'quality circles' to
integrate the rank and file into managerial values and purposes.
(14)  These all aim to trade marginal improvements in repetitive
jobs for a strengthening of managerial legitimacy (see Fox 1974b;
Poole 1975).  Also classifiable under the control approach to interpreting social technology are the various participation devices and
even, in a way, collective bargaining itself which, provided it is
'managed' correctly, can be used as a means towards legitimising
managerial actions and securing union incorporation (Nichols and
Beynon 1977;  Elliott 1976).  Having made that point, equally what
should not be ignored is the opposition to unions found among employers.  The Grunwick incident indicates the lengths to which this
opposition may be taken.  Donald Roy (1980) graphically describes
the deployment of 'fear stuff, sweet stuff and evil stuff' in an
attempt to keep unions out of the American South.  These kind of
strategies are too easily overlooked and forgotten by those who
overly concentrate on neo-human relations experiments or glibly
talk of union 'incorporation'.

   It is not necessary here to review the range of arguments but
certain points must be emphasised, for, as managerial control systems become increasingly all-embracing, sophisticated and impersonal, so too does the reconciliation of the workforce to its tasks
demand increasingly urgent reappraisal.  The control systems which
take care of economic/technical systems integration tend to pay but
little regard to what sociologists call 'social integration' (Lockwood 1964).  Human relations strategies set out to remedy this situation.

   The tenets of human relations seem to proffer a felicitous con-
gruence between worker satisfaction and the securement of managerial
objectives.  The link registering in managerial minds is that which
tantalisingly loops between:  a more 'satisfied' workforce, higher
morale, higher output, and more profit.  Pre-eminent among popular
tantalisers are Fred Herzberg, Rensis Likert and Douglas McGregor.
The 'human resource-management' packages they offer extol the virtues of various participatory schemes which seek to channel energy
into managerially defined directions.  Theory Y, Blake's managerial
grid, the use of T-Groups and job enrichment, have all formed part
of the lexicon of any even half-fashionable personnel manager.  'Job
Enrichment Pays-Off' announces Herzberg (1969) confidently.  It implies a concern not just with *job context* (such as working conditions and pay) but also *job content*.  Perhaps Human Resource Manage-

ment spokesman should be credited with leading the renaissance of
interest in the labour process!

A cognate development, and one directly pertinent to the issues
of control and prerogative, is that of 'group working schemes' or
so-called autonomous work groups.  The more advanced forms may be
responsible for their own organisation of work - the allocation of
tasks, self-supervision, discipline, examining, quality control and
ensuring adequate service operations.  As a result, they are said to
reduce indirect labour, supervision and inspection.  They should
produce more versatile and flexible working arrangements thus speed-
ing-up workflows and securing lower levels of work-in-progress.  A
'highly-successful' example of group-working has been reported at
the Emcar clothing factory in East Anglia.  It employs about 200
people making a wide range of garments on small production-runs requiring the use of a number of fabrics and machines, thus placing a
premium on versatility.  Groups were established under guidance from
the Industrial Training Research Unit in Cambridge.  Lower indirect
costs, lower labour turnover and less absenteeism were sufficient to
prompt the extension of self-organised work groups throughout the
factory in 1975.  This move 'from closely supervised section working
to self-directing groups has had a major impact upon the factory and
relationships within it' (Pearcey 1977).  Benefits to management
have been considerable, and many of their control problems and
management tasks have been reduced - 'one group even recruited an
ex-employee to join the group, relieving management of a recruiting
task' (ibid.).  The Emcar conversion (its scale makes it more than
just another 'experiment'), has been offered by the Industrial
Training Board as 'a resounding success' and a model for other
manufacturers to emulate - though some 'conditions for success'
are appendaged.

The more typically cited examples of quasi- (to be more accurate)
autonomous work group schemes, are Volvo and Saab in Sweden, Philips
in Holland, and Pye and Ferodo in Britain.  Saab and Volvo actually
built newly designed plants to take advantage of group-working
methods rather than conventional assembly lines.  These new factories were more costly to build than conventional systems, but it is
claimed that the investment paid off in revenue terms.  Whilst any
move away from the mind-numbing effect of short job-cycles and as-
sembly-line production is to be welcomed, the new 'humanisation of
work' schemes have been criticised by trade unionists (15) and sociologists alike.  One immediate suspicion is that they are anti-trade
union in intent, being devices either to forestall unionism, or to
curtail its impact.

It appears that such schemes are typically launched when management faces problems such as recruitment, labour turnover, absenteeism, high cost and low productivity (Ramsay, 1977 and 1980, sees a
cyclical pattern of interest in participation corresponding to perceived threats to managerial authority).  In other words, the initial impetus only seems to be generated when managerial problems are
manifest, not in palmy days when management thoughts turn kindly to
worker self-actualisation needs.

In any event, managements in Britain at least have moved with
considerable caution with regard to the neo-human relation devices.
Many have displayed a marked suspicion of the new working methods.

Ironically their view has been shared by some radical writers who believe that managers attempting to use the language of job enrichment, reduced supervision and other non-cash incentives could find this a counter-productive tactic (Bosquet 1980).  It has been argued for example, that in so far as workers were to take managerial claims at face value and thereby develop a heightened consciousness about not only the financial compensation for production but about the *methods* of production, they would then need to take but a short step to develop a consciousness about the *purpose* of production.  Workers long-accustomed to expect nothing more from work than extrinsic reward, 'accepting' its alienative quality, could, once they caught a glimpse of an alternative, unwarily peddled by an unthinking managerial advocate of self-actualisation, be enticed to pursue a series of demands less easily accommodated than the annual wage round.

These projected 'unintended consequences' are effectively dismissed by Nichols (1975).  His research in a chemical company well-known for its new working arrangements casts doubts upon such a prognosis.  These doubts range from an observation that changes proclaimed are not the same as changes actually implemented, to the cataloguing of divisions within the workforce and the low levels of political consciousness.  In so far as changes had occurred, these amounted to a tendency 'for workers to manage themselves for management'.  One may recall here too the Emcar workers, self-supervising and even self-recruiting.

Most companies have not moved in any real way even towards the positions taken up by the above quoted companies.  Lower participants' roles remain inherently of a low-discretion type.  Alan Fox is critical of the institutionalised distrust which this portrays.  Under such circumstances he dismisses human relations techniques as 'attempts to *retain* the advantages of large-scale organization, extreme division of labour, hierarchy and full managerial control, while at the same time avoiding their disadvantages' (1974a:99).  This judgment is in line with Oppenheimer's who found Theory Y philosophy to be 'seductive and dangerous' (1967:47).  Theory Y organisation, he argued, does not change in any way the 'macro system' which still operates the same production goals in accordance with classical economic thinking.  Only the *means* to respond to market rationality are refined.  Job recomposition, where it has taken place, may thus be interpreted as merely an adaptation of labour processes to cope with the fraying edges of the older rationality.  Coping with the social tensions generated by the systems integration of Fordism requires some attention to 'social integration' - what could be more apt than 'neo-Fordism'? (Palloix 1976).  In the extensive literature on job re-design insufficient attention has been given to that little prefix *re*.  The fact is that 'jobs' have not mysteriously been afflicted with barrenness, they are after all officially designated clusters of discrete tasks.  They have, that is, already been designed.  But they have been purposefully *designed to be narrow*, repetitive, and devoid of discretion.  All of the things which job designers say they want to design-in have in fact been designed-out.  They have been constituted this way to facilitate easy replacement, low training costs, higher productivity (given current social relations of production), and to secure em-

ployer control.  Given this background, it may be observed that the
'movement' to re-design jobs (a) only came about to surmount particular contingent conditions and (b) the caution in its introduction reflects the priority that 're-designed' jobs should not 'roll-
back' division of labour to a degree which would compromise the
hard-won gains in lowered training costs, easy replacement of labour
and the control over labour.


DEVELOPMENTS IN CONTROL SYSTEMS

While the dichotomous model is a useful way in which to conceptualise a basic contrast in control techniques, its very simplicity
renders it less capable of illuminating the developments in managerial control systems which I now want to bring into focus.  Furthermore, many of the subtler 'higher-discretion' devices could in
fact be viewed as merely emanating from the logic of bureaucracy.
Thus the control by the carrot of promotion through the career
hierarchy is made possible because of the structural factor of
pyramidal organisational shape.  Performance appraisal, selection
and training, the strategic allocation of resources and the use of
budgets, can all be regarded as *extensions* of bureaucracy. (16)  Although the latter is essentially an impersonal control system, it
rests on discipline and the most effective form is self-discipline,
that which has been internalised.  As Weber defined it, discipline
refers to 'the probability that by virtue of habituation a command
will receive prompt and automatic obedience in stereotyped forms'.
We may thus at this stage in the argument link the impersonal rule-
bound methods with the more apparently discretionary devices, viewing the latter as more *refined* appurtenances of the former.  The new
control developments are less easily classified in simple dichotomous terms.  Developments in computerisation, managerial accounting
and industrial engineering have been ignored for too long by the
industrial relations analyst and the industrial sociologist.  In
many companies computerisation has already transformed their control
system and the overall steady progress of computers in business administration can be expected to quicken in pace with the wider
availability of cheap and plentiful mini-computers (Large 1980;  CSE
Microelectronics Group 1980b;  Jones (ed.) 1980).  But the trend is
even more significant since computerisation is not being implemented
in isolation.  Rather, accountants, production controllers and industrial engineers are finding it possible to provide integrated
control systems which cannot fail to make their impact upon rule-
making activity in industrial enterprises.  The increasing sophisti-
cation of impersonal mechanical and administrative control systems
requires a model rather more elaborate than the low discretion-high
discretion dichotomy offered by the writers discussed.
    Kynaston-Reeves and Woodward (1970) provide the basis of a model
which may be usefully examined.  It is a two-dimensional model and
therefore permits a more adequate rendering of the developments in
accountancy and industrial engineering which we wish to highlight.
It is depicted (in amended form) diagrammatically in Fig. 7.1.

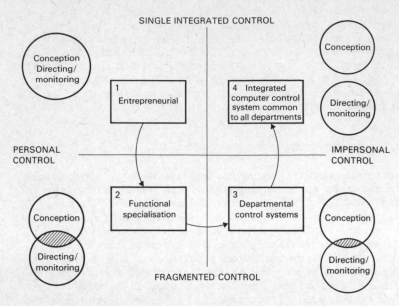

Figure 7.1   Developments in control systems

Again there is a suggestion here of a developmental trend - in an
anti-clockwise direction as indicated by the arrows from box 1 to
box 4.  Under the entrepreneurial system (box 1) the conception of
tasks and the direction and monitoring of their execution are all
undertaken by the same individual.  Control is therefore highly
personalised and unitary.  With the growth in unit size and the
specialisation of functions, departmental management have to be appointed, they rule their own sections in a personal way but there is
some breaking apart of the two spheres of conception and directing/
monitoring (box 2).  With advances in management techniques the personalised rule of departmental managers and foreman begins to give
way to formal administrative systems - standard costing, departmental budgets and the constraints of increasingly sophisticated technology (box 3).  At this third stage, conception and the direction/
monitoring of execution become even more distinct and the two
spheres become almost discrete.  Under the situations depicted by
boxes 2 and 3 there may be conflicting criteria against which foreman and operatives have to work.  These can include separate standards for quality, time and cost.  The supervisor's task is 'to
violate each of the standards as infrequently as possible' (Kynaston-Reeves and Woodward 1970:51).  Yet whilst the situation persists
there is scope for fragmented departmental bargaining by shop
stewards.  In juggling output and costs, departmental management may
feel constrained to sub-optimise, and exchange manning concessions
for production.  There may be less room for manoeuvre on such
matters in the final stage.  Here (box 4) the two spheres of conception and direction finally part.
    Continual-process technology has pre-planned control built-in to
it.  Under such a regime the administrative control systems become
increasingly sophisticated and shift from a specific function (such
as computerised stock control) to a fully integrated cross-company

control system.  At this stage the control is totally impersonal and
instructions emanate from the pre-planned logic of the system.  In
the continuous-process technologies of man-made fibre production and
brewing which I studied (Storey 1980), scope for ad hoc manpower
utilisation negotiations is extremely limited.  The controls are
built-in to the instrumentation.  However, this point should not be
exaggerated.  The application of continuous process technology
within these industries is still of a limited scope.  In brewing for
example, although the actual mashing and fermenting stages are subject to pre-planned quality control and the scope for variation in
method and manning arrangements is somewhat restricted, there are
many other areas within the breweries where the technology is totally different.  In one large modern brewery for example, of a total
workforce approximately 1,000 only 71 people were employed in the
actual brewing process.  This latter was automated and controlled
from a central console.  In contrast, other areas of this modern
complex found men knocking-in barrel stoppers with mallets and performing other jobs some distance from the totally impersonal control
system depicted in box 4 of the diagram.

Most certainly then, the model has its limitations.  Like Braverman's, it is largely confined to control at the point of production
and omits other forms of control strategy at the level of the state
for example, or devices such as replicating production facilities in
order to weaken the threat of disruption.  Moreover, even within its
more limited scope, the implied trend neglects the fact that a wide
range of control systems coexist - witness for example internal and
segmented labour markets.  Finally, certain dimensions of control,
such as discipline, rear their head in all four quadrants.

Nevertheless, some attention is bound to be directed towards the
continued search for developments in control systems if only because
of the as-yet-unknown but seemingly profound implication of new
technology and the scope it offers for more fully integrated control.  (And the model above does have the advantage of embracing
both technology and administrative control systems.)  Rapid developments in numerically-controlled machines (NC machines) are further
accelerated by advances being made in computer linkages, 'the last
stage before the full automation of plants' (Avlontis and Parkinson
1981).  NCs offer tremendous flexibility and dispense with the need
for elaborate jigs.  It is reported that the Japanese MUM (Methodology for Unmanned Metalworking) project will have a prototype unmanned plant fully operational by 1983.  With a floor area of 30,000
square metres and a staff of only 10, it will produce 2,000 different components for gear boxes and hydraulic motors, covering the
range of operations from forging, welding, presswork, machining,
assembly and painting.  Already, machine tools made today which are
of the stand-alone non-computer linked type, might be said to be ob-
solete - or very nearly so.

With these kind of developments it is imperative that careful re-
examination of technology and its relationship to the labour process
is made.

TECHNOLOGY

Technology and productive forces more generally have always enjoyed
a special place in most Marxist interpretations of social change.
Marxists have long assumed that capitalism was developing the forces
of production in 'progressive' fashion and by implication higher
stages of development should facilitate transition to socialism.
But Gorz (1972) vigorously contests these views which he says 'no
longer hold true'.  He claims to be challenging orthodoxy on a
number of points.  We can no longer accept, he maintains, that it is
the productive forces which shape the relations of production.  Nor
can it be confidently assumed that productive forces will enter
spontaneously into contradiction with capitalist relations of production.  His counter-thesis is that productive forces are shaped by
capitalist social relations and

> the imprint of the latter upon the first is so deep that any at-
> tempt to change the relations of production will be doomed unless
> a radical change is made in the very nature of the productive
> forces and not only in the way in which and in the purposes for
> which they are used (Gorz 1972:27).

In some respects these ideas are not so novel as Gorz seems to
think.  The dialectical relation between forces and relations of
production would comprise a more fruitful rendering of Marxian
theory (cf. Lazonick 1979).  But the implications of Gorz's case are
none the less significant.  The productive forces he suggests are so
infused with capitalist rationality as to be almost certain to distort any socialist revolution which attempts to utilise them unchanged.  This view contrasts with that of the Brighton Labour
Process Group (BLPG), who point to the flexibility in the potential
uses of forces of production.  They maintain, 'you don't have a
capitalist labour process simply by virtue of having an automatic
spinning jenny and self-acting mule' (1977:14).  They proceed to
argue that in the transition to socialism material production will
have to occur 'on the basis of given technologies and machine systems.  A new generation of 'socialist machinery' will not spring
into existence overnight' (Brighton Labour Process Group 1977:14).
Technology is thus not neutral to the extent that it has been designed with capitalist priorities in mind, but on the other hand, it
is not so hopelessly distorted that it permits of no other usage
given a different context.  The capitalist labour process is a combination of material instruments of production and a social organisation. (17)  In a situation where the latter component was revolu-
tionised, the former component would not be deterministic.  Tensions
emergent from non-correspondence would, however, be likely.  So Gorz
(1972) and the BLPG (1977) both concur that the 'motor of history'
is not the development of forces of production but class struggle.
They part company, however, in that Gorz is pessimistic about the
degree of contamination embodied in machine technology, whereas the
BLPG want to stress the dual dependence of forces and relations of
production in composing the capitalist labour process.  Our analysis
lends support to this latter interpretation.

   Unlike more recent accounts of organisational structure and division of labour which treat technology as an independent variable
complete with its own 'imperatives' to boot, the early political

economists regarded it as self-evidently tied to entrepreneurial
designs (Garnsey 1981).  It is this perspective which is now enjoying a renaissance.  As Braverman observes (1974:195) 'machinery
offers to management the opportunity to do by wholly mechanical
means that which it had previously attempted to do by organisational
and disciplinary means'.  Technology can be used to intensify the
bureaucratic characteristics of fragmentation and the minimisation
or elimination of discretion.  In Andrew Ure's (1861:368) notorious
statement, 'when capital enlists science in her service the refractory hand of labour will always be taught docility'.  Marx traced
this process in his famous stages from co-operation to manufacture
to machinofacture (modern industry).  This was a process involving
the separation of mental from manual labour and the harnessing of
science by capital (Marx 1976;  Sohn-Rethel 1978).  Unearthing the
'politics of technology' David Dickson argues that technological
innovation was employed not only to regularise labour and engender
discipline, but 'often as a conscious move on the part of employers
to counter strikes and other forms of industrial militancy' (1974:
79).  The threat of introducing machines could be used as a tactic
in keeping wages down.  Trade union minutes appertaining to craftsmen in the American shoe industry reveal that many were even 'prepared to reduce the piece rates for hand lasting in exchange for the
employers' agreement not to introduce machinery at that time'
(Yellowitz 1977:210).  The introduction of machines became an integral component of the class struggle.  The timing of their inception
could be used as part of the day-to-day tactics just as the wider
movement formed part of a more general strategy (Dickson 1974).  At
each level the assumptions, priorities and authority relations of
capital became embodied and crystallised in the technology that was
and is developed.  This point can be well illustrated by reference
to David Noble's (1979) study of the development and use of numerically-controlled (NC) machine tools.  He demonstrates how managers
chose to develop and deploy them in a way which centralised control
away from the worker despite the fact that the technical considerations of computer numerical control could well permit micropro-
cessor programmes to be stored and edited on the shopfloor.  There
is no question but that management saw in NC the potential to enhance their authority over production and seized upon it despite
questionable cost effectiveness' (Noble 1979:34).  The feasibility
of shopfloor control of the new Computer Numerical Control systems
is instanced at the state-owned weapons plant in Kongsberg, Norway.
Here all operators are trained in NC programming and engage in
editing (Noble 1979:47).
    There are a number of classic historical studies which shed some
light on managerial capture of technological advantage.  Most famous
are the accounts by Hobsbawm (1968, 1974), Landes (1969), Thompson
(1967, 1968) and Ricardo's celebrated chapter On Machinery (1821).
More recently the historiography of technology and its dialectical
relationship with other aspects of the labour process have flowered.
Especially notable are the collection of documents and abstracts by
Berg (1979), the work of Lazonick (1978, 1979), Yellowitz (1977) and
the collection of papers edited by Gospel (forthcoming).  Berg
(1979) explains how the Conference of Socialist Economists spawned a
separate labour process historians' group.  Meanwhile in the United

States this type of historiography has been flourishing in the jour-
nals of 'Radical America', 'Review of Radical Political Economics'
and 'Labour History'.

Articles of this kind express the essential dialectical point
that far from being neutral, technology is designed to strengthen
capital's dominance.  Its actual implementation, however, has continually provoked resistance;  this in turn may hasten the introduction of newer more labour-saving machinery (Montgomery 1979;
Lazonick 1979;  Zimbalist 1979). (18)  Contemporary instances of
this struggle are not difficult to find.  Pipeline welders reputedly
skilled and high earning, have been engaged in a national unofficial
conflict with major construction firms such as McAlpine because sub-
contractors have been hiring 'robot' automatic orbital welding machines from the United States.  Pickets argue that 'all the machine
does is to give you the same production with less plant and equipment and a smaller labour force ... we get it thrown at us that we
can't stand in the way of progress but this isn't progress, it's not
quicker or better that we are'. (19)  But project managers pursue
the Babbage principle - 'with these machines we can have less qualified people and pay considerably less'. (20)  Few employers can have
been quite so candid in their public declarations on the subject of
introducing new technology.

Machine technology may be regarded as an especially potent control device, for, while it

is a relatively simple matter to defy time and motion study technicians it is much more difficult to resist the introduction of
new technology.  The time and motion study person stands before
the worker as a blatant symbol of worker oppression by capital.
The machine, however, is a mystified oppressor ...' (Zimbalist
1979:xiii).

This insidious character of technology with regard to control has
been a key theme of Critical Theory.  The celebrated 'One-Dimension-
al Man' actually opens with this keynote sentence:  'A comfortable,
smooth, reasonable, democratic unfreedom prevails in advanced industrial civilization, a *token of technical progress*' (Marcuse 1968:19,
emphasis added).  This theme of technology as manipulative rationality is rewoven by Habermas (1980) and Schroyer (1971).  It is
important to note that not only is technology a social product,
shaped and directed by class struggle, but, equally, workshop technology is expressive of the rationality, priorities, and domination
of the wider capitalist society.  In a word, it is part of the
'totality'.  Scientism and technology are not only instruments of
control but instrumental in legitimating that control.  They replace
outworn ideologies characteristic of earlier phases of capitalism.
Scientism in its prescriptive form comprises a positivism which
functions to justify 'the extension of repressive control systems'
(Schroyer 1971:297).

The exposure of these more subtle forms of domination may require
a critical reappraisal of traditional Marxism and sociology.  Thus,
the degree of manipulative rationality embodied in contemporary
science and technology, is a phenomenon, maintains Schroyer (1971:
317) which 'Marx was simply unable to imagine'.  Marcuse and
Habermas echo this point.  They too regard Marx's analysis as requiring amendment in this respect.  In the main, Critical Theory at-

tempts to lend greater prominence to underlying purposive - rational action systems.  This tends to centralise state action in a manner which attributes to it anything but the epiphenomenal.  Politics and instrumental action, it is suggested, are inappropriately cast as merely superstructural.  The wedding of technology and capital in the 'rationally managed society' must attract central attention from those wanting to expose the intricacies of contemporary control patterns.  This is the project undertaken not only by Habermas (1970, 1971) but also by Gouldner (1976).  Top management maintain a hegemony over organisational knowledge not only by sheer monopolisation of information concerning costs, products and markets.  It goes further than that.  Reflecting the developmental model depicted in Figure 7.1, in 'The Dialectic of Ideology and Technology', Gouldner traces the transition from classic rule-centred bureaucracy which was based on an 'order and forbid' style of management, to the new industrial bureaucracies which incorporate a scientised technocracy.  This latter lends a new legitimacy to the official position. It gives rise to a new technocratic consciousness, exemplified, for Gouldner, by President Kennedy's remark:  'What is at stake in our economic decisions today is not some grand warfare of rival ideologies which will sweep the country with passion, but the more practical management of a modern economy.'  Many have concurred with such a view and pronounced the end of ideology.  But Gouldner warns of the ideological elements in technocracy:  'Science and technology' he says, 'are fantasized as the power to which all, including the hegemonic elites and their managers must bow' (1976:261).  The effect of this on political discourse has been noted by Habermas (1970) who views with some dismay the 'automation of technical choice', the self-directing consequence of the mathematically calculated approach to strategic questions.  Not only does the technocratic method provide a supporting legitimacy for social control, it also seems to dictate the series of actions which must occur all the way down the line.  Failure to comply with the dominant logic is adjudged not as a legitimate normative challenge, but as a display of incompetence and misguidedness.  And the elite are doubly-served for, the 'technicians adapt in advance, taking anticipatory account of the ideological and interest-grounded views of organizational management' (Gouldner 1976:256).  The capacity of organisational elites to play a disproportionate part in the social construction of reality can thus be understood only in the light of such processes.

## INDUSTRIAL ENGINEERING AND ACCOUNTANCY

These are two key management specialisms charged with the explicit task of designing and implementing *control systems and procedures*. Their incumbents are significant examples of the 'staff' experts and technocrats whom Gouldner viewed as launching 'bureaucracy into a fundamentally new phase in its organizational evolution' (1976:253). These specialisms, which are very different in terms of historical antecedents and personnel recruitment, training and professional institutions, in fact share some crucial common elements.  Each is a generic term which contains within it a host of specialist tech-

niques;   each is directed towards the enhancement of managerial control;   the separate disciplines even share overlapping areas such as
cost control and budgeting.  Their method of approach is often similar;   so for example, both utilise the concept of a 'standard unit'
- the accountant has his standard cost (the average or expected
value) and the industrial engineer his standard hour.  Finally, each
is undergoing development:  from being concerned with recording past
performance and taking the appropriate corrective post hoc action,
both are moving towards a more interventionalist preventive strategy.

## Industrial engineering

The industrial engineer starts out highly conscious of the premise
that labour is a 'cost' and that the objective of work activity is
to make a profit.  This message is drummed into him from every text-
book.  The task of the industrial engineer, therefore, is to design
systems of operation and to construct procedures which will monitor
costs and ensure that these are low relative to output and profits.
He seeks to make the impact of the market relevant at the level of
internal operational procedures.  Moreover, this is to be done in a
way which seemingly extends the 'scientific method' into management
control:  management must emerge systematised.

The industrial engineer's Bible is a great tome entitled
'Industrial Engineering Handbook', more commonly known to its affi-
cionados simply as 'Maynard' (its editor-in-chief).  It contains an
'official' definition of the scope of the specialism:

Industrial engineering is concerned with the design, improvement,
and installation of integrated systems of men, materials and
equipment.  It draws upon specialised knowledge and skill in the
mathematical, physical and social sciences, together with the
principles and methods of engineering analysis and design, to
specify, predict, and evaluate the results to be obtained from
such systems (Maynard 1971:1.5). (21)

This is something of a showpiece definition, dressed in idealised
career-brochure terms, rather than an informative guide to what industrial engineers actually do.  In fact the professional title
itself is somewhat self-consciously adapted by the men who are still
trying to shake off the stopwatch image of the old-fashioned efficiency expert and the time-and-motion man.  They are equally trying
to lay the ghost of F.W. Taylor, and the troubles and court hearings
which ensued upon the early implementation of Taylorism.  A new professional image is being presented to us.  At base, however, the
bread-and-butter techniques remain.  They may be summarised as follows:

(i)   Methods study and design:  the analysis of operations, motion
      study and standardisation.  Planned maintenance.  The princi-
      ple which underlies method study is that of division of
      labour.  The method worker's adage is to follow four rules:
      to divide up the job, to simplify the parts, to eliminate
      action not required, to combine the remaining refined parts.
(ii)  Work measurement:  time study.  This may involve the stop-
      watch timing of jobs on the factory floor.  More commonly

now, however, it is coming to mean predetermination of ele-
mental time standards.  That is, the breakdown of tasks into
elementary motions (e.g. standing, walking, reaching) and ar-
riving at a standard time for each task.  These elements are
then aggregated to give a standard time for a given job.

(iii)   Control determination:  production control, stock control,
quality control and budgetary control.

(iv)   Designing and implementing payment systems.  These usually
involve some incentive element if they are entrusted to the
industrial engineer.  He seeks to control activity through
the penalty or inducement of pay.

(v)   Plant layout, planning the sequencing of activities and the
routing of materials and product through the workshop.

Frequently these five basic areas will in practice be inter-
linked.  Thus management may wish to link new methods to a revised
payment system.  The common element among each of the five is the
objective of rendering to management enhanced control over the situation.  For example, a payment system may be described as out-of-
control if it produces unpredictable earnings, and earnings levels
are not linked to performance in the way that was intended.

There have been developments in more sophisticated approaches including operations research, network analysis, such as critical path
method, PERT (programme evaluation and review technique), linear
programming, and computer-linked approaches of which the spokesman
for the profession speaks so profusely.  They certainly do represent
significant technical advances, and they have saved costs.  From the
viewpoint of our present analysis, however, they can be seen simply
as more refined techniques to fulfil more accurately the same five
goals which we outlined above.

This is not to say that all industrial engineering control procedures necessarily constrain labour or represent an imposition or
an affront to it.  There is no particular merit in operating in a
rule-of-thumb manner.  This may simply lead to incompetent operations planning and periodic redundancies.  Judicious use of industrial engineering may assist in more stable labour engagement.  At
the same time, however, unregulated application of a system which
reduces activity to predetermined tables (for example there are
'Turn' tabulations which take into account the degrees turned by an
operative performing a particular motion) could raise labour control
to a level undesirable in social terms.

Whether utilising new sophisticated techniques or old-fashioned
devices, the industrial engineer's function is to systematise and
thereby increase managerial control.  Even traditional direct supervision may be transformed into standardised inspection.  Production
control is systematised through devices like route-cards, batch
books and 'instructions to works'.  Standardisation, and systemati-
sation reduce the vagaries of the labour process.  The utilisation
of labour becomes more predictable and more controllable.

Conception becomes even more separated from execution as the
above techniques are developed and implemented.  The directing and
controlling are pre-planned and built in to the system in advance.
As one industrial engineer commented, having completed the installation of a new system:  'It's foolproof, they (the stewards and workforce) will try to find ways around it but they won't succeed -

we've blocked every avenue and every move.'  As we observe in the
ensuing chapter on the reactions to control, this assessment is
somewhat exaggerated.  It leads, however, to one final and crucial
point.  Industrial engineers are of course hired by the employer -
either full-time or temporarily as consultants.  Yet they are
often portrayed, especially so in the latter guise, as independent
figures using neutral methods.  Frequently, shop stewards are themselves receptive to this imagery when dealing with consultants (far
less so apropos internal industrial engineers as we shall see).
Stewards will often allow consultants to gather information and will
co-operate with them in a way they would not consider in terms of
their own managers.  Yet the consultant researcher's problems are
defined by management, and shopfloor practices are invariably the
boundaries drawn for investigating the problem.  The information
gathered is rarely fully made available to both sides.  Stewards are
ill-equipped by their lack of training to cope with the statistical
and graphical presentations and indeed certain information is in any
case deliberately withheld in order to reduce the potential for conflicts.  This has been justified to me in terms of 'they won't
understand the concepts we are using and will therefore get the
wrong end of the stick'.  Ironically it may be the 'neutral' industrial consultant who suggests such a ploy.  In one case the managing
director wanted to act in terms of his high principles and make all
the information gathered and the computations thereby derived,
freely available.  He was advised against this by the industrial
engineer.


Accountancy

The twentieth-century developments in accountancy have brought it
closer to the internal control function.  Rudimentary accounts and
book-keeping have a long history, but the traditional task of keeping track of funds has now been supplemented not only by more
sophisticated techniques but new avenues and domains.  We may distinguish between financial accountancy and management accountancy.
The first is concerned with the raising of capital and the external
relations with shareholders.  Management accountancy on the other
hand is concerned with the development of refined techniques to
assist *internal* management in maintaining control of operations.  It
comprises two sub-parts: budgeting and costing.  I use the word
'assist' because accountancy is still officially a 'staff' function,
but, as it becomes more embroiled in planning and the control system
becomes more located at the strategic level, the traditional line/
staff dichotomy will lose some of its validity.  Accountancy already
impinges at the two main management control levels: at the planning
stage the accountant enters with the master budget and standard cost
system;  and at the level of controlling current operations he
enters with his short-term operational budget, his feedback data and
a monitoring system which is intended, in itself, to affect behaviour.  The Institute of Chartered Accountants has recognised the
accountant's role in the internal control function.  The council of
the Institute has issued a statement (1964) entitled 'Internal
Control as a Responsibility and Function of Management'.  It notes

the breadth of the control function including:  the plan of the
organisation (which we discussed above as the organisation's structure) - this is important for allocation of responsibility and for
co-ordination;  the procedures, which take in authorisations, recording devices and routine cross-checking by staff;  and thirdly
managerial *supervision* and *review,* which means examining interim
accounts, reports and statistical summaries.  Even the terminology
is instructive.  Thus the chief accountant in America is frequently
entitled the 'Controller'.  His function is to collect and interpret
data.  Even though he is not strictly a line manager, he does control, by exerting 'a force of influence that impels management
toward logical decisions ... consistent with its objectives' (Horngren 1975:12).

As Hofstede argues, 'Every plan must eventually be translated
into money terms and in this way it becomes a budget' (Hofstede
1968).  Budgets can be of varied types - sales, manufacture, inven-
tory, purchasing, capital and at the highest level, the master
budget.  A budget of any type is simply a formal quantitative expression of management plans.  Its control function enters in that
it serves to authorise, or conversely, render illegitimate, certain
expenditures and courses of action which do not concur with the official plan.  Secondly, it can count as a powerful control device
because it provides a precise quantified guide which amounts to an
impersonal command.  Departmental management hands may be tied because of this impersonal control exercised by top managerial accountants, whose actions are not (ironically) accountable to anyone
except the Board of directors.  Plant-level collective bargaining is
thus likely to occur within pre-determined parameters.  Thirdly,
budgets act as a control mechanism by measuring departmental performance, and thus departmental managers will always be attempting
to act within 'their budgets' so as to record a satisfactory performance.

So too with costing, the other major management accounting
device.  In fact budgeting and costing have much in common.  Costing
refers to the predetermination of the cost of a product.  This requires some 'standards'.  When these are used for comparison with
actual costs, the approach is described as a 'standard cost' system.
The link between budgets and standard costing may be stated simply.
If all current costs are charged to products, then the sum total of
all standard costs for one year will equal the total budget:  'they
are two ways of cutting the same pie' (Hofstede 1968:27).  While
budgets split costs department-wise, standard costs split all costs
product-wise.  The accountant using standard costing is ever alert
to 'variance' - the difference between management's official plan
and actual performance.  Where this variation from standard is not
of a stochastic (pure chance) kind, the accountant views the situation literally as 'out-of-control'.  In permitting greater sophisti-
cation in identifying the separate components of variance, the
standard cost method equips management with a powerful diagnostic
tool which will be used in order to get things back under control.

The same approach lies at the basis of other accountancy-based
managerial control strategies such as 'profit centres' and responsibility centres'.  Sub-organisation income statements, internal
pricing and administrative price systems (Gordon 1964) are attempts

to progress further from direct personal control towards impersonal
market control.

## SEGMENTED LABOUR MARKETS AND THE LABOUR PROCESS

Understanding of the dialectical relationship between the labour
process and the wider features of education and labour markets has
been significantly advanced by the recent work of Edwards (1975,
1976, 1979);  Doeringer and Piore (1971);  Edwards et al. (eds)
(1975);  Gordon, Edwards and Reich (forthcoming);  and Rubery
(1978).  These authors help to break down the perspective conventional in labour economics which regards the labour market as operating external to, and independent of, the labour process.  They
relate the sphere of circulation and exchange to the sphere of production.  The notion of 'market' implies activity at the point of
sale and purchase as opposed to activity at the point of consumption
- i.e. the labour process proper.  This conceptualisation has normally led to a search for the reasons behind the self-evident disparity in employment experiences between various groups.  Most
noticeable was and is the low pay, high unemployment, and poor job
security of blacks and of women.  Hence the search was largely confined to characteristics in the labour market or in the characteristics (qualifications, job records and so on) of 'human capital'.
Gradually the idea of 'dual labour markets' began to take hold.
    But Edwards (1979) moves well beyond this.  His essential thesis
is that the basis for different segments is not to be found in the
external labour market;  (the required degree of monopsony and monopoly respectively does not obtain to lend credence to this);
rather, the fundamental source lies in the workplace itself - i.e.
in the type of *control systems* that are used.  It is the system of
control which for instance creates the circumstances within which
education, training, experience or skills derive their salience and
significance.  So segmentation arises 'not from market forces themselves but rather from the underlying uses of labour power ... to
understand why  segmentation occurs, we must look to how labour
power is consumed in the labour process' (1979:165).
    'Dual' labour markets are replaced with three labour markets.  In
a sense the precise number need not concern us here.  One might
wonder why there should not be a dozen or more, or, at the logical
extreme, a labour market for every individual.  Determinate here are
the criteria used and the degree of patterning found.  Edwards draws
on an impressive body of research to suggest plausibility in delineating three segments:  an 'independent primary';  a 'subordinate
primary';  and a 'secondary'.  These, we are told, are of about
equal size, the secondary is thus not, as has sometimes been suggested, abnormal or 'residual'.  The segments are comprised of a
cluster of characteristics. (22)  These may be summarised in Fig.
7.2.

| Character-istics | Independent primary | Subordinate primary | Secondary |
|---|---|---|---|
| Pay | High relative to other workers | Relatively higher than secondary | Low pay |
| Career | Career pro-gression with cumulative move-ment between firms | Job ladders firm specific but with link-ages between successive jobs | Casual 'dead-end' jobs |
| Job tenure and security | Secure, good tenure, stable employment | Some job se-curity with union seniority protection. Relatively stable employ-ment. Estab-lished paths for advancement | Low job security. High labour turn-over. Few rights |
| Skill and education | Skills less quickly learned. Some control, less routinised | Semi-skilled; some technical routinisation | Low skill and education require-ments |
| Examples | Professional positions - accountants, research scien-tists, tax specialists, craft-workers | Traditional working class; unionised mass production and clerical work-ers in core firms | Service workers, especially in periphery firms - janitors, waiters and other workers with proximity to industrial reserve army |

Figure 7.2  The three labour markets

Each segment spans both blue- and white-collar work, so that the popular dichotomy is transcended by this model. Again, emphasis should be given to the point that it is not just a question of dif-ferent *outcomes* between labour markets but rather different *pro-cesses* are at work. Thus differences reside not so much in the workers but in the jobs and labour processes themselves. This can be illustrated from the fact that extra education for instance, pro-vides little return in the secondary market but does make a differ-ence for those in the primary market. Equally, even job experience itself fails to provide a stepping stone for those in the secondary market; they experience a more or less flat age-wage profile. And, significantly in the light of our earlier discussion on discipline as a form of individualising control, Edwards points out (1979:173) that workers in the secondary segment were far more likely to face dismissal for disciplinary reason than are workers in the primary sector.  In part this is because the latter are afforded protection by formalised procedures instituted by the unions.

We have already noted Edwards's explanation of the *source* of these segments - the distinct systems of control within the firms. Thus he transcends the debate about the congeries of market factors and homes-in on this single criterion.  The systems of control and the three labour-market segments may be juxtaposed to give the following matrix.

| Market segment | Simple control | Technical control | 'Bureaucratic' control |
|---|---|---|---|
| Secondary | The working poor | | |
| Subordinate primary | | Traditional, organised, proletariat | |
| Independent primary | | | Labour aristocracy and so-called 'new working class' |

Figure 7.3  Systems of control

This is a simplified version of Edwards's model, but it does indicate the typified association.  Cleaners and workers in peripheral firms are frequently found in the simple control/secondary segment; exemplifying the middle cell would be workers in auto or steel plants;  and an example of bureaucratic control and the associated independent primary segment would be jobs at IBM, craft-workers or staff jobs.  The essence of simple control in contrast with the other two, is the personal arbitrary control of supervisors who direct work, monitor it, and reward or discipline.  The other two have more subtle impersonal and institutionalised features;  the middle cell represents a compromise based on a 'bargain between core firms and industrial unions that leaves the management of the business in the employers' hands but guarantees to workers primary-market job rights' (1979:181).

There is an important critique of Braverman in Edwards's work. Edwards reveals how new forms of bureaucratic control actually *reverse* the reliance of core firms on reserve-army discipline.  They engender primary market patterns characterised by greater job security and promotion prospects.  He cites the example of Polaroid which, like other 'bureaucratically controlled' firms, has intentionally established promotion ladders and other appurtenances of an internal labour market.  The job ladder for engineers comprises five separate rungs with definitive years of experience to be served before progression between them.  In consequence of such strategies *'systems of control in the core firms now differ from those in the firms of the competitive periphery,* and in turn, labour markets have become segmented' (1979:183, emphasis added).

The model in its most basic form posits this process:  a control
system - labour characteristics which are highlighted - degree of
collective response - impact on internal labour market and control
system - and back around again.  The dialectic of control and resistance is highlighted by the example of the contrast between long-
shoreing in San Francisco and New York, wherein is demonstrated the
impact of unionism on the labour process and labour-market segmentation.  The labour process in both ports was similar prior to unionisation of San Francisco in the 1930s.  Thereafter this port ended
the simple control system and casualisation in favour of a new sub-
ordinate-primary pattern.  This was not to occur in New York until
the 1950s, being here delayed by the slow growth of unionism.


CONCLUSIONS

Five conclusions are pertinent.  First, the strategies and structures of work control may be viewed as part of a wider socio-
economic *totality*.  Disciplinary activity and the whole panoply of
devices appendaged to organisational hierarchy emerge ultimately
from the wide social base of employer control.  This involves the
company's legal ownership rights over the means of production and
their fundamental right to decide whether to invest, dis-invest,
close, expand, hire more or less labour and so on.  In an essentially supportive posture stands the state, with its coercive authority.
And underlying this is the market context.  The interrelationship of
work control at the point of production and wider societal features
also extends, however, to the schooling and higher educational
system, and to the sexual and racial divisions within labour markets.  In myriad ways work control processes and structures are inextricably linked to wider social contours.
   Nevertheless, work control is characterised not by its uniformity
but by its *variety*.  Control strategies display an unevenness between and within sectors.  Within bureaucracy itself there were seen
to be various alternative control devices available.  And beyond the
formalistic bureaucracies new forms of control were identified.
Technological developments allow more holistic integrated control
systems uniting administrative and machine control requirements.
Yet while variety was evidenced, the notion of an alternative independent congeneric form of 'responsible autonomy' was not supported.
It did not seem that such a form could justifiably be picked out as
a distinct entity counterbalancing direct control.  Rather, Braverman was to an extent correct in positing a generalised drive for
managerial control although he exaggerated the reliance upon Taylorism.  A rather less specific 'thrust for efficiency' comprising a
battery of control devices seems more in accord with the reality of
managerial control.
   An associated conclusion is the doubt cast upon a unilinear trend
towards an infinite future of de-skilling.  Certainly developments
have occurred in patterns of control but these tended to be rather
more complex and the simplest modelled format to which they could be
reduced was the matrix as amended from Kynaston-Reeves and Woodward.
This depicted managerial control developing from a single locus of
control with personal direction and monitoring, through a more frag-

mented phase with functional specialisation to a third more rationalised phase with departmental deployment of more sophisticated control systems and on to a more fully integrated control system,
highly impersonal but once more approximating a single locus of control.   However, the corrective to the unilinear view extended beyond
this, because, certain types of control device, such as discipline
for example, were found to be prominent in each phase.   Equally, all
control systems were found to contain inherent contradictions in
their implementation.   The control pattern described by Braverman
seemed to reflect somewhat uncritically the sales propaganda of
technological and systems entrepreneurs.   It reflected the aspirations for unfettered control emanating from the likes of Taylor and
machine manufacturers.   The reality upon the occasion of their
actual introduction and attempted implementation was rather more
complex.

A fourth conclusion is the emphasis given to the viability of
strategic choice in the technical and social relations of production.   Bureaucratic control systems are not necessarily the most
technically efficient in terms of least cost and the maximum output
of useful products, but reflect the priorities given to controlling
the labour process for more specific ends - most notably the accumulation of surplus-value.   In this sense structure does follow
strategy.   To choose but one more example, the reasons why education
and skill count for so little in the secondary segment of the labour
market is not so much due to technological imperatives but more to
the different strategic ways of organising the labour process.

Finally, the dialectic is manifested in the way control systems
are themselves shaped by the varying degrees of worker resistance.
Accordingly, the full consequences of an employer's chosen strategy
cannot always be foreseen.   Thus in the auto plants of the United
States in the 1930s the adopted strategy of increasing simple control and thereby maintaining it as a casual secondary segment was
diverted off-course by unionisation drives.   The firms eventually
agreed to institute seniority and to generate an internal labour
market with respect to labour allocation, lay-off and pricing.   As
Edwards demonstrated, the same firms may use different control systems in places like Korea, but attempts by GM, for instance, to try
likewise in the American South were thwarted by union organising
campaigns.   The overall extent to which worker resistance has manifested itself and the commensurate impact of the same, constitutes
the subject of the next chapter.

# Chapter 8

# STRUGGLE AND RESISTANCE

Stephen Marglin concludes his now famous article on the origins of hierarchy with this sentence - 'Under socialism (at least in its Soviet strain) no less than under feudalism and capitalism, the primary determinant of basic choices with respect to the organization of production has not been technology - exogenous and inexorable - but the exercise of power - endogenous and *resistable*' (1974: 60, emphasis added). Consideration of the extent of that resistance did not of course form part of Marglin's remit. But the issue has, in the main, also been ignored in subsequent discussions of the labour process (Nichols (ed.) 1980; Purcell and Smith (eds) 1979; Braverman 1974; Zimbalist 1979; CSE 1976). (1) And yet it is a vital subject awaiting assessment, for, the growing corpus of literature detailing the dimensions of managerial control and its apparent inexorability is not only pessimistic and partial but necessarily omits consideration of the potential of working class strategy to overcome or at least radically alter the domination so eloquently described in the studies cited above.

There are many questions to be asked. What kinds of resistance are found? How much resistance is there? How is it patterned? Against what or whom is the resistance directed? What significance does it have? Who resists most? How important are the trade unions in this regard? Why isn't there more resistance? What depth and scope does the resistance have?

There are in fact conceptual difficulties in this area. Is 'resistance' the appropriate category or does it evoke merely an image of a recalcitrant child who in the end is subject to parental will? The associated term 'response' is frequently used but again this attributes the sole initiative to management. To some degree this may be a fair reflection of reality but it does rather underplay the interreactive nature of the struggle. Low-Beer (1978) uses the term 'protest'. But David Montgomery, a renowned authority on worker-struggles in the United States finds this a condescending label to attach to working class efforts. But his term 'rebellion', may be rather too strong a term to describe many of the instances of worker refusal to co-operate with managerial plans. Other depictions have been made - for example, Bill Watson (1972) refers to 'counter-planning', and Negri (1979), uses the phrase 'the strategy

of refusal'.  Each of these terms is generic, embracing diverse actions of a planned-unplanned, collective-individual, spasmodic and
incessant nature.  They include therefore official strikes and other
union-organised forms of industrial action, but also sabotage
ca'canny, absenteeism, informal shop rules and an infinite number of
devices limited only by human ingenuity.  In the main, it is not the
difference between these terms that is important but their similarity in one key regard:  they all denote actions which interfere with
the metamorphosis of labour power into labour.  These apparently
'negative' acts consequently carry strategic significance in that
they impede the valorisation process.  It is all those forms of
worker-instigated impediments to this process which is here signalled by the term 'resistance'.

It might be thought, however, that while potential is certainly
present there has not been sufficient evidence of actual resistance
to justify spending much time on the topic.  Apart from the implied
resignation in such a stance the premise is in any case ill-founded.
There have been many significant instances of resistance which have
occurred prior to scientific management;  at its very inception;
and they have continued into present times.  At the time of its inception in particular 'not only did workers doggedly resist the employers' efforts to introduce stopwatches and incentive pay, they
also frequently formulated their own counter-proposals for industrial reorganization' (Montgomery 1979:155).  Indeed, illustrations
and analyses of many of these struggles will constitute the larger
part of this present chapter.  Marx certainly gave the subject
rather more attention than, for example, Braverman.  'The struggle
between the capitalist and the wage-labourer starts', said Marx,
'with the existence of the capital-relation itself.  It rages
throughout the period of manufacture' (1976:553).  With the introduction of machinery the worker's wrath, he observes, is directed at
the instruments of production, 'capital's material mode of existence'.  The worker is depicted as 'in revolt' against the material
foundation of the capitalist mode of production.  Marx instances
workers' revolts in the seventeenth and eighteenth centuries and he
writes of the 'large-scale destruction of machinery' in the early
years of the nineteenth century.  It took 'time and experience' he
notes, for workers to 'learn to distinguish between machinery and
its employment by capital and therefore to transfer their attacks
from the material instruments of production to the form of society
which utilizes these instruments'.  Though even at the time of his
writing he confirms that revolt occasionally still takes 'this crude
form' (Marx 1976:554-5).

More was to follow.  In direct response to the attempted introduction of Taylorism there were mass walkouts at the Norfolk navy
yard in the United States in 1915.  And there were attacks on time-
and-motion study men at Pittsburgh's American Locomotive Company in
1911 - notwithstanding a work-study agreement signed by the union
(Montgomery 1979:115).  Other instances of struggle and resistance
at this time of the early introduction of Taylorism are documented
by Aitken (1960), Palmer (1975) and Davis (1975).  More recent re-
bellions of note include inter alia that at GM's Lordstown plant,
Ohio, in the early 1970s, the rebellion against Ford's new disciplinary code at Halewood in 1981, the halting of the BL Metro line

because of speed-up in 1981, the miners' reversal of the pit-closure
plan in the winter of 1980/81, and the defeat of the Industrial
Relations Act.  The events leading to the closure of the Saltley
coke depot hardly suggest an impotent and apathetic working class.
And in Europe a number of significant landmarks of rebellion should
be remembered:  France 1968;  the general strike in Belgium 1960/61;
the occupation of Turin factories in 1920.  But in addition to these
more dramatic eruptions there are other signs of persistent resistance.  The growth of unionism and its shake-up under the impact of
the shop steward movement(s) is indicative of something other than
supine acquiescence.  Manifestations of resistance can also be found
in less organised form.  Evidence of long-standing, day-to-day lack
of compliance can be found in diverse sources.  Stanley Mathewson's
classic study of 'Restriction of Output Among Unorganized Workers',
published in 1931, gives no less than 223 detailed recorded instances of 'restriction'.  Emile Pouget in 'Sabotage' published in 1913,
outlines a syndicalist's account.  Pouget quotes an English pamphlet
of 1895 which reveals the manner in which the commodity status of
labour was turned back upon the employer:

> Now the bosses declare that labour and skill are nothing but com-
> modities like hats and shirts.  Very well we answer we'll take
> you at your word.  If labour and skill are commodities, their
> owners have a right to sell them like the hatter sells hats and
> the haberdasher sells shirts.  These merchants give a certain
> value in exchange for an equivalent value.  For the lower price
> you will have an article of either lower quality or a smaller
> quantity. (2)

In 1904, the US Commissioner of Labour published a report on 'Trade
Union Regulation and Restriction of Output'.  While it noted in
passing that limitations of production antedated trade union organisation, it confined itself to trade union manifestations and particularly the use of trade union rules.  Even Establishment maga-
zines such as 'Fortune' have been forced to recognise this refractoriness in more recent decades.  In what became characteristic of
the genre the magazine ran an article in 1970 entitled Blue Collar
Blues on the Assembly Line which analysed resistance to job discipline and the venting of feelings 'through absenteeism, high turnover, shoddy work, and even sabotage' (cited in Hunnius (ed.) 1973:
110).  Of course to be measured against such actions are the lay-
offs, rationalisations, speed-ups, plant closures and relocations
that have characterised the period since the 1970s.  In consequence,
it can be argued that in order to make any sensible assessment of
the kind of questions posed above, it is again necessary to locate
the analysis within the dialectical framework developed earlier.
The dialectic demands a linking of praxis to the totality and both
of these to the working-through of contradictions.  Thus it is
through past struggles and experience that the necessity to relate
conflict in the labour process to the totality is realised.  After
all, many of the control devices we have considered were designed
to surmount just such waywardness and recusance.  Marx noted this
dialectic between workers' struggles and employer strategies.  He
points out the large number of innovations 'whose immediate occasion
was a strike' (1976:563).  He thus argues that the employers' use of
rationalisation and machinery were not mere devices to act in competition with the worker.  On the contrary, they are:

   always on the point of making him superfluous.  It is a power
   inimical to him and capital proclaims this fact loudly and deliberately as well as making use of it.  It is the most powerful
   weapon for suppressing strikes, those periodic revolts of the
   working class against the autocracy of capital (Marx 1976:562).
Thus the vicious circle is complete:  capital continually works to
subdue labour, labour resists this fate and this resistance prompts
further repression.
   We will seek to assess the significance of workers' struggles and
resistance first by considering individualistic manifestations and
second, by considering more organised forms.


UNORGANISED RESISTANCE

Industrial relations analyses rarely depart from the institutional
level.  There have been occasional flirtations with the petit chou-
fleur of the industrial sociologist, the informal workgroup (see for
example Hill 1974), but it is rare for this tolerance to extend to
the level of the individual.  Yet the rich diversity and complexity
of work life arises because people do not respond to the farrago of
control devices in the fashion of automatons.  Individuals make an
assortment of adjustive responses to their subordinate predicaments.
Indeed, as David Mechanic has demonstrated (1962), 'lower participants' are not without their own sources of power and influence.
Perversely, those in hierarchical positions of formal authority who
conceptualise, plan, direct and in consequence are supposedly 'in
control', are themselves *dependent* upon the so-called lower participants for the implementation of their sense of order and routine.
Dependence is heightened by strategic informal coalitions which
certain staff may gradually construct and by inventive short-cuts
and operating procedures to which the formal system is blind.
   Responses such as absenteeism and quitting have to a large extent
been neglected by industrial sociologists and abandoned to economists and industrial psychologists.  Continued self-abnegation in
these areas would be regrettable.  There have been certain conceptual initiatives which could allow a more systematic study of the unorganised forms of response to control.  For example, the social
action perspective focuses on 'orientations'.  This could permit
analyses of expectations, adjustments of expectations and attempts
to shape situations to accord with expectations.  Etzioni (1961,
1975) writes of the 'orientations of the subordinate actor' ranging
from positive involvement which he labels 'commitment', to a negative involvement which he terms 'alienation'.  The locus of his concern is 'compliance' which is 'a relationship consisting of the
power employed by superiors to control subordinates and the orientation of the subordinates to this power' (1961:5).  It thus provides
a link between certain structural variables and individual action.
Rarely quoted is Etzioni's point that 'coercive power is probably
the only effective kind when the organization is confronted with
highly alienated lower participants' (1975:13).  The questions now
to be addressed are why workers should be alienated in the first
place and what responses can be expected?  Marx's theory of the real
subordination of labour has been discussed earlier and this gives a

clue to the first question.  His discussion of estranged labour in
the 'Philosophical and Economic Manuscripts' complements this.  At
the *individual* level Argyris's (1961) thesis also provides a useful
start point.  He claims there is a fundamental incompatibility between formal organisational principles and the needs of a mature
adult.  The healthy, mature personality in our culture is one which
develops, he says, from a passive infantile state to an active adult
one;  from dependency to an increased capacity for independence,
from circumscribed and limited capabilities to a repertoire of extended capabilities, from a shallow superficial involvement to a
capacity for and a requirement for a deepened sense of involvement.
The simple fact is that formal work organisations are inimical to
all these facets.  Highly circumscribed repetitive tasks deny a
meaningful level of involvement.  They disallow extended, stimulating activity.  Hierarchical authority systems demand dependence
not independence.  In effect there is an incongruence between bureaucratic control structures and the requirements of a normal
mature personality.

   Given such a structured denial of spontaneity and individuality,
and given blocked expressive aspirations, the classic psychological
prognostication is the condition of *frustration*.  This is the blocking of an organism's path towards a goal whether this goal-seeking
is conscious or unconscious (Drever 1964).  The kind of responses
evoked by frustration have been well researched.  Four basic forms
have been catalogued:  aggression, regression, fixation, resignation.  Aggression has been studied in laboratory situations by
gratuitously thwarting roused expectations, or thwarting half-
completed projects.  In the real-world factory situations participants themselves seem willing to frame accounts in these terms.
Thus in the 1978 Dagenham strike of foremen which followed the rein-
statement of an assailant, both union leaders and company managers
spoke of the aggression that can be seen building-up under assembly-
line conditions.  Regression occurs when positive attempts to 'prob-
lem-solve' constructively are abandoned in the face of continually
blocked initiatives.  When the odds seem overwhelming a person may
'regress' to a child-like state and resort to 'irresponsible' horse-
play.  This is a state where the person literally refuses to accept
responsibility for his situation or behavious.  Fixation is a display of compulsive, repetitive behaviour.  In the face of repeated
failures the person may revoke the search for alternative solutions
and respond by ritualistically repeating a set 'official' pattern
irrespective of varying conditions.  It is a defensive reaction
again demonstrating a refusal to accept responsibility given past
experiences. Resignation is a mental withdrawal and so commitment
is reduced to its absolute minimum. As a result existence at work
becomes a state of suspended animation. One particular form known
as introjection occurs when frustration is turned inwards and becomes
self-blame and depression. Whichever form it takes the apathy displayed is likely to provoke more direct supervision which in turn will
increase the frustration and thus a vicious circle is established.

   Given a widespread cultural commitment to individualism, personal
worth, encouragement of free expression, a political democracy and
some widely canvassed pretensions to egalitarian values, the new industrial recruit may experience culture shock upon arrival in the

hierarchical, markedly inequalitarian, conformist world of work.
Dissonance between expectations and experience requires some accommodation. A classic plotting of types of adaptations is R.K.
Merton's (1949) 'anomie paradigm'. From a juxtaposition of positive
and negative ends and means he derived his famous classification of
adaptations: conformity, innovation, ritualism, retreatism, rebellion. I would claim that these can be cross-tabulated with the responses to frustration discussed above. This can be shown as in
Table 8.1.

TABLE 8.1   Forms of unorganised response to frustrating work
structures

| Mode of adaptation | Ends | Means | Responses to frustration | Examples |
|---|---|---|---|---|
| 1  Conformity | + | + | Not frustrated | Obedience |
| 2  Innovation | + | - | Expediency | Modifying regulations |
| 3  Ritualism | - | + | Fixation, rigidity | Bureau-cratic at-tachment to red tape |
| 4  Retreatism/ Withdrawal | - | - | Resignation, apathy, regression | Frequent visits to toilet to smoke.  Ab-senteeism |
| 5  Rebellion | ± | ± | Aggression | Sabotage |

*Conformity* implies acceptance of prevailing goals and of approved
means. In practice it may be difficult to distinguish it from
ritualism which shows an outward sign of conformity with official
procedures, so we may consider these two behaviours together. Workers may *use* rules and procedures for their own purposes. They can
'bargain with their own conformity and use it as a tool with which
to bind management. This is just another aspect of the fight for
control. Subordinates tacitly agree to play the management game but
they try to turn it to their own advantage and to prevent management
from interfering with their independence' (Crozier 1964:185). In
other words, rules also serve to protect persons who submit to them.
Rigid organisations with impersonal rules and routine continue to
be built, in part because both superordinates and subordinates are
'trying to evade face-to-face relationships and situations of personal dependence whose authoritarian tone they cannot face' (1964:
54). Rules and routine offer a degree of protection from arbitrary
decision and afford a kind of independence. Subordinates' conformity to routine was also studied by Baldamus (1961). The tedium
of repetitive work, he found, was heightened between job cycles,
extra effort being required to start a new job cycle. During the
cycle, the phenomenon of traction created the relatively pleasant

sensation of being pulled-along.  It offers the most important
specific type of relative satisfaction in many industrial contexts
- though only in so far as the worker 'takes the external situation
for granted, the need to have a dissatisfying job at all, the necessity to keep going ...' (Baldamus 1961:65).  Like other instances of
conformity it is dependent upon the interpretations and meanings
which people bring to their job.  In a laboratory experiment reported by Baldamus, measuring reactions to repetitive tasks, subjects who thought the experiment meaningless from the start experienced more discomfort compared with those who thought they saw some
purpose in it.  The latter subjects delayed satiation for much
longer.

Rules can be used by supervisors and subordinates alike.  They
provide a bargaining tool.  Each side is likely to seek suspension
of the rule in certain instances, and on other occasions to insist
upon strict enforcement.  Further, to be bound-by-rule offers a kind
of freedom of spirit.  That is, bureaucracy offers an opportunity
for 'compulsory participation' without demanding a feeling of involvement.  This contingent parcelled-out commitment requires the
organisation to remain in a soliciting posture having, says Crozier
(1964:207), to beg for support.  Ritualistic conformity preserves a
measure of autonomy, hence people's ambivalence to participation.
Participation would require an adjustment of the psychological contract.  Understood from this standpoint Dubin's argument may in part
be vindicated.  Owing to a happy fit whereby those in undemanding
jobs have their central life interests outside work it is adjudged
unlikely that the privations of lowly status will generate any
serious measure of angst.  Dubin draws a distinction between 'necessary' and 'voluntary' action.  Motivation can be lower when actions
are of a necessary type (such as following the basic demands of industrial work).  There is a similarity here between this notion of
the low ego-demands of 'necessary acts' and Crozier's notion of the
retention of autonomy through ritualistic bureaucratic behaviour.

According to Dubin then, people solve the 'central dilemma' in
their own way and according to their own terms:  they focus on a
few central life interests and they then do not require self-
actualisation in the remaining areas of life.  He suggests that we
can easily act-out roles in formal organisations even if these are
not compatible with our personalities.  Indeed, the more easily we
can do this the less central such action is to our interests:

> Work in our society does not appear to be a central life interest
> for a substantial proportion if not a majority of our citizens.
> Their apathy and indifference result from this.  But this does
> not mitigate their effective performance as workers so long as
> their required behaviours are adequately set forth for them
> (Dubin 1961).

This conclusion has 'obvious implications' for managers concerned
with labour relations.  The vast bulk of personnel techniques designed to elicit enthusiasm from workers, rest on the assumption
that work is, or should be, an arena for self-actualisation.  If
this underlying assumption is invalid, as Dubin thinks it is, then
all the techniques built upon it are exposed as futile.  Whilst
Dubin offers a refreshingly challenging article, his case is suspect
on more than one count.  He overlooks the fact that the majority of

lower participants are structurally denied the possibility of having
work as a central life interest.  It is a voluntaristic model used
in an inappropriate sphere.  For example, Dubin posits people
*selecting* their central life interests (1961:80).  Further, as
status outside work and material allocation are closely associated
with work the scope for full involvement in non-work spheres is also
delimited by work involvement.

Despite these problems in his argument, the pointers he provides
have some value.  Industrial life, if not all beer and skittles, is
neither all conflict and strife.  Psychologists note how people
strive to maintain consistency between self-conception and their
situation.  Festinger's (1957) theory of cognitive dissonance suggests that people's adaptive responses can frequently fly in the
face of commonsense expectations.  Thus, for example, those paid
least in an experiment to endure pain were the ones more likely to
report that 'it doesn't hurt so much' (1957:153).  Hence, even those
in exploited positions have some interest in denying that explanation.  Festinger, Crozier, Merton and Dubin thus all produce theories which help to explain the high measure of conformity.  Indeed
the willingness of subjects to conform is frighteningly demonstrated
in Stanley Milgram's experiments (1963). (3)

*Innovative behaviour* implies acceptance of prescribed ends but
through the use of prescribed and illegitimate means.  This type of
adaptive action relies upon expediency and native cunning.  Donald
Roy's participative observation reports are replete with examples.
Many are associated with time study and 'making-out' on piece-rate
payment systems.  But equally, as with his study of tool allocation,
Roy was able to show how 'management logic tended to produce something less than efficiency' (1969:377).  So while innovative behaviour was frequently directed at making the job easier and better-
paid for the worker, it could also work towards functional adequacy.

*Retreatism/withdrawal* may take three forms:  complete withdrawal
(i.e. quitting), partial withdrawal (absenteeism) and psychic withdrawal (apathy and indifference while maintaining a physical presence).  In each case it is 'a privatised rather than a collective
mode of adaptation' (Merton 1949:155).  It is a form of adaptation
most likely when more institutionalised avenues are foreclosed.  In
Sykes's (1969) study of navvies the men displayed a fierce independence in the face of an unregulated, mobile and vulnerable employment situation.  They countered this by a willingness to 'jack' the
job at a moment's notice.  Indeed, the spontaneity was a source of
pride.  Quitting in industry in general may be indicative of a wider
frustration, maintains Maier.  He argues that 'the same conditions
that cause this type of turnover also cause grievances' (Maier 1973:
507).

Partial physical withdrawal through absenteeism may manifest
itself in sickness, accidental injury or just plain avoidance.  The
Tavistock Institute investigated accidents as 'a means of withdrawal
from the work situation' (Hill and Trist 1962).  They found a correlation between those workers experiencing accidents and those who
had most absences for 'no reason'.  Their diagnosis was that accidents are 'social as well as personal events....  It would seem to
follow that the quality of the relation obtaining between employees
and their workplace would in some way come 'into the question of ac-

cidents' (1962:3).  It was in order to clarify in *what* way the
social context has complicity that Nichols (1975) entered the
debate.  He highlights the limitations of the psychological and
forensic approaches, offering instead the view that 'accidents' are
the *inevitable* outcome of the 'structure of production' - i.e. the
pressure for output, the lack of worker control, the normalcy of
risky practices.  This more underlying aetiology of industrial accidents suggests they are a 'response' to the structure and authority of work organisations in a different sense.  But the veracity of
this case does not impinge on those analyses which seek to shed
light on the maldistributions of accidents within any given socio-
economic system.  The hypothesis could therefore remain that it is
in those situations where individuals are most alienated that 'accidents' are more likely to occur.  Psychic withdrawal was highlighted in Chinoy's 'Automobile Workers and the American Dream'
(1955).  He found some workers still entertaining hopes of escaping
into farming or running their own business, but the majority had
scaled down their aspirations and presented a passive face to their
work situation.  They manifested a marked lack of interest in promotion and withdrew attachment from institutionalised goals and means.
Rebellion did not follow;  rather, apathy.  Terkel's (1975:159) Ford
assembly worker illustrates the same syndrome:
  You dream, you think of things you've done.  I drift back continuously to when I was a kid and what me and my brothers did.
  Lots of times I worked from the time I started to the time of
  break and I never realized I had even worked.  When you dream
  you reduce the chances of friction....
  *Rebellion* as a mode of response is rarely a viable option for an
individual acting alone.  It may occur spontaneously but it is
likely to be viewed as sheer cussedness and the person concerned is
unlikely to be allowed an opportunity to repeat the behaviour more
than once.  If frustration runs high a person may rebel by swearing
at the foreman, refuse to do work or even resort to physical violence against person or object.  Summary dismissal is still preserved for such acts, being of the type enshrined in the 'serious
indiscipline' category of disciplinary manuals.
  One important response to a situation experienced as repressive
may be industrial sabotage.  This can take an individualistic or
collective form.  But even as an individual act it may meet with the
tacit approval, co-operation or indifference of other workers.  Industrial sabotage may provide an index of underlying industrial conflict.  One steelworker confided:  'The men don't usually talk about
this stuff;  communication is carried on through undercurrents and
understanding'.  But this doesn't necessarily detract from its significance and potency.  As the same steelworker went on to say, 'the
only way the foreman can survive - the only way he gets a fair
amount of work done in his zone - is to understand this *communica-
tion-by-sabotage*' (Montgomery 1979:156, emphasis added).  It is not
always easy to determine which actions or inactions can be regarded
as sabotage and which dismissed as 'nobody's fault', or simple
bungling.  Industrial sabotage has been defined as 'that rule-
breaking which takes the form of conscious action or inaction directed towards the mutilation or destruction of the work environment
(this includes the machinery of production and the commodity

itself)' (Taylor and Walton 1971:219). The interesting point about
this definition is the reference to 'rule-breaking'. Many steps are
taken by management which result in destruction of the product or
the cessation of production. It remains, I think, a superior definition to that offered by Pierre Dubois (1979) which is so all-
inclusive that it attempts to cover practically everything done by
workers and management which 'results in lowering the quantity or
quality of production' (1979:14). He therefore includes poor planning, less than optimum plant maintenance and even inadequate consideration of the siting of machinery. The trouble with this catho-
lic definition is that it starts from a baseline of some hypothetical efficiency standard and posits that any human action or inaction
that detracts from the attainment of this standard may be regarded
as 'sabotage'. This is to rob the term of any meaning; Geoff Brown
(1977) also relies on a somewhat elastic definition but not quite so
expandable as that of Dubois.

Discussions on the subject of industrial sabotage invariably
focus only upon worker behaviour, rarely if ever upon managerial.
(4) Yet the wholescale destruction of motor parts and accessories
by British Leyland was accepted because its expressed purpose was to
maintain market price and 'stabilise distribution outlets'. Clearly
the mere event of destruction is not sufficient to attract the label
of 'sabotage'. The same destructive act meets with moral disappro-
bation if perpetrated by workers for a respite, or for purposes of
protecting the market for labour (it has been suggested for example,
that print workers on the 'Sun' newspaper used to cut the production
run at 4 million copies in order to avoid undue damage to comrades
at the 'Mirror'), yet moral approbation, if perpetrated by managers
for purposes of protecting or shaping product markets. The pouring-
away of milk and the dumping of the agricultural 'over-production'
clearly illustrates production for profit not need. Apologists
would contend of course that maintenance of the market mechanism of
which these destructive acts form but a part, is in *the long-run*
interest of the consumer and producer. The point in terms of the
definition then is that the same destructive act is sabotage if in
violation of official *rules,* but 'normal' practice if in-accord-
with-rule. This quite clearly brings the focus back upon the origin
of these rules, the mechanisms whereby they become established, and
the question of who benefits from such rules.

'Mutilation' of the product sent out to the customer would normally be viewed as sabotage unless it was officially sanctioned as
near-enough-up-to standard given the particular circumstances (a
rush-order, pressure of other work and so on). But what of those
acts which do not damage the product but simply prevent production
altogether beyond a certain level? Managerial intervention here is
called 'production planning'. But if workers intervene their actions may be labelled either sabotage or 'restriction of output'.
There is no absolute dividing line between these two, but the latter
tends to be used when workers restrict their own expenditure of
*effort,* whereas if they hinder the machine-based production process
this is more likely to attract the 'sabotage' castigation.

Taylor and Walton suggest many 'breakdowns' are in fact consciously contrived break-times (1971:221). This is partly the case.
In one factory I was researching it was a twice-a-day routine for

workers on a conveyor-belt assembly to cut one of the drive-wires,
in order to 'take-a-breather'.  The repair was a simple and relatively inexpensive procedure taking about ten minutes, but this
means of securing a rest could presumably lend itself to improvement.  A more complex intentionality lies behind other forms of
sabotage.  As an outcome of the authority system examined in earlier
chapters, workers respond to lack of trust, and lack of discretion
by allowing a process which they know to be damaging and less efficient to proceed.  They do so because they have no 'responsibility'
(literally in the sense that the process design is not their responsibility) for the procedure.  When steelworkers allow a metal
slab that is too cold to be rolled, to proceed on its course and do
damage to machinery, and then retort:  'It's supposed to be right,
they make the decision, we couldn't care less' (ibid.), it is likely
that they mean:  'Why should we care given the structuring of responsibility?'  Such workers operate in a milieu where they are continually reminded that they are paid to do as they are told.

Industrial sabotage may not then be so 'meaningless' as it is
often portrayed.  It may have meaning in that the intention behind
it is to reduce tension, frustration or effort;  to ease the nature
of the task (instances of this kind might well figure under our
earlier category of 'innovative' behaviour);  or to gain some control over the job.  Under this latter form, Taylor and Walton include the actions of the Roberts Arundel strikers in Stockport who
attacked the outside of buildings during their long and unsuccessful
battle for union recognition.  Along with similar events in Turin
car plants, and Chadderton machine smashing during the early phases
of the Industrial Revolution, these events are characterised as
'collective bargaining by riot'.  If institutionalised channels for
protest were blocked, sabotage of this type might be expected to
increase.  And the tactics employed may not always be so bizarre as
the mooted loosening of pepperpot tops in the Claridge's Hotel dispute. (5)


ORGANISED RESISTANCE

Organised worker resistance and challenge should not necessarily be
equated with unionism.  Workers are not restricted to the closed
choice between pursuing grievances through the union structures or
alternatively restricting themselves to spontaneous individual acts
of sabotage or withdrawal.  From a year's participant observation
Bill Watson (1972) paints an evocative picture of organised
'counter-planning' in a Detroit auto plant.  This involved co-
operative action extending beyond one department to secure the unofficial 'reorganisation' of the work day to allow, for example,
significant blocks of recreation time to be carved out.  It involved
action to turn the working day, at least partly, into slots of 'en-
joyable activity' by organising 'games' such as water-fights with
hosepipes and competitions to seize-up test engines.  Perhaps more
significantly, 'counter-planning' is reported as extending to attempts to reverse a management decision on a new model.  This model
was said to be hastily planned and riddled with problems.  Having
been met with an impassive management response to 'dozens of sug-

gestions for improving the motor and modifying its design' (Watson 1972:77) workers engaged in organised acts of sabotage to 'counter-plan the production of the motor'. This involved mis-assembly, omission of parts and the cracking of distributor caps and other components on those cars which reached inspection otherwise apparently unscathed. The scale of counter-planning was such, maintains Bill Watson, that after a six-week lay-off the entire assembly for this model was dismantled and relocated with new workers brought in to man it.

The point raised in this article is that sabotage was of only secondary significance; it was merely an instrument used to much greater purpose. The nature of that purpose according to Watson is of some long-term importance. In brief he interprets such organised plant-based activity as a 'new form' which goes 'beyond unionism'. Whilst he acknowledges that early forms of independent workers' activity and sabotage existed in the late nineteenth century and under the Wobblies, what is more significant, indeed, 'unique' about current counter-planning on the shopfloor is that it is occurring *after* the establishment of mass unionism not as an incipient form of it. Moreover it can be now interpreted, he suggests as 'a definite response to the obsolescence of that social form' (Watson 1972:77). This latter observation seems a somewhat exaggerated assessment at this time, but the general tenor of the argument has some validity. Worker resistance does extend well beyond the formal union structure and in some large measure is relatively independent of it. In any event Watson's study is an important corrective to those analyses which confine discussion to corporate strategies and structures of control and thereby neglect the struggle at the point of production - i.e. the point of attempted implementation.

Mathewson's fascinating study of 'Restriction of Output Among Unorganized Workers', published in 1931, reveals that both individual and collective resistance and struggle occurred irrespective of unionisation. From extensive participant observation and interviewing of 350 workers he logged detailed information on 223 instances of restriction. They ranged over 105 establishments in 47 localities and covered 39 industries. While making his observations, the author worked as a labourer, a machine operator, a bench assembler and a skilled mechanic: he held in total 11 different jobs during the period of the investigation. He concluded that restriction was 'a widespread institution, deeply intrenched in the working habits' of Americans. In the first half of his book Mathewson describes numerous instances of restriction classified under six chapters according to the 'reasons' for restriction as generally seen from the workers' viewpoint. These comprised: pressure from fellow workers, boss-ordered restriction, wage payment, time study, fear of unemployment, and personal grievances. These six of course grossly overlap. Pressure from fellow workers and from foremen often transpired to derive from a desire to prevent lay-off and/or to protect earnings. These are the two most prominent explanations explored by Mathewson. However, some practices were simply designed to make work easier as in the case of the Mexican whose job it was to check the final tightening of the nuts on cylinder heads.

His instructions were to test all the nuts and if he found *one* or *two* loose nuts to tighten them, but if three or more were loose he was not expected to have time to tighten that many. In such cases he marked the engine with chalk and it was later set aside from the conveyor and given special attention. The superintendent found that the number of engines so set aside reached an annoying total in the day's work. He made several unsuccessful attempts to locate the trouble. Finally, by carefully watching all the men on the conveyor line, he discovered that the Mexican was unscrewing a *third* tight nut wherever he found two already loose. It was easier to loosen *one* nut than to tighten *two*' (Mathewson 1969:126).

In subsequent interviews with 65 executives Mathewson was surprised at the apparently sanguine view adopted. One line of argument he found was that restriction only became serious during the very occasional periods of lay-off and that as one senior manager expressed it, it is 'an expense that probably enters at such times like new tools and other costs incident to bringing out a new product' (p.132). In fact the academics contributing chapters to the book found it hard to understand the bosses' complacency. These latter could be found regarding it as a natural part of the market struggle - the workers seeking to adjust the supply of labour just as employers seek to adjust the supply in the product market.

Mathewson did, however, make some telling remarks. He observed workers 'successfully matching wits with management in self-protective resistance against wage-incentive plans, piece-rate cuts and prospective lay-offs' (p.152). This can be linked to one of his other conclusions: namely, 'that scientific management has failed to develop that spirit of confidence between the parties to labour contracts which has been so potent in developing good-will between the parties to a sales contract' (p.146). In fact, one of his key recommendations is a bold switch in trust similar to merchants' abandonment of caveat emptor, for the policy of the customer is always right. Could the employer institute such a policy with respect to his workers? Mathewson argues that, after all, these are in effect the self-same customers. Morgan, the President of Antioch College, wrote the conclusion to the book. He points to sheer laziness as a neglected source of restriction and yet on the other hand adopts a humanistic perspective in condemning the waste of human potential and dignity which are bound up in systematic practices of having to look-busy. He sees workers as beating capitalists at their own game - getting more for less and in the end he turns to condemn a system built on selfishness while praising the high ethical character displayed by refusing to be a passive victim and conspirator. Too much justification of restriction, he argues, will be corrosive of the regenerative spirit which in the end is humanity's final hope.

Each of the contributing commentators seem to overlook the importance of preserving some scope for autonomous regulation, the need for some measure of *control*. It is hard to imagine a 100 per cent production standard being maintained precisely as ordained without some attempt being made to vary the routine. Equally, other forms of restriction of output cannot be equated with this drive for autonomy. The production loss resulting from poor planning and the consequent injunction to workers to 'look busy' is demeaning to them and expresses their institutionalised subordination.

TOTALITY

Attention to the concept of totality allows one to confront a slice
of the questions posed at the beginning of this chapter.  Thus
brought into particular illumination are those questions concerning
the meaning and significance of 'workers' control', and the scope
and depth of workers' challenge.

Totality as used by Lukács refers, as noted earlier, to the idea
that each social formation and mode of production comprises totality
such that the complex whole is composed of interrelated parts.  The
totality is reflected in each part;  thus the whole is in the parts
and the parts in the whole.  Work organisations as mini-totalities
are thus crucial points of tension:  their vulnerability to challenge exposes the totality to subversion, but in turn they are
bolstered by ideological and material bulwarks of the totality.
This interrelationship exposes work organisations to the stress
emanating from the contractions and crises of the totality and vice
versa.

Crises of accumulation oblige management to take the initiative
in forcing *control* issues to the forefront.  The capacity to absorb
pressures through the growth process is curtailed.  The system's inherent stability or otherwise is tested more fundamentally.  Hence,
recent managerial initiatives in the realms of tighter discipline,
de-manning, speed up, and 'rationalisation' measures across a broad
front brings managerial strategy into sharper focus.  This point is
illustrated clearly in the response of BL's shop stewards' combine
to the closure plan for the Rover plant at Solihull.  In reaction to
this move in the Edwardes 'streamlining plan', the shop stewards'
combine, called for a public inquiry into the whole of 'B.L.'s long-
term strategy'. (6)  Meanwhile, the potential 'beneficiaries' at
Cowley who are destined to receive the extra work have pledged to
resist attempts to transfer production to their site.  However, it
is the increasing attention directed at the whole strategy which is
of interest.  The Edwardes plan was originally approved by the workforce in a ballot in the winter of 1979/80.  As it unfolds - or
rather develops - the whole nature of the corporate strategy is
increasingly questioned.

This process of ever-widening focus is integral to the essence of
'workers' control'.  This concept, used with extreme latitude, is
made to carry a whole range of meanings.  David Montgomery (1979)
writes of 'Workers' Control in America' referring thereby to workers' control *within* capitalism.  Others, for example Hunnius, Garson
and Case (1973), see workers' control rather as an objective, an end
state, something to be strived for.  They distinguish it from the
joint consultation or co-determination schemes of Western Europe
(for these again represent other shades of meaning of the term).
Instead, they write, 'workers' control, to us, means a fundamental
restructuring of the economic order.  In the plant it does not
simply mean replacing one set of anonymous electors with another;
it means extending democracy of participation to the shopfloor
through decentralised co-operative decision-making.  In the larger
economy - and this is equally critical - it means appropriating control of fundamental economic decisions to the people as a whole, and
deciding democratically on the allocation of resources.  A corollary

of this is that workers' control means taking this economic power
away from the tiny elite which now owns and manages the huge corporations of North America's private economy' (Hunnius et al. 1973:
324). Workers' control then, is almost another term for socialism.

From such accounts workers' control can only be meaningful if it
does confront the totality. Self-management cannot succeed in these
terms unless it is achieved both at the level of the overall system
and at unit level (Burns et al. 1979). But it is not just a question of level; it must also involve totality in the sense of scope
and depth. Thus the separation of 'industrial' from 'political'
issues would be regarded as ideological, constrictive, and impedi-
mental. As Fox (1974a:152) points out, political levels of decision-making are becoming more involved in shaping the contours to
which industry has to respond. 'Political decisions and industrial
issues being thus inextricably interwoven, unions can only fully
apply themselves to the latter by pressing also for admission to the
former.' The dialectical issue of totality is perhaps revealed most
clearly in the debate surrounding syndicalism, the workers' committee movement, guild socialism and other similar strategic attempts to bring about total radical change through direct action at
the point of production. Advocates of these schemes espoused aggressive control rather than merely defensive job control, and their
ultimate goal was the displacement of the present capitalist system
in favour of some form of workers' control.

The flowering of workers' control and guild socialist ideas occurred in Britain and other European countries around the time of
the First World War. The tumultuous events of this period could be
seen as the caryatids of the ensuing development at workplace level
after the Second World War. The most visionary and ambitious programmes revolved around the workers' committees movement on the
Clyde and other munitions and engineering centres. The official
trade unions had declared industrial peace but problems occurred
following the Treasury Agreement which relaxed trade union protective measures and introduced 'diluted' labour. Despite the fact
that in many engineering shops management did not recognise shop
stewards and maintained that their dealings at most were with 'ad
hoc deputations', the stewards established sometimes powerful workers' committees. Their aims were expounded in pamphlets by Willie
Gallacher of the Clyde Workers' Committee and J.T. Murphy of Shef-
field. In his pamphlet entitled 'Direct Action: An Outline of
Workshop and Social Organisation', Gallacher (1972) states his case
clearly: radical social change means taking the initiative

in the everyday struggle with the functionaries of the employing
class in the workshops.... It is by organizing the workers'
power of numbers in the place where power can be applied most successfully, namely in industry, that we will be able to break the
power of the employers and their puppet government (Gallacher
1919:14).

Similarly, Murphy (1972) in his pamphlet 'The Workers' Committee:
An Outline of its Principles and Structure', had written 'we are
driven back to the workshops ... the new units of organization'
(1972:18). This pamphlet by Murphy has been described as 'the chief
theoretical statement to emerge from the shop stewards' movement in
Britain during the First World War' (Hinton 1972:3). An elaborate

structure of works or plant committees composed of shop stewards
from each union and grade would be supplemented by local industry
committees, local workers' committees (from a range of industries)
and national workers' committees.  This structure was envisaged by
both Murphy and Gallacher.  'We are not antagonistic to the trade
union movement', Gallacher felt it necessary to write, but his programme implied some significant redirection for these bodies which
so 'perplex' the working class (Murphy 1972:25).

The workers' committees enjoyed some considerable support during
the First World War and they were able to organise massive district-
wide strikes.  Similar workers' councils movements, operating as
foci for revolutionary action replacing in part the traditional
socialist parties and trade unions, were found in many other countries.  Syndicalism was originally a French movement which rejected
the 'parliamentarianism' of the socialist party and emphasised
instead the centrality of the industrial struggle.  The political
battle for the state levers of power could thereby largely be by-
passed.  Their vision of socialist society contained at its core a
federated system of self-governing enterprises.  The movement found
reflection in America under the Industrial Workers of the World and
in Britain under Tom Mann's doctrine of 'industrial unionism'.  Many
syndicalists such as those in the Socialist Labour Party founded in
1903 were suspicious and even hostile to trade unions which they saw
as having complicity in the capitalist order.  But Mann believed a
base had to be built through industrial unionism in order to mount
successfully a general strike which would be the first step to
direct seizure of the means of production.  Syndicalism then, gave
'total' meaning to immediate struggles at the point of production
which, its advocates suggested, could be more important than politics at the centre.

The potential incompatibility between authentic workers' self-
management and state socialism was an issue of which Antonio Gramsci
was only too acutely aware.  He saw workers' self-management as essential on both moral and economic grounds.  Gramsci, writing at the
same time as Murphy and Gallacher, also focused on workplace
struggles.  In his famous 'Soviets in Italy' written in 1919, he
refers to the factory as the 'cell of a new state - the workers'
state' (Gramsci 1969:8).  A number of questions are left begging by
each of these pamphlets, not the least of which concerns the transition to workers' self-government, the role of managers, and the relationships with consumers generally.  The most systematic schema to
cope with such problems was that put forward by the Guild Socialists
represented notably by G.D.H. Cole.  They proposed the method of
'encroaching control', and the 'guilds' which were to run industry
would comprise those persons with specialist, technical, and managerial skill. The self-government exercised by these guilds would
be qualified by the terms of their contract with a 'state' body
whose prime duty was to protect the interests of consumers. One of
their more interesting proposals was a collective contract. This
would be part of the transitionary stage during the securement
of encroaching control. It was a type of autonomous work group,
writ large. The works committee would sign a collective contract
with the employer under which they would undertake the self-management of discipline, the allocation of labour, supervision and other

matters and in return they would receive a lump-sum payment from the employer.  It was a system of workers' control without the immediate dispossession of the entrepreneur.  The idea was taken up for a time by Gallacher himself, although he repudiated it when he eventually joined the Communist Party.  The collective contract was never fully implemented, although the shop stewards' committee at Whitehead Torpedo Works (Weymouth) produced a number of detailed memoranda outlining their proposals (Cole 1973).  The Whitehead men explain their terms as representing a response to the joint participatory proposals of the Whitely Committee, which contrivance they saw as an intended 'sedative for labour' (1973:177).  Their failure to secure implementation of their own blue-print could presumably be explained by the unwillingness of any employer to co-operate in his own eventual dispossession and demise.  For, while there may have been a future for the specialist manager under guild socialism there was no long-term future for capital.  The concept of totality can also refer to the extent of visibility accorded to, or demanded by, 'constituents' or, to use Abrahamsson and Bromstrom's term 'man-dators'.  Thus Mandel (1973:349) points out the condition that 'workers' control must be exercised by the elected delegates of the workers in full view of the entire working class and the nation as a whole, and not by a few trade union leaders meeting in secret with a few employers' leaders'.  The mechanisms for meeting this desider-atum are not as yet, however, fashioned.  But connections with Habermas's public 'communicative competence' are apparent.

The notion of totality further implies that the interactionist perspective and the associated 'negotiation of order' approach must be regarded as of only partial utility.  Indeed, the notion of ne-gotiation of order as developed by Strauss could be said to be positively misleading.  The day-to-day 'unremitting effort' of re-negotiating reality and order occurs within a context of a skewed power distribution and overarching inequality.  As Day and Day (1977) argued, the negotiation of order approach has yet to make adequate connections with the wider structures of power in economy and society.  The logic of this line of argument is, as was pointed out in chapter 1, that in the context of a 'world capitalist system' (Wallerstein 1976) even the societal level cannot be regarded as the totality.  In consequence, even a broadly-based challenge to capital in Britain may be muted by the mobility of capital.  A militant working class which, despite uneven development across industry, managed to mount a generally successful and developing challenge to capitalist control, is likely to face a dematerialisation and flight of capital.  This will involve a closure or run-down of those oper-ations where control has been most re-appropriated by workers and it will continue until the 'refactory hand of labour' has learned its lesson.  The removal of exchange controls on sterling permits this capital mobility to proceed more smoothly, though it is doubtful if the process would be significantly hindered in the longer term even without such a facility.

There are then stringent limits to workers' control under capi-talism.  Managers, it might be argued, can only relinquish preroga-tives of a highly circumscribed kind.  They must retain the right to ensure that, ultimately, production proceeds in a manner which real-ises surplus-value.  At factory or indeed company level any attempt

to impose alternative priorities, or rules which had the effect of
negating this central priority, quite simply would not, nor could
not be tolerated.  But having said that, there is a dearth of research which actually indicates the extent to which workers have
been able to challenge managerial prerogatives.  British writers on
industrial relations have largely been happier in confining themselves to logging *procedural* changes.  This remains true even today
as is witnessed by the latest study in the Warwick Industrial Relations series, Brown (ed.) (1981);  but its apogee was found in the
work of Allan Flanders (1965, 1968).  Two research reports were published in 1980, however, which helped to shed some light on this
frontier of control (Storey 1980;  Cressey and McInnes 1980c).
Cressey and McInnes's report covered 48 enterprises in Scotland.
The findings in general reflect those found in Storey (1980).  This
latter research involved a monitoring of 96 establishments between
1971 and 1978.  Previous reports of this kind had been few.  Those
coming closest had emanated from official sources:  the Government
Social Survey published in 1978 and two from the Office of Population Censuses and Surveys in the early 1970s.  These tended to show
a widening range of bargaining, but their yardstick was largely confined to job-related issues and in a sense the research was in the
tradition of that literative probing the shop steward's range of
duties (cf. Goodman and Whittingham 1969;  Partridge 1978;  Poole
1974;  Batstone et al. 1977).  Clarke, Fatchett and Roberts (1972)
examined 'workers' participation in management' more generally, and
accordingly they did include questions on financial matters and work
methods.  But their questions asked managers what they thought *ought*
to happen rather than probing what in practice actually does.  For
example, on the issue of contracting-out they observe, 'the great
majority of firms do not regard a decision to put work out to sub-
contract as one which they ought to discuss as a matter of course
with the unions or their members' (1972:94).  However, on matters
crucially located at the margin, the distinction between a general
'policy' and actual practice is especially critical.  Thus, although
only 3 per cent of their management sample considered sub-contracting as a question they *ought* to share, my own results showed that
28 per cent of managers admit that they had in fact negotiated on
this issue.  Similarly, a cognate article in 'Personnel Review' also
reports on a study which consulted managers in order to ascertain
not what they do but somewhat strangely to quiz them on what 'managers feel workers are most concerned about in relation to their
jobs'.  There was 'surprise ... to find such strength of support'
for joint consultation in view of its (actual) patchy historical
record' (Beaumont 1978:52,54).  But this becomes less surprising
when it is noted that the questionnaires were distributed to middle
managers who were at the time attending courses at Glasgow University.  Moreover, they were all involved in, or had a background in,
the personnel function.  The pitfalls associated with this kind of
research on perceptions is also revealed by the strange 'finding'
that 'control of work' is one of the mostly highly ranked issues on
a scale purporting to reveal 'similarity of aims'.

The majority of studies, then, have revealed little about the
location of the frontier of control.  At best certain snapshot studies give a static view but leave the *direction* of change in doubt.

Storey (1980) sought to repair some of these shortcomings by providing a sketch of movements in the frontier of control during the
1970s.  Given the generally depressed state of the economy during
this period and the deepening recession one would normally hypothe-
sise a debilitated shopfloor challenge.  Yet the results showed that
between 1971 and 1978 the strength of workplace shop stewards'
organisation increased and that the range of issues negotiated and
controlled by the stewards also expanded.  It was notable, however
(Storey 1980:131), that the overall increase as measured was less
than the estimates of the participants themselves would have led us
to expect.  The doctrine of managerial prerogatives dictates that
certain decision areas are, by their very nature, inappropriate for
negotiation.  This would imply that 'non-negotiable' questions must
possess some generic similarity, some underlying coherence and recognisable rationale.  Various authors have distinguished between
traditional bargaining issues versus developing ones (Slichter,
Healy, Livernash 1960);  external, market issues versus internal
governmental issues (Chamberlain and Kuhn 1965;  Fox 1974b);  and
job territory issues versus policy issues (Perlman 1968).  In fact
it was found that the old distinction between legitimate-market-
external issues, and illegitimate-managerial-internal issues, while
offering a general guide, was by 1978 heavily compromised.  Thus
questions of manning levels and discipline were reported by over
half of the managers and stewards as having in fact been subject to
negotiation.  Production techniques and methods, contracting work
out, and scheduling, had been negotiated in a quarter to a third of
establishments.  They comprised the middle group of issues 'deli-
cately poised on the edge of accepted negotiability' (Storey 1980:
133).  Issues assailed by shop stewards but in the main effectively
retained by managers included type and price of product, and the
purchase of new plant and equipment (15 per cent of managers admitted negotiations had occurred on this but 23 per cent of stewards
claimed it had occurred).  In addition, there were some areas over
which both Storey (1980) and Marsh et al. (1971) concurred that
there was some large measure of direct worker control.  These included manning, speed of work, and job demarcation.  Storey also
reported on inter-industry comparisons.  These cannot be repeated
here but it should be noted that there was sufficient contrast between industries and between establishments within the same industry
as to make it more accurate to speak of *frontiers* of control rather
than a frontier of control.

  In sum, the widening scope of workplace bargaining did appear to
have continued well into the late 1970s despite the deepening recession and mounting unemployment.  Workplace shop steward organisations too, displayed a resilience beyond what might have been
expected under orthodox labour economics theory.  What has occurred
since 1978 is more open to doubt but the survey by Cressey and
McInnes conducted in 1979 and a recent survey by W.E.J. McCarthy
(1981) conducted on behalf of the Department of Employment are in
accord with the data reported above.

PRAXIS AND SOCIAL CONSTRUCTION

A consideration of totality may be so daunting in that the interconnected parts of capitalism appear so massive and unassailable, as to
induce a state of apathetic resignation. What can be the point of
struggling for workers' control if it is not achievable under the
present system?  Gorz (1973:342) provides an answer to this question. He points out that the results of such a struggle should not
be measured only in terms of the immediate substantive outcome. He
says:

> The main result of this struggle is that it changes people, it
> changes ourselves. It is something like a self-educational pro-
> cess. Through it, we discover, or rather we invent, the working
> class's capability of self-organization, of self-determination,
> of control over the production process. We discover that workers
> are by no means as incompetent as the division of labour wants to
> make them feel....

The socially constructed incompetence 'managed' through the extreme division of labour may be thrown into sharp relief by workers'
activities in their 'own time'. Thus Woods (1981), reporting on
banger racing, observes the outstanding proficiency and confidence
of the driver-mechanics who engage in this sport. 'What is remarkable', he notes, 'is the unsystematic but thorough acquisition of
knowledge ... they are masters of improvisation. If something needs
doing, there is a way of doing it. No problem is insoluble' (1981:
387). Contrast such skill and ingenuity with the service offered by
the average domestic appliance repair 'engineer'!

The demand for workers' control may hold a central place in a
socialist strategy for the displacement of capitalism. What it
cannot do is, in itself to represent a nirvana or end state. The
objective of socialism

> has to grow out of the very needs of their fight. The demand for
> workers' control (which involves challenging the power of the
> bourgeoisie at all levels and which tends to give birth, first in
> the factory, later in the country at large, to an embryonic work-
> ers' power counterposed to bourgeois power) is the best bridge
> between the struggle for immediate demands and the struggle for
> power (Mandel 1973:348).

Thus Mandel, like Gorz above, is recommending workers' control under
capitalism as an exercise in *praxis*.

> In similar vein, Lenin points out the limitations of propaganda:
> It is not enough to *explain* to the workers that they are politi-
> cally oppressed (any more that it is to explain to them that
> their interests are antagonistic to the interests of employers).
> Agitation must be conducted with regard to every concrete example
> of this oppression (1947:57).

Lenin goes on to emphasise the necessity to expose the political dimension through concrete instances of economic oppression and agitation. In this way one could begin to transcend economism in workers' struggles. However, he believed this could only be fully
achieved through the development of a vanguard party. In the absence of this, workers' struggle and resistance would not develop
beyond 'trade union consciousness'.

These reservations find echo in Perry Anderson's statement that

'as institutions trade unions do not challenge the existence of a
society based on the division of classes, they merely express it'
(1967:264).  Observations of this kind cast doubt upon the political
significance of trade union struggles.  Marx has made known his own
misgivings about economism.  He wrote: 'The struggles over wages
within the manufacturing system presuppose manufacture and are in no
sense directed against its existence' (Marx 1976:555).  Unions seem
in practice to thrust towards ameliorating some of the excesses of
capitalism.  They can only, maintains Anderson (1967:265), 'bargain
within society but not transform it'.  Their practice, it seems true
enough, is bent largely towards regularising the social relationships of production.  Hence much time and energy is directed towards
establishing *procedures* and formalising workers' rights.  Lenin was
wrong, however, in implying that unions are logically limited to
economism.  Even Flanders pressed the point that unionism and collective bargaining are necessarily exercises in *power* relationships.
The study of *workplace* unionism in particular (see for example
Beynon 1973, and Storey 1980) leaves no doubt that struggles over
control are a fundamental and continual phenomenon.  Most certainly
the initiative to shift the frontier of control comes from both parties.  As the recession has deepened management have mounted an intensive challenge in order to roll back workers' gains in shopfloor
control.  But the vigorous resistance to this drive by Ford workers
and the miners, for example, makes the charge of economism look
facile.

The social construction aspect of the dialectical approach also
illuminates the relation between material interests and definitions
of reality.  Hence, early Taylorism was strenuously resisted by
craftsmen because it conflicted sharply with traditional modes of
operation and values.  The kind of behaviour required by the new
management approach was regarded by craftsmen as 'hoggish' and 'un-
manly' forms of conduct.  Operating more than one machine, undermining another worker's position, allowing supervisors to watch
one's work, and even accepting the piece-work form of payment - all
were 'hoggish' and 'conduct unbecoming a true craftsman' (Montgomery
1979:115).  Yet Taylorism promotes a reverse perspective:  failure
to co-operate in the desired way is 'systematic soldiering'.  These
different social constructions were grounded in divergent interests.
But additionally, they reflected the shift from an independent craft
tradition where speed, quality and technique were in the hands of
the artisan, to a developing subordination of labour (formal and
real) where attempted preservation of the same practices could be
interpreted as a disciplinary matter.  The fascination of this
period reflects the drama of a violence done to the values of an
earlier age.  'To the craftsman, time-study symbolized simultaneously the theft of his knowledge by his employers and an outrage
against his sense of honourable behaviour at work' (Montgomery 1979:
115).

A few generations later, blind to its own progeny, management is
affronted by actions and demands which challenge its 'absolute
right' to decide and command.  Another shift in reality is threatened.

The force of this challenge is in part dependent upon workers'
social imagery and consciousness.  David Lockwood (1966) outlines

three different types of worker with respect to their class images.
'Traditional proletarian' is designated as characterised by a power
model of social imagery; the 'deferential' worker holds a status
hierarchy conceptualisation; and the 'privatised' worker's outlook
approximates a 'pecuniary' model of society. Lockwood goes on to
relate these types to certain behavioural patterns. In the work
situation the privatised worker's expectations of involvement are
low as is his or her identification with fellow workers. This model
of the privatised worker was of course utilised in the famous 'af-
fluent worker' studies. The much-celebrated 'instrumental-orienta-
tion' of privatised workers at Vauxhall by implication signalled the
indifference of this 'new' working class to the deprivations of the
labour process. Only the sphere of exchange, not the sphere of production, was to count. Real subordination and the labour process
could continue to be ignored. It is thus with barely disguised
satisfaction that Andre Gorz (1973) recounts the events at Vauxhall
immediately subsequent to the conclusion of Goldthorpe's report.
Quoting 'The Times', he reports how thousands of these supposedly
integrated apathetic workers engaged in 'wild rioting' as they be-
sieged the management offices.

It is the relationship between the report and the worker behaviour which is of interest to us here. The leaked résumé of the
report was allegedly a factor in 'stimulating an explosion of class
consciousness' (Gorz 1973:334). Individually, Gorz explains, these
workers *were* apathetic. As individuals they could mount no meaningful resistance with a view to changing things. But gelled into a
collective by the report and their discussion of it, they shed these
inhibitions and took on new power and confidence. Collective action
is, as we have seen, a heuristic process. Workers learn what they
want and what they need through *praxis*. Strikes over control issues
can be, maintains Gorz, a revolutionary experience, but he also
notes that workers' councils and other devices which spring up must
either move forward to transcend capitalism or degenerate. They
cannot for long sustain a co-existence. This might explain why the
catalogue of momentous rebellion still leaves the auto-lines running, labour still divided and managerial hierarchies as refined as
ever.

But praxis is not limited to the struggle at the point of production. While this is necessarily our primary focus, it would be
wrong to infer from the discussion of totality that there exists a
perfect integration of mutually-reinforcing parts. On the contrary,
there is some considerable degree of non-correspondence between, for
example, the education system, the state and capital. Hegemony is
not complete. The schools and universities, for instance, may sow
seeds of values such as spontaneity, creativity and self-expression
which enjoy less than perfect fit with the interests of capital.
There are, for example, continuous complaints that teachers in the
main have no personal experience of industry and commerce and are
often antipathetic towards it. Similarly, the educational institutions, far from behaving as doting handmaidens of industry, may
become the centres of challenge to it. This is a theme explored in
many texts (see, for example, Habermas 1971 on student protest).
Thus the vital struggle may not necessarily emerge from the sphere
of production. Even were it so, expectations which militate against

the system may be initially forged in parts of the totality outside the workplace.


CONTRADICTIONS

The contradictions immanent in resistance and control strategies surface at a number of points.  Ultimately, as argued earlier, all attempts at the real subordination of labour founder on the rock of the final reliance of capital on workers operating, handling and/or monitoring the inanimate and inert factors of production.  The developments towards automated technology and indeed any routinised form of technology contain, as Gramsci noted, their own inherent dialectic.  He points out,

> the only thing that is completely mechanized is the physical gesture;  the memory of the trade reduced to simple gestures repeated at an intense rhythm nestles in the muscular and nervous centres leaving the brain free and unencumbered for other operations ... not only does the worker think, but the fact that he gets no immediate satisfaction from his work ... can lead him into a train of thought that is far from conformist (Gramsci 1973:809-10).

The long-term historical sweep may have witnessed an overall capture by bosses of craft-workers' knowledge and prerogatives.  But machine innovations may still cause problems.

The way in which managerial initiatives can backfire to some extent is illustrated by the history of payment-by-results.  The piece-work version of this device was initially doggedly resisted by workers.  But over time it was gradually fashioned in the well-organised engineering industry to serve worker interests to some considerable extent.  Through the principle of mutuality, shop stewards were able to insist on frequent re-negotiation of terms as jobs, materials and work conditions altered.  A situation resembling the earlier system of insider-contracting again emerged.  Shopfloor control - at least of shopfloor matters - was established on a firmer footing.  In order to reverse this and at the same time to re-gain control over costs, management sought to replace this payment system (and its associated organisation of work) with measured day work.  They had to fight as hard to rid themselves of piece-work as they had done earlier to introduce it.

Somewhat similar was the history of the introduction of bourgeois exactitude in the shape of time into work life.  The onslaught of factory hooters, bells, clocks and sundry other devices established the message that time was currency (Thompson 1967).  But workers were to turn this point around on their employers and demand appropriate 'compensation' for time 'consumed'.  Work time required in excess of standard was to be paid for at premium rates.  Moreover, selling merely labour power meant that this capacity was but sold for stipulated diurnal periods.  It was possible, therefore, to reduce exploitation by 'wasting' time.  As one of Robert Tressell's ragged trousered philanthropists says, ceasing to decorate for a spell and ready to 'hinjoy' a quiet smoke:  'This is where we get some of our own back' (1965:38).

Equally, the processes of resistance contain their own points of contradiction. The essential contradiction that has dogged worker resistance is the double-edged nature of permanent organisation. Any collectivity which moves beyond the spontaneous, risks turning into a control device not *for* labour but *over* labour. It is not necessary to subscribe to Michel's iron law to recognise this fact. Gramsci used the phrase 'industrial legality' to refer to the impact of unionism (1969:15). This is a victory for the working class in that it curbs the arbitrary exercise of management power yet it is simultaneously advantageous to management in rationalising and stabilising its domination. In this regard Blumberg (1968) noted how many of the gains won by American shop stewards amounted to no great inroads into managements' power but rather represented what he termed 'personnel rationalization'. It was almost as if the stewards had operated as an enlightened personnel management func- tion which had successfully pressed its case for rationalised ad- ministration. In fact sophisticated managers may actually gain by relying on unions to channel grievances, screen out 'unrealistic' demands, and present issues in a planned and rational way. In a logical development, despite the propaganda for public consumption, bosses, it has been noted, have much cause to 'love the closed shop' (Hart 1979).

Governments have not shown themselves averse to promoting stable official unionism. The Wagner Act of 1935 in the United States, for example, helped unions to become firmly established as part of the New Deal. In Britain too, the state has frequently declared itself in favour of promoting collective bargaining and the old Ministry of Labour and the Department of Employment, along with quasi-government bodies such as the CIR and now ACAS, have been changed and have charged themselves with facilitating it. Developments of this kind, as David Montgomery points out, are 'simultaneously liberating and cooptive for the workers' (1979:165).

But it would be facile to dismiss the official union structures simply because of these tendencies. It may be true, as Mills (1948: 8) suggested, that unions may come to act as 'managers of discon- tent'. Nevertheless, 'the union', often scorned, provides the back- cloth protection for many an action which under non-union circum- stances would be mere cavalier cavorting. The long union tradition provides the depth to the powerful social meanings and coercive po- tential carried in the terms 'strike', 'picket', 'scab' and other like conceptual weapons. Each of these draws on a considerable re- servoir of inter-subjective understanding in order to make its impact. What would collective absence from work be without the understood connotation of strike other than an aggregate absence or desertion? Apart from the obvious but exceptional mass pickets of miners, why would large numbers of workers take note of a few motley straddlers at work entrances unless they carried the aura of 'pickets'? Certainly a union on its own is nothing without active members; but equally, activists would be far more vulnerable with- out a union. (7)

Organised worker resistance contains yet another contradiction - the long standing oscillation between sectionalism and solidarity. As Tony Lane points out: 'Sectionalism was regarded as one of the cardinal sins by every conscientious trade unionist - and amply in- dulged in by all of them' (1974:267-8). This again was not a weak-

ness of individual trade union leaders but was a logical product of
the nature of the task that had been set for them.  In the absence
of a wide and coherent political programme which would have made the
interminable internecine squabbles seem petty, these struggles (such
as the laggers' dispute which in 1980 nearly split the TUC itself)
have continued to divert much energy.

The contradiction is that the social relations of production
which inevitably generate a dichotomous 'us' and 'them' situation
have at the same time fostered a long history of fragmentation.

The earliest stable unions - the New Model unions - were indeed
based largely from the start on exclusivity.  They were in a literal
sense unions of different *trades*.  To use H.A. Turner's terminology,
the 'open' unions were not successful in recruiting on a permanent
basis until the latter part of the nineteenth century.  And even
after their breakthrough and well into the twentieth century the
divergent strategies of open and closed, inclusive and exclusive,
survived.  The exclusive union organisations were directed as much
at protecting their members by keeping the rest of the working class
'out' as they were directed at employers as such.

Contradiction of a different kind is found in the issues over
which worker collectivities fight.  Unionists are frequently found
opposing capitalism and working for its replacement, yet equally
found devoting prodigious energy towards advancing their members'
interests *within* capitalism and thereby arguably helping to assuage
their discomfiture and resentment.  This in turn should leaven the
worst anomalies and assist towards stabilising the system.  This
dilemma was poignantly captured by Fritz Tarnow, a German trade
union leader speaking in 1931:

are we sitting at the sickbed of capitalism, not only as doctors
who want to cure the patient, but as prospective heirs who cannot
wait for the end and would like to hasten it by administering
poison?  We are condemned I think to be doctors who seriously
wish a cure, and yet we have to retain the feeling that we are
heirs who wish to receive the entire legacy of the capitalist
system today rather than tomorrow.  This double role, doctor and
heir, is a damned difficult task (Tarnow cited in Lane 1974:263).

But the contradictions are not confined to the nature of worker
resistance.  There is a wider dialectic between managerial initiatives on the real subordination of labour and worker behaviour
during the labour process.  Thus Mike Davis (1975) illustrates how
the unskilled rank and file - as well as craft-workers - responded
to the rationality of Taylorism and the speed-up.  His vehicle for
analysis was the Industrial Workers of the World.  They used a whole
battery of responses which ranged from major strikes at McKees
Rocks, East Hammond, Lawrence, and Detroit.  He cites an authority
on the 1909 McKees Rocks strikes who concluded that 'it was this
rigorous but logical extension of the ideas of scientific management
which led directly to the McKees Rocks strike' (1975:75).  The
Wobblies also advocated and used rank-and-file sabotage.  This
covered deliberate soldiering to protect 'traditional worker prerogatives';  it also involved a certain amount of retaliatory destruction.  The IWW leader, Big Bill Haywood, actually made a public
espousal of it in New York before a large crowd.  He announced 'I
don't know of anything that can be applied that will bring as much

satisfaction to you, as much anger to the boss as a little sabotage
in the right place at the right time.  Find out what it means.  It
won't hurt you and it will cripple the boss' (Davis 1975:81).  In
fact it transpires that the IWW indulged in property destruction
less frequently than the conservative AFL.  It is suggested that the
IWW used the talk and threat of practice as a tactic in its own
right.  This was partly a heuristic device to 'demystify the sancti-
ty of property' but also to dissuade bosses from driving too hard a
bargain.  Thus even the IWW news-sheet, 'Industrial Worker', reflected upon this phenomenon.  In the edition of 16 May 1912 it
announced:

> In Lawrence one of the reasons for the settlement of the strike on
> terms favourable to the strikers was the fact that the employers
> feared that the cloth might not be produced in the best condi-
> tions by workers who were entirely dissatisfied.

Now this in itself implies a significant end-stop upon employer attempts to secure complete subordination.  But the 'Industrial
Worker' foresaw even more mileage in this situation, for, 'this
knowledge shared by the strikers, gave to the toilers the feeling
that they were a necessary portion of the social mechanism and
brought them that much nearer the time when the workers as a class
shall feel capable of managing industry in their own interests'
(quoted in Davis 1975:84).  So here we glimpse the significance of
that aspect which Braverman denied himself - the working class as a
class *for* itself.  So too, through struggle and resistance there
emerges the possibility of workers at least beginning to envisage if
only in a most shadowy form that vital possibility of an *alternative*
way.


CONCLUSIONS

What impact have workers' struggles had?  This is undoubtedly a most
difficult question to answer, not least because it requires speculation about what might hypothetically have occurred if there had been
no resistance at all.  The record does show, however, the long-term
*resilience* of worker protest and resistance.  It antedates Taylorism, it was heightened during the phase of implementation of scientific management, and it has proved capable of surviving the onslaught of timing, measurement, rationalisation, reorganisation, the
assembly line, and all sorts of 'new technology'.  Empirical surveys
indicate something rather different to the inexorable developments
of the real subordination of labour.  Certainly there is a revealed
pattern of uneven development.  Certainly the challenge has hardly
manifested itself at top corporate levels.  But companies have experienced problems in *implementing* their preconceived plans at the
actual point of production.  While this may seem to cast labour in
a reactive rather than proactive stance, equally it gnaws at the assumed inviolate managerial 'prerogatives'.  Real subordination,
then, a century after Marx wrote on the subject is still not complete.  It is even arguable whether, overall, it has intensified.
Refining the system of formal rationality has exercised the minds
and consumed the endeavours of countless 'experts' through three or
more generations;  it too remains incomplete.

Nor does it seem adequate to conceive of the situation as one merely requiring the remaining 'gaps' to be filled.  In theoretical terms there are inherent contradictions at play.  Capital's massive power has been shown to be assailable.  It is difficult to sustain an initiative in the industrial sphere.  Through a series of lock-outs the engineering employers secured a management rights clause at national level.  In daily workshop activity its impact was whittled away.  No proletarian army had been neutralised;  the military analogy, although ubiquitously deployed, is inappropriate.  Ford's $5 day initiative, which attracted a superabundant supply of labour and the legendary ten men at the gates waiting for every malcontent's job, did not suffice to dampen the smouldering fires of discontent provoked by the assembly line and the severe discipline.  As noted, the Ford Company later switched tactics in Detroit, away from reliance on 'casual' labour and the dead weight of the reserve army, towards a primary labour market pattern as a result of union organising campaigns.  Elsewhere, the coerced signing of the Document and the Open Shop Campaign failed to break the unions.

But equally the 'victories' of the workers are shown to be far from self-sustaining.  The long and bitter struggle for union recognition in the textile mills of the American north-east eventually bore fruit.  But its reward was the prompted exodus of textile capital to the south.  In Britain, Derek Robinson, the 'scourge' of BL, was in the end sacked by BL.  Mike Cooley, Lucas convener and champion of alternative technology and the alternative corporate plan, eventually met the same fate in June 1981 having survived a similar onslaught two years previously.  And even when workers' organisations are on the ascendancy they tend to be stymied by the contradictions of economism and fractionalism.  Rebellion is rendered partial.

These apparently foreshortened challenges nevertheless serve heuristic purposes.  Workers experience the practical limits to their strength - and at the same time learn something of their organised potential.  Some of the mystique of capital is dented while praxis is advanced.

Finally, when one asks what impact workers' struggles have had, the debate is bound to engage with the question of totality.  Worker resistance at the shopfloor level is ultimately checked by the parameters of the competitive system.  The ultimate contradiction is that a successful challenge, if it persists, tends to lead to defeat.  This may be avoided if other competitors succumb to similar challenge, or if a monopoly prevails, or again, if the relief of real subordination fails for some reason to increase costs or impede accumulation.  Irrespective of particular victories or defeats the wider totality is ultimately dependent, despite the stabilising force of other institutions, on the maintenance of the sphere of production - yet it is here where the antagonistic relations of the capitalist system are at their most transparent.

# Chapter 9

# CONTROL AND DEMOCRACY

The crucial dynamic traced in the foregoing chapters emerges from an interplay between managerial control and worker resistance; between an increasingly sophisticated and integrated control system and a still-developing workplace organisation; between a seemingly inexorable production logic and guerrilla action which challenges specific applications of that logic. The path and ultimate destiny of this dynamic will have a significance far beyond the workplace; and the future shape of industrial society is bound up with the fate of this crucial contention.

The last couple of decades have witnessed a dramatic clash over the control of production. The much-vaunted managerial resurgence came hard on the heels of the 'second shop stewards' movement' which had just reached its zenith. The challenge from below met a challenge from above. The adage that control could only be regained by sharing it took on a new twist as the unions were cast more as wooers and less as the wooed. But to interpret the real political, economic and social significance of these events requires that they be placed in theoretical and historical context. One version we noted saw managerial prerogative as having suffered a secular erosion (Smith 1979). In contrast, Braverman and his followers view the twentieth century as a period of inexorable degradation of work, the ascendancy of Taylorism and the destruction of immemorial craft prerogative. Marx's theory of the real subordination of labour and Weber's rationalisation thesis, would seemingly lend support to the latter account.

Our analysis of Marx, Weber and Braverman revealed, however, a more complex and less certain picture. Garnering the numerous critiques of Braverman, we argued their ostensible variety concealed an underlying consistency - that the shortcomings in Braverman's thesis resulted from the absence of a *dialectic*. Hence, ironically, while he had sought to resurrect Marx's analysis of the labour process he left unregarded a vital part of it. Paradoxically, therefore, in order to go 'beyond Braverman', as we must, it is necessary to begin at the foundations of Marx's own scheme. To do this requires attention to the underlying raison d'être of the capitalist mode of production - accumulation. The process of accumulation proceeds from the securement of surplus-value. As the scope for the expan-

sion of absolute surplus-value through the lengthening of the working day becomes checked, employers find it necessary to seek relative surplus-value through the intensification and rationalisation
of production.  The key to this process is the distinction between
labour power and labour:  the transformation of the one into the
other is always subject to 'porosity'.  A parallel distinction is
that between the purely formal subordination and the real subordination of labour.  In order to glean relative surplus-value, the capitalist intervenes to reorganise and direct the units of labour power
he has bought in such a way as to extract a greater measure of effective labour.

Taylorism is but one - albeit a major - gambit in this necessary
process.  Braverman reified it and treated it as *the* equivalent of
capitalist control.  By the same token Friedman reified 'responsible
autonomy' as the 'alternative' strategy.  Certainly under the constraint of falling rates of profit, employers are forced to intensify work in some manner.  But the dialectical interplay of control
and rank-and-file resistance has to be taken into account.  Hence
the employers' strategies are *variegated*.  De-skilling is certainly
one ploy but equally they will try productivity bargaining, payment
by results, 'work-humanisation' programmes, 'constitutionalism'
through a wider range of bargaining with the unions, or at the opposite extreme as Donald Roy noted, they may try 'fear stuff and
sweet stuff', and currently we see the cajoling hand of unemployment
accompanied (in some but not all locations) by re-structuring and
new working methods.

Not only did Braverman reify Taylorism as *the* method, he under-
estimated the implementation problem which employers faced and do
face, and as we also argued, he tended to take at face value the
sales propaganda of the new systems' designers, the new machine-
makers and other self-interested purveyors of the vocabulary of
motive.  It can be concluded too that like most other Marxist and
non-Marxist analysts he underexplored the category 'management'.
As our investigations on managers and managerial prerogative demonstrated, these agents of capital, even when examined, have typically
been attributed with a measure of rationalised action which in reality seems exaggerated.  The 'over-rationalised conception of mana-
gerial-man' has conspired to impute to him or her a level of 'strategy' which does not accord with the image emerging from empirical
investigations.  While governmental agencies have from time to time
sought to persuade industrialists to escalate the status and influence of personnel and industrial relations specialists in order to
effect a more consistent and formalised approach to labour management, industry's take-up of such 'policies' has been decidedly
patchy.  Indeed, of late there seems to have been some reversal to
the incipient belief and reliance on line managers' responsibility
for this function.  Even the personnel orthodoxy of time off for
shop steward duties and other like tactics to incorporate the rank-
and-file challenge through the provision of 'facilities' has suffered recent set-backs.

The underlying theoretical reasons for this variety we suggest
can be located in the dialectic of control and resistance.  There
are fundamental contradictions in the real subordination of labour.
Rationalised attempts to suppress human foibles and the capricious

variability of behaviour runs up against the employers' need to exploit and at times rely upon human flexibility and ingenuity.  Moreover, even when this is not the most immediately pressing problem,
real subordination provokes disaffection and frustration.  The deleterious consequences of this latter were illuminated in chapter 8 on
resistance.  The aggression which can derive from abject subordination is well illustrated in Georgakas and Surkin's retelling of the
James Johnson case in 'Detroit:  I Do Mind Dying' (1975).  Johnson,
an auto worker at Chrysler's 'rationalised' gear and axle plant,
used an M-1 carbine to gun down two foremen and a job setter on the
afternoon shift of 15 July 1970.  At his trial Johnson was found not
to be responsible for his actions and he was committed to a state
hospital.  Shortly afterwards he was awarded workman's compensation
for the injuries done to him by the corporation.  Chrysler was
ordered to pay him $75 a week retroactive to the day of his 'break-
down'.  At a collective level the degree of resistance provoked by
scientific management was revealed through the investigations of
scholars such as Montgomery (1979) and Palmer (1975).

    The inherent contradictions of real subordination are inextrica-
bly bound to the other dialectical categories of social construction
and totality.  Employer attempts to find ways to realise surplus-
value and their relative success, or otherwise, in this endeavour
must be situated within the context of the capitalist mode of production and the wider cultural and political spheres.  Besides im-
pelling the valorisation process, the wider context gives rise to
institutions which nurture it, and yet they may come to incubate the
infant antagonist.  Thus, while Braverman served to re-focus attention on the sphere of production, a more coherent analysis would
have to relate Marx's 'two spheres' - production and circulation.
We concluded that Edwards (1975, 1979) and Lazonick (1978) had so
far been most successful in this venture.  Edwards (1975) pointed
up the close links between different forms of control at the point
of production and the different labour market structures which were
thereby created.  Other contradictions within the system are illuminated by his approach.  Under job-protection programmes and work-
experience schemes labour occasionally comes to capital gratis.  Employers are exhorted to 'help' by deigning to utilise (exploit) this
labour.  Equally, with respect to conventional wage-labour, an increasing part of the wage bill - in the USA as much as in Britain -
takes the form of the 'social wage'.  This is one of the reasons why
Edwards (1979) sees a long-run conflict between capitalism and democracy.  This is despite the point which 'one cannot avoid' - that it
is the major capitalist nations which have so far been the democratic states.  However, this may, he fears, have been a marriage of
convenience, soon to be discarded.  Social service benefits create a
'social drag' on profits and blunt reserve army discipline.  So
capitalists find it essential (at a time when it is also more precarious) to control the state.  What is likely to happen is a removal of choice to the administrative sphere - leaving the democratic 'form' gutted of 'substance'.

    Despite the prodigious edifice of control piled high over a
couple of centuries of development, industrial capitalism remains
vulnerable.  This is so in both spheres.  The same malaise of patterned inequality acts as a blight in each.  Paradoxically, it is

the failure to engage the 'surplus 10 per cent' of the workforce
which is currently building up tensions within the social order.  At
the same time it is the control of work - despite the army of superintendence, the reserve army of unemployed, the integrated and
rationalised control systems, tight discipline and the elaborate
hierarchies - which remains the Achilles heel.

This study has sought to correct the theoretical weakness whereby
the dialectic of control and resistance has been underemphasised.
Significant sections of the working class have refused to be intimi-
dated by capital's massive resources.  High capitalisation levels
and interdependent production cycles render rationalised industry
susceptible to disruption.  The various capitals have responded by
creating segmented labour markets.  For some sectors this has meant
putting 'casualisation' policies into reverse.  The cultivation of a
primary segment characterised by relative security of employment,
sophisticated procedures, job ladders and other, similar devices,
has none the less occurred against a general backcloth of mounting
unemployment.  Accordingly, there is a temptation for social analysts, affronted by dehumanised labour and anxious to achieve a
change, itchily to reach for the tocsin.  At the present time that
temptation is particularly acute.  Given the unusual scale of the
recession and the aridity of governmental response, it is understandable that so many commentators ruminate ominously of 'crisis'
and 'overdetermination'.  There may, overall, be good grounds to
forsake caution and add one's voice to this clamour.  But, in my
view, if a prognosis is constructed solely on the basis of an analysis of the labour process, there is as yet insufficient cause to
reach such a conclusion.  The nature of the link between 'de-
skilling' and revolutionary consciousness has as yet to be demonstrated.

In Brecher's (1972) view, material conditions are more important
for effecting revolutionary change than the raising of abstract
consciousness.  Higher levels of consciousness are in any case debilitated by divisions between mental and physical labour, by hierarchy, and by sexual and racial divisions.  Cultural, educational
and political structures further impede the break from commodity
fetishism.  Labour learns to self-identify and self-evaluate in
market terms.  Self-deprecation is never far away - 'if you're so
smart how come you ain't rich?' (Aronowitz 1973:410).  The implication of the material conditions argument is that industrial struggles will inevitably widen into more revolutionary objectives (Gorz,
Mallet).  But Low-Beer contends in his study of 'new-working-class'
militancy in Italy that the causal link is rather the reverse.  Instead of positing a link from work to other realms, he adduces the
opposite.  It is the experience gained outside the work situation
which, he suggests, leads to militancy within it.  Determination in
either direction is perhaps specious.  Workers will only develop a
radical replacement ideology when the *unity* of the labour process
and the political and cultural context is captured.  Thus, for example, to oppose redundancies and to engage in demands concerning
pricing and socially useful products is necessarily to engage both
with the micro-totality and the societal 'totality'.  The most dramatic instances of revolt such as the 'Great Rebellion' in Detroit
in July 1967 have involved an admixture of issues - racial oppres-

sion, urban neglect, policing methods, unemployment and employment
experiences on Detroit's assembly lines.

> In the violent summer of 1967 Detroit became the scene of the
> bloodiest uprising in a half century ... there were 41 known
> dead, 347 injured, 3,800 arrests.  Some 5,000 people were home-
> less ... while 1,300 buildings had been reduced to mounds of
> ashes and bricks ('Time Magazine', 4 August 1967).

Brixton and Toxteth are clearly but shadows of this measure of rebellion.  And despite the scale of dislocation, Detroit managed to
'contain' the situation (Georgakas and Surkin 1975).  But it did so
only after the commencement of a massive urban renewal programme
which involved industrialists and bankers in a new form of 'investment'.  Affirmative action was launched on a scale hardly conceiva-
ble in Britain.

On a more abstract theoretical level, Lukács (1971) brought to
the surface the issues of totality and reification, and Habermas
(1971, 1974, 1976) served to recast the question of base and superstructure.  Each of these studies provides pointers to the journey
beyond Braverman.  The crucial contention denoted at the opening of
this final chapter is revealed to require a more subtle response
than Braverman suggests.  Of course the journey with Habermas, as
we have seen, takes one additionally beyond Marx.  Habermas's critique of orthodox Marxism involves greater attention to superstructural considerations.  In so far as he traces the basic contradiction of capitalism to the private appropriation of wealth, his path
may be termed neo-Marxist.  But he highlights some new areas, ones
unexplored in conventional Marxist accounts.  He finds that the
basic instability in contemporary capitalism arises from the fact
that the fundamental principles of the economic and social order
could not be justified in unrestricted discourse.  'Hence the stability of the capitalist social formation depends on the continued
effectiveness of legitimations that could not withstand discursive
examination' (McCarthy 1978:358).  On the other hand, this does not
necessarily presage a 'de-totalisation', nor does it pre-judge the
'chances for a self-transformation of advanced capitalism' (Habermas
1976:40).  The possibility of an economic crisis being permanently
averted because of capital's adjustive capabilities is not pre-
cluded, though this would tend to distort the imperatives for capital realisation in a way which 'would produce a series of other
crisis tendencies'.  'Administrative processing' may arise to transfer crisis tendencies into the socio-cultural system (Habermas 1976:
40).  The end result is a legitimation crisis.

Accordingly, employer and managerial ideology bent to the task of
justifying 'managerial prerogative' is deserving of much greater
critical attention that it has so far received.  Chapter 6 attempted
to remedy this neglect.  It revealed that each of the cataclysmic
battles in the engineering industry involved at bottom a tussle over
this question.  The analyses by Braverman and Marx are ill-equipped
to tackle the issue on their own.  While a sound basis is built by
Marx, the 'administrative processing' of crisis tendencies from the
economic to the political and cultural spheres under contemporary
conditions of advanced capitalism, demands a wider framework.  Heilbroner's (1975) 'realm' of the ideological-cultural elements which
he found missing in Braverman is thus seen to be a fundamental and

not a merely incidental omission.  The dynamic element, it may be
concluded, is not the tendency towards de-skilling argued by Braverman, nor even the real subordination of labour explicated by Marx,
but a wider arena of class struggle.  Managerial control is precarious and conditional.  For the remaining days of capitalism its managers will have to face again and again the question of control.
With only a democratic *form* for protection that may not be for very
long;  with a refurbished and genuine democratic *substance* the time
horizon could be even shorter.

# NOTES

CHAPTER 1   CONTROL AND THE LABOUR PROCESS:   TOWARDS A DIALECTICAL
APPROACH

1   The issue of control has suffered relative not absolute neglect.
    There have been significant exceptions such as Carter L.
    Goodrich (1920) following the First World War.   James Hinton
    (1973) examined 'The First Shop Stewards' Movement' in that
    period.   Other studies of related importance include Bendix
    (1956) and Gouldner (1954).   And although the question of mana-
    gerial preorgative was skirted in the British literature, a
    number of American scholars have given it attention (Chamberlain
    1948;   Chandler 1964;   Slichter, Healy and Livernash 1960;
    Derber 1953, 1958, 1961).
2   'Financial Times', 5 January 1981.
3   Geoffrey Armstrong, Director of Employee Relations, BL Cars, The
    Role of Industrial Relations in the Management System, Wednesday
    26 November 1980 (transcript), Trent Business School, Open Lec-
    ture.
4   Having circumscribed the role of the stewards it is only logical
    that BL should now propose that they spend more of their time
    back at their allotted work stations (June 1980).
5   Letter dated 7 November 1980, from Ron Todd, National Organizer
    of the TGWU and Chairman FNJNC to Paul J. Roots, Employee Rela-
    tions Director, Ford Motor Company Ltd.   The author gratefully
    acknowledges Mr Todd's release of this correspondence.
6   In the light of these developments it is instructive to compare
    the different attempts to define the field of 'industrial rela-
    tions' because they reflect shifts in the understanding of the
    essential problematic.   Hence Dunlop's focus on the 'web of
    rules' which actors generate to govern their relations, high-
    lights a pluralistic perspective predicated upon the assumption
    of an underlying consensus.   This latter allows the parties to
    concern themselves with 'the establishment of procedures and
    rules' and this circumscribed activity constitutes 'the centre
    of attention in an industrial relations system' (Dunlop 1958:
    13).   In a similar vein, Flanders narrows the field to something
    dangerously near a study of collective bargaining.   But certain

technical shortcomings in this term, as originally conjured by
the Webbs, persuade him to focus on the slightly wider arena of
'job regulation'.  However, an augmented perspective which
allows account to be taken of strategic ideological devices -
such as the claim to a managerial prerogative - is made possible
by Hyman's attempt to express the core of the subject.  'Industrial relations is the study *of the processes of control over
work relations*' (Hyman 1975:12).  This is simple but precise.
It may be observed, however, that little of the literature
within industrial relations meets the challenge posed by this
definition.

7  Braverman's seminal work has stimulated an extraordinary abun-
dance of papers, articles, courses, workshops, study groups and
conferences.  Key reviews have been made by Elger (1979), Coombs
(1978), Cutler (1978), Jacoby (1977), Davies and Brodhead
(1975), Schwarz (1977), MacKenzie (1977), de Kadt (1975), Zeiger
(1976), Lazonick (1977), Heilbroner (1975), Nichols (1977).

8  See for example Nichols (1977), Palmer (1975).  Studies on the
other hand which illustrate the degree of resistance include
Davis (1975), Montgomery (1976, 1979) and Mathewson (1969).

9  While Friedman comes closer than most to developing a dialectical analysis of control and resistance his treatment is coloured
by his perspective as an economist.  As Ken Roberts (1978) has
noted, the data and analysis in Friedman (1977a) tends to bear
on trade union membership and industry-level strike statistics.

10  Cutler (1978) critiques Braverman (1974) the Brighton Labour
Process Group (1977) and the Conference of Socialist Economists
(1974) in toto.  He finds fault with the implied central location afforded to the category, labour.  The fundamental tenet of
'degradation' implies some negative departure from a 'natural'
form.  Here, as in Cutler et al. (1977), the ontological problem
concerning the elevation of an assumed natural state of labour
is surfaced.  Cutler et al. castigate this conceptualisation of
an essential character to human labour in Marx as 'anthropologi-
cal humanism'.  But Giddens (1971) has provided a pointer to a
way out of this dilemma.  The assumption that Marx's reference
to 'species being' implies a reductionism to a natural state is,
Giddens maintains, mistaken.  Arguably, the position is actually
the reverse of this, that is 'the enormously productive power of
capitalism generates possibilities for the future development of
man' (1971:15).  So alienation is not separation from a primeval
natural self;  rather the tension is 'between the potential
generated by a specific form of society (capitalism) and the
frustrated realization of that potential' (Giddens 1971:15-16).
In other words it is not a question of a static natural state
which has been distorted, but rather a failure to realise the
full potential of a socially dynamic self.

However, while this may have been Marx's position, Braverman's treatment of de-skilling does tend to be rather more
clearly a posited corrosion of a romantic ideal of craft labour.
This determinism and myth requires correction.  Braverman's work
is also in need of theoretical development in order to anchor it
more firmly within Marx's more complex account of capitalism's

dynamic.  This is especially so with respect to the link between the labor process and the valorisation process.

11  Marx of course has often been accused of peddling a materialist determinism.  But from his criticisms of Hegel and Feuerbach it is clear that he was not of this persuasion.

12  Marx, 'Capital', vol.III, C.H. Kerr and Co., New York:388.

13  Realising this, it might therefore seem rather less odd that there exist *two* apparently contradictory interpretations of the history of control.  On the one hand there is that version championed by Braverman.  This depicts industrial history as progressive degradation of work, a fragmentation of tasks, a steady loss of worker control and a campaign of seizure by management. On the other hand exists the version which interprets industrial history as a loss of *management* control.  Thus Robin Smith (1979:6) claims:

> That the managerial prerogative has changed over a period of time almost beyond recognition can be seen by considering any privately-owned enterprise in its growth pattern ... at the start of this growth the owner enjoyed total unilateral control of decision-making on all aspects of personnel - from recruitment and selection, methods of payment, training and development, and the manning of production processes, to discipline and dismissal.

CHAPTER 2   RATIONALITY AND THE REAL SUBORDINATION OF LABOUR:   WEBER AND MARX

1  It must always be remembered that Weber was constructing ideal types.  As Roth and Wittich point out in their introduction to 'Economy and Society', Weber was himself very much a *realist* noting people's tendencies to pursue myriad courses of action (Weber 1968).  And as Schutz (1943) observes, 'in our daily life it is only very rarely that we act in a rational way' although we do tend towards typified patterns of action in typified situations (1943:134-5).

2  An additional point concerning the literal source of these confusions is the question of the intellectual derivation of these concepts.  This can only be of indirect relevance to us here but it may be noted that Weber was under the sway of the neo-Kantians and of Nietzsche.  He borrowed from Kant the distinction between 'formal' and 'material' 'practical principles' and adapted them away from Kant's concern with deducing universal moral categories.  From Nietzsche he derived the antinomy between the rationalities and the element of the irrational in their outcomes (Mueller 1979;  Gerth and Mills 1948).

3  Whilst it is common to regard substantive rationality as somehow 'higher' than formed rationality, this supposition would not always fit snugly with Weber's own usage.  He noted that substantive rationality can be emotional, excitable, unpredictable and, according to Forbes (1975:222) even 'irrational'.  This latter is seemingly a contradiction in terms - an event not uncommon with the dichotomous model.  Certainly, however, the kind of ultimate ends which Weber had in mind were not always the

equivalent of those which a social reformer might hold dear.
Thus he instanced not only social justice and equality, for
these 'form only one group', others, inter alia, were actions
to preserve a hierarchy of class distinctions, or the pursuit
of power (1964:185-6).

4  A question posed of course on many occasions - see, for example,
Lindberg, Alford, Crouch and Offe (1975).


CHAPTER 3   BRAVERMAN AND BEYOND

1  There are in fact five parts to the book, but for the purposes
of our exposition Parts IV and V entitled The Growing Working
Class Occupations, and The Working Class respectively may be
collapsed into one theme - occupational and class impact.

2  They somewhat overstate their case by suggesting that the capitalist must 'seek to abolish it'.


CHAPTER 4   WORK CONTROL IN CONTEXT

1  Although this ironically extends to the denial of even this puny
and unadventurous bid for agreement (see Giddens 1974:17).

2  Dubin (1960) uses the terms 'power of', 'power to' and 'power
in' to refer respectively to the description of the parties,
outcomes and sources of power.

3  It would be a mistake to assume that managers are all advocates
of the 'power to' approach. The suspicion of the 'plus-sum' or
'power raises' approach is revealed explicitly in the succinct
statement from a speaker at the first CBI Congress in November
1977:  'Responsibility divided is responsibility lost'.

4  Similarly, Walton and McKersie (1965) identify the potential for
'integrative bargaining'. This can develop 'when the nature of
a problem permits solutions which benefit both parties.... this
is closely related to what game theorists call the varying-sum
game' (Walton and McKersie 1965:5). In turn, Chamberlain and
Kuhn (1965), who also note the 'mutual dependence' of management
and workers, discern a distinction between 'conjunctive' and
'co-operative' bargaining. Conjunctive bargaining arises not
from any sympathetic regard for the other party but from the
fear of impasse if some sort of agreement was not reached. Co-
operative bargaining, they say, arises from the parties realising that they can actually achieve their own objectives better
if they can win support from the other.
    This same theme has been taken up in Britain under the more
familiar label of 'productivity bargaining', although this perhaps more clearly stresses results rather than relationships
(Flanders 1969:315). The theme is echoed too, in the dictum of
'regaining control by sharing it', and in the strategy of 'management by agreement' (McCarthy and Ellis 1973).

5  As Schroyer (1972:93) observes, 'Despite the vilification of the
left, and to the dismay of the academy, Jurgen Habermas remains
a marxist'.

6  This is not to deny the measure of discord, however. See for example, the challenge in 'Capital and Class', Spring 1981.

CHAPTER 5   MANAGEMENT

1   Only the more recent editions of Hugh Clegg's standard text
    carry a chapter on management.  But in fact, despite the chapter
    heading, the contents lack theoretical unity;  they cover di-
    versely:  size of unit, payment systems, overtime, personnel
    management, fringe benefits and foremen.  Similarly, Jackson's
    (1977) text mirrors this situation, carrying as it does sub-
    sections on industrial concentration, foremen, personnel mana-
    gers, training and education.  There is no separate chapter on
    managers.  They share one with 'employers' associations and the
    industrial enterprise'.  Hyman's (1975) 'Industrial Relations:
    A Marxist Introduction' discusses the state, trade unions, the
    rank and file, and capital, but managers are pushed out.  There
    is nothing exceptional about these examples.  Industrial rela-
    tions literature in general has simply neglected managers as
    pertinent figures in the overall framework.
2   Managers' own perceptions of this form the forthcoming second
    part of Marshall and Stewart's article on Managers' Perceptions.
    The first part was published in 'Journal of Management Studies',
    18, 2 (1981).
3   Mant surely exaggerates here;  similar debates can be found in
    other countries too.  To take one example, Battalia and Tarrant
    (1973) in the United States, lament the drift from concreteness
    to symbols in American management.  The corporate eunuch for-
    sakes the skills of craftsmanship and personal understanding for
    the abstractions of 'communications', MBO, and other slogans.
    Nevertheless, it is a common theme in Britain.  Robert Heller
    (n.d.) puts the case for the prosecution in castigating British
    managers':  'social attitudes from the past when the successful
    businessman turned himself into a country gentleman as rapidly
    as possible, still impede the development of aggressive Ameri-
    can-style, round-the-clock, driving, get up and go management'
    (Heller:5).
4   Roger Falk (1970) in 'The Business of Management', makes a re-
    vealing distinction between management as a science and *leader-
    ship* as an art:  'good management must get the maximum possible
    from the managed, good leadership must see it is done with har-
    mony' (1970:49).  From the studies quoted above, one might be
    forgiven for suspecting that management divides itself so that
    certain functionaries can specialise in the different aspects -
    the iron fist can wear a velvet glove.
5   One might compare Winkler's (1974) study of directors;  he too
    found them cut off from genuine and active deliberation at least
    on industrial relations matters.  This, he argued, was a result
    of their active disinclination to get involved.  Isolation was a
    tactic, a short-term coping mechanism which 'permits compromises
    at lower levels on apparent pragmatic bases so that positions
    are not yielded on principle' (1974:210).  It can therefore be
    seen as an attempt to preserve managerial prerogative.  Similar-
    ly, Anthony (1977:62), noting the tactic of remaining aloof from
    the nitty gritty of negotiations, observes that 'isolation and
    ignorance have their uses'.
6   One might contrast the central core picked out by the Inter-

national Encyclopedia of the Social Sciences in their entry on Management.  They attribute this to decision-making.
7    Adam Smith, 'The Wealth of Nations', Modern Library, New York, 1937, p.423.
8    See Stephen Wood's (1979) critique of contingency theory.
9    In 'The Ragged Trousered Philanthropists', a 'novel' based on his own experience as a painter and decorator seventy years ago, Robert Tressell also vividly makes this point:

All the same it was a fact that the workmen did do their very best to get over this work in the shortest possible time, because although they knew that to do so was contrary to their own interests, they also knew that it would be very much more contrary to their interests not to do so.  Their only chance of being kept on if other work came in was to tear into it for all they were worth.  Consequently, most of the work was rushed and botched and slobbered over in about half the time that it would have taken to do it properly.  Rooms for which the customer paid to have three coats of paint were scamped with one or two.  What Misery did not know about scamping and faking the work, the men suggested to and showed him in the hope of currying favour with him in order that they might get preference over others and be sent for when the next job came in.  This is the principle incentive provided by the present system, the incentive to cheat.  These fellows cheated the customers of their money.  They cheated themselves and their fellow workmen of work and their children of bread, but it was all for a good cause - to make profit for their master (1965:366-7).

10   While Fletcher's discussion of managers as victims is useful, his thesis that management as an institution may well soon 'end' is not convincing.  The strand of his argument which anticipates demise arising from stresses and strains in the role makes heroic assumptions.  Computerisation, another aspect of his case, is altogether a different phenomenon and could equally lead to a more enhanced form of managerialism.


CHAPTER 6   MANAGERIAL PREROGATIVE

1    The debate on workers' 'job property rights' has also ignited from time to time.  Rottenberg (1962) argued that the groundswell of opinion favourable to compensating the loss of 'job property' was misplaced.  He suggested that wages carry an element to cover 'depreciation'.  The ensuing debate with Stein and Cohen followed a number of threads such as whether workers actually can be said to have property rights in their job;  whether, even if they do, compensation should be paid if the job is lost;  whether redundant workers are analogous to redundant machines;  and so on.  To a large extent the redundancy payments legislation in the advanced countries has overtaken many of the arguments in that particular debate.
2    Robert Carr issued a Code of Industrial Relations Practice in a Consultative Document, June 1971.
3    Of course on these matters there is also constraint on the

'free' exercise of management rights which derives from the law. The Employment Protection Act and the Health and Safety at Work Act furnish but two notable examples. Even without direct legislation government can shape managerial practices on promotion, training and transfer. The CBI protested angrily in 1979 when the government announced it would withdraw contracts from firms not satisfying employment practice criteria on racial matters ('Guardian', 28 February 1979). Earlier the government had attempted to enforce a pay policy using a similar tactic.

4   'New Standard Dictionary', 1962.

5   The issue has, however, enjoyed a marked revival in the journal of the Institute of Directors recently. See for example: Mr A.R.G. Raeburn, President of Shell Kosen KK. Tokyo. What Are Your Rights in running the Company? 'Director', June 1976:64-5. He argues that 'the focus of attention for management study in the next decade may have to shift from that of the past - improving the ability to manage - towards the problem of how managers can protect the opportunity to manage' (p.64); also G. Bull, Frustrated Directors Raise a Flag, 'Director', September 1976. In this article 'two members of the Institute of Directors talk frankly and in depth.... the message which they are desperate to send is ...: British management isn't in danger of emasculation; it is already losing the right to manage.... Blunt, forceful men powerfully built and outspoken, sitting in the Managing Director's big bright office they swing into the attack' (p.56).

6   Bob Wright, Fabian Lecture, 1972.

7   George Meany, 'Fortune Magazine', March 1955:92-3.

8   Ibid.

9   This is confirmed in statements made by EEF national officials during interviews with the author, and according to the negotiating committee transcripts which are reviewed later in this chapter.

10  It is also of course an industry of foremost importance. It produces some 40 per cent of the country's manufactured goods and the Federation itself has some 6,000 member firms which employ 2 million workers. The EEF has long been the most important employers' organisation in Britain.

11  'Proceedings in Conference', EEF and CSEU, 15 September 1971:3.

12  Ibid.:9.

13  As Hugh Scanlon put it: 'at all stages we are the appellants and you sit in judgement', 'Proceedings in Conference', 16 April 1970:14.

14  Clive Jenkins and B.Sherman, 'Collective Bargaining', Routledge & Kegan Paul, London, 1977:63.

15  'Proceedings in Conference', 2 April 1969:2. Although the old agreement was abandoned in 1971 and nothing put in its place until 1976, one still encounters even recent books rehearsing the familiar arguments as though they continued to apply in the 1970s. See for example: Alan Aldridge, 'Power, Authority and Restrictive Practices', Blackwell, Oxford, 1976:39. The book by Jenkins and Sherman (1977:62-3) similarly gives the impression that the criticisms of the procedure 'covering three million workers' have remained valid throughout the seventies. This

ignores the fact that while the Staff Procedure continued, the manual workers procedure did not.  I was informed by the EEF that 'so far as the Federation is concerned York is strictly historical and largely forgotten' (Letter, May 1978).  Jenkins's book is sub-titled:  What You Always Wanted To Know About Trade Unions and Never Dared to Ask;  it must be said that this is more than a teeny-weeny bit exaggerated.

16   Ibid.:3.
17   Ibid.:13.
18   'Financial Times', 16 September 1969.
19   'Proceedings in Conference', 16 April 1970:9.
20   Ibid.
21   Ibid.:18.
22   Ibid.:20.
23   Ibid., 15 September 1971:9.
24   Ibid.:10.
25   Ibid., 17 January 1973.
26   M. Chandler observes 'in effect, rights often become a grander cause with which to associate one's concept of a fair share (1964:309).
27   To equate rights with power would seem to be too restrictive. If one is robbed by dint of force it would seem odd to say that one had no rights.
28   The functional justification of rights would not, however, suffice in every instance.  Thus, for example, certain groups such as the chronically sick would have no rights because they can make no economic contribution.
29   John Locke, 'Second Treatise on Civil Government' (1690), reprinted in 'Social Contract', Oxford University Press, 1947; see also K. Olivecrona, Locke's Theory of Appropriation, 'Philosophical Quarterly', 24 July 1974.
30   Apart from the obvious problem of private monopoly control of necessary goods implied here, there are additional social and economic problems which arise under such circumstances.  Thus for example, unearned increments accrue from private property rights - and the size of these increments has little or nothing to do with the bringing forward of additional supplies.  In this way even classical economic precepts are flouted.  Further, the exercise of private rights in property may, indeed is likely to, lead to significant externalities because of physical interdependencies (Castle 1978).
31   This is particularly so when one notes the extreme degree of concentration of industrial wealth.  Frank Field (1981) quotes data showing the 'wealthiest one per cent of the population owning eighty-one per cent of company stocks and shares;  the top five per cent, ninety-six per cent of company stocks and shares;  and this percentage rose to ninety-eight per cent for the wealthiest ten per cent of the community' (1981:154).


CHAPTER 7   THE CONTROL OF WORK

1   It should be noted that, given our dialectical approach, the analytical distinction made in this and the following chapter

between control and resistance is strictly speaking impermissible.  Rather, the course of strategic control is influenced by
resistance and vice versa.  But for the purposes of exposition
this breakdown is made.

2  A number of these critiques of orthodoxy are, however, very
sketchy when it comes actually to constructing an alternative,
Marxist-informed analysis.  Thus Salaman's (1978) proposal for
a Marxist organisation theory is undiscerning with regard to the
fierce controversies and divisions as exemplified, for example,
in the clash between Cohen's (1978) attribution of primacy to
the forces of production and Levine and Wright's (1980) critique
of this;  equally it is evident in the work of Habermas, Althusser and Cutler et al.  Variations within Marxism are exemplified in Schroyer's statement that 'orthodox marxism fails to
recognize the uniqueness of late capitalism' (1971:297).
Panzieri (1976) helps spell this out.  He too claims that
'marxist thought has failed to grasp the fundamental characteristic of modern-day capitalism'.  This lies, he maintains, 'in
its capacity for salvaging the fundamental expression of the law
of surplus value, i.e. planning both at the level of the factory
and at the social level' (Panzieri 1976:22).  Variations within
the Marxist framework with respect to interpreting Taylorism and
capitalist control are also elaborated by Elger and Schwarz
(1980).

3  We accept Day and Day's (1977) thesis that, while negotiated-
order theory is illuminating, it requires developing to engage
with the wider political and material dimension of social
action.

4  Goldman and van Houten (1980) argue similarly that bureaucratic
innovation was in large part a strategic response to worker recalcitrance and not some rational evolution of techniques.  This
loops back to the discussion of Weber and Marx in chapter 2.

5  This term is permissible, although it must be used guardedly because of its frequent deployment within the functionalist paradigm (see Heydebrand 1977:102).

6  Kilpatrick and Lawson (1980), in investigating British de-indus-
trialisation, submit that most analyses have neglected the developments in the labour process and organised resistance in
British capitalism.  The decline is not a 'temporary aberration'
but can be explained, they claim, by contrasting Britain with
countries like Germany, France and the United States where the
labour movement was more effectively constrained.  Change in
Britain has been impeded 'by organized resistance and obviated
by relatively protected markets'.  In consequence, 'slow growth
is now deeply rooted in British Society' (1980:92).

7  'Guardian', 25 May 1981.

8  Attention to information flows and cybernetics in isolation from
other functions, however, necessarily yields only a partial and
technical view.  Thus we cannot accept Eilon's (1979, 1965) re-
commendation that it would be better to focus on what happens to
plans, decisions, and tasks rather than to people and departments.

9  For other schematic summaries of this kind see Goldman and van
Houten (1980, 1977), the Brighton Labour Process Group (1977)

and Millham et al. (1972).  For example, Millham and Bullock
outline five processes which can be involved in controlling
(i.e. restricting deviance):  (i) structural control over office
(selection and dismissal), (ii) rewarding and sanctioning, (iii)
institutional control (through structuring the organisations),
(iv) control by orientation (e.g. through training and the use
of special reception units), (v) informal control.  The control
device selected for priority will differ between organisations
depending upon the degree of pre-socialisation, prevailing norms
and other contingent factors.  Millham and Bullock's article, it
should be noted, carries a prescriptive intent. They seek to
identify the most 'appropriate' control mechanisms under the
circumstances.

10  One further shortcoming in the Mellish and Collis-Squires's
(1976) article is that it is not made clear whether the corrective approach itself is the main subject of the critique or
those accounts which imply that such an approach now predomi-
nates.

11  David Montgomery (1979:154) expresses the phenomenon this way:
'every worker knows that she or he remains "under surveillance"
on the job and a "pariah" without one'.

12  In 'Discipline and Punish' (1977:222) Foucault argues:
Historically the process by which the bourgeoisie became in
the course of the eighteenth century the politically dominant
class was masked by the establishment of an explicit, coded
and formally egalitarian juridical framework, made possible
by the organization of a parliamentary, representative
regime.  But the development and generalization of disciplinary mechanisms constituted the other dark side of these
processes.... And although in a formal way, the representative regime makes it possible ... for the will of all to form
the fundamental authority of sovereignty, the disciplines
provide at the base, a guarantee of the submission of forces
and bodies.  The real corporal disciplines constituted the
foundation of the formal juridical liberties (quoted in Lea
1979:76).

13  Significantly the extent of search activity in the decision-
making process has been viewed as an investment decision.  Subordinates are allowed to investigate a problem up to a point
where the expected cost of research is greater than the expected
financial returns (Charne and Cooper, The Theory of Search,
'Management Science' 1958).

14  D. Hutchins, of Hutchins Associates, writing in the BIM's
'Management Review and Digest', defines a quality circle as a
small group who meet together each week under the leadership of
a supervisor on a voluntary basis to identify (production) problems and to *recommend* their solution to management, and where
possible to implement the solutions themselves (1980, vol.8,
no.1:3-7).  There could hardly be a better rendition of the idea
of self-management for management.

15  See, for example Tony Banks, Autonomous work groups, 'Industrial
Society', July/August 1974:10-12.

16  In consequence, I tend to doubt Peter Abell's observation that
we are 'witnessing a demise' of rational domination and a 'trend
to democratic authority structures' (1979:142).

17   The repressive nature of administrative theory and its implica-
     tions for the interpretation of the 'communist experience' is
     explored by Fleron and Fleron (1972) and by Hearn (1978).
18   While Lazonick's (1979) analysis is to be recommended, this is
     not to say that it is without shortcomings.  Thus his account of
     the struggle over the introduction of the self-acting mule sug-
     gests that management's prerogative to introduce the 'most effi-
     cient machinery' was accepted in *exchange for* the 'minder's pre-
     rogative to control the division of labour on the mules' (1979:
     257).  Yet it needs to be additionally noted that in the longer
     term the former would oust the latter.  Of course, the value of
     the dialectical approach which Lazonick shares is that it under-
     scores the perpetual incompletion of domination - as the minders
     lose one set of rights other forms of labour resistance are
     fashioned to counter a new situation.
19   'Sunday Times', 31 May 1981.
20   Ibid.
21   The decimalised pagination is symptomatic of the systematised
     approach.
22   Racial and sexual discrimination comprise part, but only part,
     of this.  Such discrimination is seen as inherited from an
     earlier age but institutionalised and exploited by capitalism.
     In an earlier article entitled Individual Traits and Organiza-
     tional Incentives:  What Makes a 'Good' Worker, Edwards (1976)
     points out the need to critique neoclassical theories of the
     firm which view it as a technological relationship of people -
     nature interaction.  He views it alternatively as a social boss-
     worker relationship.  *Given* this conflictual context then the
     apparently non-efficient strategy of discrimination in sex and
     race can in fact be profitable for capital (1976:64).


CHAPTER 8   STRUGGLE AND RESISTANCE

1   There have been some exceptions, e.g. Friedman (1977) and
    Salaman (1979), but the main thrust of even these works remains
    almost fully on management control strategies and organisational
    design respectively.
2   Quoted in Emile Pouget, 'Sabotage', Chicago 1913:22, and in the
    'Introduction' to the 1969 edition of S.B. Mathewson, 'Restric-
    tion of Output Among Unorganized Workers'.
3   It would be wrong to attach a value-laden approval to conformity
    and to assume that its opposite is always a bad thing.  As the
    classic experiments by Stanley Milgram illustrate, obedience
    itself may indicate fixation and rigidity leading to a 'problem
    of conformity'.  He tested subjects' responses to the dilemma of
    whether to obey authority in circumstances which would violate
    human values by inflicting pain on others, or whether to disobey
    authority and follow individual conscience.  Subjects were led
    to believe they were involved in an experiment to test the
    effect of punishment upon learning capacity.  The 'learner' (an
    accomplice of the experimenter) was strapped to a plausible-
    looking electric chair, and the subject 'teacher' was shown how
    to administer the purported 'switches' in an adjoining room.

Voltage levels at his disposal ranged from 15 volts (labelled as 'slight shock') to 360 volts ('extreme intensity shock') to 420 volts ('danger: severe shock') and even to 450 volts ('XXX'). He was asked to increase the voltage as a punishment for a 'wrong answer'. Milgram took predictions from his colleagues on the likely behaviour of such subjects; the experts doubted that subjects would exceed 240 volts. Yet, in fact, subjects, though they became anxious at the 300-volt level ('intense shock') as the 'learner' pounded on the wall in 'agony', nevertheless proceeded to increase the voltage. Indeed, rather disturbingly, the majority (65 per cent) actually continued right up to the maximum limit at their disposal: 450 volts! (Milgram 1963: 371-8).

4   One important exception was Thorstein Veblen who, in 'The Engineers and the Price System' (1947), outlined the limitations placed on productive effort by industrial elites.

5   'Guardian', 11 April 1978.

6   'Guardian', 8 June 1981.

7   I am pleased to note that Montgomery agrees with this point.   He observes,

The very shopfloor militancy which so disturbs corporate executives and union officials alike in the 1970's could not assume the open and chronic form which makes it notorious without the presence of union and legal defences against arbitrary dismissal.   To see the role of unions in this setting as *nothing more* than disciplinary agents for management, therefore, is a facile and dangerous form of myopia' (1979: 156, emphasis in original).

# BIBLIOGRAPHY

ABELL, P. (1975), 'Organizations as Bargaining and Influence Systems', Heinemann, London.

ABELL, P. (1977), The many faces of power and liberty - revealed preferred autonomy and teleological explanation, 'Sociology', vol.13.

ABELL, P. (1979), Hierarchy and democratic authority, in T.R. Burns et al. (eds), 'Work and Power'.

ABERCROMBIE, N. and TURNER, B.S. (1978), The dominant ideology thesis, 'British Journal of Sociology', vol.29, pp.149-70.

ABERCROMBIE, N. et al. (1980), 'The Dominant Ideology Thesis', Allen & Unwin, London.

ABRAHAMSSON, B. and BROMSTROM, A. (1980), 'The Rights of Labour', Sage, Beverly Hills.

ACKER, J. and VAN HOUTEN, D.R. (1974), Differential recruitment and control: the sex structuring of organizations, 'Administrative Science Quarterly', vol.19, pp.152-63.

ACKROYD, S. (1974), Economic rationality and the relevance of Weberian sociology to industrial relations, 'British Journal of Industrial Relations', vol.IX, no.2.

ACTION SOCIETY TRUST (1956), 'Management Succession', The Trust, London.

ADLER, F. (1977), Factory councils, Gramsci and the industrialists, 'Telos', no.31.

ADVISORY, CONCILIATION AND ARBITRATION SERVICE (1977a), 'Disciplinary Practice and Procedures in Employment, Code of Practice, No.1', HMSO, London.

ADVISORY CONCILIATION AND ARBITRATION SERVICE (1977b), Code of Practice 2: 'Disclosure of Information to Trade Unions for Collective Bargaining Purposes', HMSO, London.

AITKEN, H. (1960), 'Taylorism at Watertown Arsenal', Harvard University Press, Cambridge, Mass.

ALBROW, M. (1970), 'Bureaucracy', Macmillan, London.

ALDRIDGE, A. (1976), 'Power, Authority and Restrictive Practices', Blackwell, Oxford.

ALLEN, V.L. (1975), 'Social Analysis: A Marxist Critique and Alternative', Longman, London.

ALTHUSSER, L. (1969), 'For Marx', Allen Lane, London.

ALTHUSSER, L. (1971), 'Lenin and Philosophy and Other Essays', New Left Books, London.
ALTHUSSER, L. and BALIBAR, E. (1970), 'Reading Capital', New Left Books, London.
AMIN, S. (1975), Toward a structured crisis of world capitalism, 'Socialist Revolution', vol.38, no.2, June.
ANDERMAN, S.D. (1972), 'Voluntary Dismissals Procedure and the Industrial Relations Act', PEP, London.
ANDERSON, P. (1967), The limits and possibilities of trade union action, in R. Blackburn and A. Cockburn (eds), 'The Incompatibles: Trade Union Militancy and the Consensus', Penguin, Harmondsworth.
ANDERSON, P. (1976), 'Considerations on Western Marxism', New Left Books, London.
ANSHEN, M. (1980), 'Corporate Strategies for Social Performance', Collier-MacMillan, London.
ANSOFF, H.I. (1969), 'Business Strategy', Penguin, Harmondsworth.
ANSOFF, H.I. (1979a), 'Corporate Strategy', Penguin, Harmondsworth.
ANSOFF, H.I. (1979b), 'Strategic Management', Macmillan, London.
ANTHONY, P.D. (1977), 'The Ideology of Work', Tavistock, London.
ANTHONY, R.N. (1965), 'Planning and Control Systems - A Framework for Analysis', Harvard University Press.
ARATO, A. (1972), Lukács' theory of reification, 'Telos', no.11, Spring.
ARGYRIS, C. (1957), 'Personality and Organization: The Conflict Between System and the Individual', Harper & Row, New York.
ARGYRIS, C. (1961), Personal versus organizational goals, in R. Dubin (ed.), 'Human Relations in Administration', Prentice-Hall, New Jersey.
ARGYRIS, C. (1964), 'Integrating the Individual and the Organization', Wiley, New York.
ARONOWITZ, S. (1973), 'False Promises: The Shaping of American Working Class Consciousness', McGraw-Hill, New York.
ASHDOWN, R. and BAKER, K. (1973), 'In Working Order: A Study of Industrial Discipline', Department of Employment, London.
ASHTON, T.S. (1948), 'Industrial Revolution', Oxford University Press.
AUSTIN, T. (1980), The 'lump' in the U.K. construction industry, in T. Nichols (ed.), 'Capital and Labour'.
AVLONTIS, G. and PARKINSON, S. (1981), The automatic factory dawns, 'Management Today', May 1981.
BABBAGE, C. (1835), 'On the Economy of Machinery and Manufacturers', Charles Knight, London.
BACHRACH, P. and BARATZ, M.S. (1963), Decisions and non-decisions, 'American Political Science Review', vol.LVII, pp.641-51.
BACHRACH, P. and BARATZ, M.S. (1971), The two faces of power, in F. G. Castles et al. (eds), 'Decisions, Organizations and Society', Penguin, Harmondsworth.
BAIN, G.S. (1979), 'A Bibliography of British Industrial Relations', Cambridge University Press.
BAKKE, E.W. and WIGHT, E. (1958), The function of management, in E.M. Hugh-Jones (ed.), 'Human Relations and Modern Management', North Holland Publishing Company, Amsterdam.
BAKKE, E.W., KERR, C. and ARNOLD, C.W. (eds) (1960), 'Unions, Management and the Public', Harcourt Brace, New York.

BALBUS, I.D. (1971), The concept of interest in pluralist and Marxian analysis, 'Politics and Society', vol.1, no.2, pp.151-77.
BALDAMUS, W. (1961), 'Efficiency and Effort', Tavistock, London.
BALDWIN, R.W. (1966), 'Social Justice', Pergamon Press, Oxford.
BALIBAR, E. (1978), Irrationalism and Marxism, 'New Left Review', no.107.
BAMBER, G. (1976), Trade unions for managers, 'Personnel Review', vol.5, pp.36-41.
BANKS, J. (1977), Review article in 'Times Higher Educational Supplement', 25 November.
BARAN, P. (1957), 'The Political Economy of Growth', Monthly Review Press, New York.
BARAN, P. and SWEEZY, P. (1966), 'Monopoly Capital', Penguin, Harmondsworth.
BARNARD, C.I. (1956), 'The Functions of the Executive', Harvard University Press.
BARNARD, C.I. (1968), 'The Functions of the Executive', Harvard University Press.
BARRATT-BROWN, M. (1969), Pamphlet no.4, 'Opening the Books', Institute for Workers' Control.
BARRINGTON MOORE, J. JR (1973), 'Social Origins of Dictatorship and Democracy', Penguin, Harmondsworth.
BARTHES, R. (1973), 'Mythologies', Paladin, St Albans.
BATSTONE, E. (1979), Systems of domination, accommodation and industrial democracy, in T.R. Burns et al. (eds), 'Work and Power'.
BATSTONE, E., BORASTON, I. and FRENKEL, S. (1977), 'Shop Stewards in Action:  The Organization of Work-place Conflict and Accommodation', Blackwell, Oxford.
BATSTONE, E., BORASTON, I. and FRENKEL, S. (1978), 'The Social Organization of Strikes', Blackwell, Oxford.
BATTALIA, O.W. and TARRANT, J.T. (1973), 'The Corporate Eunuch', Abelaird Schuman, New York.
BAUMGARTNER, T., BURNS, T.R. and DE VILLE, P. (1979), Work, politics and social structuring under capitalism, in T.R. Burns et al. (eds), 'Work and Power'.
BEAUMONT, P.B. (1978), Management perceptions of the institution of collective bargaining, 'Personnel Review', vol.7, no.3.
BEAUMONT, P. and GREGORY, M. (1980), The role of employers in collective bargaining in Britain, 'Industrial Relations Journal', December.
BECKER, J.F. (1977), 'Marxian Political Economy', Cambridge University Press.
BECKER, L.C. (1978), 'Property Rights', Routledge & Kegan Paul, London.
BEECHEY, V. (1977), Some notes on female labour in capitalist production, 'Capital and Class', no.3, pp.45-66.
BEECHEY, V. (1979), 'Labour and Monopoly Capital - Notes Towards a Marxist Critique', Sociology Department, University of Warwick.
BEETHAM, D. (1974), 'Max Weber and the Theory of Modern Politics', Allen & Unwin, London.
BEHREND, H. (1957), The effort bargain, 'Industrial and Labour Relations Review', vol.10, pp.503-15.
BENDIX, R. (1956), 'Work and Authority in Industry', Wiley, New York.

BENDIX, R. (1961), Industrial authority, in R. Dubin (ed.), 'Human Relations in Administration', 2nd edn, Prentice-Hall, New Jersey.
BENDIX, R. (1966), 'Max Weber: An Intellectual Portrait', Methuen, London.
BENN, S.I. and PETERS, R.S. (1959), 'Social Principles and the Democratic State', Allen & Unwin, London.
BENSON, J.K. (1975), The inter-organizational network as a political economy, 'Administrative Science Quarterly', no.20, pp.229-49.
BENSON, J.K. (1977), Organizations: a dialectical view, 'Administrative Science Quarterly', vol.22, pp.1-18.
BERG, M. (ed.) (1979), 'Technology and Toil in Nineteenth Century Britain', CSE Books, London.
BERGEN, H.B. (1940), Managerial prerogatives, 'Harvard Business Review', March.
BERGER, P.L. and LUCKMAN, T. (1967), 'The Social Construction of Reality', Allen Lane, London.
BERGER, P. and PULLBERG, S. (1966), Reification and the sociological critique of consciousness, 'New Left Review', vol.35, pp.56-71.
BERLE, A. and MEARS, G.C. (1932), 'The Modern Corporation and Private Property', Macmillan, New York.
BETTELHEIM, C. (1975), 'The Transition to Socialist Economy', Harvester Press, Sussex.
BEYNON, H. (1973), 'Working For Ford', Allen Lane, London.
BEYNON, H. and WAINWRIGHT, H. (1979), 'The Workers' Report on Vickers', Pluto Press, London.
BHASKAR, R. (1978), 'A Realist Theory of Science', Harvester, Hassocks.
BIERSTEDT, R. (1950), An analysis of social power, 'American Sociological Review', vol.15, no.6.
BITTNER, E. (1973), The police on Skid Row, in Salaman and Thompson (eds), 'People and Organisations', Longman, London.
BLACKABY, F. (ed.) (1979), 'De-Industrialization', NIESR Economic Policy Papers, Heinemann, London.
BLACKBURN, R. (1972), A brief guide to bourgeois ideology, in R.C. Edwards et al. (eds), 'The Capitalist System', Prentice-Hall, Englewood Cliffs, N.J., pp.36-46.
BLAKE, R.R. and MOUTON, J.S. (1964), 'The Managerial Grid', Gulf, Houston, Texas.
BLAU, P.M. (1964), 'Exchange and Power in Social Life', Wiley, New York.
BLAU, P.M. and SCHOENHERR, R. (1971), 'The Structure of Organizations', Basic Books, New York.
BLAU, P.M. and SCHOENHERR, R.A. (1973), New forms of power, in G. Salaman and K. Thompson (eds), 'People and Organizations', Longman, London.
BLAU, P.M. and SCOTT, W.R. (1963), 'Formal Organizations', Routledge & Kegan Paul, London.
BLOCK, F. and HIRSCHHORN, L. (1979), New Productive forces and the contradictions of contemporary capitalism: a post-industrial perspective, 'Theory and Society', vol.7, no.3.
BLUMBERG, P. (1968), 'Industrial Democracy: The Sociology of Participation', Constable, London.
BLYTON, P. (1980), The co-existence of managers and managed in a single trade union branch, in M.J.F. Poole and R. Mansfield (eds), 'Managerial Roles in Industrial Relations'.

BORASTON, I., CLEGG, H.A. and RIMMER, M. (1975), 'Workplace and Union', Heinemann, London.
BOREHAM, P. (1980), The dialectic theory and control:  capitalist crisis and the organization of labour', in D. Dunkerley and G. Salaman (eds), 'International Yearbook of Organization Studies 1980'.
BOREHAM, P. and DOW, G. (1980), The labour process and capitalist crisis, in P. Boreham and G. Dow (eds), 'Work and Inequality'.
BOREHAM, P.R. and DOW, G. (eds) (1980), 'Work and Inequality', Macmillan, Melbourne.
BOSANQUET, N. and STANDING, G. (1972), Government and unemployment, 1966-70:  a study of policy and evidence, 'British Journal of Industrial Relations', vol.10, no.2.
BOSQUET, M. (1977), 'Capitalism in Crisis and Everyday Life', Harvester Press, Hassocks, Sussex.
BOSQUET, M. (1980), The meaning of job enrichment, in T. Nichols (ed.), 'Capital and Labour'.
BOTTOMORE, T. (1974), 'Marxist Sociology', Macmillan, London.
BOWEN, P. (1974), The steelworker and work control, 'British Journal of Industrial Relations', vol.12, no.2, pp.249-67.
BOWEN, P. (1976), 'Social Control in Industrial Organizations', Routledge & Kegan Paul, London.
BOWLES, S. and GINTIS, H. (1976), 'Schooling in Capitalist America', Routledge & Kegan Paul, London.
BOWLES, S., GINTIS, H. and MEYER, P. (1975), The long shadow of work:  education, the family and the reproduction of the social division of labour, 'Insurgent Sociologist', no.5, Summer.
BRADLEY, K. (1980), A comparative analysis of producer co-ops, 'British Journal of Industrial Relations', July.
BRAHAM, P. (1975), Immigrant labour in Europe, in G. Esland et al. (eds), 'People and Work', Holmes McDougall, Edinburgh, pp.119-33.
BRANNEN, P., BATSTONE, E., FATCHETT, D. and WHITE, P. (1976), 'The Worker Directors:  A Sociology of Participation', Hutchinson, London.
BRAVERMAN, H. (1974), 'Labour and Monopoly Capital:  The Degradation of Work in the Twentieth Century', Monthly Review Press, New York.
BRAVERMAN, H. (1976), Two Comments, 'Monthly Review', vol.28, no.3.
BRECHER, J. (1972), 'Strike!', Straight Arrow Books, San Francisco.
BRECHER, J. (1979), Uncovering the hidden history of the American workplace, 'Review of Radical Political Economics', vol.10, no.4.
BRIGHT, J. (1958a), Does automation raise skill requirements?, 'Harvard Business Review', vol.36, no.4.
BRIGHT, J. (1958b), 'Automation and Management', Harvard University Press.
BRIGHTON LABOUR PROCESS GROUP (1977), The capitalist labour process, 'Capital and Class 1', Spring, pp.3-42.
BRITISH INSTITUTE OF MANAGEMENT (1977), 'Employee Participation: The Way Ahead', British Institute of Management, London.
BROWN, G. (1977), 'Sabotage', Spokesman, Nottingham.
BROWN, R.K. (1978), From Donovan to where?  Interpretations of industrial relations in Britain since 1968, 'British Journal of Sociology', vol.29, no.4, December.
BROWN, W. (1972), A consideration of custom and practice, 'British Journal of Industrial Relations', vol.10, pp.42-61.

BROWN, W. (1973), 'Piecework Bargaining', Heinemann, London.
BROWN, W. (ed.) (1981), 'The Changing Contours of British Industrial Relations', Blackwell, Oxford.
BROWN, W.A., EBSWORTH, R. and TERRY, M. (1978), Factors shaping shop steward organization in Britain, 'British Journal of Industrial Relations', vol.16, no.2, July.
BUCHANAN, A. (1979), Revolutionary motivation and rationality, 'Philosophy and Public Affairs', vol.9, no.1, Fall.
BULLOCK, LORD (1977), 'Report of the Commission of Inquiry on Industrial Democracy', Cmnd 6706, HMSO, London.
BURAWOY, M. (1978), Towards a marxist theory of the labour process: Braverman and Beyond, 'Politics and Society', vol.8, nos 3-4.
BURGESS, K. (1969), Technological Change and the 1852 Lockout in the British Engineering Industry, 'Int. Journal of Social History', vol. 14, no.2.
BURKE, R.J. (1970), Methods of resolving superior-subordinate conflict, 'Organizational Behavior and Human Performance', July, pp. 393-411.
BURNS, T. and STALKER, G.M. (1961), 'The Management of Innovation', Tavistock, London.
BURNS, T.R. and RUS, V. (1979), Introduction and overview, in T.R. Burns et al. (eds), 'Work and Power'.
BURNS, T.R. et al. (eds) (1979), 'Work and Power: The Liberation of Work and the Control of Political Power', Sage Publications, London.
BURRELL, G. (1980), Radical organization theory, in Dunkerley and Salaman (eds) (1980a).
CAITS (1980a), 'Trade Union Strategy in the Face of Corporate Power', Centre for Alternative Industrial and Technological Systems, North East London Polytechnic.
CAITS (1980b), 'Co-operation or Co-option', Centre for Alternative Industrial and Technological Systems, North East London Polytechnic.
CAMBRIDGE POLITICAL ECONOMY GROUP (1974), 'Britain's Economic Crisis', Bertrand Russell Peace Foundation, London.
CAMERON (LORD) (1974), 'Report of a Court of Enquiry', Cmnd 131, HMSO, London.
CANNON, I.C. (1967), Ideology and occupational community, 'Sociology', May, vol.15, no.2.
CARCHEDI, G. (1975), Reproduction of social classes at the level of production, 'Economy and Society', vol.4, no.4, pp.361-417.
CARCHEDI, G. (1977), 'On the Economic Identification of Social Classes', Routledge & Kegan Paul, London.
CASTLE, E.N. (1978), Property rights and the political economy of resource scarcity, 'American Journal of Agricultural Economics', vol.60, no.1.
CASTLES, S. and KOSACK, O. (1973), 'Immigrant Workers and Class Struggles in Western Europe', Oxford University Press.
CERTO, S.C. (1980), 'Principles of Modern Management', Wm. C. Brown Company, Dubuque, Iowa.
CHAMBERLAIN, N.W. (1948), 'The Union Challenge to Management Control', Harper, New York.
CHAMBERLAIN, N.W. (1963a), The union challenge to management control, 'Industrial and and Labour Relations Review', vol.16, no.2.
CHAMBERLAIN, N.W. (1963b), Management rights and labour arbitration, 'Industrial and Labour Relations Review', vol.16, no.2.

CHAMBERLAIN, N.W. and KUHN, J.W. (1965), 'Collective Bargaining', 2nd edn, McGraw-Hill, New York.
CHANAN, M. (1976), 'Labour Power in the British Film Industry', British Film Institute.
CHANAN, MICHAEL (1980), Labour, power and aesthetic Labour in film and television in Britain, 'Media, Culture and Society', vol.2, no.2.
CHANDLER, A.D. (1962), 'Strategy and Structure: Chapters in the History of the Industrial Enterprise', MIT Press, Cambridge, Mass.
CHANDLER, A.D. (1977), 'The Visible Hand: The Managerial Revolution in American Business', Harvard University Press, Cambridge, Mass.
CHANDLER, A.D. and DAEMS, H. (1980), 'Managerial Hierarchies', Harvard University Press.
CHANDLER, M. (1964), 'Management Rights and Union Interests', McGraw-Hill, New York.
CHANNON, D.F. (1973), 'The Strategy and Structure of British Enterprise', Macmillan, London.
CHAPMAN, S.D. (1972), 'The Cotton Industry in the Industrial Revolution', Macmillan, London.
CHESLER, M.A. et al. (1978), Power training: an alternative path to conflict management, 'California Management Review', vol.XXI, no.2.
CHILD, J. (1969a), 'British Management Thought', Allen & Unwin, London.
CHILD, J. (1969b), 'The Business Enterprise in Modern Industrial Society', Collier McMillan, London.
CHILD, J. (1972), Organisation structure and strategies of control, 'Administrative Science Quarterly', vol.17, pp.163-77.
CHILD, J. (1973), Strategies of organizational control and organizational behaviour, 'Administrative Science Quarterly', March.
CHINOY, E. (1955), 'Automobile Workers and the American Dream', Doubleday, New York.
CLARK, D.G. (1966), 'The Industrial Manager: His Background and Career Pattern', Business Publications, London.
CLARKE, R.O. (1957), The dispute in the engineering industry 1897-98, 'Economia', vol.24, May.
CLARKE, R.O., FATCHETT, D.J. and ROBERTS, B.C. (1972), 'Workers' Participation in Management in Britain', Heinemann, London.
CLAWSON, D. (1980a), 'Bureaucracy and the Labour Process: The Transformation of U.S. Industry 1860-1920', Monthly Review Press, New York.
CLAWSON, D. (1980b), Class struggle and the rise of bureaucracy, in D. Dunkerley and G. Salaman (eds), 'International Yearbook of Organizational Studies'.
CLEGG, H.A. (1960), 'A New Approach to Industrial Democracy', Blackwell, Oxford.
CLEGG, H.A. (1975), Pluralism in industrial relations, 'British Journal of Industrial Relations', vol.13.
CLEGG, H.A. (1976), 'Trade Unionism Under Collective Bargaining', Blackwell, Oxford.
CLEGG, H.A. (1978), 'Trade Unions Under Collective Bargaining', Blackwell, Oxford.
CLEGG, S. (1975), 'Power, Rule and Domination', Routledge & Kegan Paul, London.
CLEGG, S. (1979), 'The Theory of Power and Organizations', Routledge & Kegan Paul, London.

CLEGG, S. and DUNKERLEY, D. (1980), 'Organization, Class and Control', Routledge & Kegan Paul, London.
CLEGG, S., DUNKERLEY, D. (eds) (1977), 'Critical Issues in Organizations', Routledge & Kegan Paul, London.
CLEMENTS, R.V. (1958), 'A Study of Their Careers in Industry', Allen & Unwin, London.
CLIFF, T. (1970), 'The Employers' Offensive', Pluto Press, London.
COATES, K. (ed.) (1968), 'Can the Workers Run Industry?', Institute for Workers Control, Nottingham.
COATES, K. and TOPHAM, P. (1974), 'The New Unionism:  The Case For Workers' Control', Penguin, Harmondsworth.
COHEN, G.A. (1978), 'Karl Marx's Theory of History:  A Defence', Oxford University Press.
COHEN, J. (1972), Max Weber and the dynamics of rationalized domination, 'Telos', no.14 (Winter).
COLE, G.D.H. (1948), 'A Short History of the British Working Class Movement 1789-1947', Allen & Unwin, London.
COLE, G.D.H. (1957), 'The Case for Industrial Partnership', Macmillan, London.
COLE, G.D.H. (1972), 'Self Government in Industry', Hutchinson, London (first published by Bell and Sons 1917).
COLE, G.D.H. (1973), 'Workshop Organization', Hutchinson, London (first published by Clarendon Press in 1923).
COLLETTI, L. (1972), 'From Rousseau to Lenin', New Left Books, London.
COLLETTI, L. (1973), 'Marxism and Hegel', New Left Books, London.
COMMISSION OF THE EUROPEAN COMMUNITIES (1975), 'Employee Participation and Company Structure', Luxembourg.
COMMISSION ON INDUSTRIAL RELATIONS (1972), Report No.31: 'Disclosure of Information', HMSO, London.
COMMISSION ON INDUSTRIAL RELATIONS (1973a), 'Industrial Relations at Establishment Level:  A Statistical Survey', HMSO, London.
COMMISSION ON INDUSTRIAL RELATIONS (1973b), Report No.34:  'The Role of Management in Industrial Relations', HMSO, London.
CONFERENCE OF SOCIALIST ECONOMISTS (1976), 'The Labour Process and Class Struggle', Stage One, CSE, London.
CONFERENCE OF SOCIALIST ECONOMISTS (1980a), 'The Alternative Economic Strategy:  A Labour Movement Response to the Economic Crisis', CSE London Working Group.
CONFERENCE OF SOCIALIST ECONOMISTS (1980b), 'Microelectronics, Capitalist Technology and the Working Class', CSE, London.
CONSERVATIVE POLITICAL CENTRE (1968), 'Fair Deal at Work, The Conservative Approach to Modern Industrial Relations', Conservative Political Centre, London.
CONSERVATIVE POLITICAL CENTRE (1976), 'One Nation at Work', London.
CONSTAS, H. (1958), Max Weber's two conceptions of bureaucracy, 'American Journal of Sociology', vol.52, January, pp.400-9.
COOLEY, M. (1980), 'Architect or Bee', Langley Technical Services, Slough.
COOMBS, R. (1978), 'Labour and Monopoly Capital', New Left Review, vol.107, pp.79-97.
COPEMAN, G. (1975), 'Employee Share Ownership and Industrial Relations', Institute of Personnel Managers, London.
COTGROVE, S. (1973), Anti-Science, 'New Society', 12 July, pp.82-4.

COTGROVE, S. (1975), Technical rationality and domination, 'Social Studies of Science', vol.5.

COUNTER INFORMATION SERVICES (1974), 'British Leyland:  The Beginning of the End?', Counter Information Services, London.

CRESSEY, P. and MACINNES, J. (1980a), Industrial democracy and theories of power and control in the workplace, 'Discussion Paper 3', Centre for Research in Industrial Democracy and Participation, University of Glasgow.

CRESSEY, P. and MACINNES, J. (1980b), Voting for Ford, 'Capital and Class', no.11, Summer, pp.5-34.

CRESSEY, P. and MACINNES, J. (1980c), 'Employee Participation in Scottish Industry and Commerce:  A Survey of Attitudes and Practice', Centre for Research in Industrial Democracy and Participation, University of Glasgow.

CRICHTON, A. (1968), 'Personnel Management in Context', Batsford, London.

CROMPTON, R. and GUBBAY, J. (1977), 'Economy and Class Structure', Macmillan, London.

CROUCH, C. (1977), 'Class Conflict and the Industrial Relations Crisis', Heinemann, London.

CROUCH, C. (1979a), 'The Politics of Industrial Relations', Fontana, London.

CROUCH, C. (1979b), The State, Capital and Liberal Democracy, in Crouch (ed.), 'State and Economy in Contemporary Capitalism'.

CROUCH, C. (ed.) (1979c), 'State and Economy in Contemporary Capitalism', Croom Helm, London.

CROZIER, M. (1964), 'The Bureaucratic Phenomenon', Tavistock, London.

CULLEN, D.E. and GREENBAUM, M.L. (1966), 'Managements' Rights and Collective Bargaining:  Can Both Survive?', State School of Industrial and Labour Relations, Ithaca, New York.

CUMMINGS, L. and GREENBAUM, J. (1978), The struggle over productivity:  workers management and technology, in Union for Radical Political Economics (eds), 'U.S. Capitalism in Crisis', URPE, New York.

CUTLER, A. (1978), The romance of labour, 'Economy and Society', vol.7, no.1.

CUTLER, A., HINDESS, B., HIRST, P. and HUSSAIN, A. (1977/8), 'Marx's Capital and Capitalism Today', 2 vols, Routledge & Kegan Paul, London.

CYERT, R.M. and MARCH, J.G. (1963), 'A Behavioural Theory of the Firm', Prentice-Hall, Englewood Cliffs, N.J.

DAHL, R. (1957), The concept of power, 'Behavioural Science', vol.2, July.

DAHL, R. (1961), 'Who Governs?', Yale University Press.

DAHRENDORF, R. (1959), 'Class and Class Conflict in Industrial Society', Routledge & Kegan Paul, London.

DALTON, M. (1959), 'Men Who Manage', Wiley, New York.

DANIEL, W.W. and MCINTOSH (1972), 'The Right to Manage', MacDonald/ PEP, London.

DAVIDSON, A.B. (1972), The varying seasons of Gramscian studies, 'Political Studies', vol.XX, no.4, December, pp.448-61.

DAVIES, M. and BRODHEAD, F. (1975), Labour and Monopoly Capital:  a review, 'Radical America', vol.9.

DAVIS, M. (1975), The stopwatch and the wooden shoe:  scientific management and the industrial workers of the world, 'Radical America', no.9, pp.69-95.

DAY, R.A. and DAY, J.V. (1977), A review of the current state of negotiated order theory:  an appreciation and a critique, 'Sociological Quarterly', vol.18, pp.126-42.

DE KADT, M. (1975), Management and labour, 'Review of Radical Political Economics', vol.7, no.1.

DE KADT, M. (1976a), Management in monopoly capital:  the problem of the control of workers in large corporations, PhD Thesis, New School for Social Research, New York.

DE KADT, M. (1976b), The importance of distinguishing between levels of generality, 'Review of Radical Political Economics', vol.7, no.1.

DE LOREAN, J.Z. (1979), 'On a Clear Day You Can See General Motors, J.Z. De Lorean's Look Inside the Automotive Giant', J.P. Wright, Wright Enterprises, Michigan.

DEMSETZ, H. (1967), Towards a theory of property rights, 'American Economic Review', vol.57, May, pp.347-59.

DEPARTMENT OF EMPLOYMENT (1971), Manpower Paper No.5:  'The Reform of Collective Bargaining at Plant and Company Level', HMSO, London.

DEPARTMENT OF EMPLOYMENT (1975a), 'Making Work More Satisfying', HMSO, London.

DEPARTMENT OF EMPLOYMENT (1975b), 'Work Restructuring Projects and Experiments in the United Kingdom', HMSO, London.

DERBER, M. (1955), 'Labour Management Relations at Plant Level Under Industry-wide Bargaining', University of Illinois, Urbana.

DERBER, M. (1960), Management and union rights in industrial establishments, 'Current Economic Comment', May.

DERBER, M., CHALMERS, W.E. and EDELMANN, M.T. (1961), Union participation in plant decision making, 'Industrial and Labour Relations Review', vol.15, no.1.

DERBER, M., CHALMERS, W. and STAGNER, R. (1954), 'Labour-Management Relations in Illini City' (2 vols), University of Illinois Institute of Labour and Industrial Relations.

DEROSSI, F. (1981), 'The Technocratic Illusion:  A Study of Managerial Power in Italy', M.E. Sharpe, London.

DE VROEY, M. (1975), The separation of ownership and control in large corporations, 'Review of Radical Political Economics', vol.7, no.2.

DICKSON, D. (1968), 'Social Problems', vol.16, pp.143-56.

DICKSON, D. (1974), 'Alternative Technology and the Politics of Technical Change', Fontana, London.

DICKSON, D. (1975), Technology and social reality, 'Dialectical Anthropology', vol.1, no.1.

DICKSON, L. et al. (1979), The governments working papers on employment protection legislation, 'Industrial Law Journal', vol.8, pp.246-8.

DISCO, C. (1979), Critical theory as ideology of the new class:  rereading Jurgen Habermas, 'Theory and Society', vol.8, no.2.

DOBB, M. (1947), 'Studies in the Development of Capitalism', Routledge & Kegan Paul, London.

DOERINGER, P. and PIORE, M. (1971), 'Internal Labour Markets and Manpower Analysis', Lexington Books, Mass.

DREVER, J. (1964), 'A Dictionary of Psychology', Penguin, Harmondsworth.

DRONBERGER, I. (1971), 'The Political Thought of Max Weber', A
Appleton, New York.
DRUCKER, P. (1950), Management must manage, 'Harvard Business
Review', vol.23, no.2, March.
DRUCKER, P. (1954), 'The Practice of Management', Harper & Row, New
York.
DRUCKER, P. (1974), 'Management: Tasks, Responsibilities,
Practices', Heinemann, New York.
DUBIN, R. (1957), Power and union-management relations, 'Administra-
tive Science Quarterly', vol.2, pp.66-81.
DUBIN, R. (1960), A theory of conflict and power in union-management
relations, 'Industrial and Labour Relations Review', vol.13, no.4.
DUBIN, R. (1961), 'Human Relations in Administration', 2nd edn,
Prentice-Hall, Englewood Cliffs, N.J.
DUBOIS, P. (1979), 'Sabotage in Industry', Penguin, Harmondsworth.
DUNKERLEY, D. and SALAMAN, G. (eds) (1980a), 'The International
Yearbook of Organization Studies 1979', Routledge & Kegan Paul,
London.
DUNKERLEY, D. and SALAMAN, G. (eds) (1980b), 'The International
Yearbook of Organization Studies 1980', Routledge & Kegan Paul,
London.
DUNLOP, J.T. (1958), 'Industrial Relations Systems', Holt, New York.
DURKHEIM, E. (1933), 'The Division of Labour in Society', Macmillan,
New York.
EASLEA, B. (1973), 'Liberation and the Aims of Science', Chatto &
Windus, London.
EDWARDS, R.C. (1972), Alienation and inequality: capitalist
relations of production in bureaucratic enterprises, PhD Thesis,
Harvard University.
EDWARDS, R.C. (1975), The social relations of production in the firm
and labour market structure, 'Politics and Society', vol.5.
EDWARDS, R.C. (1976), Individual traits and organizational
incentives: what makes a good worker?, 'Journal of Human
Resources', Winter.
EDWARDS, R.C. (1979), 'Contested Terrain: The Transformation of the
Workplace in the Twentieth Century', Heinemann, London.
EDWARDS, R.C. et al. (eds) (1975), 'Labour Market Segmentation',
D.C. Heath, Lexington, Mass.
EHRENREICH, B. and EHRENREICH, J. (1977), The professional-
managerial class, 'Radical America', vol.11, no.2.
EILON, S. (1965), Control systems with several controllers, 'The
Journal of Management Studies'.
EILON, S. (1979), 'Management Control', Pergamon, London.
EISON, A. (1978), The meanings and confusions of Weberian
'rationality', 'British Journal of Sociology', vol.29, no.1, March.
ELBAUM, B. and WILKINSON, F. (1979), Industrial relations and
uneven development: a comparative study of the American and British
steel industries, 'Cambridge Journal of Economics', vol.3.
ELGER, A. (1975), Industrial organizations - a processual approach,
in J.B. McKinlay (ed.), 'Processing People', Holt, Rinehart &
Winston, New York.
ELGER, A. (1979), Valorization and deskilling: a critique of
Braverman, 'Capital and Class', no.7, Spring.
ELGER, A. and SCHWARZ, B. (1980), Monopoly capitalism and the impact

of Taylorism:  notes on Lenin, Gramsci, Braverman and Sohn-Rethel, in T. Nichols (ed.), 'Capital and Labour'.

ELKINS, A. (1980), 'Management:  Structures, Functions, and Practices', Addison-Wesley, Reading, Mass.

ELLIOTT, D. and ELLIOTT, R. (1976), 'The Control of Technology', Wykeham, London.

ELLIOTT, J. (1978), 'Conflict or Co-operation?  The Growth of Industrial Democracy', Kogan Page, London.

ELLIOTT, R. (1976), A case study of management and worker attitudes to managerial authority and prerogatives, PhD Thesis, University of London.

ELSON, D. (ed.) (1980), 'Value:  The Representation of Labour Under Capitalism', CSE Books, London.

ENGELS, F. (1892), 'The Condition of the Working Class in England in 1844', Allen & Unwin, London.

ENGELS, F. (1969), On authority, in L.S. Feuer (ed.), 'Marx and Engels:  Basic Writings on Politics and Philosophy', Fontana, London.

ENGINEERING EMPLOYERS' FEDERATION AND CONFEDERATION OF SHIPBUILDING AND ENGINEERING UNIONS, 'Proceedings in Conference, Transcripts of Negotiations' (various meetings).

ENGLAND, J. and WEEKES, B. (1981), Trade unions and the state:  a review of the crisis, 'Industrial Relations Journal', January/ February.

ETZIONI, A. (1961), 'The Comparative Analysis of Complex Organizations', Free Press, New York.

ETZIONI, A. (1975), 'The Comparative Analysis of Complex Organizations', wnd edn, Free Press, New York.

FALK, R. (1970), 'The Business of Management', Penguin, Harmondsworth.

FARNHAM, D. (1978), Can managers collect their strength?, 'Management Today', February, pp.29-34.

FEINBERG, J. (1966), Duties, rights and claims, 'American Philosophical Quarterly', vol.3, no.2.

FESTINGER, L. (1957), 'A Theory of Cognitive Dissonance', Row, Peterson, Evanston, Illinois.

FIELD, F. (1981), 'Inequality in Britain:  Freedom, Welfare and the State', Fontana, London.

FINE, B. et al. (eds) (1979), 'Capitalism and the Rule of Law', Hutchinson, London.

FLANDERS, A. (1965), 'Industrial Relations:  What is Wrong with the System?  An Essay on its Theory and Future', Faber, London.

FLANDERS, A. (1968), Collective bargaining:  a theoretical analysis, 'British Journal of Industrial Relations', vol.VI, no.1.

FLANDERS, A. (ed.) (1969), 'Collective Bargaining.  Selected Readings', Penguin, Harmondsworth.

FLANDERS, A. (1970), 'Management and Unions', Faber, London.

FLANDERS, A. (1974), The tradition of voluntarism, 'British Journal of Industrial Relations', November.

FLERON, F.J. and FLERON, L.J. (1972), Administrative theory as repressive political theory:  the communist experience, 'Telos', vol.12, pp.63-92.

FLETCHER, C. (1973), The end of management, in J. Child (ed.), 'Man and Organization', Allen & Unwin, London.

FOLEY, B. and MAUNDERS, K. (1977), 'Accounting Information, Disclosure and Collective Bargaining', Macmillan, London.

FORBES, R.P. (1975), The problem of laissez faire bias in Weber's concept of rationality, 'Sociological Analysis and Review', vol.5, pp.219-36.

FORD U.K. (1980), 'Disciplinary Procedure/Code', Supervisors Bulletin, Plant No.642, Halewood, Liverpool.

FOSTER, J. (1974), 'Class Struggle and the Industrial Revolution', Weidenfeld & Nicolson, London.

FOSTER, J. (1976), British imperialism and the labour aristocracy, in J. Skilling (ed.), 'The General Strike 1926', Lawrence & Wishart, London.

FOUCAULT, M. (1977), 'Discipline and Punish', Allen Lane, London.

FOX, A. (1966), Managerial ideology and labour relations, 'British Journal of Industrial Relations', vol.4.

FOX, A. (1971), 'A Sociology of Industry', Collier-MacMillan, London.

FOX, A. (1973), Industrial relations: a social critique of pluralist ideology, in J. Child (ed.), 'Man and Organisation', Allen & Unwin, London.

FOX, A. (1974a), 'Man Mismanagement', Hutchinson, London.

FOX, A. (1974b), 'Beyond Contract', Faber, London.

FOX, A. (1979), A note on Industrial relations pluralism, 'Sociology', January.

FOX, A. and FLANDERS, A. (1969), The reform of collective bargaining: from Donovan to Durkheim, 'British Journal of Industrial Relations', vol.7, no.2.

FREEDLAND, M. (1975), Reasonableness of dismissal: the code of practice and good personnel management, 'Industrial Law Journal', no.4.

FREEDMAN, A. (1979), 'Managing Labor Relations: Organization, Objectives and Results', The Conference Board, New York.

FREIDSON, E. (1977), The division of labour as social interaction, in M.R. Haing and J. Dofny (eds), 'Work and Technology', Sage, London.

FREUND, J. (1968), 'The Sociology of Max Weber', Allen Lane, London.

FREUND, P. and ABRAMS, M. (1976), Ethnomethodology and Marxism: their use for critical theorizing, 'Theory and Society', vol.3, no.3.

FRIEDMAN, A.L. (1977a), 'Industry and Labour: Class Struggle at Work and Monopoly Capitalism', Macmillan, London.

FRIEDMAN, A. (1977b), Responsible autonomy versus direct control over the labour process, 'Capital and Class', Spring.

FRIEDMAN, H. and MEREDEEN, S. (1980), 'The Dynamics of Industrial Conflict: Lessons from Ford', Croom Helm, London.

FRIEDMAN, M. (1962), 'Capitalism and Freedom', University of Chicago Press.

FROST, P. (1980), 'The representation of managerial interests', in M.J.F. Poole and R. Mansfield (eds), 'Managerial Roles in Industrial Relations'.

GALLACHER, W. (1978), 'Revolt on the Clyde', Lawrence & Wishart, London.

GALLACHER, W. and CAMPBELL, J.R. (1972), 'Direct Action: An Outline of Workshop and Social Organization', Pluto Press (first published by the National Council of the Scottish Workers Committees, 1919).

GAMBLE, A. and WALTON, P. (1976), 'Capitalism in Crisis', Macmillan, London.

GARNSEY, E. (1981), The rediscovery of the division of labour, 'Theory and Society', vol.10.

GEORGAKAS, D. and SURKIN, M. (1975), 'Detroit - I Do Mind Dying:  A Study in Urban Revolution', St Martins Press, New York.

GEORGE, K.D. (1974), 'Industrial Organization', Allen & Unwin, London.

GERTH, H. and MILLS, C.W. (eds) (1948), Introduction in Weber, 'Max Weber:  Essays in Sociology'.

GIDDENS, A. (1968), Power in the recent writings of Talcott Parsons, 'Sociology', vol.113, pp.257-72.

GIDDENS, A. (1971), 'Capitalism and Modern Social Theory', Cambridge University Press.

GIDDENS, A. (1973), 'The Class Structure of the Advanced Societies', Hutchinson, London.

GIDDENS, A. (1974), Elites in the British class structure, in P. Stanworth and A. Giddens (eds), 'Elites and Power in British Society', Cambridge University Press.

GILROY, P. (1980), Managing the 'underclass':  a further note on the sociology of race relations in Britain, 'Race and Class', vol.22, no.1.

GINTIS, A. (1972), Activism and counter-culture:  the dialectics of consciousness in the corporate state, 'Telos', no.12, Summer.

GINTIS, H. (1976), The nature of labour exchange and the theory of capitalist production, 'Review of Radical Political Economics', vol. 8, no.2.

GLYN, A. and SUTCLIFFE, B. (1972), 'British Capitalism, Workers and the Profits Squeeze', Penguin, Harmondsworth.

GOLDING, D. (1980a), Authority, legitimacy and 'The Rights to Manage', at Wenslow Manufacturing Co., 'Personnel Review', Winter.

GOLDING, D. (1980b), Establishing blissful clarity in organizational life:  managers, 'Sociological Review', vol.28, no.4.

GOLDMAN, P. (1976), 'Ideology, Bureaucracy and Sociology:  A Critique of Bourgeois Organizational Theory and Research', Presented at the Annual Meeting of the American Sociological Association, New York, August.

GOLDMAN, P. and VAN HOUTEN, D. (1977), Managerial strategies and the worker:  a Marxist analysis of bureaucracy, 'The Sociological Quarterly', vol.18.

GOLDMAN, P. and VAN HOUTEN, D. (1980), Bureaucracy and domination: managerial strategy in turn-of-the-century American industry, in D. Dunkerley and G. Salaman (eds), 'International Yearbook of Organization Studies', pp.108-41.

GOLDTHORPE, J.H. (1974), Industrial relations in Great Britain: critique of reformism, 'Politics and Society', vol.4, no.4.

GOODEY, C. (1974), Factory committees and the dictatorship of the proletariat 1918, 'Critique', vol.3.

GOODMAN, J.B.F. and WHITTINGHAM, T.G. (1969), 'Shop Stewards in British Industry', McGraw-Hill, London.

GOODMAN, J.F.B., ARMSTRONG, E.G.A., DAVIS, J.E. and WAGNER, A. (1977), 'Rule-making and Industrial Peace', Croom Helm, London.

GOODRICH, C.L. (1920), 'The Frontier of Control', Bell and Sons, London (republished by Pluto Press 1975).

GORDON, D. (1972), 'Theories of Poverty and Underemployment: Orthodox, Radical and Dual Labour Market Perspectives', D.C. Heath, Lexington, Mass.

GORDON, D. (1976), Capitalist efficiency and socialist efficiency, 'Monthly Review', vol.28, no.3, pp.19-39.

GORDON, D., EDWARDS, R.C. and REICH, M. (forthcoming), 'Labour Market Segmentation in American Capitalism'.

GORDON, M.J. (1964), The use of administrative price systems to control large organizations, in C.R. Bonini (ed.), 'Management Controls: New Directions in Basic Research', McGraw-Hill, New York.

GORZ, A. (1970), Workers' control, 'Socialist Revolution', vol.1, no.6.

GORZ, A. (1972), Technical intelligence and the capitalist division of labour, 'Telos', no.12, pp.27-41.

GORZ, A. (1973), Workers' control is more than just that, in Hunnius et al. (eds), 'Workers' Control'.

GORZ, A. (ed.) (1976), 'The Division of Labour: The Labour Process and Class Struggle in Modern Capitalism', Harvester Press, Hassocks, Sussex.

GOSPEL, H. (1974), Employers' organizations: their growth and function in the British system of industrial relations in the period 1918-39, PhD Thesis, University of London.

GOSPEL, H. (1978), European managerial unionism: an early assessment, 'Industrial Relations', vol.27, pp.360-71.

GOSPEL, H. (ed.) (forthcoming), 'Managerial Strategies and Industrial Relations: An Historical and Comparative Survey'.

GOULDNER, A.W. (1954), 'Patterns of Industrial Bureaucracy', Free Press, Chicago.

GOULDNER, A.W. (1955), Metaphysical pathos and the theory of bureaucracy, 'American Political Science Review', vol.49, pp.496-507.

GOULDNER, A.W. (1965), 'Wildcat Strike', Free Press, New York.

GOULDNER, A.W. (1971), 'The Coming Crisis of Western Sociology', Heinemann, London.

GOULDNER, A.W. (1976), 'The Dialectic of Ideology and Technology', Macmillan, London.

GOVERNMENT SOCIAL SURVEY (1968), 'Workplace Industrial Relations', HMSO, London.

GOWER, L.C.B. (1969), 'Principles of Modern Company Law', Stevens, London.

GOWLER, D. and LEGGE, K. (eds) (1975), 'Managerial Stress', Gower Press, London.

GRAMSCI, A. (1969), 'Soviets in Italy', Institute for Workers' Control, Nottingham.

GRAMSCI, A. (1971), 'Selection from the Prison Notebooks', Lawrence & Wishart, London.

GRAMSCI, A. (1977), 'Political Writings 1910-1920', Lawrence & Wishart.

GREENWOOD, J. (1977), 'Worker Sit-Ins and Job Protection', Gower Press, London.

GUEST, D. (1980), 'The Role and Effectiveness of Personnel Managers', LSE, London.

HABER, S. (1964), 'Efficiency and Uplift: Scientific Management in the Progressive Era 1890-1920', University of Chicago Press.

HABERMAS, J. (1970), Towards a theory of communicative competence, in H.P. Dreitzel (ed.), 'Recent Sociology No.2', Collier-MacMillan, London.
HABERMAS, J. (1971), 'Toward a Rational Society', Heinemann, London.
HABERMAS, J. (1974), 'Theory and Practice', Heinemann, London.
HABERMAS, J. (1976), 'Legitimation Crisis', Heinemann, London.
HABERMAS, J. (1980), Psychic thermidor and the rebirth of rebellious subjectivity, 'Berkeley Journal of Sociology', vol.XXV.
HAIMANN, T., SCOTT, W.G. and CONNOR, P.E. (1978), 'Managing the Modern Organization', Houghton Mifflin, Boston.
HAMMOND, J.L. and HAMMOND, B. (1925), 'The Town Labourer', Longman, London.
HANNAH, L. (1974), Mergers in British manufacturing industry 1880-1918, 'Oxford Economic Papers', vol.26.
HANNAH, L. (1976), 'The Rise of the Corporate Economy', Methuen, London.
HANNAH, L. (1980), Visible and invisible hands in Great Britain, in A.D. Chandler and H. Daems, 'Managerial Hierarchies'.
HARASZTI, M. (1977), 'A Worker in a Worker's State: Piece Rates in Hungary', Pelican, Harmondsworth.
HARBISON, F.H. and MYERS, C.A. (eds) (1959), 'Management in the Industrial World', McGraw-Hill, New York.
HARDIN, G. (1968), The tragedy of the commons, 'Science', vol.162, pp.1243-8.
HARMON, C. (1979), Mandel's late capitalism, 'International Socialism', vol.2, no.1.
HARRIS, N. (1980), Crisis and the core of the world system, 'International Socialism', Winter.
HART, M. (1979), Why bosses love the closed shop, 'New Society', 15 February.
HARTMAN, H. (1974), Managerial employees: new participants in industrial relations, 'British Journal of Industrial Relations', vol.12, no.2.
HAWKINS, K. (1971), Company bargaining: problems and perspectives, 'British Journal of Industrial Relations', vol.IX, no.2, July.
HAYEK, F. (1960), 'The Constitution of Liberty', Regnery, Chicago.
HEARN, F. (1978), Rationality and bureaucracy - Maoist contributions to a Marxist theory of bureaucracy, 'Sociological Quarterly', vol. 19, pp.37-54.
HEILBRONER, J. (1975), Men at work, 'New York Review of Books', vol. 21, no.22.
HELLER, R. (n.d.), 'Management in Britain: The Real Challenge', Ashbridge Management College, Papers in Management Studies.
HENRY, S. (1981), 'Disciplining Deviance at Work: The Changing "Technology" of Industrial Social Control', Mimeo, Working Paper, Centre for Occupational and Community Research, Middlesex Polytechnic.
HERDING, R. (1972), 'Job Control and Union Structure', Rotterdam University Press.
HERZBERG, F. (1969), Job enrichment pays off, 'Harvard Business Review', March/April.
HEYDEBRAND, W. (1977), Organizational contradictions in public bureaucracies, 'Sociological Quarterly', vol.18, no.1, pp.83-107.
HEYDEBRAND, R. and TUMMONS, P. (1975), Introduction to the Muller and Neusüs discussion, 'Telos', no.25.

HICKSON, D.J. (1966), A convergence in organization theory, 'Administrative Science Quarterly', vol.11, pp.224-37.
HICKSON, D.J. et al. (1971), A strategic contingencies theory of intra-organizational power, 'Administrative Science Quarterly', vol. 16, pp.216-29.
HILL, J. and HOOD, J. (1952), Management rights, in F. Elkouri (ed.), 'How Arbitration Works', Bureau of National Affairs, Washington D.C.
HILL, J.M.M. and TRIST, E.L. (1962), 'Industrial Accidents, Sickness and Other Absences', Tavistock, London.
HILL, S. (1974), Norms, groups and power:  the sociology of work-place industrial relations, 'British Journal of Industrial Relations', vol.12, no.2.
HILL, S. (1981), 'Competition and Control at Work', Heinemann, London.
HIMMELSTRAND, U. et al. (1981), 'Beyond Welfare Capitalism', Heinemann, London.
HINTON, J. (1972), Introduction to J.T. Murphy, 'The Workers' Committee'.
HINTON, J. (1973), 'The First Shop Stewards' Movement', Allen & Unwin, London.
HINTON, J. (1976), Reply to Monds, 'New Left Review, no.97.
HIRSCH, F. and GOLDTHORPE, J.H. (eds) (1978), 'The Political Economy of Inflation', Martin Robertson, London.
HIRSCH, P. (1975), Organization analysis and industrial sociology: an instance of cultural lag, 'American Sociologist', no.10, pp.3-12.
HOBSBAWM, E.J. (1968), 'Labouring Men', Weidenfeld & Nicolson, London.
HOBSBAWM, E.J. (1974), 'Labour's Turning Point 1880-1900', Harvester, Hassocks, Brighton.
HODGSON, G. (1976), Exploitation and embodied labour time, 'Bulletin of the Conference of Labour Economists', vol.5, no.1.
HODGSON, G. (1979), 'Socialist Economic Strategy', Labour Party Discussion Series No.2, ILP, Leeds.
HOFSTEDE, G.H. (1968), 'The Game of Budget Control', Tavistock, London.
HOLLIS, M. and NELL, E. (1975), 'Rational Economic Man', Cambridge University Press.
HOLUBENKO, M. (1975), The Soviet working class:  discontent and opposition, 'Critique', vol.4.
HOPKIN, E. (1969), 'A History of the Lancashire Cotton Industry and the Amalgamated Weavers' Association', Amalgamated Weavers Association, Manchester.
HORKHEIMER, M. and ADORNO, T. (1979), 'Dialectic of Enlightenment', New Left Books, London.
HORNGREN, C.T. (1975), 'Accounting for Management Control', Prentice-Hall, New Jersey.
HUBBARTT, W.S. (1981), The delicate art of firing, 'Administrative Management', vol.XLII, no.4.
HUNNIUS, G., GARSON, G.D. and CASE, J. (eds) (1973), 'Workers' Control:  A Reader on Labour and Social Change', Random House, New York.
HYMAN, R. (1971), 'Marxism and the Sociology of Trade Unionism', Pluto Press, London.

HYMAN, R. (1973), Industrial conflict and the political economy, in R.Miliband and J. Saville (eds), 'Socialist Register', Merlin Press, London, pp.101-53.
HYMAN, R. (1974), Workers' control and revolutionary theory, 'Socialist Register', Merlin Press, London.
HYMAN, R. (1975a), 'Industrial Relations:  A Marxist Introduction', Macmillan, London.
HYMAN, R. (1975b), Trade unions, sociology and political economy, in J.B. McKinlay (ed.), 'Processing People', Holt, Rinehart & Winston, New York.
HYMAN, R. (1975c), 'Social Values and Industrial Relations', Blackwell, Oxford.
HYMAN, R. (1976), Trade unions, control and resistance, in Open University, 'Politics of Work and Occupation', Course Unit 14, Open University Press, Milton Keynes.
HYMAN, R. (1979), The politics of workplace trade unionism, 'Capital and Class', no.8.
INDUSTRIAL SOCIETY (1978), 'Effective Discipline', Industrial Society, London.
INSTITUTE OF CHARTERED ACCOUNTANTS IN ENGLAND AND WALES (1964), 'Internal Control as a Responsibility and Function of Management', Council Statement, 9 December.
I.W.C. MOTORS GROUP (1980), 'A Workers' Enquiry into the Motor Industry', CSE/IWC, London.
JACKSON, M.P. (1977), 'Industrial Relations', Croom Helm, London.
JACOBY, R. (1977), Review of Braverman, 'Telos', no.3.
JACQUES, E. (1951), 'The Changing Culture of a Factory', Tavistock, London.
JAY, M. (1973), 'Dialectical Imagination', Heinemann, London.
JAY, M. (1974), Some recent developments in critical theory, 'Berkeley Journal of Sociology', vol.18.
JOHNSON, T. (1977), What is to be known?  The structural determination of social class, 'Economy and Society', vol.6, pp.194-233.
JONES, T. (1980), 'Microelectronics and Society', Open University Press, Milton Keynes.
JORDAN, B. (1981), 'Automatic Poverty', Routledge & Kegan Paul, London.
KAHN-FREUND, O. (1969), Industrial relations and the law: retrospect and prospect, 'British Journal of Industrial Relations', vol.8, no.3.
KAY, G. (1979), 'The Economic Theory of the Working Class', Macmillan, London.
KELLY, J. (1978), Understanding Taylorism:  some comments, 'British Journal of Sociology', vol.29, pp.203-7.
KELLY, J. (1979), Automation and social integration:  technology re-examined, 'Personnel Review', vol.8, pp.44-8.
KILPATRICK, A. and LAWSON, T. (1980), On the nature of industrial decline in the UK, 'Cambridge Journal of Economics', vol.4, pp. 85-102.
KITWOOD, T. (1980), Necessary and contingent aspects of technical practice, 'International Journal of Social Economics', no.1, pp. 37-46.
KNIGHT, I. (1979), 'Company Organization and Worker Participation', HMSO, London.

KOUZMIN, A. (1980), Control in organizational analysis:  the lost politics, in D. Dunkerley and G. Salaman (eds) (1980), 'The International Yearbook of Organization Studies'.

KURZWELL, E. (1977), Foucault:  ending the era of man, 'Theory and Society', vol.4, no.3.

KYNASTON-REEVES, T. and WOODWARD, J. (1970), The study of managerial control, in J. Woodward (ed.), 'Industrial Organization:  Behaviour and Control', Oxford University Press.

LAMMERS, C.J. (1967), Power and participation in decision-making in formal organizations, 'American Journal of Sociology', vol.73, no.2.

LANDES, S. (1969), 'The Unbound Prometheus', Cambridge University Press.

LANE, D.S. (1971), 'The End of Inequality?  Stratification Under State Socialism', Penguin, Harmondsworth.

LANE, D.S. (1978), 'Politics and Society in the USSR', 2nd edn, Martin Robertson, London.

LANE, D. and O'DELL, F. (1978), 'The Soviet Industrial Worker', Martin Robertson, Oxford.

LANE, T. (1974), 'The Union Makes Us Strong', Arrow, London.

LARGE, P. (1980), 'The Micro-Revolution', Fontana, London.

LARNER, R.J. (1970), The effects of management control on the profits of large corporations, in M. Zeitlin (ed.), 'American Society Inc.', Markham, Chicago.

LASKI, H.J. (1967), 'A Grammar of Politics', Allen & Unwin, London.

LAWRENCE, P.R. and LORSCH, J.W. (1967), 'Organization and Environment:  Managing Differentiation and Integration', Harvard University Press.

LAZONICK, W. (1977), The appropriation and reproduction of labour, 'Socialist Revolution', no.38.

LAZONICK, W. (1978), The subjection of labour to capital:  the rise of the capitalist system, 'Review of Radical Political Economics', vol.10, no.1.

LAZONICK, W. (1979), Industrial relations and technical change:  the case of the self-acting Mule, 'Cambridge Journal of Economics', vol. 3, no.3.

LEA, J. (1979), Discipline and capitalist development, in Fine et al. (eds), 'Capitalism and the Rule of Law', Hutchinson, London.

LEGGATT, T. (1978), Managers in industry:  their background and education, 'Sociological Review', vol.26, pp.807-25.

LEGGE, K. (1978), 'Power, Innovation and Problem Solving in Personnel Management', McGraw-Hill, New York.

LEIJNSE, F. (1980), Workplace bargaining and trade union power, 'Industrial Relations Journal', May/June.

LENIN, V.I. (1965), 'Collected Works', vol.27, Progress Publishers, Moscow.

LEVINE, A. and WRIGHT, E.O. (1980), Rationality and class struggle, 'New Left Review', no.123.

LEVINE, S. and WHITE, P.E. (1961), Exchange as a conceptual framework for the study of interorganizational relationships, 'Administrative Science Quarterly', vol.5, pp.583-601.

LINDBERG, L., ALFORD, R., CROUCH, C. and OFFE, C. (1975), 'Stress and Contradiction in Modern Capitalism', D.C. Heath, New York.

LINDOP, E. (1979), Workplace bargaining - the end of an era?, 'Industrial Relations Journal', vol.10, no.1.

LIPSTREU, C. (1963), Management rights:  conflict or co-operation?, 'Labour Law Journal', April.
LITTERER, J. (1961), Systematic management:  the search for order and integration, 'Business History Review', vol.35, pp.461-76.
LITTLER, C. (1978), Understanding Taylorism, 'British Journal of Sociology', vol.29.
LITTLER, C. (1980a), The bureaucratisation of the shop floor:  the development of modern work systems, PhD Thesis, London University.
LITTLER, C. (1980b), Internal Contract and the Transition to Modern Work Systems, in D. Dunkerley and G. Salaman (eds), 'International Yearbook of Organization Studies', pp.157-85.
LITTLER, C. and SALAMAN, G. (1982), Bravermania and beyond:  recent theories of the labour process, 'Sociology', vol.16, no.2.
LOCKWOOD, D. (1964), Social integration and systems integration, in G.K. Zollschan and W. Hirsch (eds), 'Explorations in Social Change', Routledge & Kegan Paul, London.
LOCKWOOD, D. (1966), Sources of variation in working class images of society, 'Sociological Review', vol.14, November.
LOCKYER, K. et al. (1981), UK managers are ignoring basic production techniques, 'Works Management', April, vol.34, no.4.
LOEWITH, K. (1970), Rationalization and freedom, in D. Wrong (ed.), 'Max Weber', Prentice-Hall, New Jersey.
LONDON CSE GROUP (1979), Crisis, the labour movement and the alternative economic strategy, 'Capital and Class', no.8.
LOVERIDGE, R. (1979), 'Business Strategy and Community Culture:  Manpower Policy as a Structured Accommodation to Conflict', University of Aston Management Centre Working Paper, no.146.
LOVERIDGE, R. (1980), What is participation? review of literature and some methodology problems, 'British Journal of Industrial Relations', November.
LOW-BEER, J. (1978), 'Protest and Participation', Cambridge University Press.
LUKACS, G. (1971), 'History and Class Consciousness', Merlin Press, London.
LUKES, S. (1970), Some problems about rationality, in B.R. Wilson (ed.), 'Rationality', Blackwell, Oxford.
LUKES, S. (1974), 'Power:  A Radical View', Macmillan, London.
LUPTON, T. (1963), 'On the Shop Floor', Pergamon Press, Oxford.
MCCARTHY, T. (1978), 'Critical Theory of Jurgen Habermas', Heinemann, London.
MCCARTHY, W.E.J. (1966), 'The Role of Shop Stewards in British Industrial Relations', Research Paper I, HMSO, London.
MCCARTHY, W.E.J. (1981), The Trade union dinosaur evolves, 'New Society', 14 May.
MCCARTHY, W.E.J. and ELLIS, N.D. (1973), 'Management by Agreement', Hutchinson, London.
MCCLOSKEY, J.H. (1965), Rights, 'Philosophical Quarterly', vol.15.
MCCOULLOUGH, A.E. and SHANNON, M. (1977), Organizations and protection, in S. Clegg and D. Dunkerley (eds), 'Critical Issues in Organizations', Routledge & Kegan Paul, London.
MCGIVERING, I.C., MATTHEWS, C.G.J. and SCOTT, W.H. (1969), 'Management in Britain', Liverpool University Press.
MCKENDRICK, N. (1961), Josiah Wedgwood and factory discipline, 'The Historical Journal, vol.IV, no.1.

MACKENZIE, G. (1975), World images and the world of work, in G. Esland et al., 'People and Work', Homes McDougall, Edinburgh.
MACKENZIE, G. (1977), The political economy of the American working class, 'British Journal of Sociology', vol.28, no.2, pp.244-52.
MCLELLAND, D. (1979), 'Marxism after Marx', Macmillan, London.
MCNEIL, K. (1978), Understanding Organizational Power:  Building on the Weberian legacy, 'Administrative Science Quarterly', vol.23, pp.65-90.
MCNULTY, M.S. (1975), A question of managerial legitimacy, 'Academy of Management Journal', vol.18, pp.579-88.
MCPHERSON, C.B. (1973), 'Democratic Theory:  Essays in Retrieval', Clarendon Press, Oxford.
MCPHERSON, C.B. (1978), 'Property', University of Toronto Press.
MACCOBY, M. (1977), 'The Gamesman:  The New Corporate Leaders', Simon & Schuster, New York.
MAIER, C.S. (1970), Between Taylorism and technocracy:  European ideologies and the visions of industrial productivity in the 1920's, 'Journal of Contemporary History', vol.5, pp.27-8.
MAIER, N.R.F. (1949), 'Frustration:  the Study of Behaviour Without a Goal', McGraw-Hill, New York.
MAIER, N.R.F. (1973), 'Psychology in Industrial Organizations', Houghton Mifflin, Boston.
MAITLAND, I. (1980), Disorder in the British workplace:  the limits of consensus, 'British Journal of Industrial Relations', November.
MANDEL, E. (1973), The debate on workers' control, in G. Hunnius et al. (eds), 'Workers' Control:  A Reader on Labour and Social Change', Random House, New York.
MANDEL, E. (1975), 'Late Capitalism', New Left Books, London.
MANDEL, E. (1978), 'The Second Slump:  A Marxist Analysis of Recession in the Seventies', New Left Books, London.
MANN, M. (1970), The social cohesion of liberal democracy, 'American Sociological Review', vol.35, pp.423-39.
MANN, M. (1973), 'Consciousness and Action Among the Western Working Class', Macmillan, London.
MANSFIELD, R. (1980), 'Who are the managers?', in M.J.F. Poole and R. Mansfield, 'Managerial Roles in Industrial Relations:  Towards a Definitive Survey of Research and Formulation of Models', Gower, Farnborough.
MANT, A. (1977), 'The Rise and Fall of the British Manager', Macmillan, London.
MARAVALL, J. (1979), The limits of reformism:  parliamentary socialism and the Marxist theory of the state, 'British Journal of Sociology', vol.30, no.3.
MARCH, J.G. and SIMON, H.A. (1958), 'Organizations', Wiley, New York.
MARCUSE, H. (1965), Industrialization and capitalism, 'New Left Review', vol.30, pp.3-17.
MARCUSE, H. (1968), 'One Dimensional Man:  The Ideology of Industrial Society', Sphere Books, London.
MARCUSE, H. (1972), 'Negations', Penguin, Harmondsworth.
MARGLIN, S. (1971), What do bosses do?  The origins and functions of hierarchy in capitalist production, Harvard Institute of Economic Research, Discussion Paper No.22.
MARGLIN, S. (1974), What do bosses do;  the origins and functions of

hierarchy in capitalist production, 'Review of Radical Political
Economics', vol.6, no.2.
MARRIS, R. (1964), 'The Economic Theory of "Managerial" Capitalism',
Macmillan, London.
MARSH, A.I. (1966), 'Disputes Procedures in Action', Research Paper
2, pt I, HMSO, London.
MARSH, A.I. and MCCARTHY, W.E.J. (1968), 'Disputes Procedures in
Action', Research Paper 2, pt 2, HMSO, London.
MARSH, A.I., EVANS, E.O. and GARCIA, P. (1971), 'Workplace
Industrial Relations in Engineering', Kogan Page, London.
MARSH, A.I. and GILLIES, J.G. (1977), 'Involvement of Line and Staff
Managers in I.R.', Paper Presented to SSRC Management Function in IR
Conference at Cumberland Lodge 14-16 December.
MARSHALL, J. and STEWART, R. (1981), Managers job perceptions
part I:  their overall frameworks and working strategies, 'Journal
of Management Studies', vol.18, no.2.
MARTIN, R. (1977), 'The Sociology of Power', Routledge & Kegan Paul,
London.
MARX, K. (1955), 'The Poverty of Philosophy', Progress, Moscow.
MARX, K. (1959), 'Capital', vol.3, Progress, Moscow.
MARX, K. (1972), 'Theories of Surplus Value', vols 1-3, Lawrence &
Wishart, London.
MARX, K. (1973), 'Grundrisse:  Foundations of the Critique of
Political Economy', Penguin, Harmondsworth.
MARX, K. (1976), 'Capital:  A Critique of Political Economy', vol.1,
Penguin, Harmondsworth.
MARX, K. and ENGELS, F. (1974), 'The German Ideology', Lawrence &
Wishart, London.
MATHEWSON, S.B. (1969), 'Restriction of Output Among Unorganized
Workers', Carbondale and Edwardsville:  Southern Illinois University
Press (first published 1931).
MAYNARD, H.B. (1971), 'Industrial Engineering Handbook', McGraw-
Hill, New York.
MECHANIC, D. (1962), Sources of power of lower participants in
complex organizations, 'Administrative Science Quarterly', vol.17,
no.3.
MEEK, R.L. (1973), 'Studies in the Labour Theory of Value', 2nd edn,
Lawrence & Wishart, London.
MELLING, J. (1980), Non-commissioned officers:  British employers
and their supervisory workers 1880-1920, 'Social History', vol.IV,
no.3.
MELLISH, M. and COLLIS-SQUIRES, N. (1976), Legal and social norms in
discipline and dismissal, 'Industrial Law Journal', vol.5, pp.
164-77.
MELOSSI, D. (1979), Institutions of social control and the
capitalist organizations of work, in B. Fine et al. (eds),
'Capitalism and the Rule of Law', Hutchinson, London, pp.90-9.
MELROSE-WOODMAN, J. (1978), 'Profile of the British Manager',
British Institute of Management, London.
MENNELL, S. (1974), 'Sociological Theory:  Uses and Utilities',
Nelson, London.
MERKLE, J.A. (1968), The Taylor strategy:  organizational innovation
and class structure, 'Berkeley Journal of Sociology', vol.13, pp.
59-81.

MERTON, R.K. (1949), 'Social Theory and Social Structure', Free Press, Chicago.

MESZAROS, I. (1970), Lukács' concept of dialectic, in G.H.R. Parkinson (ed.), 'George Lukács: The Man, His Work, and His Ideas', Weidenfeld & Nicolson, London.

MILGRAM, S. (1963), Behavioural study of obedience, 'Journal of Abnormal Social Psychology', vol.67, pp.371-8.

MILIBAND, R. (1969), 'The State in Capitalist Society', Weidenfeld & Nicolson, London.

MILIBAND, R. (1977), 'Marxism and Politics', Oxford University Press.

MILIBAND, R. (1978), A state of de-subordination, 'British Journal of Sociology', vol.XXIX, no.4, pp.399-409.

MILLER, D.C. and FORM, W.H. (1964), 'Industrial Sociology', Harper & Row, New York.

MILLER, J. (1975), Review of legitimation crisis, 'Telos', no.25, Fall.

MILLHAM, S. et al. (1972), Social control in organizations, 'British Journal of Sociology', vol.23, no.4.

MILLS, C.W. (1948), 'New Men of Power', Kelley, New York.

MILLS, C.W. (1953), 'White Collar', Oxford University Press, New York.

MILLS, C.W. (1940), Situated actions and vocabularies of motives, 'American Sociological Review', pp.904-13.

MILLS, C.W. (1970), The contribution of sociology to studies of industrial relations, 'Berkeley Journal of Sociology', vol.15, pp.11-32.

MINKIN, L. (1974), The British labour party and the trade unions: crisis and compact, 'Industrial and Labour Relations Review', vol.28.

MINTZBERG, H. (1973), 'The Nature of Managerial Work', Harper & Row, New York.

MINTZBERG, H. (1976), The structure of 'unstructured' decision-processes, 'Administrative Science Quarterly', vol.21.

MONDS, J. (1976), Workers' control and the historians: a new economism, 'New Left Review', no.97.

MONTGOMERY, D. (1974), The new unionism and the transformation of workers' consciousness in America 1909-1922, 'Journal of Social History', Summer.

MONTGOMERY, D. (1976), Workers' control of machine production in the nineteenth century, 'Labour History', vol.17, Fall, pp.486-509.

MONTGOMERY, D. (1979), 'Workers' Control in America', Cambridge University Press.

MORRIS, R.J. (1979), 'Class and Class Consciousness in the Industrial Revolution, 1750-1850', Macmillan, London.

MOUZELIS, N. (1975), 'Organization and Bureaucracy', Routledge & Kegan Paul, London.

MUELLER, G.H. (1979), Rationality in the work of Max Weber, 'European Journal of Sociology', vol.20, pp.149-71.

MULLER, W. and NEUSÜS, C. (1975), The illusion of state socialism and the contradiction between wage labour and capital, 'Telos', no.25, Fall.

MURPHY, J.T. (1972), 'Preparing for Power', Pluto Press, London.

MURPHY, J.T. (1972), 'The Workers Committee', Pluto Press, London (first published 1917).

NEGRI, T. (1979), The Strategy of the Refusal, in 'Working Class Autonomy and the Crisis', Red Notes:CSE Books, London.

NELSON, D. (1975), 'Managers and Workers: Origins of the New Factory System in the United States, 1880-1920', University of Wisconsin Press, Madison.

NICHOLS, T. (1969), 'Ownership, Control and Ideology', Allen & Unwin, London.

NICHOLS, T. (1977), Labour and monopoly capital, 'Sociological Review', pp.192-4.

NICHOLS, T. (1975), The 'socialism' of management: some comments on the new 'human relations', 'Sociological Review', May.

NICHOLS, T. (ed.) (1980), 'Capital and Labour', Fontana, London.

NICHOLS, T. and ARMSTRONG, P. (1976), 'Workers Divided', Fontana, London.

NICHOLS, T. and BEYNON, H. (1977), 'Living with Capitalism: Class Relations and the Modern Factory', Routledge & Kegan Paul, London.

NIVEN, M.N. (1967), 'Personnel Management 1913-63', IPM, London.

NOBLE, D.F. (1977), 'America by Design: Science, Technology and the Rise of Corporate Capitalism', Knopf, New York.

NOBLE, D.F. (1978), Social change in machine design, 'Politics and Society', vol.8, no.3.

NOBLE, D.F. (1979), Social choice in machine design: the case of automatically controlled machine tools, in A. Zimbalist (ed.), 'Case Studies on the Labour Process'.

NOZICK, R. (1974), 'Anarchy, State and Utopia', Basic Books, New York.

O'CONNOR, J. (1973), 'The Fiscal Crisis of the State', St Martins Press, New York.

O'CONNOR, J. (1974), 'The Corporation and the State: Essays in the Theory of Capitalism and Imperialism', Harper, New York.

O'CONNOR, J. (1975), Productive and unproductive labour, 'Politics and Society', vol.5, pp.297-336.

OFFE, C. (1973), The abolition of market control and the problem of legitimacy, 'Kapitalistate', vol.1, pp.109-16.

OFFE, C. (1975a), Further comments on Muller and Neusüs, 'Telos', no.25.

OFFE, C. (1975b), Introduction to legitimacy versus efficiency, in L. Lindberg et al. (eds), 'Stress and Contradiction in Modern Capitalism'.

OFFE, C. (1976a), 'Industry and Inequality: The Achievement Principle in Work and Social Status', Edward Arnold, London.

OFFE, C. (1976b), Political authority and class structure, in P. Connerton (ed.), 'Critical Sociology', Penguin, Harmondsworth.

OFFE, C. (1976c), Crises and crisis management: elements of a political crisis theory, 'International Journal of Politics', vol.6, pp.29-67.

OFFE, C. and RONGE, V. (1975), Theses on the theory of the state, 'New German Critique', vol.6, pp.137-47.

OFFICE OF POPULATION CENSUSES AND SURVEYS (1974), 'Workplace Industrial Relations 1972', HMSO, London.

OPCS (1975), 'Workplace Industrial Relations 1973', HMSO, London.

O'NEILL, J. (1974), For Marx against Althusser, 'The Human Context', vol.6, no.2, pp.385-98.

OLSEN, M.E. (1970), 'Power in Societies', Macmillan, London.

OPINION RESEARCH CENTRE (1977), 'A Survey of the Motivation of British Management', ORC, London.

OPPENHEIMER, M. (1967), The Y theory: enlightened management confronts alienation, 'New Politics', vol.1, no.4.

PAHL, R.E. and PAHL, J.M. (1971), 'Managers and Their Wives: A Study of Career and Family Relationships in the Middle Class', Penguin, Harmondsworth.

PALLOIX, C. (1976), The labour process: from Fordism to neo-Fordism, in CSE Pamphlet No.1, 'The Labour Process and the Class Struggle', London, Stage 1, pp.46-67.

PALMER, B. (1975), Class conception and conflict: the thrust for efficiency, managerial views of labour and the rebellion 1903-22, 'Review of Radical Political Economy', vol.7, no.2.

PANITCH, L. (1976), 'Social Democracy and Industrial Militancy', Cambridge University Press.

PANITCH, L. (1977), Profits and politics: labour and the crisis of British capitalism, 'Politics and Society', vol.7, pp.477-507.

PANITCH, L. (1980), The state and the future of socialism, 'Capital and Class', Summer.

PANITCH, L. (1981), Trade unions and the capitalist state, 'New Left Review', no.125, pp.21-43.

PANZIERI, R. (1976), Surplus value and planning: notes on the reading of 'Capital', in Conference of Socialist Economists, 'The Labour Process'.

PARKIN, F. (1972), 'Class Inequality and Political Order', Paladin, London.

PARTRIDGE, B. (1978), The activities of shop stewards, 'Industrial Relations Journal', vol.8, no.4.

PARTRIDGE, H. (1980), Italy's Fiat in Turin in the 1950's, in T. Nichols (ed.), 'Capital and Labour', Fontana, London.

PAYNE, P.L. (1978), Industrial Entrepreneurship and Management in Great Britain, in P. Mathias and M.M. Postar (eds), 'Cambridge Economic History of Europe', vol.VII, pt I, Cambridge University Press.

PEARCEY, D. (1977), Self-organized work groups in the clothing industry, 'British Boot and Shoe Institute', May-June.

PEDLER, M. (1973), Shop stewards as leaders, 'Industrial Relations Journal', vol.4, pp.43-60.

PERLINE, M. (1971), Organized labour and managerial prerogatives, 'California Management Review', June.

PERLMAN, S. (1968), 'A Theory of the Labour Movement', Kelley, New York (first published 1928).

PERLMAN, S. (1949), 'A Theory of the Labour Movement', Kelley, New York (first published 1928).

PETERSON, R.B. (1967), The status of managerial rights in Swedish collective bargaining, PhD Thesis, University of Wisconsin, Madison.

PETTIGREW, A. (1973), 'The Politics of Organizational Decision Making', Tavistock, London.

PETTIGREW, A. (1975), 'Occupational Specialization as an Emergent Process', in G. Esland et al. (eds), 'People and Work', Holmes McDougall, Edinburgh.

PICCONE, P. (1971), Phenomenological Marxism, 'Telos', no.9.

PICCONE, P. (1972), Dialectic and materialism in Lukács, 'Telos', no.11.

PICCONE, P. (1976), Gramsci's Marxism:   beyond Lenin and Togliatti, 'Theory and Society', vol.3, pp.485-512.
PLUMRIDGE, M.D. (1966), Disciplinary practice, 'Personnel Management', September.
POLLARD, S. (1965), 'The Genesis of Modern Management', Edward Arnold, London.
POOLE, M. (1974), Towards a sociology of shop stewards, 'Sociological Review', vol.22.
POOLE, M. (1975), 'Workers' Participation in Industry', Routledge & Kegan Paul, London.
POOLE, M. (1979), Industrial democracy:  a comparative analysis, 'Industrial Relations', vol.18, no.3.
POOLE, M. and MANSFIELD, R. (eds) (1980), 'Managerial Roles in Industrial Relations:  Towards a Definitive Survey of Research and Formulation of Models', Gower, London.
POOLE, M., MANSFIELD, R., BLYTON, P. and FROST, P. (1981), 'Managers in Focus', Gower, Aldershot.
POULANTZAS, N. (1975), 'Classes in Contemporary Capitalism', New Left Books, London.
PROCEEDINGS IN CONFERENCE (various dates), Transcripts of negotiations, Engineering Employers' Federation and the Confederation of Shipbuilding and Engineering Unions, London.
PUGH, D.S., HICKSON, D.J. and HININGS, C.R. (1969), An empirical taxonomy of work organizations, 'Administrative Science Quarterly', vol.14, pp.115-26.
PURCELL, J. (1982), 'The Management of Industrial Relations in the Modern Corporation', Paper presented at the British Universities Industrial Relations Association Conference, 5 July, Norwich.
PURCELL, J. (forthcoming), Managers and industrial relations - a review, 'British Journal of Industrial Relations'.
PURCELL, J. and EARL, M.J. (1977), Control systems and industrial relations, 'Industrial Relations Journal', vol.8, no.2.
PURCELL, J. and SMITH, R. (eds) (1979), 'The Control of Work', Macmillan, London.
RAMSAY, H. (1977), Cycles of control:  worker participation in sociological and historical perspective, 'Sociology', vol.11, no.3.
RAMSAY, H. (1980), Participation:  the pattern and its significance, in T. Nichols (ed.), 'Capital and Labour'.
REICH, M. (1973), A theory of labour market segmentation, 'American Economic Review', vol.64, May, pp.359-65.
RESEARCH PAPER 10 (1968), 'Shop Stewards and Workshop Relations', HMSO, London.
RICARDO, D. (1911), 'On the Principles of Political Economy and Taxation', Dent, London, chapter 31, On Machinery.
ROBERTS, K. (1978), Review of Friedman, 'Sociology', vol.12, no.3.
ROBERTS, K. et al. (1977), 'The Fragmentary Class Structure', Heinemann, London.
ROBINSON, A. (1969), Rationality in politics and in formal models of the political process, MA Thesis, McGill University.
ROSE, H. and S. (1972), The radicalisation of science, 'The Socialist Register', pp.105-31.
ROSE, H. and ROSE, S. (1980), Against an oversocialized conception of science, 'Communication and Cognition', vol.13, nos 2/3.
ROTTENBERG, S. (1962), Property rights in work, 'Industrial and Labour Relations Review', vol.15, no.5.

ROUSSEAU, J.J. (1947), 'The Social Contract', Oxford University Press (first published 1762).

ROVATTI, P.A. (1972), Fetishism and economic categories, 'Telos', no.14, Winter.

ROWBOTHAM, S. et al. (1979), 'Beyond the Fragments', Merlin, London.

ROWTHORN, B. (1974), Neo-classicism, neo-Ricardianism and Marxism, 'New Left Review', vol.86, pp.63-87.

ROWTHORN, B. (1976), Review: Late Capitalism, 'New Left Review', vol.98, pp.59-83.

ROWTHORN, B. (1980a), 'Capitalism, Conflict and Inflation: Essays in Political Economy', Lawrence & Wishart, London.

ROWTHORN, B. (1980b), The alternative economic strategy, 'International Socialism', no.8, pp.385-94.

ROY, D. (1952), Quota restriction and goldbricking in a machine shop, 'American Journal of Sociology', vol.57, pp.427-42.

ROY, D. (1953), Work satisfaction and social reward in quota achievement: an analysis of piecework incentive, 'American Sociological Review', vol.18, pp.507-14.

ROY, D. (1954), Efficiency and the 'fix': informal inter-group relations in a piecework machine shop, 'American Journal of Sociology', vol.60, pp.255-66.

ROY, D. (1969), Making-out: a counter system of workers' control of work situations and relationships, in T. Burns (ed.), 'Industrial Man', Penguin, Harmondsworth.

ROY, D. (1973), 'Banana' time: job satisfaction and informal interaction, in G. Salaman and K. Thompson (eds), 'People and Organisations', Longman, London.

ROY, D. (1980), Fear stuff, sweet stuff and evil stuff: management's defenses against unionization in the South, in T. Nichols (ed.), 'Capital and Labour', Fontana, London.

ROYAL COMMISSION ON THE DISTRIBUTION OF INCOME AND WEALTH (1975-78), (The Diamond Commission). Reports 1-6.

ROYAL COMMISSION ON TRADE UNIONS AND EMPLOYERS' ASSOCIATIONS (1968), 'Report', Cmnd 3623, HMSO, London.

RUBERY, J. (1978), Structured labour markets, worker organization and low pay, 'Cambridge Journal of Economics', March.

RUDIN, B. (1972), Industrial betterment and scientific management as social control 1890-1920, 'Berkeley Journal of Sociology', vol.XVII, 1972/73.

RUSSELL, J. (1978), The coming of the line: the Ford Highland Park plant, 1910-14, 'Radical America', vol.12, May-June, pp.29-45.

RUSSELL, R. and HOCHNER, A. (1979), Participation, influence and worker ownership, 'Industrial Relations', vol.18, no.3, Autumn.

RUTIGLIANO, E. (1977), The ideology of labour and capitalist rationality in Gramsci, 'Telos', no.3.

RYDER, D. (1975), 'British Leyland: The Next Decade', HMSO, London.

SALAMAN, G. (1978), Towards a sociology of organizational structure, 'Sociological Review', vol.28, no.3.

SALAMAN, G. (1979), 'Work Organizations: Resistance and Control', Longman, London.

SALAMAN, G. (1981), 'Class and the Corporation', Fontana, London.

SARTRE, J.-P. (1976), 'Critique of Dialectical Reason', New Left Books, London.

SAYLES, L.R. (1964), 'Managerial Behaviour: Administration in Complex Organizations', McGraw-Hill, New York.

SCHROYER, T. (1968), Alienation and the dialectical paradigm, PhD Dissertation, New School for Social Research, New York.
SCHROYER, T. (1970), Toward a critical theory for advanced industrial society, in H.P. Dreitzel (ed.), 'Recent Sociology No.2', Collier-MacMillan, London.
SCHROYER, R. (1971), The Critical Theory of Late Capitalism, in George Fischer (ed.), 'The Revival of American Socialism', Oxford University Press, New York, pp.297-321.
SCHROYER, T. (1972a), The dialectical foundations of critical theory: Jurgen Habermas' metatheoretical investigations, 'Telos', no.12, Summer.
SCHROYER, T. (1972b), Marx's theory of the crisis, 'Telos', no.14, pp.106-25.
SCHUTZ, A. (1943), The problem of rationality in the social world, 'Economica'.
SCHUTZ, A. (1967), 'Collected Papers Vol.1, The Problem of Social Reality', Martinus Nijhoff, The Hague.
SCHUTZ, A. (1972), 'The Phenomenology of the Social World', Heinemann, London.
SCHWARZ, B. (1977), On the monopoly capitalist degradation of work, 'Dialectical Anthropology', vol.2, no.2.
SCOTT, C. (1979), The labour process, class conflict and politics in the Peruvian sugar industry, 'Development and Change', vol.10, pt.1, pp.57-89.
SEIDMAN, S. and GRUBER, M. (1977), Capitalism and individuation in the sociology of Max Weber, 'British Journal of Sociology', vol. XXVIII, no.4, pp.498-508.
SELUCKY, R. (1974), Marxism and self-management, 'Critique', vol.3.
SHILLINGLAW, G. (1972), 'Cost Accounting: Analysis and Control', Irwin, Illinois.
SIMON, H.A. (1957), Authority, in C.M. Arensberg (ed.), 'Research in Industrial Human Relations', Harper & Row, New York.
SIMPSON, D.H. (1979), The Pattern of Constraint on Management Decisions in the Newspaper Industry, PhD Thesis, University College, Cardiff.
SINGELMANN, P. (1980), Intraorganizational coercion and interorganizational structure, in Dunkerley and Salaman (eds) (1980a).
SINGH, A. (1977), U.K. industry and the world economy: a case of de-industrialization, 'Cambridge Journal of Economics', June.
SKLAIR, L. (1971), The sociology of the opposition to science and technology: with special reference to the work of Jacques Ellul, 'Comparative Studies in Society and History', vol.13.
SLICHTER, S.H., HEALY, J.L. and LIVERNASH, E.R. (1960), 'The Impact of Collective Bargaining on Management', The Brookings Institute, Washington D.C.
SLOAN, Alfred P. (1963), 'My Years with General Motors', Sidgwick & Jackson, London.
SMITH, A. (1937), 'The Wealth of Nations', Random House, New York.
SMITH, C.G. and TANNENBAUM, A.S. (1963), Organisation control structure - a comparative analysis, 'Human Relations', vol.16, no.4, pp.299-316.
SMITH, R. (1978), 'Work Control and Managerial Prerogative in Industrial Relations', Durham University Business School, Working Paper Series, no.3.
SMITH, R. (1979), The maximization of control in industrial

relations, in J. Purcell and R. Smith (eds), 'The Control of Work'.
SOFER, C. (1970), 'Men in Mid-Career:  A Study of British Managers
and Technical Specialists', Cambridge University Press.
SOHN-RETHEL, A. (1976), The dual economics of transition, in
Conference of Socialist Economists, 'The Labour Process and Class
Struggle'.
SOHN-RETHEL, A. (1978), 'Intellectual and Manual Labour:  A Critique
of Epistemology', Macmillan, London.
SPENCER, A. (1981), What non-executive directors don't do,
'Management Today', May.
SPURING, L. (1977), 'Phenomenology and the Social World:  The
Philosophy of Merleau-Ponty and its Relation to the Social
Sciences', Routledge & Kegan Paul, London.
SRZEDNICKI, J. (1971), Rights and rules, 'Philosophical Quarterly',
vol.21.
STEDMAN-JONES, G. (1975), Class struggle and the industrial
revolution, 'New Left Review', no.90.
STEWART, R. (1967), 'Managers and Their Jobs:  A Study of the
Similarities and Differences in the Ways Managers Spend Their Time',
Macmillan, London.
STEWART, R. (1974), The manager's job:  discretion versus demand,
'Organizational Dynamics', Winter.
STEWART, R. (1976), 'Contrasts in Management', McGraw-Hill,
Maidenhead.
STEWART, S., PRANDY, K. and BLACKBURN, R. (1980), Social stratifica-
tion and careers into management, in M. Poole and R. Mansfield
(eds), 'Managerial Roles in Industrial Relations'.
STINCHCOMBE, A.L. (1970), Bureaucratic and craft administration of
production, in O. Grusky and G.A. Miller (eds), 'The Sociology of
Organizations', Free Press, New York.
STOLZMAN, J.D. (1975), Objective and subjective concepts of interest
in sociological analysis, 'Sociological Analysis and Theory', vol.5.
STONE, K. (1973), The origins of job structures in the steel
industry, 'Radical America', November-December.
STONE, K. (1974), The origin of job structures in the steel
industry, 'Review of Radical Political Economics', vol.6, no.2.
STOREY, J. (1976), Workplace collective bargaining and managerial
prerogative, 'Industrial Relations Journal', vol.7, no.4.
STOREY, J. (1979), 'Managerial Prerogatives in Britain', Social
Science Research Council Report, London.
STOREY, J. (1980), 'The Challenge to Management Control', Kogan
Page, London.
STOREY, J. (1981), 'The Challenge to Management Control',
Hutchinson, London.
STOREY, J. and STOREY, A. (1980), Higher education in Britain and
the United States:  selectivity versus universality, 'Journal of
General Education', vol.XXXII, no.3.
STOREY, A., CROUCH, H. and STOREY, J. (1981), An analysis of some
cultural determinants of pay differentials, 'International Journal
of Women's Studies', vol.4, no.3.
STRAUSS, A.L. et al. (1973), The hospital and its negotiated order,
in E. Friedson (ed.), 'The Hospital in Modern Society', Free Press,
Chicago, pp.147-69.
SULLIVAN, T. (1973), Collective bargaining and disclosure of

information.  A view from labour economics, 'Personnel Review',
Summer.
SUTTON, F.X., HARRIS, S.E., KAYSON, C. and TOBIN, J. (1956), 'The
American Business Creed', Harvard University Press.
SWINDLER, A. (1973), The concept of rationality in the work of Max
Weber, 'Sociological Inquiry', vol.43, no.1, pp.35-42.
SWINGEWOOD, A. (1975), 'Marx and Modern Social Theory', Macmillan,
London.
STRAUSS, G. (1979), Workers' participation:  symposium introduction,
'Industrial Relations', vol.18.
SUDNOW, D. (1973), Normal crimes, in G. Salaman and K. Thompson
(eds), 'People and Organizations', Longman, London.
SUTCLIFFE, R.B. (1971), 'Industry and Underdevelopment', Addison-
Wesley, London.
SWARTZ, D. (1981), The eclipse of politics:  the alternative
economic strategy as socialist strategy, 'Capital and Class', no.13.
SYKES, A.J.M. (1969), Navvies:  their work attitudes, 'Sociology',
vol.III, no.1.
TANNENBAUM, A.S. (1968), 'Control in Organizations', McGraw-Hill,
New York.
TANNENBAUM, A.S. (1974), 'Hierarchy in Organizations', Jossey Bass,
San Francisco.
TARLING, R. and WILKINSON, F. (1978), The social contract:  post war
incomes policies and their inflationary impact, 'Cambridge Journal
of Economics', vol.1, pp.395-414.
TAYLOR, F.W. (1911), 'Principles of Scientific Management', Harper,
New York.
TAYLOR SYSTEM HEARINGS (1912), Hearings Before the Special Committee
of the House of Representatives, 62nd Congress, Washington D.C.
Government Printing.
TAYLOR, L. and WALTON, P. (1971), Industrial sabotage, in S. Cohen
(ed.), 'Images of Deviance', Penguin, Harmondsworth.
TENBRUCK, F.H. (1980), The problem of thematic unity in the works of
Max Weber, 'British Journal of Sociology', vol.31, no.3.
TEPPERMAN, J. (1976), Organizing office workers, 'Radical America',
vol.10, pp.3-20.
TERKEL, S. (1975), 'Working', Wildwood House, London.
THERBORN, G. (1978), 'What Does the Ruling Class Do When it Rules?',
New Left Books, London.
THOMAS, K.W. (1978), Introduction:  symposium on conflict in
organizations, 'California Management Review', vol.XXI, no.2.
THOMAS, R.E. (1976), 'The Government of Business', Philip Alan,
Oxford.
THOMPSON, J.D. (1956), Authority and power in identical organisa-
tions, 'American Journal of Sociology', vol.62, pp.290-301.
THOMPSON, E.P. (1967), Time, work discipline and industrial
capitalism, 'Past and Present', no.38, pp.56-97.
THOMPSON, E.P. (1968), 'The Making of the English Working Class',
Penguin, Harmondsworth.
THORNLEY, J. (1981), 'Workers' Co-operatives:  Jobs and Dreams',
Heinemann, London.
THURLEY, K. and WOOD, S. (1977), Business strategy and industrial
relations strategy, Paper Presented at SSRC Conference held at
Cumberland Lodge, 14-16 December.

THURLEY, K. and WOOD, S. (eds) (forthcoming), 'Management Strategy and Industrial Relations', Cambridge University Press.

TIMPERLEY, S. (1980), Organisation strategies and industrial relations, 'Industrial Relations Journal', vol.XI, no.5.

TOPHAM, T. (1976), 'The Organized Worker', Arrow Books, London.

TORRENCE, G.W. (1959), 'Management's Right to Manage', Bureau of National Affairs, Washington D.C.

TOWERS, B., WHITTINGHAM, T.G. and GOTTSCHALK, A.W. (1972), 'Bargaining for Change', Allen & Unwin, London.

TRADES UNION CONGRESS (1967), 'Trade Unionism', TUC, London.

TRADES UNION CONGRESS (1969), 'Programme for Action', TUC, London.

TRADES UNION CONGRESS (1977), 'Industrial Democracy: Including Supplementary Evidence to the Bullock Committee', TUC, London.

TRADES UNION CONGRESS (1973), 'Good Industrial Relations: A Guide For Negotiators', 4th reprint, TUC, London.

TRADES UNION CONGRESS (1980), 'The Crisis of Monetarism and the TUC Alternative', TUC, London.

TRESSELL, R. (1965), 'The Ragged Trousered Philanthropists', Panther, London.

TUCHFELD, J.E. (1969), Background to the crisis, in K. Coates (ed.), 'Democracy in the Motor Industry', IWC, Nottingham.

TURNER, B.A. (1971), 'Exploring the Industrial Subculture', Macmillan, London.

TURNER, H.A., ROBERTS, C. and ROBERTS, D. (1977), 'Management Characteristics and Labour Conflict: A Study of Managerial Organization, Attitudes and Industrial Relations', Cambridge University Press.

UDY, S.H. (1959), Bureaucracy and rationality in Weber's organization theory, 'American Sociological Review', vol.24, December, pp. 791-5.

UNION FOR RADICAL POLITICAL ECONOMICS (1978), 'U.S. Capitalism in Crisis', Union for Radical Political Economics, New York.

URE, A. (1861), 'The Philosophy of Manufacturers', Bohn, London.

URWIN, H. (1970), 'Plant and Productivity Bargaining', Transport and General Workers' Union, London.

VON BEYME, K. (1980), 'Challenge to Power', Sage, London.

VUSKOVIC, B. (1976), Social inequality in Yugoslavia, 'New Left Review', pp.26-44.

WACHTEL, H.M. (1975), Class consciousness and stratification in the labour process, in R.C. Edwards et al. (eds), 'Labour Market Segmentation'.

WALLERSTEIN, I. (1974), 'The Modern World-System', Academic Press, London.

WALLERSTEIN, I. (1974), The rise and future demise of the world capitalist system, 'Comparative Studies in Society and History', vol.16.

WALLERSTEIN, I. (1975), A world system perspective in the social sciences, 'British Journal of Sociology', vol.27.

WALTON, R.E. and MCKERSIE, R.B. (1965), 'A Behavioural Theory of Labour Negotiations', McGraw-Hill, New York.

WATSON, B. (1972), Counter-planning on the shop floor, 'Radical America', vol.5, pp.77-85.

WATSON, T.J. (1977), 'The Personnel Managers', Routledge & Kegan Paul, London.

WEBER, M. (1922), 'Wirtschaft und Gesellschaft', Tübingen, Mohr.
WEBER, M. (1943), 'Max Weber: Essays in Sociology', translated and
with an introduction by H.H. Gerth and S. Wright Mills, Routledge
& Kegan Paul, London.
WEBER, M. (1964), 'The Theory of Social and Economic Organisation',
translated by A.M. Henderson and Talcott Parsons, Free Press, New
York.
WEBER (1968), 'Economy and Society', Bedminster Press, New York.
WEDDERBURN, D. and CRAIG, C. (1974), Relative Deprivation in Work,
in D. Wedderburn (ed.), 'Poverty, Inequality and Class Structure',
Cambridge University Press.
WEIGHTS, A. (1978), Weber and legitimate domination: A theoretical
critique of Weber's conceptualisation of 'Relations of Domination',
'Economy and Society', vol.7, no.1.
WEIR, D. (1976), Radical managerialism: middle managers' percep-
tions of collective bargaining, 'British Journal of Industrial
Relations', vol.14, pp.324-38.
WELSH, J. (1979), 'The Destruction of Social Reality: Berger and
Luckmann', The Transforming Sociology Series of the Red Feather
Institute for Advanced Studies in Sociology, no.48.
WESTERGAARD, J. (1970), The rediscovery of the cash nexus, in R.
Miliband (ed.), 'The Socialist Register', Merlin, London.
WESTERGAARD, J. and RESLER, H. (1975), 'Class in a Capitalist
Society', Penguin, Harmondsworth.
WHYTE, W.H. (1956), 'The Organization Man', Anchor, New York.
WIGHAM, E. (1973), 'The Power to Manage', Macmillan, London.
WILDERS, M.G. and PARKER, S.R. (1975), Changes in workplace
industrial relations 1966-72, 'British Journal of Industrial
Relations', vol.13, no.1.
WILKINSON, E.C. (1939), 'The Town That Was Murdered', Gollancz,
London.
WILLIAMS, R. (1971), 'Politics and Technology', Macmillan, London.
WILLIAMS, R. (1976), 'Keywords: A Vocabulary of Culture and
Society', Fontana, London.
WILLIAMSON, O.E. (1975), 'Markets and Hierarchies', Free Press, New
York.
WILLIAMSON, O.E. (1980), The organization of work: a comparative
institutional assessment, 'Journal of Economic Behaviour and
Organization', vol.1, no.1.
WILLIS, P. (1977), 'Learning to Labour', Saxon House, Farnborough.
WILSON, B.R. (ed.) (1977), 'Rationality', Blackwell, Oxford.
WILSON, H.T. (1977), 'The American Ideology: Science, Technology
and Organization as Modes of Rationality in Advanced Industrial
Societies', Routledge & Kegan Paul, London.
WILSON, H.T. (1980), Functional rationality and sense of function,
some comments on ideological distortion, in D. Dunkerley and G.
Salaman, 'The International Yearbook of Organization Studies 1980'.
WILSON, V.S. (1973), The relationship between scientific management
and personnel policy in North American administrative systems,
'Public Administration', vol.51.
WING, C. (1837), 'Evils of the Factory System Demonstrated by
Parliamentary Evidence', Frank Cass, London; republished 1967.
WINKLER, H. (1974), The ghost at the bargaining table: directors
and industrial relations, 'British Journal of Industrial Relations',
vol.12, pp.191-212, July.

WITTE, J.F. (1980), 'Democracy, Authority and Alienation in Work:
Workers' Participation in an American Corporation', University of
Chicago Press.
WOLF, R.D. (1975), Marxian crisis theory:  structure and implica-
tions, 'Review of Radical Political Economics', vol.10, no.1.
WOLFF, R. (1968), 'The Poverty of Liberalism', Beacon Press, Boston.
WOOD, L.C. (1956), A study of managerial prerogatives as a system
of ideas, unpublished PhD Thesis, University of Wisconsin.
WOOD, S. (1979), A reappraisal of the contingency approach to
organization, 'Journal of Management Studies', October.
WOOD, S. (1980a), Managerial reactions to job redundancy through
early retirement, 'Sociological Review', November.
WOOD, S. (1980b), Corporate strategy and organizational studies, in
D. Dunkerley and G. Salaman, 'International Yearbook of Organization
Studies 1980'.
WOOD, S. (1981), 'An Overview of the Study of Management in British
Industrial Relations', A Paper Originally Presented to the SSRC
Conference on Management Functions in Industrial Relations,
Cumberland Lodge, 14-16 December 1977.
WOOD, S. (ed.) (forthcoming), 'The Degradation of Work', Hutchinson,
London.
WOODS, P. (1981), Mad Mick, Tracy and Kamikaze Les, 'New Society',
4 June.
WOODWARD, J. (1965), 'Industrial Organization:  Theory and
Practice', Oxford University Press.
WOODWARD, J. (1970), 'Industrial Organization, Behaviour and
Control', Oxford University Press.
WRIGHT, E. (1974), To control or to smash bureaucracy:  Weber and
Lenin on politics, the state, and bureaucracy, 'Berkeley Journal of
Sociology', vol.19, pp.69-108.
WRIGHT, E. (1978), 'Class, Crisis and the State', New Left Books,
London.
WRONG, D.H. (1968), Some problems in defining social power,
'American Journal of Sociology', vol.73, pp.673-81.
WYCKO, W. (1975), The work shortage, class struggle and capital
reproduction, 'Review of Radical Political Economics', vol.7, no.2.
YELLOWITZ, J. (1977), Skilled workers and mechanization:  the
masters in the 1880's, 'Labour History', vol.18, Spring, pp.197-213.
YEO-CHI KING, A. (1977), A voluntarist model of organization:  the
Maoist version and its critique, 'British Journal of Sociology',
vol.28, no.3.
YOUNG, N. (1967),  Prometheans or troglodytes?  The English working
class and the dialectics of incorporation, 'Berkeley Journal of
Sociology'.
YOUNG, S. (1963), The question of managerial prerogatives,
'Industrial and Labour Relations Review', vol.16, no.2, pp.240-53,
January.
ZALD, M.N. (ed.) (1970), 'Power in Organizations', Vanderbilt
University Press, Nashville.
ZEIGER, A. (1976), Labour and monopoly capital, 'Labour History',
vol.17, no.4.
ZEITLIN, M. (1974), Corporate ownership and control:  the large
corporation and the capitalist class, 'American Journal of
Sociology', vol.79, no.5.

ZIMBALIST, A. (1975), The limits of work humanization, 'Review of Radical Political Economics', vol.7, pp.50-60.
ZIMBALIST, A. (ed.) (1979), 'Case Studies in the Labour Process', Monthly Review Press, New York.
ZIMMERMAN, D. (1973), The practicalities of rule use, in G. Salaman and K. Thompson (eds) (1973), 'People and Organisations', Longman, London.

# INDEX

236